Lecture Notes in Computer Science 5090

Commenced Publication in 1973
Founding and Former Series Editors:
Gerhard Goos, Juris Hartmanis, and Jan van Leeuwen

Editorial Board

David Hutchison
  Lancaster University, UK
Takeo Kanade
  Carnegie Mellon University, Pittsburgh, PA, USA
Josef Kittler
  University of Surrey, Guildford, UK
Jon M. Kleinberg
  Cornell University, Ithaca, NY, USA
Alfred Kobsa
  University of California, Irvine, CA, USA
Friedemann Mattern
  ETH Zurich, Switzerland
John C. Mitchell
  Stanford University, CA, USA
Moni Naor
  Weizmann Institute of Science, Rehovot, Israel
Oscar Nierstrasz
  University of Bern, Switzerland
C. Pandu Rangan
  Indian Institute of Technology, Madras, India
Bernhard Steffen
  University of Dortmund, Germany
Madhu Sudan
  Massachusetts Institute of Technology, MA, USA
Demetri Terzopoulos
  University of California, Los Angeles, CA, USA
Doug Tygar
  University of California, Berkeley, CA, USA
Gerhard Weikum
  Max-Planck Institute of Computer Science, Saarbruecken, Germany

Roland T. Mittermeir Maciej M. Sysło (Eds.)

Informatics Education – Supporting Computational Thinking

Third International Conference on Informatics
in Secondary Schools – Evolution and Perspectives, ISSEP 2008
Torun, Poland, July 1-4, 2008
Proceedings

 Springer

Volume Editors

Roland T. Mittermeir
Institut für Informatik-Systeme
Universität Klagenfurt
Klagenfurt, Austria
E-mail: roland@isys.uni-klu.ac.at

Maciej M. Sysło
Faculty of Mathematics and Computer Science
Nicolaus Copernicus University
Torun, Poland
E-mail: syslo@mat.uni.torun.pl

Library of Congress Control Number: 2008929575

CR Subject Classification (1998): K.3, K.4, J.1, K.8

LNCS Sublibrary: SL 1 – Theoretical Computer Science and General Issues

ISSN   0302-9743
ISBN-10   3-540-69923-6 Springer Berlin Heidelberg New York
ISBN-13   978-3-540-69923-1 Springer Berlin Heidelberg New York

This work is subject to copyright. All rights are reserved, whether the whole or part of the material is concerned, specifically the rights of translation, reprinting, re-use of illustrations, recitation, broadcasting, reproduction on microfilms or in any other way, and storage in data banks. Duplication of this publication or parts thereof is permitted only under the provisions of the German Copyright Law of September 9, 1965, in its current version, and permission for use must always be obtained from Springer. Violations are liable to prosecution under the German Copyright Law.

Springer is a part of Springer Science+Business Media

springer.com

© Springer-Verlag Berlin Heidelberg 2008
Printed in Germany

Typesetting: Camera-ready by author, data conversion by Scientific Publishing Services, Chennai, India
Printed on acid-free paper   SPIN: 12327676   06/3180   5 4 3 2 1 0

Preface

Informatics Education – Supporting Computational Thinking contains papers presented at the Third International Conference on Informatics in Secondary Schools – Evolution and Perspective, ISSEP 2008, held in July 2008 in Torun, Poland.

As with the proceedings of the two previous ISSEP conferences (2005 in Klagenfurt, Austria, and 2006 in Vilnius, Lithuania), the papers presented in this volume address issues of informatics education transcending national boundaries and, therefore, transcending differences in the various national legislation and organization of the educational system. Observing these issues, one might notice a trend. The proceedings of the First ISSEP were termed *From Computer Literacy to Informatics Fundamentals* [1]. There, broad room was given to general education in ICT. The ECDL, the European Computer Driving License, propagated since the late 1990s, had penetrated school at this time already on a broad scale and teachers, parents, as well as pupils were rather happy with this situation. Teachers had material that had a clear scope, was relatively easy to teach, and especially easy to examine. Parents had the assurance that their children learn "modern and relevant stuff," and for kids the computer was sufficiently modern so that anything that had to do with computers was considered to be attractive. Moreover, the difficulties of programming marking the early days of informatics education in school seemed no longer relevant. Some colleagues had a more distant vision though. They already proposed in their papers to weave conceptual knowledge into the strictly application-focused instruction of how to handle computers; and how to handle widely used general application software.

A trend of the still young second millennium to be witnessed external to school is that personal computers have penetrated households and citizens are increasingly using the Internet not only as a professional resource but also privately as an information resource as well as an infrastructure for communicating with relatives and friends, along with companies and public authorities. Politicians encouraged this and publicized e-learning as "learning of the future." As technical competence for e-learning was missing in the broad base of educators, e-learning was initially pushed into the domain of those who could handle computers, i.e., teachers of informatics. The proceedings of the Second ISSEP, *Informatics Education – The Bridge between Using and Understanding Computers* [2], reflect this situation in so far as they focus, next to discussions about the breadth of informatics education, on programming instruction and programming contests, but also on ICT and on e-learning.

The fact that informatics education, due to its relationship with technical devices, is bound to act swiftly in response to societal trends can be seen from the proceedings of the Third ISSEP. While the call for papers still voiced the theme "Informatics Education – Contributing Across the Curriculum", it is well justified to label these proceedings *Informatics Education – Supporting Computational Thinking*. Placing a focus on "computing" might seem at first glance like returning to the roots of informatics education forced by some stubborn teachers, blindly excited about programming. It is not! It is a reaction (and to some extent an anticipation) of the fact that not only personal computers have penetrated homes but quite often laptops have penetrated school bags. Even more important, the cell phone (mobile phone, in some countries referred to as "handy"), a device highly popular not only with children, can no longer be considered simply as a telephone, i.e., as a device for oral communication. It has gradually become a universal communication device. Its SMS facility makes it a teletype devise, its camera a multi-media device, and its addressability an Internet access device. School is not needed to teach kids how to handle this highly powerful and therefore also quite complex device. Kids learn this from their peers. This phenomenon, however, places new challenges on informatics education.

Consequently, the basics of using computers can no longer benefit from the excitement of using sophisticated technical equipment. The mobile phone in the possession of children has already become a more sophisticated device for a spectrum of limited tasks than a mere PC. What remains? If informatics education is constrained to ICT-education, it is training about skills that are not terribly motivating for a substantial portion of a class. Studies have shown that too much ICT training does specifically turn off girls [3, 4]. A personal experience I had recently in this respect involved a young lady asking me on the basis of her school education in informatics "How can you be so excited about such a dull subject?"

Several authors in these proceedings respond to these challenges by addressing the issue of what informatics education has to offer young people beyond the skills of how to use computers. The answers have a broad range. Computing in the sense of algorithmic constructions are among them as well as focusing on physical constructions by building small robots. Others focus rather on the intellectual challenge of anticipation and combining critical thinking, motherhood, and possibly also some mathematics before venturing into a brute force (algorithmic) solution. In summary, one might see a trend toward "back to the roots" of algorithms and programming. But these concepts are not to be seen from the computer scientist's perspective or from the perspective of preparing pupils for a computer science profession. They are rather to be seen from the teacher's perspective, preparing students for a life in an environment loaded with information and information technology and for preparing them with problem-solving strategies that got cultivated in the computing domain but whose scope extends computing by far.

Due to the trends mentioned above as well as to effective training measures of in service teachers, e-learning got out of the focus of informatics teachers. The didactical challenges involved with e-learning still require further discussion. But these discussions better take place in didactical conferences of the respective discipline. Only some infrastructural issues remain in the realm of informatics experts, and these were discussed at the conference.

The 32 papers contained in this volume consist of 28 contributed papers, selected out of 63 submissions and 4 invited contributions. They were reviewed by at least three members of the Program Committee and can be grouped into the sections introduced below.

The section on "Informatics, a Challenging Topic" starts with the paper by Syslo and Kwiatkowska. In this opening lecture, the authors introduce readers to the development of informatics education in Poland. The paper nicely shows, with this national example of Poland, some of the observations mentioned above and urges informatics instruction to instill computational thinking on students. The fact that computing skills

Table 1. Highly efficient compression functions

i	j	$h_i =$	secure
1	4	$E_v(m_i) \oplus v$	N
2	8	$E_v(m_i) \oplus m_i$	N
3	20	$E_v(h_{i-1}) \oplus v$	N
4	28	$E_v(h_i) \oplus h_{i-1}$	N
5	52	$E_v(v) \oplus v$	N
6	56	$E_v(v) \oplus m_i$	N
7	60	$E_v(v) \oplus h_{i-1}$	N
8	12	$E_v(m_i) \oplus h_{i-1}$	N
9	16	$E_v(m_i) \oplus m_i \oplus h_{i-1}$	N
10	64	$E_v(v) \oplus m_i \oplus h_{i-1}$	N
11	24	$E_v(h_{i-1}) \oplus m_i$	Y
12	32	$E_v(h_{i-1}) \oplus h_{i-1} \oplus m_i$	Y
13	36	$E_v(h_{i-1} \oplus m_i) \oplus v$	Y
14	40	$E_v(h_{i-1} \oplus m_i) \oplus m_i$	Y
15	44	$E_v(h_{i-1} \oplus m_i) \oplus h_{i-1}$	Y
16	48	$E_v(h_{i-1} \oplus m_i) \oplus h_{i-1} \oplus m_i$	Y

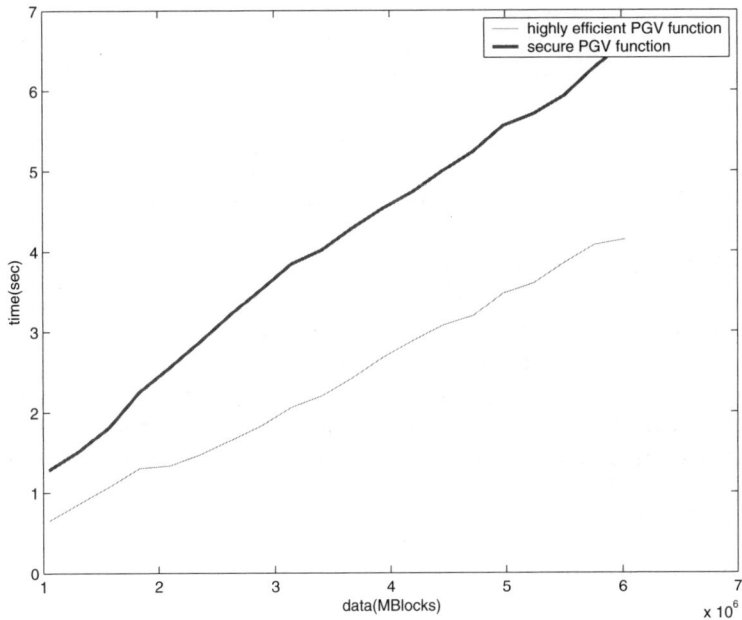

Fig. 4. Comparison between two compression functions

$11 - 16$ schemes in table 1 can be used to implement indifferentiable Zipper hash function which implies collision-resistant hash function. Black etc. claimed that it is impossible to build a collision-resistant hash function with the have to be nurtured already with young pupils is alluded to in the paper by Dagiene and Futschek. They discuss tasks for the Bebras contest, addressed at pupils of grade 5 to 12, stratified into 3 age groups. Diks and Madey report in their keynote on work with Polish contestants at International Olympiads in Informatics (IOI). They show how students are prepared to perform well in such international competitions and how their career as informatics professionals progresses.

The next section focuses on informatics as a technical discipline in presenting "Didactical Merits of Robot-Based Instruction." Programming is not seen as the way to instruct computers but as the way to move a technical device, the robot. The advantage with robot programming, which is of course computer programming in a special way, is not only that the effects of the program can be seen immediately – this would also apply, e.g., to spreadsheet programming – but that students have to think in terms of integrated systems.

Rhine and Martin describe a series of learning modules created in the context of an interactive robotics course. They focus specifically on the integrative aspects of mathematics, geometry, physics, and informatics. Wu, Tseng, and Huang report on different learning effects observed with students working with physical robots and those working just with robot simulators. Kamada, Aoki, Kurebayashi, and Yamamoto describe their (inexpensive) robot building kit and its programming language. In the following paper, members of this group, Kurebayashi, Aoki, Kamada, Kanemune, and Kuno, report on a learning unit using this robot construction kit for building a tri-axial robot. They report that students had a better understanding about automatically controlled systems after taking this course. Thus, they met their aims of knowledge transfer.

Issues concerning "Transfer of Knowledge and Concept Formation" is the linking theme of the next section. Knowledge transfer from solving abstract problems to concrete design issues is addressed in Ginat's keynote. Departing from the statement that design is a fundamental skill in computer science, he analyzes students' skills to find all simple non-intersecting polygons that can be drawn on a grid structure consisting of 3×3 equidistantly placed points such that the area enclosed equals a fixed amount (2 cm^2). He uses the relationship between forms identified by students and forms missed by them to hypothesize different skill deficiencies of the experimental subjects.

The paper by Sendova, Stefanova, Nikolova, and Kovatcheva reports on a course establishing ICT skills with teachers. It is placed in the transfer section, however, because the actual theme of this contribution is on the transfer of ideas to enhance motivation. This general concept can be successfully applied in any other kind of informatics instruction. Its essence is to motivate learners by integrating them into the educational process in such a way that they transcend the role of observers by becoming constituent members of the teaching venture in a form where teaching and learning flows into each other.

Schulte's duality reconstruction also departs from an ICT vantage point. On the basis of analyzing a word processor, he introduces the notion of didactical lenses which allow students to perceive structural as well as functional aspects of the material covered. Thus, the perspective of the engineer and the perspective of the application specialist become visible and students can thus construct a multifaceted image of the discipline.

Romeike considers transfer issues from a motivational perspective. In school, students quite often are forced to solve problems that are too remote from their personal problems to trigger motivation. The different performance children show in solving challenges of their daily life (such as using a mobile phone to its full extent) and in solving typical simple algorithmic problems lets the author conclude that instead of pre-canned artificial algorithmic problems, school should offer open challenges with a stepwise progression of difficulty. Gruber also looks at various approaches to raise the motivation of pupils, zooming in particularly on in-classroom differentiation.

The section on "Object Orientation and Programming" starts out with *Hubwieser's* paper on an analysis of learning objectives in object-oriented programming. The motivation of the analysis resulted from the need of writing a textbook. However, the message conveyed transcends this immediate problem domain. Conducting a similar analysis might help in various situations to protect teachers from rushing into the most modern developments of the professional side of the discipline without considering didactical consequences and without considering whether students can be accompanied along the whole trip from showing them a concept and making them convincingly aware of the usefulness of this concept.

Weigend takes a modeling perspective in pleading to make a distinction between the existential aspects of a state and its possessive elements. Benaya and Zur's deliberations are based on empirical results, studying the performance and problems faced by students, who already know how to program in an algorithmic language, in a course that introduced them to object-oriented programming in Java.

Yovcheva proposes what she refers to as a "spiral approach" of teaching programming. Departing from simple mathematical problems, a spiral of increasing complexity is defined in such a way that youngsters learn programming in small chunks, the bites being small enough to be comprehended and big enough to solve the problem at hand. A different angle of introducing students to algorithmic problem solving is presented by Haberman, Muller, and Averbuch. They recommend fostering critical thinking of students by dragging them away from starting programming too quickly. The authors challenged students with a core example backed up with variations. The problems are set such that the text of the examples varies only moderately, while the solution to the problems become, with some variations, almost trivial for those who apply good motherhood and some mathematical reasoning; in other cases, a slight modification of the problem substantially raises the complexity of the required solution.

The section closes with two papers following slightly different strands of ideas. Adamaszek, Chrzastowski-Wachtel, and Niewiarowska intend to help novice programmers stumbling over pointers and related concepts by introducing VIPER, a visual interpreter for Pascal. Blonskis and Dagiene report on an analysis of programs developed by students during their maturity exams.

The following section, "Strategies for Writing Textbooks and Teacher Education," starts out with two contributions reporting the authors' reflections and recommendations for textbooks introducing students to informatics. Freiermuth, Hromkovic and Steffen explain in a keynote lecture their way of teaching fundamental concepts using LOGO as didactical vehicle. In doing so, they also establish bridges between computer science and mathematics. Noteworthy is their remark that a systematic way of teaching avoids gender problems in programming courses. Kalas and Winczer also strive for an introductory text that should "build respect for informatics as a science and as a subject." But they follow a different strategy. While the group from ETH is liberal with space needed to express their ideas, the colleagues from Bratislava submit to the trend of short messages. They show how to fit 10 chapters into a total of 48 pages while still striving at a constructivist approach, following the progressive pattern of using, understanding, and creating information technology.

A totally different approach is presented in the paper by Nishida, Idosaka, Kofuku, Kanemune and Kuno. They strive to popularize Bell, Witten and Fellows' concept of "Computer Science Unplugged" and report the experience they obtained with this approach in three schools.

The section closes with papers on teacher training. Ragonis and Hazzan report on a course for preparing pre-service computer science teachers for Israeli high schools. It covers a broad spectrum of topics from an informatics didactics perspective. While in this course, programming, though addressed from various angles, is just one among several topics, the ensuing paper by Kolczyk focuses specifically on how informatics teachers should present algorithms. It departs from the vantage point that planning, i.e., proper anticipation of situations yet to come and reflecting about potential alternatives of reaction, is a key capability to be developed before programming. On this basis, the paper shows how planning may be trained in small progressive steps. This approach to programming starts already at the primary level and progresses to later phases of the curriculum. The paper by Grgurina reports on teacher training at the University of Groningen. After an explanation of the Dutch system of teacher formation, a concept of highly supervised training on the job is described.

Almost antithetic to the Dutch approach are the reports from Latvia and from Lithuania. Both apply e-learning technology to upgrade their teachers. The paper from the Latvian colleagues, placed in the e-learning section, specifically addresses the problem of smoothening the difference between Riga and the countryside. Dagiene, Zajančkauskiene, and Žilinskiene focus on this technology as a means and an end in so far as they argue for e-learning as a powerful and purposeful way of motivating teachers to use the technology they are to familiarize students with for their own learning. The details of the targets to be achieved by this program are reported in the paper opening the next section.

The section on "National and International Perspectives on ICT Education" starts with a paper from Dagiene, reporting on the implementation of the national strategy for the introduction of information and communication technologies into the Lithuanian educational system. This contribution, reporting on a progressive strategy of introducing IT in grade 5 to 10, is followed by a report on a project assessing spreadsheet knowledge and skills of French secondary school students, presented by Tort, Blondel and Bruillard. The study shows that, when ICT is to be used in a mode remote from those domains where it has penetrated private life, formal education is still a necessity. This section closes with a paper by Micheuz, arguing for a harmonization of informatics education in Europe on the terminology level as well as on the level of concepts. The NCTM standard for mathematics is proposed as an example from a related discipline. Various initiatives aiming at structuring informatics education are mentioned.

The proceedings close with tree papers dealing with "e-Learning" issues. This section starts with a contribution from Eibl and Schubert reporting on design criteria for e-learning systems considering security aspects. Damaševičius and Štuikys aim for reusable learning objects, reporting their experience of producing generative components. Lavendels, Sitikovs, and Krauklis report on the use of information technologies for reducing the gap between teachers in the capital of Latvia and country-side teachers. It is noteworthy to mention that this is the initiative of a university, to broaden the base of their students by providing pupils from the countryside with access to modern education in informatics.

A conference like this is not possible without many hands and brains working for it or without the financial support of graceful donors. Hence, I would like to thank particularly the General Chair and the members of the Program Committee and all the additional reviewers for ensuring the quality of papers accepted. Among them, Carol Sperry deserves specific mention as she helped some authors to improve linguistic aspects of their text. Special thanks are due to the Organizing Committee led by Anna Beata Kwiatkowska and to Annette Lippitsch for editorial support for these proceedings.

The conference was made possible due to the support of several sponsors whose help is gratefully acknowledged. Finally, hosting of the conference by the Faculty of Mathematics and Computer Science, Nicolaus Copernicus University in Torun is gratefully acknowledged.

April 2008   Roland Mittermeir

References

1. Mittermeir, R.T. (ed.): ISSEP 2005. LNCS, vol. 3422. Springer, Heidelberg (2005)
2. Mittermeir, R.T. (ed.): ISSEP 2006. LNCS, vol. 4226. Springer, Heidelberg (2006)
3. Antonitsch, P., Krainer, L., Lerchster, R., Ukowitz, M.: Kriterien der Studienwahl von Schülerinnen und Schülern unter spezieller Berücksichtigung von IT-Studiengängen an Fachhochschule und Universität; IFF-Forschungsbericht, AAU-Klagenfurt (März 2007)
4. Schulte, C., Knobelsdorf, M.: Das informatische Weltbild von Studierenden. In: Schubert, S. (ed.) Didaktik der Informatik in Theorie und Praxis, Proc. INFOS 2007. LNI, vol. P 112, pp. 69–79. Springer, Heidelberg (2007)

Organization

ISSEP 2008 was organized by the Nicolaus Copernicus University, Toruń, Poland.

ISSEP 2008 Program Committee

Maciej M. Sysło (Co-chair)	Nicolaus Copernicus University, Toruń, Poland
Roland T. Mittermeir (Co-chair)	Universität Klagenfurt, Austria
Andor Abonyi-Tóth	Eötvös Loránd University, Hungary
Peter Antonitsch	Universität Klagenfurt, Austria
Juris Borzovs	University of Latvia, Riga, Latvia
Laszlo Böszörmenyi	Universität Klagenfurt, Austria
Norbert Breier	Universität Hamburg, Germany
Mike Chiles	Western Cape Education Department, South Africa
Piotr Chrząstowski-Wachtel	Warsaw University, Poland
Bernard Cornu	CNED-EIFAD (Open and Distance Learning Institute), France
Valentina Dagienė	Institute of Mathematics and Informatics, Lithuania
Krzysztof Diks	Warsaw University, Poland
Zide Du	China Computer Federation, China
Steffen Friedrich	Technische Universität Dresden, Germany
Karl Fuchs	Universität Salzburg, Austria
Patrick Fullick	University of Southampton, UK
Gerald Futschek	Technische Universität Wien, Austria
David Ginat	Tel-Aviv University, Israel
Bruria Haberman	Holon Institute of Technology and The Davidson Institute of Science Education at The Weizmann Institute of Science, Israel
Juraj Hromkovič	ETH Zürich, Switzerland
Peter Hubwieser	Technische Universität München, Germany
Feliksas Ivanauskas	Vilnius University, Lithuania
Ivan Kalaš	Comenius University, Bratislava, Slovakia
Susumu Kanemune	Hitotsubashi University, Tokyo, Japan
Ewa Kołczyk	University of Wrocław, Poland
Ala Kravtsova	Moscow Pedagogical State University, Russia
Anna Beata Kwiatkowska	Nicolaus Copernicus University, Toruń, Poland
Ville Leppanen	University of Turku, Finland
Jan Madey	Warsaw University, Poland
Peter Micheuz	Universität Klagenfurt and Gymnasium Völkermarkt, Austria
Joerg R. Mühlbacher	University of Linz, Austria

Zdzisław Nowakowski — Center for Lifelong Learning, Mielec, Poland
Ana Isabel Sacristan — Center for Research and Advanced Studies (Cinvestav), Mexico
Tapio Salakoski — Turku University, Finland
Sigrid Schubert — Universität Siegen, Germany
Aleksej Semionov — Moscow Institute of Open Education, Russia
Carol Sperry — Millersville University, USA
Oleg Spirin — Zhytomyr Ivan Franko University, Ukraine
Aleksandras Targamadzė — Kaunas University of Technology, Lithuania
Armando Jose Valente — State University of Campinas, Brazil
Tom Verhoeff — Eindhoven University of Technology, The Netherlands
Anne Villems — University of Tartu, Estonia
Andrzej Walat — Center for Informatics Education and Applications of Computers, Warsaw, Poland

Additional Reviewers

Michal Adamaszek — University of Warsaw, Poland
Ernestine Bischof — Universität Klagenfurt, Austria
Karin Freiermuth — ETH Zürich, Switzerland
Karin Hodnigg — Universität Klagenfurt, Austria
Kees Huizing — Eindhoven University of Technology, The Netherlands
Toshiyuki Kamada — Aichi University of Education, Japan
Yasushi Kuno — University of Tsukuba, Japan
Shuji Kurebayashi — Shizuoka University, Japan
Yoshiaki Nakano — Senri Kinran University, Japan
Anna Niewiarowska — University of Warsaw, Poland
Tomohiro Nishida — Osaka Gakuin University, Japan
Björn Steffen — ETH Zürich, Switzerland
Takeo Tatsume — Tokyo University of Agriculture and Technology, Japan

Organizing Committee

Anna Beata Kwiatkowska (Chair); Maria Berndt-Schreiber, Michał Dudkiewicz, Maciej Koziński, Wiesława Osińska, Grzegorz Osiński, Oliwia Piwińska, Mariusz Piwiński, Andrzej Polewczyński, Krzysztof Skowronek, Maciej M. Sysło, Danuta Zaremba; all UMK, Torun.

Main Sponsor

ISSEP 2008 and the publication of its proceedings were partly supported by the Faculty of Mathematics and Informatics, Nicolaus Copernicus University, Torun, Poland.

Table of Contents

Informatics, a Challenging Topic

The Challenging Face of Informatics Education in Poland 1
    Maciej M. Sysło and Anna Beata Kwiatkowska

Bebras International Contest on Informatics and Computer Literacy:
Criteria for Good Tasks 19
    Valentina Dagienė and Gerald Futschek

From Top Coders to Top IT Professionals 31
    Krzysztof Diks and Jan Madey

Didactical Merits of Robot-Based Instruction

Integrating Mathematical Analysis of Sensors and Motion in a Mobile
Robotics Course 41
    Don Rhine and Fred Martin

Visualization of Program Behaviors: Physical Robots Versus Robot
Simulators 53
    Cheng-Chih Wu, I-Chih Tseng, and Shih-Lung Huang

Development of an Educational System to Control Robots for All
Students 63
    Toshiyuki Kamada, Hiroyuki Aoki, Shuji Kurebayashi, and
    Yoshikazu Yamamoto

Proposal for Teaching Manufacturing and Control Programming Using
Autonomous Mobile Robots with an Arm 75
    Shuji Kurebayashi, Hiroyuki Aoki, Toshiyuki Kamada,
    Susumu Kanemune, and Yasushi Kuno

Transfer of Knowledge and Concept Formation

Design Disciplines and Non-specific Transfer 87
    David Ginat

Like a (School of) Fish in Water (or *ICT-Enhanced Skills* in Action) 99
    Evgenia Sendova, Eliza Stefanova, Nikolina Nikolova, and
    Eugenia Kovatcheva

Duality Reconstruction – Teaching Digital Artifacts from a
Socio-technical Perspective 110
    Carsten Schulte

What's My Challenge? The Forgotten Part of Problem Solving in
Computer Science Education 122
  Ralf Romeike

Bringing Abstract Concepts Alive. How to Base Learning Success on
the Principles of Playing, Curiosity and In-Classroom Differentiation ... 134
  Peter Gruber

Working with Objects and Programming

Analysis of Learning Objectives in Object Oriented Programming 142
  Peter Hubwieser

To Have or to Be? Possessing Data Versus Being in a State – Two
Different Intuitive Concepts Used in Informatics 151
  Michael Weigend

Understanding Object Oriented Programming Concepts in an Advanced
Programming Course 161
  Tamar Benaya and Ela Zur

Spiral Teaching of Programming to 10–11 Year-Old Pupils After Passed
First Training (Based on the Language C++) 171
  Biserka Boncheva Yovcheva

Multi-facet Problem Comprehension: Utilizing an Algorithmic Idea in
Different Contexts 180
  Bruria Haberman, Orna Muller, and Haim Averbuch

VIPER, a Student-Friendly Visual Interpreter of Pascal 192
  Michał Adamaszek, Piotr Chrząstowski-Wachtel, and
  Anna Niewiarowska

Analysis of Students' Developed Programs at the Maturity Exams in
Information Technologies 204
  Jonas Blonskis and Valentina Dagienė

Strategies for Writing Textbooks and Teacher Education

Creating and Testing Textbooks for Secondary Schools – An Example:
Programming in LOGO... 216
  Karin Freiermuth, Juraj Hromkovič, and Björn Steffen

Informatics as a Contribution to the Modern Constructivist
Education... 229
  Ivan Kalas and Michal Winczer

New Methodology of Information Education with "Computer Science Unplugged" 241
  Tomohiro Nishida, Yukio Idosaka, Yayoi Hofuku, Susumu Kanemune, and Yasushi Kuno

Disciplinary-Pedagogical Teacher Preparation for Pre-service Computer Science Teachers: Rational and Implementation 253
  Noa Ragonis and Orit Hazzan

Algorithm – Fundamental Concept in Preparing Informatics Teachers... 265
  Ewa Kolczyk

Computer Science Teacher Training at the University of Groningen..... 272
  Nataša Grgurina

Distance Learning Course for Training Teachers' ICT Competence 282
  Valentina Dagienė, Lina Zajančkauskienė, and Inga Žilinskienė

National and International perspectives on ICT Education

Teaching Information Technology and Elements of Informatics in Lower Secondary Schools: Curricula, Didactic Provision and Implementation 293
  Valentina Dagienė

Spreadsheet Knowledge and Skills of French Secondary School Students 305
  Françoise Tort, François-Marie Blondel, and Éric Bruillard

Harmonization of Informatics Education – Science Fiction or Prospective Reality?... 317
  Peter Micheuz

E-Learning

Development of E-Learning Design Criteria with Secure Realization Concepts 327
  Christian J. Eibl and Sigrid E. Schubert

On the Technological Aspects of Generative Learning Object Development 337
  Robertas Damaševičius and Vytautas Štuikys

Informational Technologies for Further Education of Latvian Province Teachers of Informatics 349
  Jurijs Lavendels, Vjaceslavs Sitikovs, and Kaspars Krauklis

Author Index 357

The Challenging Face of Informatics Education in Poland

Maciej M. Sysło[1,2] and Anna Beata Kwiatkowska[2]

[1] Institute of Computer Science, University of Wroclaw
F. Joliot-Curie str. 15, 50-383 Wroclaw, Poland
`syslo@ii.uni.wroc.pl`
[2] Faculty of Mathematics and Computer Science, Nicolaus Copernicus University
Chopin str. 12/18, 87-100 Torun, Poland
`aba@mat.uni.torun.pl, syslo@mat.uni.torun.pl`

Abstract. In this paper, a learning and teaching framework is described which is aimed at increasing student interest in studying computer science as a discipline, or at least in better understanding how a computer and its tools work and can be used in solving problems which may occur in different areas.

In the beginning of information education in Poland, in the mid 80's, the informatics curricula for schools and teaching were focused on computer science. Then, in the beginning of the 90's, with the growing popularity and wide use of end-user friendly software, the emphasis in education has moved from computer science to information technology, from constructing computer solutions to using ready-made tools, from computer science for some students to information technology for all. We demonstrate here, however, how teaching and learning information technology can be used to enhance algorithmic and computational thinking in solving with computers, problems which arise in various school subjects, learning disciplines and in real life.

We strongly believe that the learning methodology presented here, about computer use by students and applying computers and information technology to solving problems, would be a good motivation and preparation for their future decisions to study computing and become computer specialists.

1 Introduction

We begin with a comment on **terminology**. In Poland, 'informatics' (pl. *informatyka*) is used for 'computer science' and also for almost all disciplines and subjects, especially in education, which have anything to do with computers. There is for instance: applied informatics (in practice, 'applied informatics' in subject A, means 'the use of computers in subject A'), computer physics, chemical informatics, medical informatics, etc. In this paper, the term 'informatics' is equivalent to 'computer science' and we use 'computer science' when we want to emphasize scientific aspects of the discussion. The term 'computing' however, which embraces 'computer science', 'software engineering', 'information systems', 'information technology' and some other computer-related titles, is not popular in Poland and has no official counterpart, with the exception of 'computational science' which is sometimes used for computations related to scientific problems.

In our paper [15], presented at the 1st ISSEP Conference in Klagenfurt (2005) we focused our attention on the question: *how much informatics is needed to use information technology?* In particular we investigated:

- to what extent should one learn a discipline (informatics) to be able to use its applications (information technology), and
- how to prepare teachers of informatics and information technology, as well as teachers of other subjects who are equipped with the technology for their new role as moderators of students' learning, to use information technology in different situations.

Today, other questions and their answers are more important for the computer science community as well as for society as a whole. In this paper, we are also motivated by recently growing interests to answer a fundamental question: *Is Computer Science Dying?* This question is formulated as a result of a gradual decline in the number of students applying to earn a computer science degree.

The main goal of this paper is to 1) show that students in middle and high schools can begin to learn basic informatics principles and start to master **computational thinking** (see [19] and Section 2.2) while learning how to use computers and their applications (information technology), and 2) how to apply informatics tools and methods in studying and learning other subjects and solving problems from various disciplines and areas. We are convinced that the approach presented in this paper can help students to add computational thinking to the traditional three Rs: (i.e. **r**eading, **w**riting and **a**rithmetic) as an additional basic skill needed by everyone. Moreover we believe that in this way we may better prepare our school students to choose a future career as either computer scientists or computer specialists.

Our considerations are based on our experience in:

- working on syllabi and text books on informatics and information technology for schools;
- teaching informatics and information technology in schools;
- preparing future teachers, in-service training of working teachers, and our experiences in guiding and supporting teachers of informatics and information technology.

The approach described in this paper has been implemented in some schools in Poland which use our textbooks [7-9]. The main obstacle to expanding this approach to a larger number of schools is the lack of teachers – teachers of informatics and other subjects, who are adequately prepared in computational thinking. Teacher preparation in computational thinking will be the subject of another paper.

The paper is organized as follows. In Section 2 we focus on the development of computer science with a special emphasis on its role and place in education. In Section 3 we briefly present the education system in Poland and the role of informatics education. In Section 4 we describe general ideas illustrated by examples of our approach in learning and teaching information technology which is oriented to developing computational thinking. Finally some conclusions are formulated.

2 Computer Science, Education, Computational Thinking

In this section we first comment on a recent question regarding whether computer science is a dying discipline, then present the main challenges of computer science education and finally discuss the role of computational thinking in meeting these challenges.

2.1 Is Computer Science in Crisis?

In Poland in the 1960's, computer science at universities was a part of the discipline of mathematics, and popular among mathematicians and other scientists who used computers as tools for their theoretical research and practical calculations. It was the 'new fashion' to enhance research papers with the results of computations performed by a computer, to add some computer oriented theoretical calculations, and to also include some computer codes (programs, e.g. in Algol or in Fortran). The majority of Ph.D. theses in almost all disciplines included some computer calculations designed and performed by members of computer science departments.

After a few years, computer science departments were set apart from mathematics departments, and today there is a mathematics and informatics faculty at almost all Polish universities. Although most of the professors in computer science departments have made their scientific careers (Ph.D., habilitation and the professor title) in mathematics, in actuality, the scientific cooperation between members of these two departments, even within the same faculty, is rather incidental.

Since its beginning, computer science has often been confused with computer programming and computer technology. Computer science curricula are largely responsible for this image of the discipline popular today in our society. They were developed at a time when, for most students, the study of computer science was the first introduction to computing and there was no software available. Today, most students enter university with years of computer experience usually gotten outside of schools, since computer technology is a part of their lives. Moreover, students and universities have access to high-level tools which can be used to design and produce complex applications for business, science and entertainment without the knowledge of logic, discrete mathematics, programming methodology, or computability, which belong to every computer science curriculum. Complex graphic designs (e.g. produced by a photographer Ryszard Horowitz) and animations (e.g. *The Cathedral*, 2002 by Tomasz Bagiński, an Oscar-nominated short movie) can be created with no knowledge of object-oriented design.

Today, one of the challenges to a curriculum in computer science is to catch up to the new technology and the other is to adjust it to rapidly changing markets and users' expectations. Moreover, as a starting point, the initial preparation of students must also be taken into account.

A new curriculum should widen the computer science student's view of the world. Scientists and students in university faculties of computer science still work on developing theoretical solutions to problems which are not always practical. On the other hand, the computer industry moves its focus to delivery and service. Moreover, some computer science departments, especially at undergraduate colleges, become information technology departments and mainly develop resources to meet the needs of the market and customers. They use computer tools as black boxes and they teach only a little of discrete mathematics, algorithmics, formal programming methods and languages, Turing machines, etc.

One may expect that in the future new computing departments will be interdisciplinary, drawing ideas from various disciplines and contributing a computing foundation to those disciplines. They will look outwards to address computing applications.

Some people argue that there is no longer a need for a large number of computer scientists working on foundations of the discipline and developing basic products such as programs, algorithms, libraries, systems, languages, compilers, as it was in the 1960's and 1970's. However, there is still a demand for experts and specialists in various areas of computer use and applications who are competent in the range of the university curriculum in computer science. Therefore, there is still and will be in the future a need for students and graduates in all areas of computing. If so, how should we prepare students in high schools who wish to choose university computer science as their future career?

2.2 Computer Science Education

Today, many people, among them policy makers (even some in education), teachers, academics and parents do not consider computer science as an independent science and, therefore, as a separate school subject. Most of them confuse computer science and information technology and limit informatics education to making computers and the Internet available to students and teachers in class rooms and at home. The fundamental problem is that they do not distinguish between using computer and network technology and studying the general principles of computing.

When in the 80's and 90's, computer science was confused with computer programming there was a strong opposition among education policy makers and parents to teaching informatics. They argued that only a few high school graduates would choose a career as a programmer. The same people claimed that the use of computers in schools should not be separated from other subjects.

Twenty years ago, very few students had used a computer, either in schools or at home, before they entered university. For the last 10 years, the main emphasis in K-12 education was on computer literacy, which is focused mainly on using applied (office) software and the Internet. As a result, most high school graduates are quite fluent in using computers to play, search the web and communicate, but their actual knowledge about the discipline of computer science and about what happens inside a computer and in the net and web – or actual knowledge of the discipline of computer science – is on a very low level. As a result, graduates have no real interest in pursuing computer science as a career choice. In fact they are not even fluent in using information technology as defined in [1], see also [5]. They don't see themselves creating a new culture or new technology, only working with the technology that has already been invented. Evidently it is easier to follow than to innovate and invent, to take risks. Youth's infatuation with technology does not extend to their desire to learn the discipline of computer science – we need to discover how to motivate students to go 'beyond the screen' and investigate how computers and software work so they can create their own computer solutions.

It is also the case that students have tasted enough information technology while growing up to want something different at the university level. To change this, information technology and informatics in primary, middle and secondary schools should prepare students for further study in information technology-related fields instead of being satisfied with the knowledge and skills they have already learned. Sometimes students are disappointed and discouraged with the information technology subjects in schools. They do not see any future in studying this subject more deeply, even for use in the discipline they are most interested in, becoming a member of the IT profession, that is, to become a user of information technology with a solid, professional base in computer science [5].

We have to take into consideration that the factors for choosing computer science as a study field today are different.

Informatics education in schools does not clear up the myths about computer science and most of the students in high schools graduate with no clear answers to the popular statements formulated as "relations": CS = programming, CS = IT (ICT), CS = computer literacy, CS = a tool for studying other subjects, CS ≠ scientific discipline. The White Paper by the CSTA [13] lists a number of challenges and requirements that must be met if we want to succeed in bridging the gaps in education and improve education in informatics as a computer science discipline:

- students should acquire a broad overview of the field of CS;
- informatics instruction should focus on problem solving and algorithmic thinking;
- informatics should be taught independently of specific application software and programming languages and environments;
- informatics should be taught using real-world problem situations;
- informatics education should provide a solid background for the professional use of computers in other disciplines.

One of our goals in this paper is to show how we partly meet these challenges in our approach to informatics education for all students in schools in Poland – informatics education in this paper stands for both computer science and communication and information technology.

2.3 Computational Thinking

Our approach to informatics education in schools, from the beginning in the mid 60's through the mid 90's, was to put the emphasis on algorithms and **algorithmic thinking** as the main components of computer science. The other important components were also present – computers (together with operating systems and programming environments) as machines for running algorithms and programming languages – as tools for expressing algorithms to communicate them to computers and to other programmers. In fact there was no other application software available in those years.

Algorithmic thinking is understood as thinking in terms of existing or new algorithms and as the ability to analyze problems from an algorithmic point of view, which is how to apply known algorithms for their solution, how to devise a new algorithmic solution for a new problem situation, to implement that solution, and then to run and test it on a computer.

In the late 90's, after a few years of struggling to find a proper place for information technology in our education system, it was realized that skills known as **computer** (or **information technology**) **literacy**, which is the capability to use today's technology in one's own field, are not a sufficient preparation of the young generation, or the work force, or any other users of computers to help them adapt to changes in technology. The notion of **fluency with information technology** was adopted for "a process of lifelong learning in which individuals continually apply what they know to adapt to changes and acquire more knowledge to be more effective at applying information technology to their work and personal lives." [1] Fluency with information technology requires three kinds of knowledge: contemporary skills (the ability to use today's computer applications), foundational concepts (the basic principles and ideas of computers, networks, and information), and intellectual capabilities (the ability to apply information technology in complex situations). Information technology fluency is therefore the capability to learn and use new technology as it evolves throughout one's professional lifetime. Moreover, it also includes the ability to use algorithmic thinking and programming to solve problems.

A much wider view on computing competencies has been proposed by Jeannette Wing in her paper on computational thinking [19]. Earlier, one of the EU directives suggested in the late 90's that the traditional skills for everyone known as the 3Rs (i.e. **r**eading, w**r**iting and a**r**ithmetic) should be extended to 3R+TI by adding skills in applying information technology. Wing has taken this step further by proposing to consider **computational thinking** and thus extending algorithmic thinking and fluency with information technology to competencies which are built "on the power and limits of computing processes, whether they are executed by a human or by a machine." [19]. She argues "Just as the printing press facilitated the spread of the 3Rs ... computing and computers facilitate the spread of computational thinking."

One can observe the influence of computational thinking on other disciplines. On the other hand, computer scientists' interest in other disciplines is driven by their belief that other scientists can benefit from computational thinking. For instance, in mathematics, as formulated by R.W. Hemming in 1959, *the purpose of computing is insight, not numbers*. In our paper presented at the 2nd ISSEP Conference [16] we discussed a number of topics, which are usually considered as a part of informatics education in schools and show how they can contribute to mathematics education. All the topics described in [16] are included in the textbook for informatics [8], addressed to high school students in Poland. However these topics are still absent in teaching mathematics and in mathematics textbooks used by our students.

Computational thinking includes a range of mental tools that reflect the breadth of computer science, for example, reduction and decomposition of a complex problem in order to solve it efficiently, approximating when an exact solution is beyond the reach of the computer, recursion as a method of inductive thinking and its computer implementation, representation and modeling some aspects of a problem to make it tractable, and heuristic reasoning to develop a solution.

We illustrate in Section 4 how we expose all our middle and high school students, not only those interested in computer science, to computational thinking: with methods, models and tools within informatics education (information technology classes). We agree with Jeannette Wing [19] and believe that computational thinking may "inspire the public's interest in the intellectual adventure of the field of computer science" and as a result may also encourage more high school students to consider a future career in computer science.

3 Informatics Education in Poland – In the Past and Today

The first regular informatics classes (two hours a week) in Poland were organized in two high schools in Wroclaw in the mid sixties, just 'a day after' the first three mainframe commercial computers (Elliott 803, made in the UK) were installed in the University of Wroclaw and in two scientific institutions (in Warsaw and Gdańsk). The main topics of instruction were algorithms and programming in Algol 60, applied to numerical calculations (e.g., polynomials, interpolation, numerical integration, and their applications).

The first national curriculum for informatics as an independent subject was proposed by the Polish Computer Society in 1985. For the next 10 years (micro)computers were mainly used in teaching informatics (computer science) as an independent subject and only occasionally were they used as a support in teaching other subjects. Then the development of user-friendly human-computer interfaces as well as the Internet became the main factors that influenced the way computers were used in our schools. In the mid 90's, the term 'information technology', meaning 'informatics for all students', was accepted by the education policy makers in Poland. Today 'information technology' is widely used in our education system as meaning 'information and communication technology' which means, as it does in other countries – computer science education for all, not only students.

3.1 Informatics in the Education System in Poland

Today, the education standard in the core national curriculum related to informatics education is formulated as follows:

> **the responsibility of schools is to guarantee students the possibility of using information and communication technology, and to prepare them to live in the information society**

It is expected that schools are oriented towards across-curriculum integration of computers, information technology, and the Internet with the learning and teaching of all subjects.

Formal education (since 1999) starts in Poland at the age of 7. The school system at the primary and secondary levels consists of three stages:

- primary school – 1-6 grades (age 7 to 13);
- middle school (in Polish: *gimnazjum*) – 7-9 grades (age 13 to 16);
- high school – 10-12 grades (to 13 in certain vocational schools) – (age 16 to 19).

As in the majority of European countries, informatics or information technology is included in our national core curriculum as an independent subject:

- in primary schools – **informatics**, at least 2 hours per week for one year; actually the scope of this subject is restricted in the curriculum to information technology topics – how to use application and educational software, for instance, in other school subjects;
- in middle schools – **informatics**, at least 2 hours per week for one year; the curriculum of informatics for middle schools contains a section on algorithmics, algorithmic thinking and solving problems with computers; although programming is

not included in the curriculum, an introduction to Logo is a part of the instruction in some schools and those students take the first steps in programming;
- in high schools – **information technology**, at least 2 hours per week for one year; it is recommended that at this level of school education, information technology should be mainly used to enhance other subjects with the use of computers;
- in high schools – **informatics** (understood as computer science), an elective subject, taught only in some high schools; students may also take an external final examination (*matura* in Polish) in informatics.

Therefore, information technology, as a separate subject, is now taught in all types of schools in Poland. Therefore, since 2005, Poland has met the EU standard (see the EU eLearning initiative [4]) that all students leaving the school system (formal education) are digitally literate.

3.2 The Era of Informatics (Computer Science) in the Past

At the very beginning of informatics education in some of our high schools in the mid 60s', due to the obvious difficulty in using computers personally and the lack of human-computer interfaces, the main emphasis was put on writing programs for numerical calculations and algorithmics was restricted to numerical methods.

Then for more than fifteen years (1985 – 2002), informatics (in fact, elements of informatics – EI) was a part of the curriculum in Poland (for all schools with computers) and was taught in elementary schools (1-8 – mainly during the last two years), and in high schools (9-12 – for one, two, three and even four years). A textbook was published (the first edition appeared in 1988) and it is perhaps interesting to mention that this textbook had a new printing each year and more than 100 000 copies have been sold; it is unusual for a textbook on informatics to remain unchanged on the market for so long. It was due to the approach adopted in this book, which was mainly on understanding how computers and software work and how to use computer tools in problem solving. In that sense the content of the book was (and still is) universal: the history of computers and informatics, how computers are designed and how they work (operating systems), playing and learning (turtle graphics – Logo), from problems to programs (elements of programming), designing one's own directory (data base), calculations in mathematics, computing faster (elements of algorithmics), easy and effective managing of a small business (spreadsheet).

A new series of textbooks for informatics in high schools has been recently written with the same approach in mind [8]. We are in quite a comfortable situation since the topics of information technology education are now taught as an independent subject and are included in a different text book [9], and therefore we could omit them from the textbook on informatics.

3.3 The Era of Information Technology

As a part of the Education Reform, the core curriculum was published in 1997, and presently, with respect to informatics education, the main goal is: to guarantee students the possibility of using information and communication technology, and to prepare them to live in the information society.

In developing the curriculum for information technology and informatics education it was very useful to have the model for information technology development as presented in the UNECSO Curriculum [18]. This model provides a framework which shows the interrelationship of various components within a system and aids understanding by all parties involved in education: students, parents, teachers, educational administrators and policy-makers.

The UNESCO model [18] consists of four stages: emerging, applying, integrating, and transforming. It also describes stages of teaching and learning and can be applied to learning and using information technology (by students as well as by teachers), teaching information technology and teaching with the help of information technology. The model can also help to understand why students, teachers, schools and other users of information technology have to follow a similar route of information technology development in their personal and professional lives. For instance, in the case of the preparation of teachers, they first have to learn about computers (*emerging stage*) to be able to use them in their subjects (*applying stage*), and then they begin to *integrate technology* with other teaching areas and finally the school becomes ready to play a transforming role in the community and society.

"The introduction of computers to schools in the 80's created high expectations for improving education. Today however those expectations have not yet been fulfilled – it is argued that this is mainly due to unrealistic assumptions about learning as a passive process of information absorption. It is believed that to improve the results of learning, **computers should be embedded** in, instead of only added to, learning environments as tools that elicit and support in students the active processes of knowledge construction and skill development." [15]

4 Implementing Computational Thinking

In our approach to informatics education we make a general assumption that informatics (= computer science) deals mainly with creating 'new products' related to computers (such as hardware, programs and software, algorithms, notions, theories, etc.) and information technology is mainly applying and using 'informatics (computer related) products'. Although this distinction does not define either informatics or information technology, it is very useful in describing the methodology of learning and teaching both subjects. Moreover, one may argue – it is quite important for student achievement – that information technology, especially its sophisticated tools, may be used to create highly involved computer products. However, their novelty and ingenuity contribute to the discipline to which they belong, rather than to computer science.

4.1 General Approach to Informatics Education

We describe here a general approach to teaching and learning information technology and informatics (computer science in high schools) as independent subjects.

4.1.1 Elements of Style in Using Information Technology

In our approach to teaching and using information technology [7, 9] we convince a learner to elaborate her/his **style of working with information**. Application software programs, such as editors (text and graphics), spreadsheets, presentation programs, usually have several options which support a user in improving her/his style (e.g., styles, templates, wizards, etc.). Elements of style are also very important when working with information on the Internet, and in searching, publishing and communicating on the web. A proper use of style options in software systems also depends on the subject area to which an elaborated information belongs, and such products benefit very much from a proper choice of styles.

We also expect students taking informatics (computer science) in high schools to have their own style in working with information, for instance in computer programs, data bases, spreadsheets, and multimedia presentations.

4.1.2 Creating "Computer Products"

In teaching informatics we use a standard methodology, called **algorithmic problem solving**, for the systematic development of a computer program (in general, a computer solution) for an algorithmic problem, which covers the entire process of designing and implementing the solution, from beginning to end. This methodology is aimed at generating good solutions, characterised by three fundamental properties: readability (the solution is understandable to anyone who is familiar with the problem domain and computer tools used), correctness (the solution satisfies the problem specification), and efficiency (the solution doesn't waste computing resources, time and space). The methodology consists of six stages:

1. *Problem situation.* Analyze and understand the problem statement, input and output description, limitations.
2. *Specification.* Develop a precise specification of the problem based on the understanding of its statement and analysis made in Stage 1. The problem specification consists of the input specification, the output specification and relations between input and output. The specification is then used in the next stages as a program specification.
3. *Design.* Design a computer solution (program) of the problem – choose an algorithmic technique (e.g. recursion) and algorithms together with the proper data structures. Decide which computer application should be used.
4. *Coding.* Write a complete computer solution based on the results of Stage 3. Translate, test and evaluate the computer solution, and test the correctness of the solution. Already available building blocks (e.g. elements of subroutine libraries) may be used as a complete solution or its parts.
5. *Testing.* Systematically verify and test your solution. Use the specification to verify if the correct answer is produced for specified problem inputs. Some problem benchmarks can be used to test the solution and to compare it with other solutions of the problem.
6. *Presentation.* Write a documentation of your solution and users' manual. The solution and the whole process which led to it can also be the subject of a presentation which is then shown to a teacher and to other students.

This methodology applies to problems which can be solved by designing an algorithm which is then implemented in a programming language as a computer program and run on a computer.

The main idea of our approach is that a similar methodology can be used to solve a majority of tasks and problems which are in the range of information technology rather than informatics (computer science) and end up with computer solutions that are not necessarily computer programs in the traditional sense, for instance: documents, configurations of an educational program, data bases, web pages, and multimedia presentations. Solving tasks and problems of information technology with the methodology which is inherent in computer science is an opportunity to expose students to computational thinking.

4.1.3 New Facets of Old Computer Science Notions

We extend the meaning of two computer science concepts, problem solving and programming, to see them in a wider context of using computers to solve tasks and problems which are not necessarily algorithmic in nature and introducing all students to computational thinking.

The core of computer science is about problem solving with computers. On the other hand, students deal with problems in almost all subjects and quite often a computer is a suitable tool for solving those problems. We may assume that, regardless of the discipline, **a problem** occurs when one has to provide an answer/solution based on what one has learned but is not told how to apply what was learned to solve the problem. A problem should contain a certain difficulty, not just be a simple task. When a computer is to be used in solving a problem we should also extend the range of the problem to finding an answer on how to provide its computer solution. In such a situation, our methodology described in this paper can be used to obtain a solution and to develop computational thinking while solving problems from various disciplines with the help of computers.

We want to also extend the meaning of a program and **programming**. A computer is a machine which only runs programs. It is fed with some basic programs and any user may use her/his own programs. New programs are usually the result of programming and they are often written in a programming language, a language which computers can understand. In schools however there is not enough time to teach a programming language and students are not prepared enough to learn programming. However, there are plenty of opportunities to teach how one can communicate with a computer by means of programs which are created by using tools other than programming language tools. We 'claim' that the following computer objects are programs: spreadsheet, data base, interactive and dynamic presentation, website, and also documents and graphics which are the elements of programming office packages. Hence again, one may use our methodology in teaching and learning how to obtain these objects which is the subject of information technology classes. Therefore information technology lessons may be used to develop computational thinking. This observation has an important meaning to school education since information technology is a subject taken by all students for many years.

Our meaning of programming a computer within information technology with no use of a programming language has a psychological advantage over programming in the traditional sense since learning a programming language is considered by the majority of students and their parents as the first step to a computer science career, but our goal is only to expose all students to computational thinking.

4.2 Computational Thinking in Informatics Education

In this section we present some examples of topics taken from the textbooks [7-9] to illustrate how the general approach described in Section 4.1 can be used to develop computational thinking.

4.2.1 The Use of Office Application Software

As mentioned above, while working with application (office) software, students are able to develop elaborations on their style by using system-embedded options, which support this development: styles, templates, wizards. As a result, 'computer products' generated by application software for various subjects benefit from a proper choice and use of styles.

On the other hand, teachers and their students may use a more general approach to obtain a computer product. Let us assume that a group of students, members of a school bicycle club, want to present the club in an electronic form (e.g. as a booklet, presentation, web page), which can be accessed from the school web site. The students' work may proceed according to the following stages (see Section 4.1.2):

1. *Problem situation.* Students discuss what kind of information about the club, and in which form (text, graphics, animation, films), they want to present it. They also decide how to proceed in obtaining information they do not yet have but wish to include in their presentation. Copyrights are also considered.
2. *Specification.* As a result of Stage 1, the content of the presentation is precisely described at this stage, together with some relations (links) between different portions of information.
3. *Design.* Students decide which computer application is the most suitable for their presentation (e.g. MS Publisher, MS PowerPoint, a webpage editor). Depending on the tool they choose, they now can plan a presentation and prepare the building bricks in an electronic format.
4. *Coding.* The computer presentation is constructed based on the design elaborated in Stage 3 and using information prepared in electronic formats. Moreover, students test whether the presentation works correctly.
5. *Testing.* In this stage students systematically verify and test the presentation to see if it satisfies its specification as determined in Stage 2.
6. *Presentation.* The presentation and the whole process which led to it now becomes the subject of a presentation shown to a teacher and to other students.

4.2.2 Sorting Techniques, Demo Software Packages

Sorting appears in many real-world situations and may be treated from different points of view: practical applications, operations and techniques performed, complexity (number of operations performed), practical efficiency, etc. We usually demonstrate different sorting techniques using educational software (see Fig. 1 and 2). Students like to discuss and discover the order in which the elements are compared and exchanged. They count the number of basic operations and they are surprised that it may take a while to sort an already sorted sequence of elements, before they realize that a computer cannot see that the sequence is already sorted.

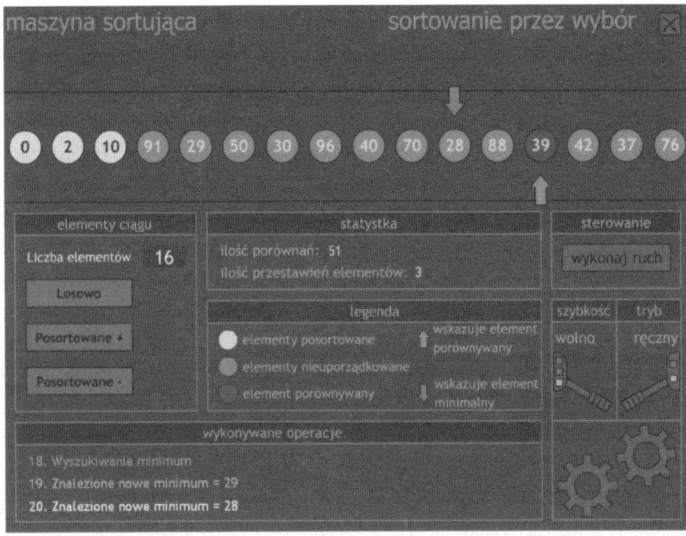

Fig. 1. Demonstration of the selection sort, and the algorithm for finding the smallest element

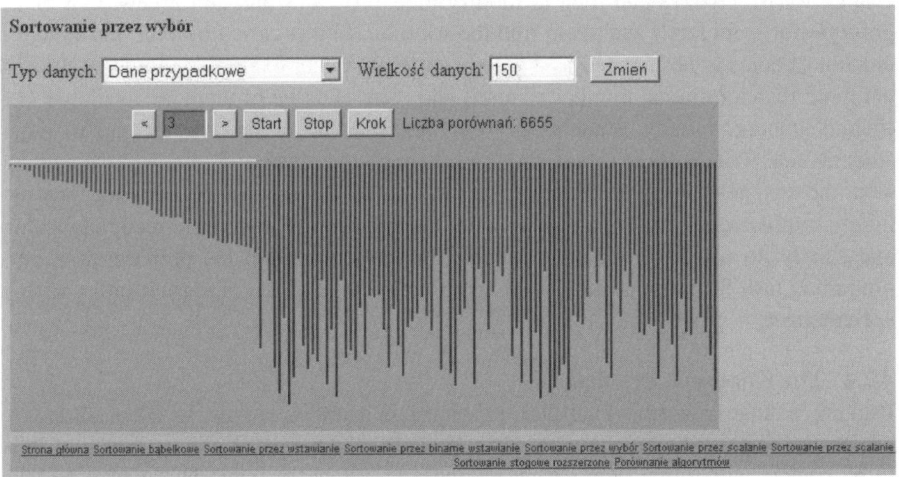

Fig. 2. Demo package for sorting algorithms (bubble, selection – in the figure, merge, insertion, binary insertion, heap, quicksort)

In our textbooks [7-9] we use a number of demos for showing how some of the algorithms work. In fact, these demos may be considered as unfinished programs, since students can program by defining their final versions choosing values of parameters.

4.2.3 The Change-Making Problem

The following is a problem situation presented to students in middle school [7]: given is a change *V*, find the least number of notes and coins of our currency which constitute the value V. We assume that each type of note and coin is available in unlimited quantity. We first ask students to discuss how they usually get their change in a shop (*Problem situation*). Quite often they remember situations in which they got many small coins, for instance in shops that sell newspapers and other small items such as chewing gum and pops, or in a school shop. The discussion leads to better understanding the problem, its formulation (i.e. *a specification* consisting of input, output and the relation between them) and hints how to solve it. Students easily come to a heuristic strategy which says that if you want to have the smallest amount of notes and coins you have to proceed in a greedy way – in each step the largest possible note or coin is used to form the change V. They verify the strategy making changes for different values of V. The *design stage* of solving this problem ends with a precise description of the greedy algorithm which solves the problem. Then in the *coding stage*, the algorithm is coded as a spreadsheet. This problem is thus used to demonstrate that a spreadsheet, such as MS Excel, may be used to program an algorithm[1]. In the next stage students *test their programs* (spreadsheets) using different instances of V. Finally we return to the specification and ask the students if their programs for a given value V really find the smallest possible number of notes and coins which constitute V. Most of them answer YES but they have difficulty in convincing the other students that they are right[2]. We ask them to use their programs to make a change for 61 groszys and then to modify their programs and add a new coin of 21 groszys (for gamblers!) and again find the solution. In this case, however, the smallest amount of coins is not formed as a greedy solution. Other examples show that we can get more than a minimal number of notes and coins if some of them are available in a limited amount. Finally, students *present* their finding to the teacher and to other students and write a short report about what they have done and obtained. In conclusion, the change-making problem appears to be very interesting for students, they are highly motivated to discuss possible solutions and then to code the greedy algorithm and finally, to test it on different values. Students also like this problem as a programming task for a spreadsheet – this problem is an example of **algorithmics with a spreadsheet**.

4.2.4 The Knapsack Problem

Packing a knapsack (the knapsack problem) is another simple problem situation, which can be solved by using a greedy approach: a knapsack of a given capacity W is to be packed with some items, each having a value and weight. The goal is to take items of the total weight at most W and the highest possible total value. In this case students usually come up with one of three strategies: first take the most valuable item, first take the lightest item, or first take the item with the largest value to weight ratio. Then, in the stage of *algorithm design*, they work hard to find a problem instance for which none of these greedy strategies produces the best solution. Greedy solutions can be easily coded in a spreadsheet. Some students are also able to follow and develop a dynamic programming algorithm for the knapsack problem.

---

[1] We have a number of other algorithmic problems which can be solved by using a spreadsheet as a programming tool, for instance calculating a square root (see [16]).
[2] The change-making problem is computationally one of the hardest combinatorial problems.

4.2.5 History of Computers and Informatics

Elements of the history of informatics can inspire and motivate students. There is much to learn from computing history and its deep ties with the historical development of other disciplines, such as mathematics, engineering, physics, biology and many others.

In informatics (computer science), in contrast to rapidly changing technology, one can identify timeless and invariant basic elements (e.g. notions, ideas, physical and mental constructions) which constitute a meaningful base of the discipline and its didactics. All traditional subjects with a long tradition in education, such as mathematics and physics, are full of everlasting ideas and constructions. Computer science with its close ties to these disciplines may share some of the common principles, such as information representation (e.g. binary, positional), information transmission (e.g. protocols), etc. [10]

All our textbooks [7-9] contain context references to historical ideas, notions, people, facts, and pictures, which are not only limited to the history of computing but also to historical events in other disciplines which have some connections to calculating machines, computers and computing. A set of 12 two-sided posters, entitled *History of computing: ideas, people, machines* has been published (see Fig. 3) and schools are encouraged to buy and hang them in computer labs.

There are only a few facts in the history of computing closely related to Poland and Polish. We think that at least two of them are very important contributions of Polish

Fig. 3. A poster from the set: *History of computing: ideas, people, machines*

scientists to the general history of computing. First, it was the introduction of the **Polish Notation** by Jan Łukasiewicz in the 1920's, which was later modified to form the **Reverse Polish Notation** (RPN). There are still many calculators available on the market with RPN. It is a challenging question for our students: why do such calculators have no key with the equal sign[3]. We also show them a number of these calculators (HP, Sinclair, MK). Unfortunately, we have no example of a calculator with RPN which was invented and produced in Poland!

Another, very important innovation in computing was "Polish Bomba", which was to simulate the Enigma, done by Marian Rejewski (see Figure 4) and his colleagues in the late 1930's and is considered the beginning of **computer cryptography**.

There are plenty of other opportunities in schools: when talking about other disciplines, one can mention historical facts, events or people, recognized in the history of computing and computers for their achievements. For example, we have Napier and his logarithms and then slide rules, Blaise Pascal with his calculator Pascalina, Wilhelm G. Leibniz and his stepped drum used in mechanical calculators (in Curta) until their last days in 1972, Babbage who tried to correct mechanically some very messy navigation and astronomy tables, Mark Twain, the first author who typed an entire book on a typewriter (old text editor) and Ernest Hemingway who said of his Corona 3 typewriter, "It is the only psychiatrist I would ever submit to". In fact we are using today a QWERTY computer keyboard invented in the second half of the XIX century, one in which all the letters of the word TYPEWRITER are located in one row, the QWERTY row!

Fig. 4. Marian Rejewski has a monument in Bydgoszcz (near Toruń), where he was born

---

[3] With respect to the first author, who had spent some time in Japan, it is also quite interesting to demonstrate to students that the Japanese read mathematical expressions as if they have been written in the RPN form, for instance 2+2=4 is read as 2 2 + 4 =.

Most important is to include historical facts from computing into the general history of human innovations and achievements and also to mention the contribution and impact of achievements in the domain of computing to the history of mankind. Although no general-purpose computer was constructed before the end of the WWII, the use of computing devices, such as "Polish Bomba" and a special-purpose computer called Colossus, helped the war to be ended two years earlier.

5 Conclusions

We have presented in this paper the way in which informatics can be taught today in secondary schools in Poland. The main focus moves from only using informatics tools by students to applying a general strategy of solving problems with the use of computers, to problems which arise in various school subjects, learning disciplines and in the real world.

The approach which we present can be viewed as an implementation of the computational thinking approach to learning and teaching about computers and with computers. We also strongly believe that this way of talking with students about computers and their role in solving problems may be a good motivation and preparation for their future decisions to study computing and become computer specialists.

References

1. Being Fluent with Information Technology, National Academy Press, Washington, DC (1999)
2. Clark, M.A.C., Boyle, R.D.: Computer Science in English High Schools: We Lost the S, Now the C Is Going. In: Mittermeir, R.T. (ed.) ISSEP 2006. LNCS, vol. 4226, pp. 83–93. Springer, Heidelberg (2006)
3. Cohen, A., Haberman, B.: Computer Science – A language of Technology (preprint)
4. Commission of the European Communities, eLearning – designing tomorrow's education, Brussels, SEC, 318 final (2000)
5. Denning, P.J.: Who Are We? Comm. ACM (2001)
6. Denning, P.J.: Great principles in computing curricula. In: Proceedings of SIGCSE 2004, Norfolk, Virginia, USA, pp. 336–341 (2004)
7. Gurbiel, E., Hardt-Olejniczak, G., Kołczyk, E., Krupicka, H., Sysło, M.M.: Informatics (in Polish). Textbook for middle school, WSiP, Warszawa (2007)
8. Gurbiel, E., Hard-Olejniczak, G., Kołczyk, E., Krupicka, H., Sysło, M.M.: Informatics (in Polish). Textbook for high school, WSiP, Warszawa, vol. 1 & 2 (2002-2003)
9. Gurbiel, E., Hardt-Olejniczak, G., Kołczyk, E., Krupicka, H., Sysło, M.M.: Information technology. Textbook for high school, WSiP, Warszawa (2007)
10. Humbert, L., Micheuz, P., Puhlmann, H.: Why history matters in school informatics. In: Medichi Workshop 2007 (Methodic and Didactic Challenges of the History of Informatics), Klagenfurt University, April 12-13 (2007)
11. McGettrick, A., Boyle, R., Ibbett, R., Lloyd, J., Lovegrove, G., Mander, K.: Grand Challenges in Computing – Education, British Computer Society (2004)
12. Snyder, L., Aho, A.V., Linn, M., Packer, A., Tucker, A., Ullman, J., van Dam, A.: Being Fluent with Information Technology. In: Committee in Information Technology Literacy, National Academy of Sciences. National Academy Press, Washigton (1999)

13. Stephenson, C., Gal-Ezer, J., Haberman, B., Verno, A.: The New Education Imperative: Improving High School Computer Science Education, Final Report of the CSTA Curriculum Improvement Task Force, CSTA, ACM (February 2005) http://csta.acm.org/Publications/White_Paper07_06.pdf
14. Syslo, M.M. (ed.): Standards for Information Technology and Informatics in Teacher Preparation, Ministry of Education and Sport in Poland, Warsaw (2003)
15. Syslo, M.M., Kwiatkowska, A.B.: Informatics Versus Information Technology – How Much Informatics Is Needed to Use Information Technology – A School Perspective. In: Mittermeir, R.T. (ed.) ISSEP 2005. LNCS, vol. 3422, pp. 178–188. Springer, Heidelberg (2005)
16. Syslo, M.M., Kwiatkowska, A.B.: Contribution of Informatics Education to Mathematics Education in Schools. In: Mittermeir, R.T. (ed.) ISSEP 2006. LNCS, vol. 4226, pp. 209–219. Springer, Heidelberg (2006)
17. Tucker, A., Deek, F., Jones, J., McCowan, J., Stephenson, C., Verno, A.: A Model Curriculum for K-12 Computer Science, Report of the ACM K-12 Education Task Force Computer Science Curriculum Committee, ACM (2003)
18. UNESCO, Information and Communication Technology in Education. A Curriculum for Schools and Programme of Teacher Development, IFIP/UNESCO (2002)
19. Wing, J.M.: Computational thinking. Communications of the ACM 49, 33–35 (2006)

Bebras International Contest on Informatics and Computer Literacy: Criteria for Good Tasks

Valentina Dagienė[1] and Gerald Futschek[2]

[1] Informatics Methodology Dept., Institute of Mathematics and Informatics, Lithuania
Dagiene@ktl.mii.lt
[2] Institute of Software Technology and Interactive Systems, Vienna University of Technology, Austria
Gerald.Futschek@tuwien.ac.at

Abstract. The Bebras International Contest on Informatics and Computer Literacy is a motivation competition in informatics that addresses all lower and upper secondary school pupils divided into three age groups: Benjamin (age 11-14), Junior (age 15-16) and Senior (for upper secondary level). Using a computer the pupils have to solve 15 to 21 tasks of different levels within 45 minutes. Two general types of problems have been used: interactive tasks and multiple-choice tasks. Creating interesting and attractive tasks that are also motivating and funny for the pupils is very challenging. The paper deals with criteria for good tasks. Some examples of tasks are presented and discussed as well.

Keywords: Teaching informatics, Computer education, Contest on computer literacy, Developing tasks.

1 Introduction

The quality of tasks is crucial for the success of all task-based competitions. Usually competitions have several goals and the tasks have to fulfill a wide variety of criteria. The tasks must reflect the goals of the competition and should be adequate for the applicants. Seeking to motivate students to learn science issues more deeply competitions are one of the best ways to capture their attention [3, 4, 12]. In educational competitions, tasks should attract students and drive them to learn and explore as well to develop skills in the particular area [6]. Children are attracted by competitions and get easier involved in discussions and become more active [11].

The Bebras International Contest on Informatics and Computer Literacy addresses pupils grade 5 to 12 (13 in some countries) and aims to motivate the participants to be interested in typical informatics problems. The Bebras Contest has a similar structure as the Kangaroo Contest in the field of Mathematics [9]. The students have to solve a series of tasks of three different difficulty levels. Each task takes between 1 to 4 minutes to be solved. Finding interesting and adequate tasks that can be solved in a few minutes seems to be much harder in the field of informatics than in the field of Mathematics. This paper shows criteria for good tasks and gives examples for good task development.

2 Experiences of the International Bebras Contest

The idea of the International Bebras Contest on Informatics and Computer Literacy originated in Lithuania 2003 (The name Bebras – in English "beaver" – is connected with the hard-working, intelligent, goal seeking and lively animal living around lakes and rivers in Lithuania and other countries). It took almost a year to create tasks and to prepare technology to implement it: the first contest started in October 2004. The organizers had the goal to make the Bebras Contest an international one. The well-known Baltic Olympiad in Informatics was organized in Lithuania in May 2005 [1]. It was a good opportunity to advertise the Bebras Contest at least for participants of the Olympiad (Denmark, Estonia, Finland, Germany, Latvia, Sweden, and Poland). During the Baltic Olympiad the international Bebras workshop for creating tasks was organized. Four more countries were invited and participated in the Bebras workshop (Austria, Egypt, Israel, and The Netherlands). Participants spent a lot of time discussing the structure and development of the contest as well as preparing tasks. It was decided to run the Bebras Contest each autumn (October-November).

In spring 2006, the second International Bebras Contest workshop was organized in Lithuania and the International Bebras Organizing Committee was established [8]. The main goal of the workshops is to develop a set of tasks for the coming Bebras Contest. After a year the third international Bebras workshop was organized again in the same place as previously. Two more countries joined the workshop: Slovakia and Ukraine.

At the moment some countries have already been running the international Bebras contest for their pupils, some are still in a preparation stage. In 2007, the Bebras Contest was very successful in Germany – 21 802 participants (www.informatik-biber.de), in Estonia – 2978 participants (www.miksike.ee), as well as in Lithuania – 7015 participants [8], in Poland – around 7000 participants (www.bobr.edu.pl), in the Netherlands – 2405 participants (www.beverwestrijd.nl), in Austria – 1400 participants (http://at.beverwedstrijd.nl/).

3 Categories of Tasks

Children and students are using computers and technology every day. Some of them have a better understanding, other are plain users. However users need also some thinking skills while applying technology. The best way to develop thinking skills is to solve problems. The ability of pupils to solve problems in real-life settings is of prime concern to educators and policy makers. Interest and engagement are very important in problem solving [3, 5].

Problem solving is an individual's capacity to use cognitive processes to confront and resolve real, cross-disciplinary situations where the solution path is not immediately obvious [2].

When teaching informatics and computer literacy via problem solving, it is very important to choose interesting tasks (problems) for motivating learning. Therefore, one should try to present problems from various fields of science and life, with a lot of real data.

Interest in competitions essentially depends on problems. Attraction, invention, tricks, surprise should be desirable features of each problem presented to competitors. The problems have to be selected carefully, taking into account the different aspects of each problem, i.e. what educational power it contains and how to interpret its attractiveness to students (whether it stimulates the motivation of learning).

Problems can be of different types: starting from the most common questions of computers and their applications in the daily life to specific integrated problems related to history, languages, arts, and, of course, mathematics. It is very important to choose the problems in such a way that the participants of the competition could have the same chance to solve the tasks, irrespective of the operating system or computer programs used by them.

In informatics, there is also the problem of syllabus. Even if there is an education standard for informatics at school in some countries, there till now there is no common agreement what should be included in an integrated syllabus using information technologies. We can use some guidelines e.g. the UNESCO recommendations [7].

In the first and second international Bebras contests some problems were related to the usage of various most common programs, others were related to hardware and software, and some of them were connected with the culture and language. So it could happen that some problems would not be applicable in some countries: some might appear too simple, and some – too complicated.

At the second international Bebras workshop (2006), a brainstorming session was held to generate ideas for different types of tasks that could be used in the contests. Also the classification of tasks was started to elaborate and some topics groups were suggested [10].

The classification proceeded further in the third Bebras workshop and in discussions between members of the Bebras Organizing Committee. In September 2007, some active members of the Bebras Organizing Committee have launched the meeting in Potsdam and elaborated the following proposal for topics of the Bebras contests on informatics and computer literacy.

INF	**Information comprehension**	
	Representation (symbolic, numerical, visual)	
	Coding, encryption	
ALG	**Algorithmic thinking**	
	Including programming aspects	
USE	**Using computer systems**	
	e.g. search engines, email, spread sheets, etc.	
	General principles, but no specific systems	
STRUC	**Structures, patterns and arrangements**	
	Combinatorics	
	Discrete structures (graphs, etc.)	
PUZ	**Puzzles**	
	Logical puzzles	
	Games (mastermind, minesweeper, etc.)	
SOC	**ICT and Society**	
	Social, ethical, cultural, international, legal issues	

This list of task categories improves the task types given in [10] in the respect that it forms a small number of groups of tasks of nearly the same importance and gives the categories names that are easily understandable even by pupils.

The selection of tasks is very important: a set of tasks must cover as many sub-areas of informatics as possible, including algorithms and programming methods, and what is most important, the pupils should acquire the skills of using them. The problems have to be selected taking into account the different aspects of each problem. Two large groups of problems were distinguished: 1) interactive problems (for making something with computer and technologies); 2) multiple choice questions.

The problems have to be selected carefully, with regard to different aspects of each problem (*i.e.*, what educational power it has) and interpretation of its attractiveness to pupils (whether it stimulates the motivation of learning).

4 Criteria for Good Bebras Tasks

The following list of criteria reflects the experiences of the International Bebras Organizing Committee in developing successful Bebras tasks:

Table 1. Criteria for good Bebras tasks on informatics and computer literacy that are used by the International Bebras Organizing Committee. The criteria that start with the word "should" may be not fulfilled by all Bebras tasks.

Good tasks ...	Explanation
are related to informatics, computer science or computer literacy	As stated in the aims, the Bebras contest is a competition on informatics and computer literacy.
allow learning experiences	In solving the tasks one should learn something interesting. Learning gives satisfaction and is never boring.
can be solved in 3 minutes	3 minutes is the average time to solve a task.
have a difficulty level (3 levels)	Level A (1/3): simple, all pupils of the target group should be able to solve. Level B (1/3): intermediate, challenging tasks that need some thinking to solve. Level C (1/3): hard to solve, only the best can solve these tasks.
are adequate for the age of contestants (3 age groups)	Bebras has 3 age groups: • Benjamin: grade 5 to 8, • Junior: grade 9 to 10, • Senior: grade 11 to 13. Some tasks may be suitable for more than one age group. They may differ in difficult level.
are independent from any curriculum	The International Bebras Contest cannot support all curricula of a large number of countries. The Bebras tasks are oriented on the usual ability of pupils of the addressed age groups.

Table 1. (*continued*)

Good tasks ...	*Explanation*
are independent from specific IT systems	Of course all tasks don't rely on pre-knowledge of details of specific IT systems. No specific operating system, programming language or application software is taken for granted. All system specific terms must be explained within a task.
have easy understandable problem statements	A problem statement should be presented as easy as possible: easy understandable wording, easy understandable presentation of the problem (maybe use of pictures, examples, embedded in a proper story, use of a simulation or an interactive solving process), a problem statement should never be misleading.
are presentable at a single screen page	A single task should never exceed a single screen page. Scrolling is not reasonable in a contest situation.
are solvable at a computer, without other hardware, additional software or paper and pencil	Bebras tasks are independent from specific operating or application systems. Use of additional software should not be necessary. Also a calculator should not be necessary to use. Mental arithmetic should be sufficient for all calculations. Cheating is much easier within a computer lab if paper and pencil is allowed.
are politically correct	Good tasks contain no gender, racial or religious stereotypes.
should be funny	Some sort of excitement or fun should be provoked by a good task or by solving the task. It should never be boring.
should have pictures	Tasks that involve pictures are more attractive. The pictures should play a role in understanding or solving the task. It should not be a mere illustration. Pictures are supporting visual thinking.
should have interactive elements (simulations, solving activities, etc)	Multiple-choice is in many cases not adequate. Sometimes it is appropriate to input a number or a word or have a choice of a list of possibilities. Often the result can be produced by operating a simulation of a machine that should be operated properly.
should give immediate feedback	After solving a task correctly the participant should have the certainty of having solved the task correctly.

Furthermore a good Bebras task should not be tricky. A tricky task is usually too hard to be solved by thinking, but the knowledge of a very specific detail allows the solution.

To discuss this list of criteria we give some examples of tasks that were given at beaver competitions. The first one lacks some of these criteria, the others are almost perfect.

4.1 Example Task: Tomorrows Weather

We consider the following multiple choice task:

> *Assume that the weather would follow the rule:*
>
> *"If there is a sunny day, the day after will be sunny too"*
>
> *If it is sunny today, what could you infer?*
>
> **A.** *It is always sunny*
> **B.** *Yesterday it was sunny*
> **C.** *From now on it will always be sunny*
> **D.** *It will never be sunny again*
>
> *(One of the answers is correct)*

Fig. 1. The Tomorrows Weather task that was given at Bebras contest 2007

At the first glance it seems that this task is a pure logic thinking question, but the requested sort of thinking is exactly the same as it is necessary to understand loops in algorithms and programs. Therefore the task category is partly algorithmic thinking (ALG) and partly puzzles (PUZ) because of its logical puzzle characteristic. If one is not sure that C is the correct answer it should be possible to exclude the wrong answers by falsification of the answers A, B and D.

This task does not fulfill all optional criteria for good tasks:

- It has no picture involved
- It has no interactive elements

In the Bebras competition 2007 in Austria this task (a German translation) was used in the age groups Benjamin and Senior. In both age groups it was the task with the highest number of wrong answers.

Due to this fact we can say that also some other criteria are not completely fulfilled:

- It is not funny (interesting) to solve the task (what is funny when the idea of the task was not grasped by so many pupils?)
- The problem statement is not easily understandable (maybe there were problems to understand the term "infer")
- It does not allow enough learning experiences (what can be learned when nearly all participants failed to solve the task?)

Due to this list of not fulfilled criteria it is now - after the competition - questionable if this was really a good Bebras task.

The Weather task yielded also another interesting result: it was the only task that had more correct solutions in the younger group (22%) than in an elder group (10%). It is very surprising that it was this logic oriented task that was easier for the younger pupils to find the correct solution.

4.2 Example Task: Islands in a Lake

Now we give an example of a possibly perfect interactive task:

> *Beaver discovered a number of islands in a lake and decided to build bridges to connect them. While building bridges Beaver follows the rules: the bridges must be built keeping the directions East-West and North-South and they shouldn't overlap each other.*
>
> *Help Beaver to build as many bridges as possible. Use the mouse to connect pairs of islands.*

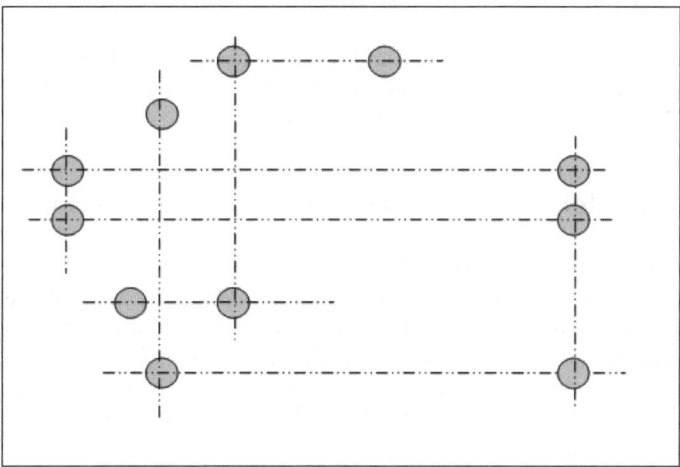

Fig. 2. An interactive task, age group Junior, difficulty level A (simple)

It is an algorithmic thinking (ALG) task, since a solution strategy incorporates strategies to find all different ways of building bridges. The possibility of interactively building bridges that are counted automatically and that can also be reset allows a sort of game-based learning.

4.3 Example Task: Shape Manipulation

Anne created a program, which includes just three operations:
- *rotation of the shape 90 degrees to the right*
- *rotation of the shape 90 degrees to the left*
- *mirroring of the shape*

These operations can be performed unlimitedly.

Which one of these shapes is IMPOSSIBLE to attain while experimenting with the given shape?

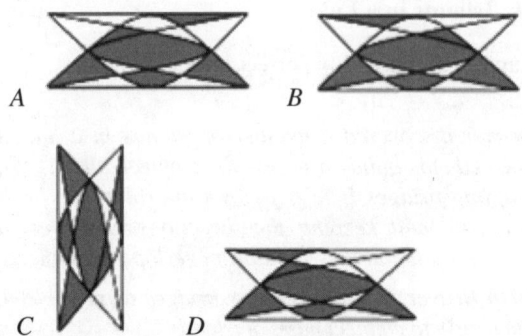

Fig. 3. A multiple choice task, age group Benjamin, difficulty level C

This multiple choice task does not involve any interactive elements. The challenge in this task is not doing but imagining the possible effects of the operations. It is a way of thinking that is also necessary in testing software.

5 Challenges for the International Bebras Task Development

Each year the international Bebras workshop develops a set of new tasks and questions. The group of international experts in pedagogy and computer science follows a process that allows creativity in finding new tasks and ensures a high quality of the output. It is not easy to create tasks that fulfill all criteria. Even the mandatory criteria are often hard to meet. But all tasks that do not fulfill the mandatory criteria have to be dropped. Often it is a process of several versions from an imperfect task formulation to an acceptable formulation.

The mandatory criteria that are usually hard to meet are:

- the task can be solved within 3 minutes
- the problem statement is easy understandable
- the task is presentable at a single screen page
- the task is solvable at a PC without use of other SW or paper and pencil
- the task is independent from specific systems

Practical tasks in informatics are usually not solvable within 3 minutes. So the tasks for the Bebras contest have to concentrate on smaller learning items. Due to the independence from specific systems the focus of the tasks is not the work in real systems but the understanding of the principles, ideas and concepts that are involved in informatics systems.

The easy understandability of tasks is in all contexts a very important goal. Not only the wording but also the presentation of the task that may include interactive elements is important. Since the pupils should be able to solve a task in an average time of 3 minutes, the formulation of a task should be as short as possible but at any rate no longer than a single screen page. Since the Bebras contest is performed at PCs there should be no need for paper and pencil to solve a task. It should not be easier to solve a task on paper than without paper. Usually it is possible to provide suitable interactive elements on the PC so that a solution on the PC is easier.

Of course the desirable criteria are much harder to meet; two of them are discussed here:

- should be funny,
- should have interactive elements

What is funny differs from person to person. But it is important that the authors of the tasks think about the possible feelings of the pupils when they are confronted with the tasks. The Bebras Contest should motivate the pupils to be interested more deeply in informatics. This goal can only be reached if the tasks are interesting and provoke some excitement. Pure knowledge tasks are often not as exciting as tasks where thinking is necessary to solve them. Most of the Bebras tasks give new situations the pupils have never seen before, so thinking is the only way to find the correct solution.

The interactivity is very typical for computers, so it is clear that a computer oriented contest should apply interactive elements to explain or solve tasks. Very often these interactive elements are "funny" to use and make the understandability of the problem statement much easier.

Especially the interactive elements need a lot of effort in the implementation of the tasks. But due to the attractiveness of interactive tasks the high effort for implementing the interactive part is worth to be done.

6 Example of a Task Development

Now we describe the development of a task from the initial idea for that task to an intermediate, not satisfactory state to the final formulation.

6.1 Idea for a Data Structure Task and First Formulation

At the beginning was the idea for a task that involves the data structure "Heap". For a given binary tree with values at the nodes we wanted to ask how many exchanges of values are necessary to achieve a "Heap".

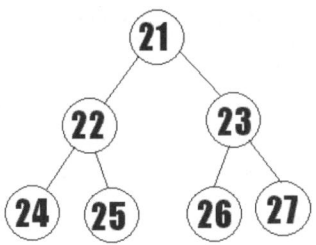

Fig. 4. The binary tree that should be transformed to a "Heap"

Since we cannot expect that the addressed pupils are familiar with the data structure of a "Heap" we had to give a definition of a "Heap".

> *The picture shows a binary tree with values in the nodes. A binary tree is called a "Heap" if each parent node has a value greater than or equal to both child nodes. The given binary tree is not a "Heap". Give the minimum number of value exchanges (of any two nodes) that produces a "Heap".*
>
> *Answers: A) 2   B) 3   C) 4   D) 5*

Fig. 5. The first formulation of the Heap task

This formulation requires pre-knowledge of the graph theoretical terms "node" and "binary tree", so this task may be suitable only for pupils of the senior age group.

The main problem with this task is that it is not easy understandable. There is only a textual definition of a "Heap"; an example of a "Heap" may be very useful. If we would use an example with other values than the given binary tree, the problem description would be extremely lengthy and the presence of two different trees would possibly be disturbing and misleading. If we would present the final Heap with the values at the final positions of the given tree, this task would be understandable and very easy to solve but there would be no learning about the "Heap" data structure possible.

As we found the idea of this task very interesting and suitable for the Bebras contest we had to work on a better presentation of this task.

6.2 Final Formulation with the Technique of Telling a Suitable Story

Finally we tried to find a suitable story that makes the understanding of a "Heap" more intuitively and more easily. The idea for the story was "to take a group photo of the young beavers". This led to the final formulation of the Beaver's Group Photo task:

> *To make a group photo of 7 beavers it is necessary that the smaller beavers stand in front and the larger beavers in back. Unfortunately the beavers stand in a wrong order. In the graphics below those beavers are connected by a line where the back beaver should be larger than the front beaver. The only operation to rearrange beavers you can do is exchanging any two beavers of the group.*
> *What is the minimum number of exchange-operations, that after all, the beavers are ready for taking picture?*
> *Please perform a minimum number of exchange-operations by clicking on pairs of beavers.*

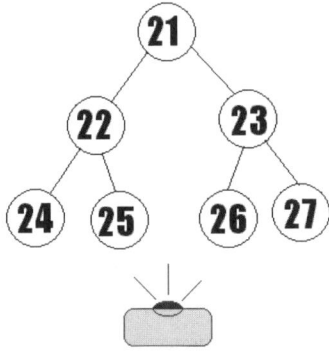

Fig. 6. The final formulation of the Heap task, that is easier understandable, it involves an interactive solution

This task was given at the Bebras Contest 2006 in all three age groups. Even the youngest pupils could solve this task due to its easy formulation using the photographer story.

To avoid use of paper and pencil in solving this task a good Bebras system should provide a possibility to interactively exchange the beavers. An automatic counter could count the number of exchanges that can be used to find the solution. In fact not all Bebras systems used by the Bebras countries in 2006 supported the interactive exchange of beavers.

7 Summary

We discussed the special challenges for the group of people who create tasks for the Bebras Contest. They have the goal to find interesting ("funny") tasks in the field of Informatics and Computer Literacy that are challenging and can be solved in a very short time. A list of criteria for good tasks helps them to create and quality check the created tasks.

In some cases a suitable story may make a presentation of a task much easier so that also younger participants may solve the problem.

We are open for all kinds of proposals and ideas of collaboration and hope to find friends and partners in all countries. Integration of information technologies into the teaching process and understanding technology while using computers should be our target. We should collaboratively try reaching it.

We are ready to share our experience, technology, and future plans with all who are interested. We expect that it will foster your own competitions similar to the Bebras contest or will encourage you to join us. We are sure that a well-organized competition with interesting, playful, exciting problems, and attractive awards will invite children of all countries to reason about proper use of computers and to explore and to understand realities, possibilities, and failings of technology.

Acknowledgements

First of all the authors would like to thank all members of the International Bebras Organizing Committee. Each and every one of them contributed to this project. Especially the authors would like to thank Hans-Werner Hein, Wolfgang Pohl, Ries Kock, and Maciej Syslo who took part in the discussions of criteria for good Beaver tasks.

References

1. Bulotaitė, J., Diks, K., Opmanis, M., Prank, R.: Baltic Olympiads in Informatics, Inst. of Math. and Inf., Vilnius, Lithuania (1997)
2. Casey, P.J.: Computer programming: A medium for teaching problem solving. In: Computers in the Schools, vol. XIII, pp. 41–51. The Haworth Press, New York (1997)
3. Dagiene, V.: Information Technology Contests – Introduction to Computer Science in a Attractive Way. Informatics in Education 5(1), 37–46 (2006)
4. Dagiene, V.: Competition in Information Technology: an Informal Learning. In: EuroLogo 2005: the 10th European Logo Conference. Digital Tools for Lifelong Learning, Warsaw, August 28–31, 2005, pp. 228–234 (2005)
5. Dagiene, V., Skupiene, J.: Learning by competitions: Olympiads in Informatics as a tool for training high grade skills in programming. In: Boyle, T., Oriogun, P., Pakstas, A. (eds.) 2nd International Conference Information Technology: Research and Education, London, pp. 79–83 (2004)
6. EI:SPIEL game (in German) (accessed 2008-01-15), https://www.ei-spiel.de
7. van Weert, T., Anderson, J. (eds.): Information and communication technologies in education: A planning guide. UNESCO (2002)
8. International IT contest Bebras (2006) (accessed 2008-01-15), http://www.bebras.lt
9. International Kangoroo Mathematics contests (accessed 2008-01-15), http://www.sms.edu.pk/IKMC_sms.php
10. Opmanis, M., Dagienė, V., Truu, A.: Task Types at Beaver Contests Standards. In: Dagienė, V., Mittermeir, R. (eds.) Proc. of the 2nd Int. Conference Informatics in Secondary Schools: Evolution and Perspectives, Vilnius, pp. 509–519 (2006)
11. Pohl, W.: Finding Talented Young People for Informatics. In: Open IFIP-GI-Conf. on Social, Ethical and Cognitive Issues of Informatics and ICT, Book of Abstr., Univ. of Dortmund, Germany, July 2002, p. 77 (2002)
12. Reed, W.M., Burton, J.K.: Educational computing and problem solving. The Haworth Press, New York (1998)

From Top Coders to Top IT Professionals

Krzysztof Diks and Jan Madey

Institute of Informatics, University of Warsaw, Banacha 2, 02-097 Warsaw, Poland
{diks,madey}@mimuw.edu.pl

Abstract. This paper presents the history of successes of young Poles in the field of computer science (particularly, in programming) in the past 15 years and indicates the grounds for their outstanding achievements. We will also discuss conditions which should be fulfilled in order for successes of young computer scientists to evolve into achievements in their professional life, corresponding to their abilities and ambition. It seems that Polish experiences are universal enough to be adopted also by some other countries and could be helpful in the process of selecting gifted IT students and in work with them.

1 Introduction

In school year 1993/1994 the first Polish Olympiad in Informatics [1] was organized. The Olympiad is a national competition in informatics for high school students, recognized and financially supported by the Ministry of National Education. Around 12000 students have taken part in all editions of the Olympiad organized so far. Since school year 1995/1996 Polish high school students have been bringing gold medals from the International Olympiad in Informatics [2] every year. The biggest successes of Polish contestants are the victories at the International Olympiad in Informatics in 2006 (Filip Wolski defeated 282 contestants from 74 countries) and 2007 (Tomasz Kulczyński defeated 283 contestants from 77 countries). Academic successes of former Olympiad contestants prove how good the participants of the Polish Olympiad in Informatics are. The biggest achievements include victories of Warsaw University[1] teams in the ACM International Collegiate Programming Contest [3] in 2003 (Tomasz Czajka, Andrzej Gąsienica-Samek, Krzysztof Onak won a team victory in Beverly Hills, defeating in the finals 69 teams selected in the process of elimination from 3850 teams representing 1329 schools from 68 countries) and 2007 (Marek Cygan, Marcin Pilipczuk, Filip Wolski won a team victory in Tokyo, defeating in the finals 88 teams selected in the process of elimination from 6099 teams representing 1756 schools from 82 countries). Poles have also been successful in such world competitions as TopCoder Open [4], Google Code Jam 2005 [5], Microsoft's Imagine Cup [6] and the IEEE Computer Society Annual International Design Competition [7].

---
[1] The name "Warsaw University" has been recently changed by the Senate of the University into the "University of Warsaw" which became the official one in English and hence will be used in this paper.

The role of competitions in selecting and educating particularly gifted high school and university students cannot be underestimated. These educational events require knowledge and skills greatly exceeding what is taught at schools and universities. As an example, in [8] one can find minimum requirements which are to be met by participants of the International Olympiad in Informatics. A good competition always relates to the basis of the discipline which it concerns and the knowledge and skills acquired through participation therein are not volatile and constitute grounds for further field-related development. What is of even greater importance is for the competition to engage and develop skills necessary in the future professional activity of these young people: diligence, constant striving for self-development, self-discipline, hunger for knowledge, self-improvement, ability to work in a team, honesty, ambition, eagerness to compete, striving for success. Taking part in a good competition should pose intellectual challenge to a young person, whilst success should distinguish. On the other hand, competition organizers should make sure that participants have the ability to get to know one another and make close contacts which can bear fruit in their professional life. All of the aforementioned competitions meet these criteria.

No competition should be the goal as such. Discovered talents must be perfected, which means providing talented young people with possibilities of education at the highest world level, contacts with the best researchers in the field, internships and trainings in top companies having an actual impact on the development of the field, challenging tasks to be solved, and finally providing young people with financial means enabling their full engagement in professional work corresponding to their ambition, knowledge and abilities.

In this article we present a review of the most important Polish and world competitions in informatics. We provide their short characteristics and present the most significant successes of Poles in these competitions. Furthermore, we attempt to characterize the main factors which form the basis of successes of young Polish computer scientists. Finally, we deliberate on what can be done in order for successes of young people to evolve into professional achievements in their adult life.

2 Competitions in Informatics

The most important competitions in informatics for high school and university students are these involving elements of algorithmics and programming. In competitions of this type participants are presented with a certain number of tasks to be solved, each of which consists of a short story presenting the problem situation which is to be solved. The solution to a task is usually an algorithm in the form of a program written in a (algorithmic) programming language chosen by a contestant from the set offered by the organizers of the contest. The most commonly used programming languages are C and C++. In recent years a decreasing interest in the Pascal language and an increased popularity of the Java language could be observed. Correctly compiled programs are then run against tests prepared by the organizers and unknown to the contestants. Tests are chosen in a manner enabling detection of incorrect programs

Task: COD

Every permutation $A = (a_1, ..., a_n)$ of numbers $1, ..., n$ can be coded by a sequence $B = (b_1, ..., b_n)$ in which b_i equals the number of all a_j such that ($j < i$ & $a_j > a_i$), for $i = 1, ..., n$.

Example
The sequence $B = (0, 0, 1, 0, 2, 0, 4)$ is the code of the permutation $A = (1, 5, 2, 6, 4, 7, 3)$.

Task
Write a program that:

- reads from the text file COD.IN the length n and successive elements of the sequence B,
- examines whether it is a code of some permutation of numbers $1, ..., n$,
- if so, it finds that permutation and writes it in the text file COD.OUT,
- otherwise it writes in the file COD.OUT one word NO.

Input
In the first line of the text file COD.IN there is a positive integer $n <= 30000$. It is the number of elements of the sequence B. In each of the following n lines there is one nonnegative integer not greater than 30000. It is the successive element of the sequence B.

Output
The file COD.OUT should contain: in each of n consecutive lines - one element of the permutation A, whose code is the sequence B written in the file COD.IN, or word NO, if the sequence B is not a code of any permutation.

Examples

For the file COD.IN:
6
0
0
1
2
1
3

The file COD.OUT should contain:
1
6
4
2
5
3

For the file COD.IN:
2
1
0

The file COD.OUT should contain:
NO

and differentiation of solutions of different efficiency complexity, with main focus on time complexity, whereas memory complexity is restricted by explicitly specified limitations of memory used by the program. Depending on the competition, a solution is assessed in a binary manner (all tests passed/some tests failed) or it receives a number of points based on its quality. In order to make the readers familiar with the style of competition tasks, we present one of the tasks from the 2nd Polish Olympiad in Informatics.

People interested in combinatorics should discover at once that the task COD concerns reconstructing a permutation from its inversion vector. In order to solve this task one has to find out a bijection between permutations and inversion vectors. The simplest way leading to this discovery (one has to examine the given inversion vector from the end to the beginning) gives an algorithm working in n^2 time. However, there are algorithms running in time $O(nlogn)$. In order to design such an algorithm knowledge about binary search trees is needed. We also have to keep in mind that it is not sufficient for a contestant to discover the right algorithm — he or she has to write a correct program implementing the invented algorithm. Even professional programmers are not able to write programs without errors at once. In order to get correct programs they have to remove syntax errors, run several tests to remove logical faults and finally examine the efficiency of the solution. Every participant of an algorithmic/programming competition follows this path. At a small scale, contestants go through implementation stages of actual programming projects, which include:

- task analysis (finding connections between permutations and inversion vectors),
- consideration of possible solutions and selection of the best one (searching for algorithms, choice of data structures, analysis of complexity, selection of programming language),
- implementation of the selected solution (writing the program in the chosen programming environment, deleting compilation errors, testing),
- submission of work results to the user (sending the written program to competition judges).

This simple example already shows that in order to be successful in algorithmic and programming competitions, one must possess the following skills:

- ability to analyze algorithmic tasks precisely (knowledge of mathematics and logical reasoning are especially helpful in this process),
- ability to program in at least one high level programming language,
- knowledge of at least one programming environment as well as ability to compile, debug and implement programs in this environment,
- knowledge of basic techniques of algorithm and data structure design.

Winners of prestigious competitions possess the above skills at the level represented by the best professionals in the field.

Below we present short characteristics of the 5 most prestigious competitions in informatics for high school and university students as well as the most significant achievements of Poles in these competitions.

2.1 Olympiads in Informatics

The Olympiad in Informatics is a competition targeted at high school students. Winners (the first four) of national programming competitions represent their countries at the International Olympiad in Informatics (IOI) [2]. The Polish Olympiad in Informatics (POI) [1] consists of three stages. At each stage contestants are presented with a number of tasks. The first stage is usually organized in October and November. It gathers over a thousand of contestants. The contestants are presented with five or six tasks that should be solved at home within a month and sent for evaluation. About 360 contestants are qualified to the second stage of the competition. The second stage is organized in six regional centers located at universities cooperating with the POI and takes three days. The first day is a preparation day — the contestants are to solve one or two tasks during a three-hour session. However, the results are not counted in the competition. During the second and the third day the contestants are to solve two or three tasks during five-hour sessions. Solutions are collected from all the centers and evaluated centrally. About 70 contestants are qualified to the third stage of the competition. The final, third stage is organized in one place and takes five days. Similarly to the second stage, there are three competition days. The two other days are for pleasure. The first competition day is also a preparation day, during which contestants have to solve one or two tasks in three hours. Each of the other two competition days contestants have to solve three tasks in five hours. The four best contestants represent Poland at the International Olympiad in Informatics (IOI) which takes place every summer. The finals of the POI follow rules of the IOI. Every year the IOI gathers the best computer science pupils from the whole the world. The first International Olympiad in Informatics took place in year 1989, four years before the POI started. Since then Polish students have won 23 gold, 22 silver and 19 bronze medals and in the years 2006 and 2007 Poles were the overall winners of the IOI — Filip Wolski and Tomasz Kulczyński respectively.

2.2 The ACM International Collegiate Programming Contest (ICPC)

ICPC [3] is the oldest and the most prestigious computer science competition in the world and it is considered to be world championship in team programming. ICPC is targeted at university students and it is a team competition. Each team consists of three students representing the same university. ICPC is a two-stage competition. The first stage involves regional eliminations. There are a few dozen of such eliminations and they take place on all inhabited continents. Teams which prove to be the best in the eliminations (which always include the winners and a few further teams depending on a strength of the origin and the number of participating teams) advance to the finals. Both the eliminations and finals are carried out in the same manner. Each three-member team has one computer at its disposal, five hours of time and from 8 to 12 tasks to be solved. Solutions of particular tasks are evaluated at real time and teams are informed about the result of task evaluation: accepted, run-time error, time-limit exceeded, wrong answer, presentation error. Particular tasks are evaluated as accepted or rejected. The team which completes the most tasks wins the competition. In the event that more teams complete the same number of tasks, they will be ranked based on the shorter total time spent on solving completed tasks. However, each rejected submission of a completed task results in a 20-minut time penalty.

The history of the ACM competition goes back to 1977 and is inseparably connected with Bill Poucher, the originator and animator of the competition. At the beginning the competition was meant for teams from the United States (between 10 and 20). In academic year 2006/2007 the 31st Annual ACM International Collegiate Programming Contest hosted 6099 teams representing 1756 universities from 82 countries, out of which 88 teams advanced to the finals in Tokyo. In the academic year 1994/1995 Poles, the University of Warsaw team to be precise, took part in the ACM competition for the first time, instantly advancing to the finals and finishing at 11th place. The University of Warsaw teams have uninterruptedly taken part in the finals of this competition ever since. Only two universities from North America beat the University of Warsaw as far as frequency of participation is concerned, namely Virginia Tech and the University of Waterloo. The biggest successes of the University of Warsaw (and Poland) are victories in the ACM competition finals in 2003 and 2007. The winning team of 2003 included Tomasz Czajka (the winner of the Polish Olympiad in Informatics in school year 1999/2000), Andrzej Gąsienica-Samek (the winner of the Polish Olympiad in Informatics in school years 1994/1995, 1996/1997 and 1997/1998), Krzysztof Onak (2nd place in the Polish Olympiad in Informatics in school years 1997/1998 and 1999/2000). Academic world champions in team programming in 2007 were: Marek Cygan (participant of the 2nd stage of the Polish Olympiad in Informatics in school years 2001/2002 and 2002/2003), Marcin Pilipczuk (5th place in the Polish Olympiad in Informatics in school year 2001/2002, 13th place in school year 2002/2003), Filip Wolski (the winner of the Polish Olympiad in Informatics in school years 2004/2005 and 2005/2006, the winner of the International Olympiad in Informatics in 2006). Other significant achievements in this competition include 2nd place of the Jagiellonian University team (Arkadiusz Pawlik, Bartłomiej Walczak, Paweł Walter) in 2006, 5th place of the team from the University of Wrocław in 2005 (Paweł Gawrychowski, Jakub Łopuszański, Tomasz Wawrzyniak), 6th, 7th and 10th place of teams from the University of Warsaw in 2001, 2006 and 2004 subsequently. All members of these teams took part in the Polish Olympiad in Informatics while they were high school students.

2.3 TopCoder

The TopCoder competition [4] is one of the youngest yet extremely popular competitions in the world. The number of registered contestants representing over 200 countries is at present about 145.000. TopCoder is a competition for individuals and features 3 categories: Algorithm, Design and Development. The Algorithm category is the most popular one. It involves participants playing programming matches which take place once a week on average. Each match lasts around one and a half hour and is divided into two phases: coding phase and challenge phase. In the coding phase participants are presented with three tasks: easy, of medium difficulty and difficult, for 250, 500 and 1000 points respectively. In order to obtain a positive number of points, the task must be solved correctly. The number of points for a correctly solved task depends on the time spent on solving it. In the challenge phase participants can see programs of other match participants and may question their correctness. For each detection of an incorrect solution one can receive additional points, whereas incorrect reports result in deduction of points. The participant with the most points becomes the winner of the match. Ranking of all participants is created on the basis of results of the matches already played. Ranking points of students form the basis for ranking of universities and countries. Since February 2005 University of Warsaw has been ranked first in the TopCoder university ranking and Poland has been ranked second, slightly falling behind Russia. As of the day of writing this article (March 2008), there are 3 Poles among the top ten participants (Marek Cygan — on the third position, Tomasz Czajka, Tomasz Kulczyński), each of whom has been a participant of the Polish Olympiad of Informatics.

2.4 Imagine Cup

Imagine Cup [6] is a competition organized by Microsoft. It is targeted at university students and encompasses 9 categories: Software Design, Embedded Development, Game Development, Project Hoshimi, IT Challenge, Algorithm, Photography, Short Film, and Interface Design. As can be concluded from the names of particular categories, the competition is addressed to both developers of IT tools and their users. The aim of the competition is to stimulate creativeness of its participants. Poland has also had spectacular successes in this competition. In 2007 Poles won in the following categories: Algorithm (Przemysław Dębiak), Photography (Iwona Bielecka, Małgorzata Łopaciuk), Short Film (Julia Górniewicz, Jacek Barcikowski).

2.5 Computer Society International Design Competition (CSIDC)

A few years ago IEEE computer society started searching for a new competition formula for IT academic teams different from that of ICPC. As result of this effort the CSIDC [7] competition had its debut in 2000. Participants of the competition were to design and create a particular computer controlled device as a part of their academic classes. Participating universities were drawn from those willing to take part in the competition (in order to have a number of participants specified in advance, usually around 200 world-wide). They received proper equipment kits and programming packages from the organizers.

After a few months each of the participating teams presented a report which was then evaluated by experts from industry and academy. The ten projects evaluated best advanced to the finals. In the finals each team had a chance to present the results of its work live. After proper debate experts chose the winner.

It turns out that also in this competition Polish computer scientists had great successes. Teams from Poznań University of Technology advanced to the finals six times, winning in the second and fourth edition of CSIDC (years 2001, 2004) and finishing second in 2002 and 2005 as well as third in 2000. Unfortunately, due to financial reasons the competition is not organized since 2007.

3 Anatomy of Success

In this chapter we attempt to answer a question: what is the secret of successes of young Polish computer scientists? Without doubt numerous successes of young people repeated every year are not a coincidence. They also didn't happen overnight. It seems that the most important and long-term undertaking which had a great impact on the development of computer science among youth in Poland was the organization of the Olympiad in Informatics in 1993. The Olympiad is an institution which in cooperation with the Ministry of National Education, the best universities in the country (the University of Warsaw, Jagiellonian University, the University of Wrocław, Poznań University of Technology, AGH University of Science and Technology), teachers and IT industry selects IT gifted high school students and takes care of their development in an organized manner. These goals are realized by providing pupils with the opportunity of noble rivalry in solving challenging computer science tasks. These tasks are prepared both by world-class computer scientists and former participants of the Olympiad, who participate successfully in academic competitions. Moreover, former contestants of the Olympiad participate actively in Olympiad-related works by preparing model solutions of tasks presented at the Olympiad and they are the authors of the sophisticated software used during the Olympiad for the purposes of automatization of work, particularly automatic evaluation of contestants' solutions.

Besides the Olympiad, a very important role in the development of the most gifted young people is played by the Polish Children's Fund [9] — an organization which for already 25 years takes care of gifted pupils (not only with IT talent). During workshops and camps organized by the Fund, the participants have the chance to familiarize themselves with these fields of computer science which they do not necessarily have to encounter while taking part in competitions. A vast majority of the aforementioned winners of different contests were participating in the Fund's programme — many of them (e.g. Tomasz Czajka, Andrzej Gąsienica-Samek, Marcin Pilipczuk, Filip Wolski) since early childhood. The Polish Children Fund is a unique organization not only in Poland. Its activities are based on cooperation with numerous higher educational and/or research institutions, as well as with individual academics willing to offer their time and experience to work with particularly talented children and young people.

The Olympiad conducts intensive educational activity. Each year post-Olympiad materials are published and contain detailed analysis of solutions to tasks presented at the Olympiad as well as model programs. Former Olympiad contestants run an Internet educational portal for beginners in the field of programming and algorithmics [10], thanks to which even pupils from small towns and villages have the chance to discover the secrets of "real" computer science. Every year finalists of the Olympiad have the opportunity to participate in summer camps combining recreation and education, during which they attend lectures prepared by researchers and older students. They may also develop their algorithmic and programming skills by taking part in practical programming workshops.

People involved in the Olympiad's work are very often authors or translators of the most important IT handbooks, thanks to which young people can study in their mother tongue.

The first person who can notice the talent of a student and help him/her choose the right development path is the teacher. That is why the Olympiad organizes workshops for teachers, during which they can familiarize themselves in practice with the specificity of computer science competitions.

Such broad activity would not be possible without financial support. Activity of the Olympiad in Informatics is financed from both public means (grant from the Ministry of National Education) and private means from top IT companies in Poland. At this point the significant role of the IT system integrator PROKOM SOFTWARE S.A., a company that has been co-organizing the Olympiad since 1997, must be emphasized.

What is also of great importance is the fact that the best Olympiad contestants, winners of programming competitions, form an elite and are role models for future generations. Being a part of the elite is beneficial. This statement is reflected in the policies of the top universities in the country which admit finalists of the Olympiad to university without qualification procedure. The Faculty of Mathematics, Informatics and Mechanics of the University of Warsaw itself yearly admits around 50 finalists, who belong the group of the best students. Such a group of gifted students gives teachers the opportunity to prepare classes at the highest level and expect a lot of their students.

To sum up, the keys to success include:
- dedicated people (researchers, teachers, students, pupils),
- dedicated organizations (universities, the Ministry of National Education, schools),
- financial security (the Ministry, sponsors — PROKOM SOFTWARE Company, ATM S.A.),
- quality (both task quality assurance and organization quality).

4 What Further

In order to achieve success at high school and university level, it's enough to have a group of dedicated people, good organization, official and financial support. The most gifted young people are admitted to top universities in the country, which guarantee high quality of their education. Achievements in competitions guarantee financial support (scholarships) as well as possibility of internships in the best IT companies in the world. Every year a few dozen of students of the University of Warsaw complete internships in the largest and the best companies such as Google, Nvidia, Microsoft, or IBM. While still at university, they manage to find employment without any problems. However, the question remains whether it is the kind of employment that corresponds to their skills and ambition. Sometimes it is. It is no secret that successes of Polish students in programming competitions were among the most important reasons why some well-known IT companies (like Google or IBM) decided to open research and development centers in Poland. The 20% rule of Google consisting in the possibility to devote 20% of work time to fulfill one's ideas is a good method of stimulating creativeness and making good use of the knowledge and skills of gifted young people. All large companies should be encouraged to follow this example and trust the knowledge and skills of talented people for their own and general development.

The most natural place of employment of the most talented individuals are universities. The Faculty of Mathematics, Informatics and Mechanics of the University of Warsaw employs a lot of former Olympiad contestants. For instance, the research work of former Olympiad contestants Marcin Mucha and Piotr Sankowski about computing the maximum matching [11] contains breakthrough results for this field.

There could be many more such works. However, financial conditions create a barrier. Salary offered by universities to young researchers does not allow them to fully concentrate on science. Provision of financial and organizational conditions for "adult" development of competition and Olympiad winners is a challenge for many countries, particularly the new EU countries. Results achieved by these people in their youth proved that good organization and financial support bring successes recognized and acknowledged in the whole world. Investing in their adult lives will bring successes enabling Poland and other new EU countries to become members of the leading countries of the IT era.

References

1. Polish Olympiad in Informatics, http://www.oi.edu.pl/
2. International Olympiad in Informatics, http://www.ioinformatics.org/
3. The ACM International Collegiate Programming Contest, http://icpc.baylor.edu/icpc/
4. TopCoder, http://www.topcoder.com
5. Google Code Jam (2005), http://www.topcoder.com/pl/?module=Static&d1=google05&d2=overview
6. Imagine Cup, http://imaginecup.com/
7. The IEEE Computer Society Annual International Design Competition, http://www.computer.org/portal/pages/ieeecs/education/csidc/
8. Verhoeff, T., Horváth, G., Diks, K., Cormack, G.: A Proposal for an IOI Syllabus. Teaching Mathematics and Computer Science IV(1), 193–216
9. Polish Children's Fund, http://www.fundusz.org/
10. Youth Academy of Informatics, http://www.main.edu.pl
11. Mucha, M., Sankowski, P.: Maximum Matchings via Gaussian Elimination. In: Proceedings of the 45th Annual IEEE Symposium on Foundations of Computer Science (FOCS 2004) (2004)

Integrating Mathematical Analysis of Sensors and Motion in a Mobile Robotics Course

Don Rhine[1] and Fred Martin[2]

[1] Graduate School of Education
[2] Department of Computer Science
University of Massachusetts Lowell, 1 University Avenue, Lowell MA 01854 USA

Abstract. We describe a series of learning modules created as part of a semester-long course, "Interactive Robotics," which was offered to 32 high school juniors and seniors in the fall of 2007. The course integrates hands-on experiences using practical mobile robots with meaningful theoretical learning. Our analysis of the learning modules focuses on the mathematical knowledge that students employed as they solved robotics problems. Through the context of these problems, students worked with concepts of base numbering systems, data analysis and curve-fitting, and analytic geometry. We demonstrate how these mathematical ideas naturally emerge from the laboratory assignments that we developed, and illustrate the nature of student thinking that is facilitated by this approach.

1 Introduction

From middle school onward, scholastic institutions are organized by scientific discipline. Thus mathematics is taught separately from physics, even though these two topics are deeply intertwined. Indeed, Newton and Leibniz's calculus was originally conceived to explain physical phenomena. Today, secondary students study abstract math in a sequence of courses, but independently study science, technology or quantitative social sciences.

This separation of content and ideas into disciplinary boxes is deeply embedded into our academic institutions and has been variously characterized as an "unchallengeable high ground" and an "impregnable fortress" [10]. James Beane claims that subject areas or disciplines "are actually territorial spaces carved out by academic scholars for their own purposes" and that "their boundaries limit our access to broader meanings" (cited in [10]).

Nevertheless, progressive educators and reseachers, at both secondary and tertiary institutions, are challenging this presumptive structure of knowledge. Venville *et al.* argue that the "integration of content from the science, mathematics and technology learning areas is well-grounded in the philosophy of middle schooling," and have conducted research to demonstrate stronger learning results from curriculum integration approaches [9].

At the undergraduate level, engineering educators are deeply concerned with both declining enrollments and students' lack of ability to connect traditional theoretical curricula to practical applications upon commencement. There is a substantial effort underway over the last twenty years to revamp first-year (and sometimes second-year) engineering curricula to combine hands-on experiences with theoretical presentation.

Many universities across the United States and Europe have created integrated, design-rich experiences in the first years of their undergraduate engineering programs—so-called "cornerstone" projects [2]. Some examples among many are Northwestern [1], University of California Berkeley [7], and MIT [11]. In a 2005 article, Froyd and Ohland survey the practices of 14 undergraduate programs in the United States that have taken an integrative approach to the first year (or beyond) of an engineering curriculum [3].

As described by Raucent, the purpose of curriculum integration at the first-year undergraduate level (the cornerstone design experience) is different from the now-accepted, last-year "capstone design." Instead of simply a focus on the work product, there is an increased emphasis on the learning process:

> Objectives of classical projects are usually to apply and synthesize knowledge acquired during courses. Such projects are therefore result oriented. However, within the framework of [our] project-based learning, the project should be oriented towards the acquisition of new knowledge and competencies. In this context, the result of a project is the solution (e.g. a prototype, a contest) and *the learning process* [8]. (emphasis added)

In this fashion, universities try to bridge the unfortunate bifurcation of the vocational and academic tracks often present in secondary institutions. Historically, this division is based in 19th century assumptions that "industrial economies require the separation of mental and manual labour," and it is not surprising that there are sharp gaps in perceived status of these paths [12].

Zinser and Poledink lament the impact of this separation: "Without a strong academic foundation, technical programs can have a narrow focus on entry-level job skills and may limit students' potential for postsecondary education; and, without an occupational context, academic education can lose its relevance and applicability to situations in which students are interested" [13].

But there is a much deeper lost opportunity with the current state of affairs, in which academically strong students are deprived of connections to tactile learning, and more practically-oriented students are not offered the opportunity to develop their strengths with symbolic reasoning.

As described by Hoyles et al., there is a dialectic between learners and artefacts, an "instrumental genesis", which is described as the "mutual transformation of learner and artefact in the course of constructing knowledge with technology." The following is written in the context of understanding student learning of mathematical ideas when using computer algebra systems, but is equally relevant in understanding any interaction between students and interactive, computational systems:

There is a process of *instrumentalisation*, in which (in our terms) the subject *shapes* the artefact for specific uses, and simultaneously a process of *instrumentation*, in which the subject is *shaped by* actions with the artefact. This dialectic by which learner and artefact are mutually constituted in action is referred to as *instrumental genesis* [4]. (original emphasis)

Instrumental genesis is a basis for understanding the learning that occurs as students develop a computationally-enabled system (the robot) which then "plays back" their representations to them. If the students' robots perform as they expect, then they can conclude that their reasoning is sound. On the other hand, if the robot does not perform as anticipated, then students are encouraged to debug their own understanding and/or the formal representation of it that they have provided to the computational system (i.e., the code).

To summarize, we argue that these tactile and computational experiences are crucial for student learning, not merely for inspirational purposes (though those are welcome), but more profoundly to allow students the opportunity of having an impartial external actor (the computational system or robot) that reflects the students' understanding back to them.

In the heart of this paper which follows, we describe the instructional context for this particular curriculum integration project, and then detail some of the mathematical thinking we have encouraged our students to pursue.

2 Our Context

The TEAMS Academy (Technology, Engineering and Math-Science) is a new state-funded college program for academically advanced high school students. Juniors and seniors from 12 local high schools take specially-designed courses at UMass Lowell. Course topics include robotics, environmental engineering and biotechnology, electronics geared toward building devices for disabled people, and mechanical and materials engineering design. Classes meet for 90 minutes each morning; students then return to their high schools for traditional coursework.

TEAMS courses are quite different from typical high school and freshmen college courses. High schools offer traditional preparatory courses, often with limited applications to problems or cross-curricular content. University freshmen also are expected to take college level versions of these courses (e.g., Physics I and Calculus I), and would not have the opportunity to take applied project-centric courses until their junior or senior year. Thus, TEAMS courses offer high school students something they cannot obtain either at their high school, or as a first-year college student at the typical university.

Most TEAMS 11th grade students have completed high school courses in algebra, geometry, advanced algebra, biology, and chemistry. Half the students took introductory physics in the 8th or 9th grade. Twelfth graders typically completed courses in pre-calculus, and some an Advanced Placement biology or chemistry course. Our 12th graders are typically enrolled in full-year courses in calculus and physics courses.

3 The Interactive Robotics Course

The Interactive Robotics course introduces students to robots as autonomous devices, and has them implement interesting and useful behaviors in robotic devices. It is a lab course and is based on the iRobot "Create" mobile robot platform. Students investigate different sensors and actuators and use them to make the robot interact with its environment. They learn about robot control architectures and how to write control software in the C language.

A key premise of the TEAMS Academy is to provide opportunities for students to apply their pre-existing math and science skills while exploring challenging, new concepts in a project-based environment. As students experienced the interaction between hardware and software, we sought out ways to show them applications of mathematics and physics. We also chose a non-conventional pedagogical approach by introducing the students to C programming through robots.

The TEAMS course was instructed by co-author Rhine, who has a background in electrical engineering and has taught mathematics and physics courses at Tyngsborough High School for seven years. (For detailed curriculum materials, please contact the authors.) Interactive Robotics uses Matarić's *The Robotics Primer* as a text [6]. We offered two sections, each with 16 TEAMS students. Only three students had significant exposure to programming, and three others had limited exposure to programming or script-type languages. One student had experience with a robotics club.

Following we present a discussion of the co-construction of mathematical knowledge and hands-on work with the robotics hardware and software systems. We present four vignettes: (1) the use of base number systems to communicate with the low-level robot software, (2) the use of analytic geometry to understand the robot's motion patterns, (3) normalizing sensor values for motor power control, and (4) using graphing and algebraic analysis to model sensor performance.

3.1 Base Number Systems and the iRobot Create Open Interface

We used the iRobot Create educational robot base as the primary robot instructional hardware for the course. The Create is a modified version of the consumer "Roomba" home vacuuming robot (Figure 1). In the Create robot, the vacuum is replaced with a cargo bay and a DB-25 connector to give access to power, internal sensors, and a serial communication interface (Open Interface, or OI).

Students began with the OI, gaining rudimentary control of the robot through a series of commands similar to microprocessor opcodes. Using a terminal emulation program, students sent each opcode and its respective data bytes serially in a choice of binary, decimal, and hexadecimal formats. (Later in the course, after mastering the OI, students plugged in the "Command Module"—a microprocessor board—and learned C programming.)

Only 3 students had any exposure to base n number systems, but the remaining students quickly adapted their 3rd grade knowledge of base 10 decimal digits (ones digit, tens digit, hundreds digit, etc.) and advanced algebra knowledge of

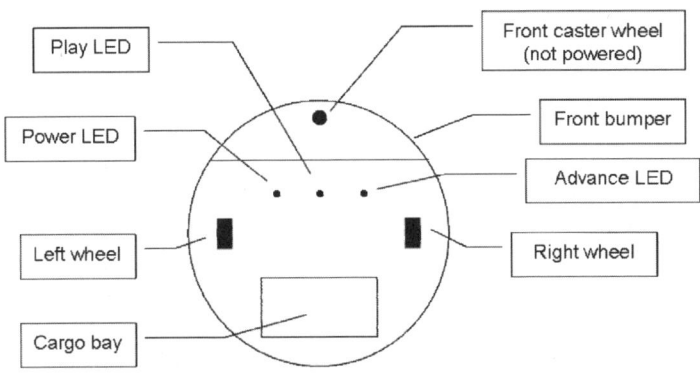

Fig. 1. The iRobot Create Robot

exponential functions to construct numbers in any desired base. A useful starting point was to have the students work as a group to populate a table of numeric conversions (Table 1).

Table 1. Homework Assignment to Introduce Students to Base Numbering Systems

Powers of 2		Write out the first sixteen positive numbers			
2^0	1	binary	base 5	decimal	hex
2^1	2	0000	0	0	0
2^2					
2^3					
2^4					
...	...	...	...	...	...
2^{15}	32,768	1111	10	16	F

Students recognized patterns in each column of the binary number and extrapolated results for the rest of the table. It was interesting to see the students' reactions as they filled out the hexadecimal equivalents of the decimal numbers 10 through 15. In both classes, students used a variety of shapes to represent the hexadecimal digits A through F. The students also concluded that groups of four binary digits (four bits, or a nibble), correspond to a single hexadecimal digit. This led to a discussion of simple microprocessor architecture, and grouping of 8 bits into a "byte" and two bytes into a "word."

We asked the students to create a base-to-base conversion tool using a technology of their choice. They delivered various solutions including hand-written tables, Excel spreadsheets, Java applets, script-based programs for graphing calculators, and C programs.

In another exercise, students had to find the largest decimal number that could be represented using a six digit number in base 2, 5, 8, 10, 16, and n.

Students noted that $999,999_{10} = 1,000,000_{10} - 1 = 10^6 - 1$, and concluded that the largest m-digit number that can be represented in base n is $n^m - 1$. The students used this result to understand the limits on magnitude for numbers passed as inputs or outputs for arithmetic integer operations in C, passing data to and from the Create robot, analog to digital conversions, etc.

Finally, students were asked to develop a method that could be used to represent negative (signed) binary and hexadecimal numbers when using only 16 bits (4 hexadecimal digits). Students developed a variety of ideas, including the use of a sign bit and methods related to the two's complement method. The instructor facilitated a student discussion that led to an algorithm to find two's complement and sixteen's complement signed numbers. Students concluded that an m-digit signed base n number could range from $-(m^{n-1})$ to $+(m^{n-1} - 1)$.

After this introduction, students began to use the OI opcodes to control the Create. Three of the 28 available commands are shown in Table 2.

Table 2. Sample iRobot Create Open Interface Commands

Command	Opcode (dec)	Byte 1	Byte 2	Byte 3	Byte 4
LEDs	139	LED bits (0 – 10)	LED color (0 – 255)	LED brightness (0 – 255)	n/a
Drive	137	Velocity (-500 to $+500$ mm/sec)		Radius (-2000 to $+2000$ mm)	
Drive Direct	145	Right Wheel Velocity (-500 to $+500$ mm/sec)		Left Wheel Velocity (-500 to $+500$ mm/sec)	

For example, to drive the Create robot forward in a straight path at a velocity of 100 mm/second, a student could use Drive Direct and specify left and right wheel velocities of 100 mm/sec. The student would send opcode 145 followed by four data bytes to specify the left and right wheel speeds either in decimal or hexadecimal format as shown:

```
145   0     100    0     100   (5 bytes sent serially as decimal numbers)
0x91  0x00  0x64   0x00  0x64  (5 bytes sent serially as hex numbers)
```

To rotate the robot clockwise about its wheelbase center, one might use Drive Direct with a right wheel velocity of -300 mm/second ($FFD4_{16}$) and a left wheel velocity of $+300$ ($012C_{16}$) mm/second as follows:

```
137   255   156    1     44    (5 bytes sent serially as decimal numbers)
0x89  0xFF  0xD4   0x00  0x64  (5 bytes sent serially as hex numbers)
```

This second example demonstrates two interesting concepts that the students needed to master to control the robot:

1. Because wheel speeds could range from -500 to $+500$ mm/sec, the opcode architecture required two bytes rather than one (16 bits can represent signed numbers from $-32,768$ to $+32,767$ while signed 8 bits numbers range from -128 to $+127$).

2. Because the bytes are sent one-by-one (serially), splitting the high and low data bytes forced students using base 10 to go through an unwieldy conversion process to send the opcode's data bytes in decimal format. As a result, many students gravitated to binary/hexadecimal number systems that are the true language of microprocessors.

As students explored various OI commands, they found that "numbers" could also represent bitwise digital switch settings used by the Create's microprocessor. For example, the eight data bits of Data Byte 1 for the LED command (opcode 139) have the following functions:

Bit	7	6	5	4	3	2	1	0
LED	–	–	–	–	–	Advance	–	Play

If a student wished to turn on the Advance LED and turn off the Play LED, the binary representation of Data Byte 1 could be xxxxx1x0 (where an "x" represents the non-applicable data bits that can represent either 0 or 1).

Our students learned how to chain together series of commands to cause interesting (but hardly complex or autonomous) actions, and were able to use values returned by built-in sensors to interact with the environment. At this point, students had developed a deep understanding of the hardware and how to implement simple "programs," but realized the OI script was an inherently limited way to control the robot. These skills and understanding of the limitations provided a natural transition to the topic of C programming.

3.2 Exploration of Robot Motion and Geometry

As mentioned, the Create provides two methods to control the motion of the robot. Drive Direct (opcode 145) actuates the left and right wheel motors independently as demonstrated above. The iRobot Roomba vacuum cleaner often travels in arcs and spirals as part of its floor coverage algorithm. The Drive command (opcode 137) implements this useful movement technique: data word 1 sets the robot's velocity, and word 2 sets the turning radius.

As students experimented with the Drive and Drive Direct commands, we asked them to think about the following:

1. How does the Create robot interpret the "radius" sent by the user?
2. How does the Create interpret a "velocity" sent by the user?
3. Derive a mathematical relationship between the Drive and Drive Direct commands.

It was important for the students to experimentally verify that their preconceived notions of velocity and radius were correct (many students found that the iRobot engineers' design differed from their expectations). Students set up a variety of experimets to compare the outputs for the two commands. The methods used to derive the relationship varied as well based on their prior math and physics skills and their ability to model a physical problem.

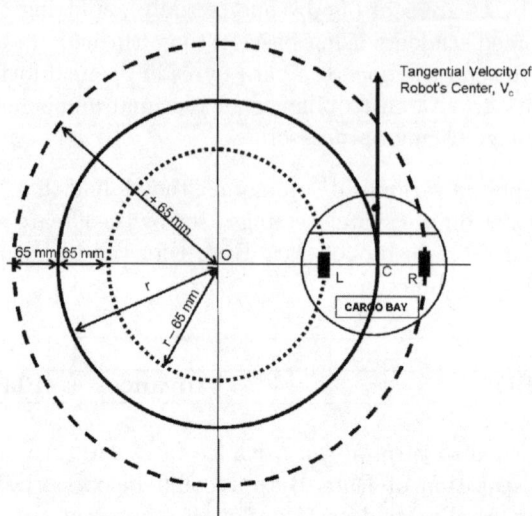

Fig. 2. Representative Student Diagram of Robot Driving Through an Arc

In two or three cases, students did not fully grasp the concept of the problem and provided insufficient answers. The rest of the students examined the geometry of the situation and took different approaches when solving the problem. Most students developed a diagram to help model the situation similar to that shown in Figure 2.

Most students used the following observation to develop a mathematical model: as the robot travels around in a circle (the solid circle in Figure 2), the time it takes for the robot's center, C, to make one revolution is the same time it takes for the left and right wheels to make one revolution. Therefore the wheels must travel faster (or slower) than the center because it must travel a longer (or shorter) distance in the same time.

For a given turning radius, r, the students calculated the distance traveled by the center of the robot, the robots right wheel, and the robot's left wheel (the circumferences of the solid, dashed, and dotted concentric circles, respectively). Using the observation above and the physical relationship between time, distance and velocity, the students concluded:

$$time\_for\_one\_revolution = \frac{2\pi r}{V_C} = \frac{2\pi(r+65)}{V_R} = \frac{2\pi(r-65)}{V_L}$$

where V_C, V_R, and V_L are the velocities of the robot center, right wheel, and left wheel, respectively, and 65 represents half the Create's wheelbase in mm.

About a third of the students employing this method used a specific numeric example rather than generalizing the problem using algebra. Another third of the students found the relationship above, but did not use the system of three equations to find the general relationship between the Drive and Drive Direct

Commands. The remainder of the students successfully completed the derivation and found the following relationship:

$$Drive(V_C, r) = DriveDirect(V_L = \frac{V_C(r-65)}{r}, V_R = \frac{V_C(r+65)}{r})$$

A few advanced students recognized that the velocity of the center of the robot must be equal to the average of the velocities of the left and right wheels. From this relationship they used implicit differentiation to reach the same general conclusion shown above.

Some used physics and a constant angular velocity to model the problem. The angular velocity, ω, in radians/second, or rpm for points L, R, and C are equal. The students showed using unit analysis that $\omega r = VT$, where r is any length radius and VT is the tangential velocity at that radius. Solving for ω yields: $\omega = VT/r$. Therefore, at points C, R, and L they found:

$$\omega = \frac{V_C}{r} = \frac{V_R}{(r+65)} = \frac{V_L}{(r-65)}$$

3.3 Normalizing Sensor Values for Motor Control

The Create robot has several built-in sensors and also has several ports for connecting to a variety of external sensors and actuators. The students used these different sensors to collect data from the operating environment and use that information to control the behavior of the robot.

For example, the students experimented with Cadmium Sulfide (CdS) photoresistors to sense the amount of visible light incident on the device. These two-lead devices can be modeled as a resistance that varies from a few hundred ohms in bright light to a few hundred thousand in the dark.

From the Create's technical manual, students learned that the analog sensor port reports this change in resistance as a varying voltage ranging from 0v to 5v. The Create converts the analog voltage into a 10-bit unsigned digital number (0 to $2^{10} - 1$, or 0 to 1,023). The students experimentally observed that these sensors returned digital values ranging from approximately 200 units (dark) to 900 units (bright) as shown in Figure 3, data line (a).

We asked the student to create a algebraic function to convert these raw sensor values (200 to 900) into a useable output to set the speed of a wheel. For example, in complete darkness, the wheel should drive at a speed of -100 mm/second (away from the light), but bright light should have the opposite effect (speed = $+100$ mm/second, toward light). For values in between, there should be a proportional response. The students could use these results to implement Braitenberg vehicles with photophobic and photophilic reactions.

To help the students visualize the problem, the instructor drew number lines (a) and (c) shown in Figure 3, and asked the students to find a way to manipulate the input (a) into the desired output (c). As a group they developed a solution by applying basic algebraic function translation and transformation concepts:

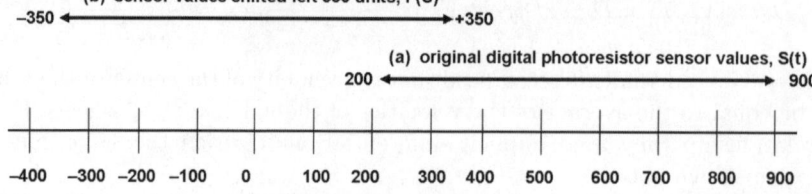

Fig. 3. Photoresistor to Motor Power Conversion

1. Subtract 550 units from the sensor value to center the function on the origin as shown in number line (b); i.e, $F(S) = S(t) - 550$
2. The range of values spans 700 units, but needs to be scaled down to 200 units. Divide by 700 to normalize the range, then multiply by 200; i.e., $V(t) = \frac{F(S)}{700} 200 = \frac{2}{7}(S - 550)$

Students used this method to implement proportional control in their C program. Here is a sample line of code (the first parameter is left wheel velocity controlled by the digital photoresistor input):

```
cr8_drive_direct(2*sensor/7, right_wheel_velocity);
```

3.4 Linearizing Raw Sensor Data

The students also used analog Sharp infrared distance sensors to implement wall following and object detection. The students collected data and found that the sensor output to be non-linear and inverted as shown in Figure 4. (Note that the sensor's operating range is 10–80 cm). Although the nonlinearity could be useful under certain circumstances, a linear output is generally easier to use for proportional control and to convert to actual distance measurements.

In class discussions, students were encouraged to develop a mathematical model of the empirical sensor measurements. Then they could algebraically find the inverse of the model to recover the original distance inputs to the sensor. This process would yield a sensor reading to distance function. The instructor led the students through the process:

1. Find the equation of a function that accurately models the operating region of the curve. The students suggested using a polynomial (parabola) and a rational functions (hyperbola).
2. The instructor used a general form for a hyperbola below to model the function. S represents the sensor output provided by the Create robot, and d is the input distance:

$$S(d) = \frac{k}{ad+b} + c$$

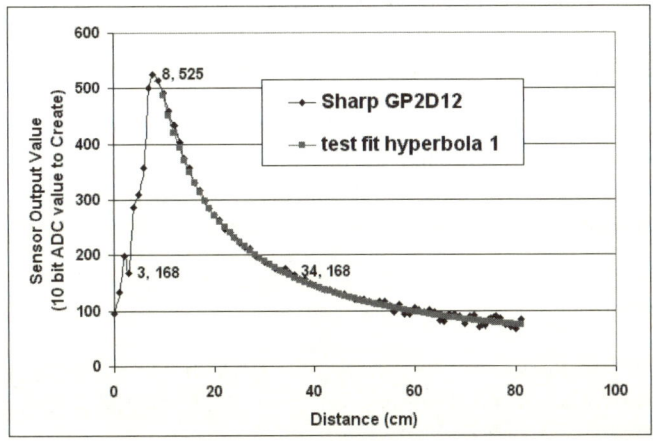

Fig. 4. Data from Sharp GP2D12 Distance Sensor with Hyperbolic Fit

After selecting approximate values for constants k, a, b, and c, the instructor used a spreadsheet linked to a graph to manually fine tune the values to fit the curve. Students with TI-89 graphing calculators were able to run a hyperbolic regression to verify the instructors final values of $k = 18,500$, $a = 3$, $b = 8$, and $c = 0$.

3. The students calculated the inverse function:

$$F(S) = \frac{k - b(S - c)}{a(S - c)}$$

4. By taking a composition of the data provided by the sensor and the inverse function, the students correctly concluded that $F(S(d)) = d$. Several students used this methodology to recover the actual distance values and use these values to effectively control the behavior of the Create robot as it sensed obstacles in its environment.

4 Conclusions

We have developed an advanced high school-level robotics course called Interactive Robotics, which was delivered to 32 high school students. The course has a focus on making connections between concepts inherent in the robotic materials and a corresponding mathematical understanding of these ideas. As much as possible, we have encouraged our students to develop their own mathematical analysis to explain the robot behaviors. We have also supported them with our own explanations of the concepts involved.

We believe this curriculum integration approach has strong pedagogical value. Having a mathematical basis for understanding physical phenomena is at the core of engineering practice. At the same time, students learn that mathematics has practical value. In many regards, the approach mirrors the "model-eliciting activities" of mathematics educator Richard Lesh, where students develop a locally contextual mathematics, based on their own existing mathematical knowledge, to make sense of a problem situation [5].

We are particularly encouraged by the dialectic between practical work and mathematical understanding that we observed in our students. This at the the core of our approach. We believe all education would be improved by giving students materials that can carry their ideas into the world.

References

1. Colgate, E., McKenna, A., Ankenman, B.: IDEA: Implementing design throughout the curriculum at northwestern. International Journal of Engineering Education 20(3), 405–411 (2004)
2. Dym, C.L., Agogino, A.M., Eris, O., Frey, D.D., Leifer, L.J.: Engineering design thinking, teaching, and learning. Journal of Engineering Education 94(1), 103–120 (2005)
3. Frond, J.E., Ohland, M.W.: Integrated engineering curricula. Journal of Engineering Education 94(1), 147–164 (2005)
4. Hoyles, C., Noss, R., Kent, P.: On integration of digital technologies into mathematics classrooms. International Journal of Computers for Mathematical Learning 9, 309–326 (2004)
5. Lesh, R., Harel, G.: Problem solving, modeling, and local conceptual development. Mathematical Thinking and Learning 5(2–3), 157–189 (2003)
6. Matarić, M.: The Robotics Primer. MIT Press, Cambridge (2007)
7. McKenna, A., McMartin, F., Agogino, A.: What students say about learning physics, math, and engineering. In: 30th ASEE/IEEE Frontiers in Education Conference (2000)
8. Raucent, B.: What kind of project in the basic year of an engineering curriculum. Journal of Engineering Design 15(1), 107–121 (2004)
9. Venville, G., Wallace, J., Rennie, L., Malone, J.: Bridging the boundaries of compartmentalized knowledge: Student learning in an integrated environment. Research in Science & Technological Education 18(1), 23–35 (2000)
10. Venville, G.J., Wallace, J., Rennie, L.J., Malone, J.A.: Curriculum integration: Eroding the high ground of science as a school subject? In: Annual Conference of the Australian Association for Research in Education, December 2001, Fremantle, WA (2001)
11. Verghese, G.C.: Stepping out with a new undergraduate curriculum. MIT Department of Electrical Engineering and Computer Science Newsletter 9(1) (Fall 2007)
12. Young, M.: A curriculum for the 21st century? towards a new basis for overcoming academic/vocational divisions. British Journal of Educational Studies 41(3), 203–222 (1993)
13. Zinser, R., Poledink, P.: The ford partnership for advanced studies: A new case for curriculum integration in technology education. Journal of Technology Education 17(1) (Fall 2005)

Visualization of Program Behaviors: Physical Robots Versus Robot Simulators

Cheng-Chih Wu[1], I-Chih Tseng[1], and Shih-Lung Huang[2]

[1] National Taiwan Normal University, Information and Computer Education,
162 Heping East Road, Sec. 1, Taipei, Taiwan
{chihwu,samuel}@ice.ntnu.edu.tw
[2] Taipei Municipal Dali High School,
2, Changshun St., Taipei, Taiwan
braingrant179@yahoo.com.tw

Abstract. This study compared the effects of using physical robots (LEGO Mindstorms) and robot simulators (LEGO Mindstorms Simulator, LMS) in teaching novice programming concepts. A quasi-experiment design was implemented in this study. Four classes of high school students, totaling 151 students, participated in the study. Two classes of 76 students used the physical robots to learn programming, whereas the other two classes of 75 students used LMS. The students' post-experiment achievement tests, replies on questionnaires, and focus group interview data were collected and analyzed. The findings of the study were: (1) no significant difference was found on students' performance between the physical robot group and the simulator group, (2) the physical robot group demonstrated more positive attitudes toward the learning activities, and (3) the physical robot group indicated that they could better imagine the program behaviors.

Keywords: Programming, Robot, Simulator, LEGO Mindstorms.

1 Introduction

In recent years, computer science educators have advocated the use of robots in CS1 and CS2 courses, especially in teaching novices programming concepts [1, 2, 3, 4]. Some [5] further proposed that robotics-oriented projects could be used to motivate and enhance the learning of certain knowledge areas recommended in *ACM Computing Curriculum 2001* [6]. The use of robots addresses the problems or difficulties that novice programmers face such as weak logical reasoning and coding before designing; and students find working with robots interesting and fun [3].

Early use of the concept of robots in teaching programming originated from the development of the "mini-language" approach. The idea of the mini-language approach is to design a small and simple language to support the beginning of learning programming. Mini-languages provide insight into programming for the general population and to teach algorithmic thinking [7]. The programming environment of mini-languages is often accompanied with a micro-world, where students learn to program by studying how to control a robot, which can be a turtle, a ladybug, or other agents, acting in the micro-world. Students can actually "see" how their programs were executed by observing the behaviors of the programmed robot in the micro-world. For example, in Papert's LOGO [8], students command a turtle robot to draw figures on the screen. In *Karel the Robot* (http://www.mtsu.edu/~untch/karel/), the robot lives in a micro-world consisting of streets, walls, and beepers. The robot can move along the streets, detect walls, and pick up, move, and put down beepers. Concepts such as procedures and basic control structures can be quickly introduced to students by using the *Karel* micro-world. The visual representation of the robot's world offers many benefits, among them are: the animation provides visual feedback on the correctness of an algorithm and students can often see where their program goes wrong simply by watching the animation [2]. Since students may eventually learn to program with general-purpose programming languages, it was proposed to use a subset of a general-purpose language to replace the mini-language approach [7]. In fact, various versions of Karel have been developed based on different programming languages such as C, C++, and Java.

A good way to make the virtual robot more attractive for young students is to use a real world robot [7]. The more practical and concrete the learning situations are, the more learning takes place [9]. The game-like feature of the real robots motivates students to invest time and mental efforts on learning [10]. The benefits of using real robots have been supported by the availability of standardized, low-cost robot construction kits during the last decade. For example, the newly released LEGO Mindstorms NXT kit (http://www.lego.com), with a 32-bit microprocessor (NXT brick), 3 interactive servo motors, 4 sensors (sound, ultrasonic, light, and touch sensors), wheels, USB and Bluetooth support, and 519 construction pieces – everything needed for constructing a robot, costs approximately USD 250. It allows the user to build fully autonomous robots with all computing power located within the machine. Many CS educators have used LEGO Mindstorms to teach students programming concepts and the reported effects are mostly positive [9, 11, 12].

Although there are many claimed benefits for using the physical robots to teach novice programming, little empirical evidence has shown that its effects are indeed better than the robot simulators on the screen. If the effects of both teaching tools are the same, it may not be worth spending money on purchasing the physical robots. This study reports our preliminary attempt to compare the effects of using the LEGO Mindstorms (LM) robot and its simulator – LM Simulator in teaching novice programming concepts.

2 Methodology

A quasi-experiment design was implemented in this study. Four classes with a total of 151 10th grade high school students who enrolled in an *Introduction to Computers* course participated in the experiment. Two classes of 76 students used the LM robots (LMR group) to learn programming concepts, whereas the other two classes of 75 students used the LM simulator (LMS group). The experiment was conducted over a seven-week period in which students met two hours per week. All the learning activities were directed by the same teacher who was experienced in using the LM tools.

We collected various data sources to analyze the effects between the two groups, including the post-experiment achievement test scores, student questionnaires, and focus group interviews with students. Below, we describe the LM robots, the LM simulator, and the learning activities implemented in the study.

2.1 LEGO Mindstorms Robots

The LMR group used the LEGO Mindstorms RCX module which consisted of a 16 bit microprocessor (RCX brick), a light sensor, a touch sensor, and other LEGO components. The robot can use its light sensor to track the path of a street and use its touch sensor to detect the wall so that it can walk in a maze. We decided to provide students with pre-assembled robots (see Fig. 1) instead of having students build their own robot. This allows students to focus their attention on programming the robot. In order to use Java with the Mindstorms robots, the original firmware in the RCX brick was replaced with another firmware – leJOS which is a tiny Java Virtual Machine for the LEGO Mindstorms RCX. LeJOS is an open source project and can be freely downloaded from www.sourceforge.net. Due to the limited number of LM robots we had, students in the LMR group share the robots, that is, two students used one LM robot. However, each student was provided with a PC when writing programs.

Fig. 1. The pre-assembled robot for the LMR group

2.2 LEGO Mindstorms Simulator

As to the LM simulator group, we adopted the LEGO Mindstorms Simulator (LMS, http://ddi.uni-paderborn.de/software/lego-mindstorms-simulator.html) as the learning

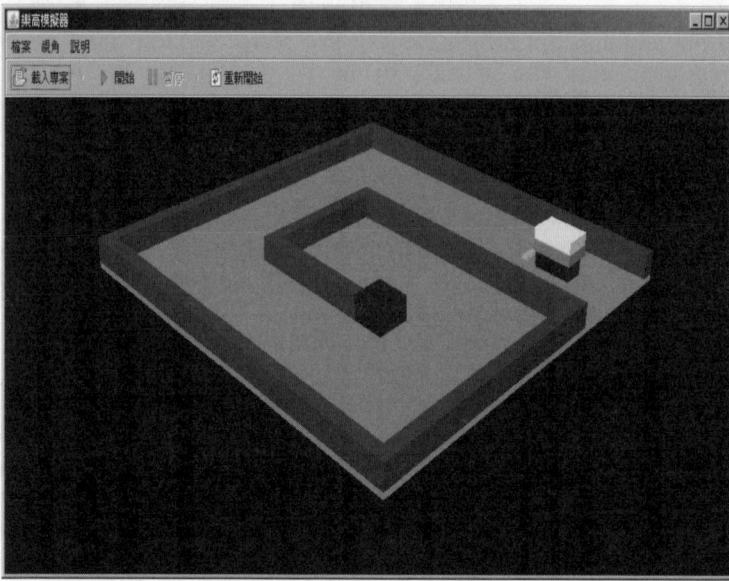

Fig. 2. The LEGO Mindstorms Simulator for the LMS group

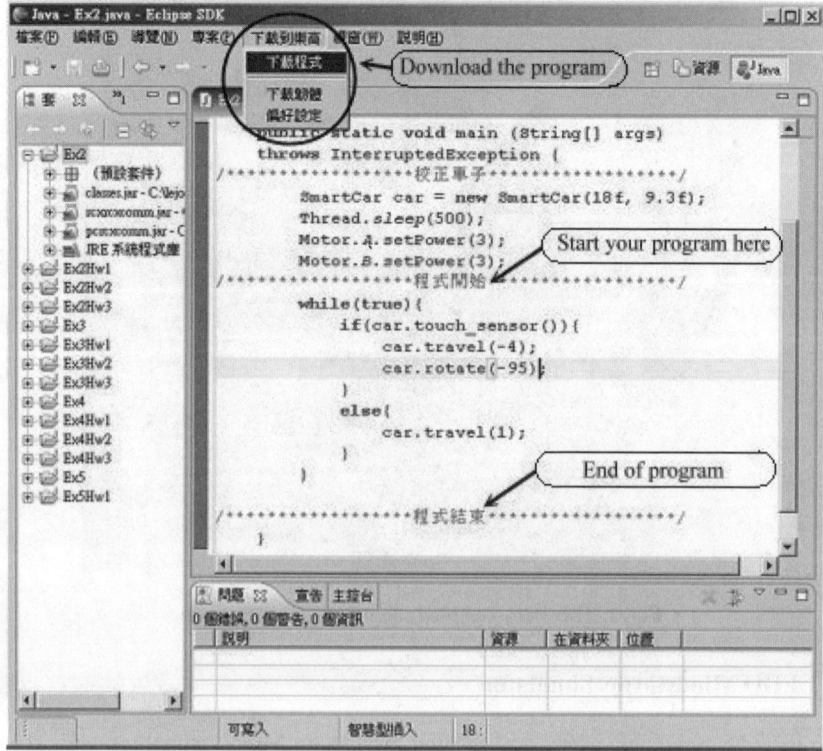

Fig. 3. Editing/compiling/downloading a robot program in Eclipse

tool. The LMS was developed by a research group at the University of Paderborn. The simulator is written in Java to simulate leJOS programs with simple 3D-Models (see Fig. 2). LMS enables students to write programs in Java that will run in a graphic simulator and in the LM robot. The simulator can simulate a robot and other actors, such as walls and streets. A Java program written for controlling the LM robot in the real world environment can also be used to control the virtual robot running in a similar scene on the simulator screen. Thus, the major difference between the two groups is: the LMR group ran their programs in the real world, and the LMS group ran their programs on LMS on a computer screen.

Both groups used Eclipse (http://www.eclipse.org/, see Fig. 3) to edit/compile/ download their programs. We had revised Eclipse source codes and several plug-ins so that students could download their compiled programs to the LM robot and the LMS with simple operations.

2.3 Learning Activities

The learning activities were designed to enable students to learn basic programming concepts, that is, variables, expressions, assignment, and control structures. Because our focus was on teaching algorithmic thinking, not the Java language, we limited students' use of Java components on the following: if-else, if-else-if, while, arithmetic/relational/Boolean operators, integer variables, and assignment. When writing programs for solving a problem, we provided a template for students to use. All the necessary declaration and system settings for the program were given in the template. Students only had to program the codes on the algorithm block (see Fig. 3, "Start your program here").

LeJOS provides basic commands to control the LM robot. For example, for the robot to make a right turn, you need to give a command to stop the right motor (wheel) and a command to start the left motor (wheel), and yet another command to keep the current status for a certain amount of time. We considered these commands too primitive and not intuitive enough for students to manipulate the robot, especially if our focus was on algorithmic thinking. To reduce the learning load and make the control of the robot more intuitive, we provided students with the following seven methods (adapted from [13]):

Motor.A.setpower (n): Set the power of left motor to n level.
Motor.B.setpower (n): Set the power of right motor to n level.
car.travel (±n): The robot move forward (+) or backward (-) n centimeters.
car.rotate (±n): The robot turns clockwise (-) or counter-clockwise (+) n degrees.
car.stop (): The robot stops.
car.touch_sensor (): Return TRUE if the robot touches something, else False.
car.light_sensor (): Return the light intensity it detects.

The learning activities consist of five units as shown in Table 1. Each unit was conducted with the following steps: First, the teacher demonstrated how to write a program to solve an example problem. The codes of example programs were available for students in the example folder. Next, students were given an assignment, which was similar to the example problem and could be easily solved by revising the example program. Finally, students were given a second assignment to write a whole program. To solve the assignment, students would need to use the concepts/instructions taught in the unit. An optional third assignment was offered for students who had finished the second assignment before the teacher concluded the unit.

Fig. 4 is the maze assignment given to the LMR group in Unit 2, whereas Fig. 2 is the same assignment for the LMS group. To solve the problem, students would need to use the conditional structure to determine whether the touch sensor touches a wall and use a simple iterative structure (*while(true)*) to make the robot continue going. Fig. 5 is the "Tracking the road" assignment given to the LMR group in Unit 4. Students would need to make use of the light sensor to "see" the road to complete the assignment.

Table 1. Programming and robot concepts covered in each unit

Unit	Programming concepts	Robot concepts	Time
1	1. Editing programs (Eclipse) 2. Sequential structure	1. LMR/LMS environment 2. Basic control (move, turn, stop)	3 hrs
2	1. Conditional structure (if-else) 2. Boolean expression 3. Iteration structure (while)	1. Use of a touch sensor 2. Detecting walls	4 hrs
3	1. Variables 2. Conditional structure (if-else-if)	Walking in a maze	2 hrs
4	1. Code reusing 2. Review on control structures	1. Use of a light sensor 2. Tracking the road	3 hrs
5	A small project	Combining use of touch sensor and light sensor	2 hrs

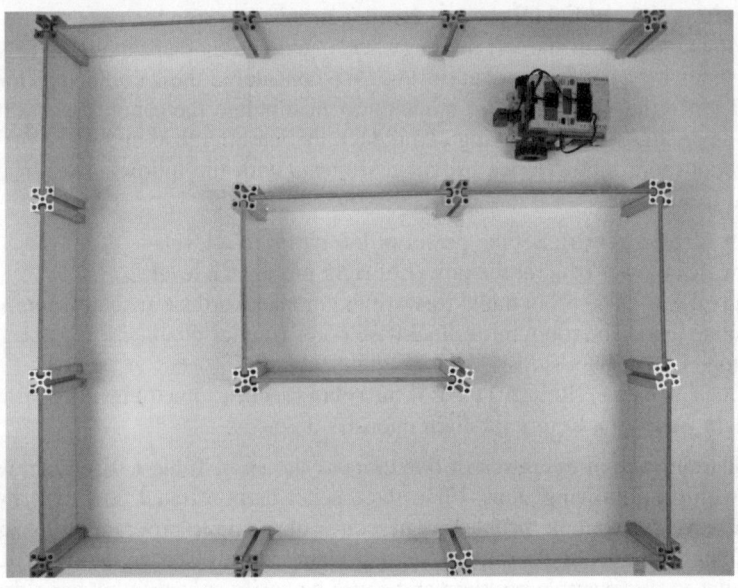

Fig. 4. The maze assignment for the LMR group

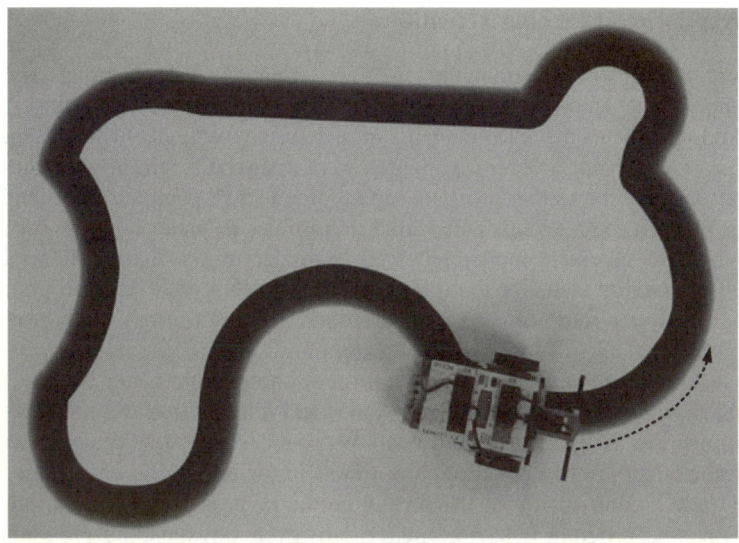

Fig. 5. The "Tracking the road" assignment for the LMR group

3 Results and Discussion

3.1 Achievement Test

The post-experiment achievement test consists of two parts. One is for testing students' comprehension of programs the other is for testing a generation of programs. Since our experiment lasted only 14 hours, we decided to cover only near-transfer tasks in the achievement test, except for one task in the program generation part. The near-transfer tasks were the ones which were similar to the examples or assignments given in the learning activities. A t test was performed to test the differences of the achievement scores between the two groups. Table 2 presents the summary results. The t test results show that there were no significant differences between the LMR group and the LMS group in terms of the program comprehension ($t(149) = 0.08$, $p = .94$), program generation ($t(149) = 0.56$, $p = .58$), and the total ($t(149) = 0.38$, $p = .71$) scores. Obviously, students achieved similar performance levels in learning programming using either the physical robots or the robot simulator.

Table 2. The t test results on students' post-experiment test scores

Test (total scores)	Group	Mean	SD	t
Program comprehension (7)	LMR	5.37	1.74	0.08
	LMS	5.35	1.61	
Program generation (8)	LMR	5.68	2.13	0.56
	LMS	5.49	2.08	
Total (15)	LMR	11.05	3.63	0.38
	LMS	10.84	3.31	

3.2 Perceptions of Learning Activities

In the post-experiment questionnaire, we asked students in both groups about their perceptions of the learning activities and their attitudes toward learning. Students were asked to fill out the questionnaire on a Likert-type scale, which ranged from *strongly agree* to *strongly disagree*. Scores were assigned 5 for *strongly agree*, 4 for *agree*, etc. Table 3 shows the statistical results of students' perceptions of the learning activities. Overall, both groups considered themselves to understand the robot methods and the Java statement moderately well in the learning activities (Items 1 and 2) and could reasonably visualize the robot's behaviors when viewing a program (Items 3 and 4) – the mean score of each item is around 3.5 to 4 (*agree*). Both groups were neutral on the difficulty of the assignment (Item 5).

The t test results reveal that the physical robot group could better imagine the program behaviors (Item 3, $t(149) = 1.98$, $p < .05$) and felt that they did not have enough time to finish the assignments (Item 6, $t(149) = 3.88$, $p < .01$), as compared to the robot simulator group. It seemed running robots in the real world environment might enhance student construction of the mental model of programming, and thus enable them to imagine program behaviors better. However, downloading programs to the RCX brick via the easy interfered infrared and testing programs with the physical robots required students to take extra time on the tasks. The newly released LEGO Mindstorms NXT brick, which uses USB to download programs, may resolve the problems that resulted from using infrared.

Table 3. The t test results on students' perceptions of the learning activities

Item	Group	Mean	t
1. I understood the robot methods in the activities.	LMR	4.12	0.90
	LMS	3.99	
2. I understood the Java statements in the activities.	LMR	3.71	0.93
	LMS	3.56	
3. I could imagine how the robot would move by viewing the program.	LMR	3.76	1.98*
	LMS	3.48	
4. Viewing the robot running my program helped me find the bugs.	LMR	3.50	0.68
	LMS	3.39	
5. In all, the assignments were not difficult.	LMR	3.09	1.90
	LMS	2.79	
6. I did not have enough time to finish the assignments.	LMR	3.70	3.88**
	LMS	3.17	

*$p < .05$, **$p < .01$

3.3 Attitudes Toward Learning

Table 4 presents the summary results of students' attitudes toward the learning activities. The results show that both groups of students felt a great sense of achievement when seeing the robot running their programs, but no significant difference was found between the two groups (Item 7, $t(149) = 1.92$, $p = .057$). The results also indicate that the physical robot group experienced having more fun on the programming tasks (Item 8, $t(149) = 3.39$, $p < .01$) and wished to learn more about robot programming (Item 9, $t(149) = 3.40$, $p < .01$) as compared to the robot simulator group. No significant difference was found between the two groups when asked if they would like to learn more about other programming (Item 10, $t(149) = 1.28$, $p = .20$). Overall, the physical robot groups demonstrated more positive attitudes on learning.

Table 4. The t test results on students' attitudes about the learning activities

Item	Group	Mean	t
7. I felt a sense of achievement when seeing the robot running my program.	LMR	4.22	1.92
	LMS	3.91	
8. Programming with the robot was fun.	LMR	3.84	3.39**
	LMS	3.17	
9. I wish to learn more about robot programming.	LMR	3.54	3.40**
	LMS	2.89	
10. Besides robot programming, I wish to learn more about other programming.	LMR	3.62	1.28
	LMS	3.39	

**$p < .01$

4 Conclusions

In this study, we compared the effects of using the physical robots and the robot simulators in teaching novice programming. The post-experiment survey questionnaire shows that students in the physical robot group had more fun with the learning activities, wished to learn more about robot programming, and considered themselves imagining the program behaviors better as compared to the simulator group. However, there was no significant difference found between the two groups in terms of the post-experiment achievement. The present study conducted the experiment for a short period of time (14 hours) and only measured students' near-transfer performance. It is suggested that future studies extend the experiment time so that the learning effects may become more evident and the far-transfer performance can also be measured.

Acknowledgement

This study was funded by the National Science Council of Taiwan under the grant number NSC 95-2520-S-003-008-MY3.

References

1. Lawhead, P.B., Duncan, M.E., Bland, C.G., Goldweber, M., Schep, M., Barnes, D.J., et al.: A Road Map for Teaching Introductory Programming Using LEGO© Mindstorms Robots. ACM SIGCSE Bulletin 35(2), 191–201 (2003)
2. Becker, B.W.: Teaching CS1 with Karel the Robot in Java. ACM SIGCSE Bulletin 33(1), 50–54 (2003)

3. Schep, M., McMulty, N.: Use of LEGO Mindstorms Kits in Introductory Programming Classes: A tutorial. Journal of Computing Sciences in Colleges 18, 323–327 (2002)
4. Linder, S.P., Nestrick, B.E., Mulders, S., Lavelle, C.L.: Facilitating Active Learning with Inexpensive Mobile Robots. Journal of Computing Sciences in Colleges 16, 21–33 (2001)
5. Klassner, F., Anderson, S.D.: LEGO Mindstorms: Not just for K-12 Anymore. Robotics & Automation Magazine 10, 12–18 (2003)
6. ACM/IEEE Task Force: Computing Curricula 2001. ACM/IEEE (2001)
7. Brusilovsky, P., Calabrese, E., Hvorecky, J., Kouchnirenko, A., Miller, P.: Mini-languages: A Way to Learn Programming Principles. Education and Information Technologies 2, 65–83 (1997)
8. Papert, S.: Mindstorms: Children, Computers, and Powerful Ideas. The Harvester Press Ltd. (1980)
9. Lahtinen, E., Ala-Mutka, K., Jarvinen, H.-M.: A Study of the Difficulties of Novice Programmers. ACM SIGCSE Bulletin 37(3), 14–18 (2005)
10. Dagdilelis, V., Sartatzemi, M., Kagani, K.: Teaching (with) Robots in Secondary Schools: Some New and Not-So-New Pedagogical Problems. In: Fifth IEEE International Conference on Advanced Learning Technologies (ICALT), pp. 757–761 (2005)
11. Flowers, T.R., Gossett, K.A.: Teaching Problem Solving, Computing, and Information Technology with robots. Journal of Computing Sciences in Colleges 17, 45–55 (2002)
12. Fagin, B.S., Merkle, L.: Quantitative Analysis of the Effects of Robots on Introductory Computer Science Education. Journal on Educational Resources in Computing (JERIC) 2, 1–17 (2002)
13. Bagnall, B.: Core LEGO Mindstorms Programming. Prentice-Hall, Englewood Cliffs (2002)

Development of an Educational System to Control Robots for All Students

Toshiyuki Kamada[1], Hiroyuki Aoki[2], Shuji Kurebayashi[3], and Yoshikazu Yamamoto[4]

[1] Aichi University of Education
tkamada@acm.org
[2] Korea University
hiroyuki.aoki@inc.korea.ac.kr
[3] Shizuoka University
eskureb@ipc.shizuoka.ac.jp
[4] Keio University
yama@ics.keio.ac.jp

Abstract. Machines controlled by computers are spreading in almost all areas of our society. However, students are not aware of the existence of such devices. At present, we have developed an educational system for secondary schools that can implement realistic computer controlled, autonomous mechanics. The system is composed of a controller board as hardware and a structured control language on top of the Dolittle programming language as software. Mechanics controlled by the controller board can be arranged according to the teacher's wishes. The biggest contribution of our system is its low-cost; students can bring their work home and use the system. In this paper, the design concept of our educational system and the design details are described. We then include the results of a survey which was taken at workshops for lower secondary school teachers.

1 Introduction

Controlling Robots is an effective way to learn computer programming [1]. In addition, it becomes increasingly clear that the learning experiences of controlling robots encourage students' understanding of electro-mechanic products. It means that we need educated people who have knowledge of how computers and communication devices work especially since they are embedded in the machines which surround us such as automobiles, train systems, vending machines, elevators, home electric appliances, etc. By knowing the relationship between hardware and software, we hope people will have a good perspective on how to approach the issue if there is some trouble with their devices.

Our previous approach was giving children materials to build a simple mobile robotic car with two wheels and put a simple computer controller board onto it and have them program the car's motion. The cars were not so precise and they could not go in a strait line [7]. The children started to solve this problem in with both, a hardware and a software approach. We reasoned that, from this experience we reasoned that the children would have a good mental model of systems where the hardware and software are tightly coupled.

However, we learned that simply controlling a robotic car did not satisfy the high scholastic achievement of these students because such robots can be programed only for simple motions that move around on the field.

Thus, in order to accommodate those students, we have developed a new controller board and programming language as well as more extensive teaching materials so that teachers can conduct various lessons according to their own ideas.

In this paper, we decribe the design concept of our teaching materials which are composed of a triaxial robot controller board as hardware and a structured robot-control language as software. Then, we report the evaluation of this concept through experimental workshops for technology teachers.

2 Fundamental Design Policy as a Teaching Material

We think that the significance of learning control with embedded computers in secondary information education is not only to understand the principle of computers and machines separately, but also computers and machines as organized systems as a whole, and that these systems are utilized in our daily life. In order to realize this meaning, we have developed our new teaching material under the fundamental design policies as follows:

- Each student must be able to design and craft their own machines
- Each student must be able to touch electronic parts on the controller board
- Each student must wire circuits of electorical elements of their machines by himself or herself
- The teaching material must be low-cost; each student must be able to bring her or his works (machines) back to her or his home
- The robot-control language must be easy to learn as only short periods of time are available

In designing the above policies, we have kept in our mind that (1) every technology regarding mechanics, electric circuits and existance of the computer should be glass boxed (not black boxed), and (2) technology itself should be learned in a short time. The necessity of (2) helps teachers to implement classes using our teaching material easily. We assume the class could be conducted within 10 hours (2 hours for learning the programming language, 4 hours for building the robotic car, and 4 hours for programming the robot).

We assume that the target of control in school lessons is an autonomous mobile robot with an arm. This kind of robot uses two motors for moving around on the field and another motor for raising and lowering the arm which lifts and carries an object. By using this mechanism, teachers can plan their lessons by starting from a conventional biaxial mobile robot car and proceeding to using a third motor.

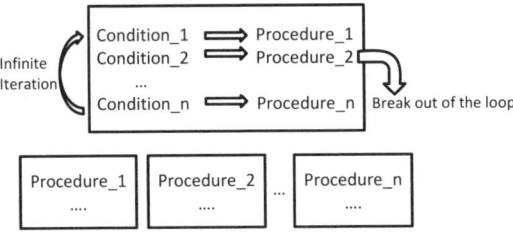

Fig. 1. Typical Architecture of Robot-Control Program with Multiple Sensors

We chose Microchip PIC 16F630 as a microcontroller to satisfy the requirements listed above. The basic structure of the controller board was defined as in Fig. 2. The detailed structure of this board will be shown in Section 3. We named this "MYUROBO controller board" [5].

Meanwhile, concerning the software, a robot-control programming language must have the feature of structured control flow.

Control programs for autonomous robots have a typical structure of branching according to multiple sensor inputs (including the changing of the internal status values of the robot according to its behavior) and taking corresponding actions (Fig. 1). However, many robot programming environments use conditional jump instructions to control program flow, and the structure explained above is difficult to construct with such primitive instructions. The situation actually holds for the MYUROBO controller board.

An answer to the problem is to prepare higher-level language with structured control flow, which is translated to the robot instructions by the compiler. We did that first with the MYU BASIC processor [6], and then with the Dolittle [2][3][4] language.

Consequently, we have developed a translator written in Dolittle to generate MYUROBO instructions with a structured robot control language on top of the Dolittle system. The strong points of our new language are that the language largely uses Dolittle syntax and the Dolittle environment, so users do not have to learn a new programming environment or new syntax (although some differences exist between the robot language and the original Dolittle).

A brief description of Dolittle and how Dolittle can program robots is shown in Section 4.

3 The Firmware of MYUROBO

The MYUROBO controller board is composed of a microcontroller, 4 input ports, and 6 output ports. The output ports have three pairs of connectors; each pair controls one DC motor for forward and reverse rotation. In the microcontroller, the flash memory and the EEPROM are embedded. The flash memory includes MYUROBO firmware which implements a virtual CPU interpreter and program loader. Actual robot programs are written as virtual CPU instructions

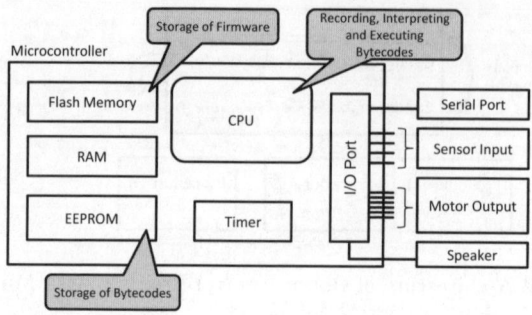

Fig. 2. The Microcontroller of MYUROBO and the Role of Each Part

(bytecodes); they are loaded into the EEPROM and executed by the interpreter. Fig. 2 shows the architecture of the microcontroller in MYUROBO and the role of each component.

3.1 Bytecode Interpreter of MYUROBO

The bytecode interpreter of MYUROBO offers a virtual CPU which has functionalities of memory transfer and calculating operations. The conceptual diagram of the implemented virtual CPU is shown in Fig. 3. The virtual CPU is modeled according to a register machine. The numerical and logical operations which are executed on the A register (Accumulator) changes status flags (C for carry and Z for zero). The status flags affect the behavior of conditional branch instructions.

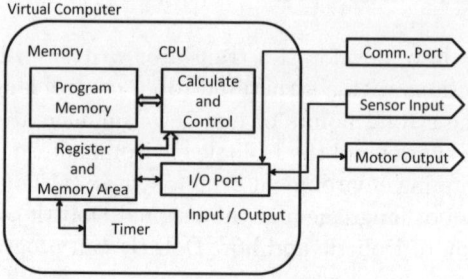

Fig. 3. The Conceptual Diagram of Virtual CPU Realized by the MYUROBO Firmware

3.2 Instructions Defined in the Bytecode

The implemented bytecode has mainly two categories of instructions. In one case optimized instructions for robot control such as motor control or branch by the status of sensor input are used. Alternatively, one may use instructions which are

Table 1. Summary of MYUROBO Instructions (excerpt)

Instruction	Function	Instruction	Function
startrobot	start of robot program	i blockstart	start of the block i
endrobot	end of robot program	blockend	end of the block
n forward	rotate both wheels forward (in $n \times 0.1$ seconds)	i executeblock	execute block i
		$i\ n$ repeatblock	repeat block i in n times
n back	rotate both backward	exitblock	exit from a current block
n turnright	turn the robot to the right	n A	set n to A register
n turnleft	turn the robot to the left	n ADD	add n to A
n stop	stop the robot	n SUB	substitute n from A
		INCA	increment A
$n\ m$ tone	play with m-width pulse	n CMP	compare A with n
i label	label with i	n AND	bitwise AND
i jump	jump to label i	n OR	bitwise OR
$i\ j$ jumpifhigh	jump to label i if the status of sensor j is high	JZ	jump if zero
		JNZ	jump if not zero
$i\ j$ jumpiflow	jump to label i if the status of sensor j is low	JC	jump if carry is set
		JNC	jump if carry is not set

the same as in other general purpose CPUs, such as transferring data between registers or numerical and logical operations.

Table 1 is a summary of typical MYUROBO instructions.

The allocation of bytecodes and naming of mnemonics corresponding to them are carefully defined as upward compatible to our previous "biaxial robot controller board" [1]. All bytecodes allocated in the previous board are included in the new bytecode system.

4 Dolittle Programming Language

"Dolittle" is an object-oriented programming language designed for school education. It has many fascinating features for school children such as turtle graphics, coloring drawn figures, animated graphics, music, etc. These are prepared in the Dolittle programming system as prototype objects.

Dolittle is a Java application. Users of Dolittle must prepare a Java runtime environment in each PC.

4.1 Sample Program on the Screen

Fig. 4 is a sample program of Dolittle and the result of the execution. Line (1) creates a copy of prototype "turtle" and assigns it to the variable "Turtle1". Line (2) creates a copy of the prototype "button" with "left" labeled and moves it to the position of $(-120, 50)$. This object is assigned to the variable "LeftButton". In line (4) and (5), buttons are defined "click" methods by assigning a fragment of a program surrounded by brackets. The right side of line (4) and (5) are named "block". By assigning a block object into a property of the object, the

```
Turtle1 = turtle ! create.                              // (1)
LeftButton = button ! "left" create -120 50 moveby.     // (2)
RightButton = button ! "right" create 20 50 moveby.     // (3)
LeftButton:click = [ Turtle1 ! 10 leftturn ].           // (4)
RightButton:click = [ Turtle1 ! 10 rightturn ].         // (5)
timer ! create [ Turtle1 ! 10 forward ] execute.        // (6)
```

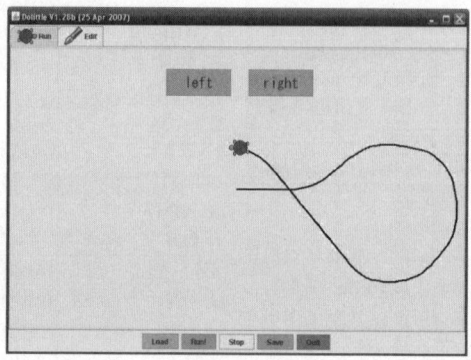

Fig. 4. Sample Program of Dolittle

method definition is accomplished. The "click" method is automatically invoked by pressing its corresponding button on the screen. In the line (6), the "timer" object repeats the specified block during 10 seconds in every 0.1 seconds by default (of course, the duration and period can be specified). The specified block is "[`Turtle1 ! 10 forward]`", the turtle moves forward 10 pixels in every 0.1 seconds.

As seen in Fig. 4, the basic syntax of Dolittle is like "`obj ! arg ... msg.`". The object "`obj`" receives message "`msg`" with some arguments. This word order seems to be strange in English, but we Japanese use this word order in our native language. Currently, Dolittle supports three languages — Japanese, Korean and English. Japanese and Korean have the same word order. Students can write their programs by using their native characters; Japanese can write programs in the Japanese alphabet, and Koreans can use the Korean alphabet.

4.2 Robot Control Using Dolittle

Dolittle has a "serialport" prototype object. This object has methods of "open", "close", "write" and "read". By using this object, Dolittle, running on a PC, can communicate with external devices with a serial port.

The MYUROBO controller board has a program loader; it reads bytecodes from its serial port and records them to the embedded EEPROM.

Hence, if Dolittle sends bytecodes for the MYUROBO board with a serialport object, the user can program robot control code for MYUROBO with Dolittle.

5 Programming Environment for MYUROBO Controller Board

5.1 Programming Environment with Dolittle

At first, we developed a simple robot language (mnemonic) translator on top of Dolittle. The main idea was to define a method for each of the mnemonics, and the method outputs corresponding op-code to the serial port, optionally with accompanying operand data.

The actual sample code is shown in Fig. 5. In our Dolittle environment, the "serialport" object is predefined. We defined additional methods whose names are the same as the mnemonics. In these methods, we wrote codes to send correspondent bytecodes and accompanying operand data to the serial port. Then, the programmer can write a robot control code as three steps, such as (1) opening the serial port, (2) doing some mnemonics method invocations, (3) closing the port. In Fig. 5, mnemonics are written in a separate method named "transfer". By using this technique, the programmer can concentrate on writing mnemonics because the other part of the program (before "startrobot" and after "endrobot") is completely the same in every program.

5.2 Structured Control and MYU BASIC

The Dolittle environment explained in the previous section was quite usable for simple programs targeted to two-motor robots. However, when the programmer starts to handle multiple sensors in the code, it becomes complicated and the readability of it degrades.

To overcome the problem, a programming language with structured control flow was necessary.

In answer to the problem, we first developed "MYU BASIC" [6] by modeling this language in a way similar to structured Basic.

```
robo = serialport ! create.
robo:transfer = [ !
  startrobot
    20 forward
    10 stop
    20 back
    10 stop
  endrobot
].
robo ! "com1" opensesame.
robo ! transfer.
robo ! closesesame.
```

Fig. 5. Example Program of MYUROBO Code in Dolittle

5.3 Design of Structured Robot-Control Language on Dolittle Syntax

From the experience with MYU BASIC, we learned that there is a good effect on the readability of the code by using structured syntax. Then, we returned to Dolittle.

At first, we examined a syntax following original Dolittle as robot-control language, but we abandoned this idea because we noticed that there is a semantic difference between the concepts of object-oriented programming in Dolittle and the autonomy of the robot. In the Dolittle program, multiple objects communicate with each other by message passing. On the other hand, in the robot-control program, a robot object describes the entire robot. If the robot object communicates with the other objects in Dolittle, it means that the robot has to communicate with the Dolittle system on the PC while it is executing. This contradicts the autonomy of the robot.

Consequently, we have determined the "MYU" object, which inherits the original "serialport" object and is designed to implement all structured commands, as methods of this object. The designed structured syntax is shown in Table 2.

Table 2. Structured Robot-Control Language on Dolittle

Function	Syntax
Condition	[! n ifhigh] then [! ...] execute
	[! n iflow] then [! ...] else [! ...] execute
Iteration	[! n ifhigh] whilerepeat [! ...] execute
	[! ...] n repeat
Terminating Iteration	break

The syntax of the conditional branch and the iteration resembles the original Dolittle except for the position of "!" sign and the absence of a period at the end of the line.

```
robo = MYU ! "com1" create.
robo:collision_avoidance = [ !
    [ ! 1 iflow ] whilerepeat
        [ ! 10 back 10 turnright ] execute
].
robo:program = [ !
    startrobot
    [ !
        forward
        [! 2 ifhigh ] then [ ! collision_avoidance ] execute
    ] repeat
    endrobot
].
robo ! program.
```

Fig. 6. Example Program of Structured Robot-Control Language on Dolittle

Development of an Educational System to Control Robots for All Students 71

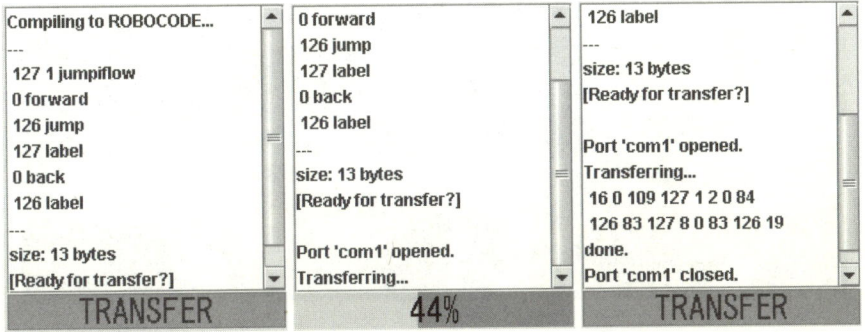

Fig. 7. Visual Elements of the MYU Object

Furthermore, in order to enable composing compound conditions, we introduced "and" and "or" methods.

An example program using this structured language is shown in Fig. 6. This program includes a definition of a subroutine by method definition, a method invocation, two conditional branches, and an iteration.

Fig. 7 shows the visual element of the "MYU" object. On the left is an appearance at the moment the converted code is shown, the second image is an appearance while transferring bytecodes, and the last is an appearance at the moment that transferring has finished.

6 Workshops for Lower Secondary School Teachers

In order to assess the usefulness and practicality of our educational system, we have had two workshops for lower secondary school teachers. One was held in August 2006 for five participants at Fukuyama city in the Hiroshima prefecture and the other was held in November 2006 for eight participants at Fujieda city in the Shizuoka prefecture.

In the workshop, participants built their robots by copying the model robot we had prepared. Then, they learned how to program robots with Dolittle and erabolated their programs and mechanism to complete the assignment which was to have to robot lift up a can, find a storage box with a touch-sensor and put the can in the box. The workshop and the model robot is shown in Fig. 8.

All participants could complete the assignment on time. After each workshop, we asked the participants to evaluate our materials by answering a questionnaire. As a result, almost all participants (11 from 13) answered "building the robot is not difficult" and "programming is rather easy" (12 participants). Moreover, from their answers, they felt our materials would be effective in technology and computer classes.

At present, some lower secondary school teachers have started or completed robot control classes and some are planning to conduct such classes.

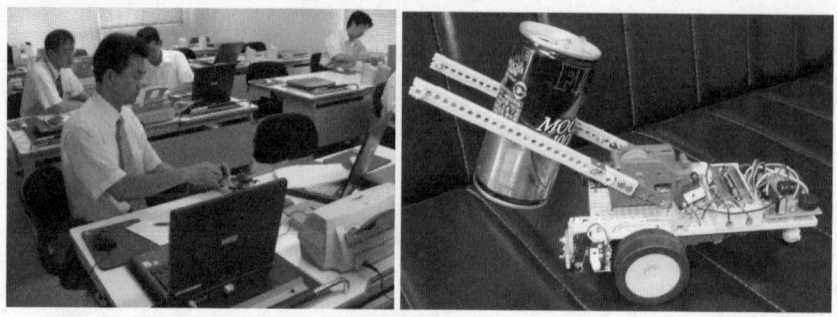

Fig. 8. Venue of Workshop and Model Robot

7 Discussion

We think the MYUROBO controller board is compact and useful for working with secondary school classes. It is low-cost so that all students can buy it and use it in their homes. However, communicating to the PC is a problem. Serial ports are legacy devices now. Students would have to buy a converter cable to use the board at home. Consequently, we need a USB interface for our board, but the cost is a barrier.

The structured robot-control language has a good reputation with school teachers. However, there are some problems.

First, there is a difference in syntax between the robot-control language and the original Dolittle. The robot object "MYU" is a standalone one. It cannot send and receive messages between other objects that are running on the PC. In the robot-control program, the code to send a message to another object causes a compiler error in the translator. Then, the receiver of the messages must be the robot object itself. That is why the "!" sign is always attached to the top of the block (as the code "[!").

The second problem relates to the handling of registers and memory. This is because all of the instructions of the robot object are methods of the robot object. In order to handle registers and memory, the programmer has to write a code to calculate using the "A" register (accumulator). This is not intuitive. There would be a need for writing expressions in robot control code as happens in other high-level languages. However, we do not know how to handle expressions well in the current implementation.

8 Related Works

The most popular educational robot system would be LEGO MindStorms, RCX and NXT. But these are too large and too expensive for our purpose. Our teaching material, including the MYUROBO controller board, costs about 20 Euros. We think that this reasonable cost is the strongest argument for our system. Moreover, when classes use our system, children get experience not only with plastic blocks but also with metal plates, screws, solder etc. By handling these various materials, we hope children will have a more realistic experience with the robot. Our materials for the robots are not standardized and so every child's robot becomes the unique one. Then, the controlling software for the robot is customized for that particular robot. This should add to the good effect on learning computer programming.

The Cricket [8] is small enough but the bytecode interpreter on the Cricket is optimized for the LOGO language. Hence, it would be difficult to implement the translator from other high-level language such as Dolittle.

9 Conclusion

We have developed an educational system to learn robot-control for secondary education. The system is composed of a MYUROBO controller board and a structured robot-control language on Dolittle.

The benefit of the MYUROBO controller board is its low-cost and that it is language free. Language free means that because the firmware of the controller board realizes a virtual CPU which runs its bytecode interpreter, the user can program with any kind of high-level language by developing the compiler or converter from the language to the bytecode.

The benefit of a structured robot-control language is that it is easy to learn, as proven from the results of the questionnaire summary from the two teacher workshops.

But there are problems, such as a different syntax from the original Dolittle and difficulty in handling variables and expressions in the implementation using the Dolittle system. Enhancing the Dolittle system or developing an independent compiler would be needed to overcome these problems. We are going to design a new structured robot-control language based on a fully object-oriented model.

Acknowledgement

We would like to thank Mr. Shuji Inoue for his kind cooperation in developing a MYUROBO controller board and MYU BASIC processor. We also appreciate the contribution of the teachers who participated in our workshops. Lastly, we would like to extend our gratitude to Dr. Fred Martin for giving us lots of useful comments on this paper.

References

1. Kurebayashi, S., Kamada, T., Kanemune, S.: Learning Computer Programming with Autonomous Robots. In: Mittermeir, R.T. (ed.) ISSEP 2006. LNCS, vol. 4226, pp. 138–149. Springer, Heidelberg (2006)
2. Kanemune, S., Kuno, Y.: Dolittle: An Object-Oriented Language for K12 Education. In: EuroLogo 2005, Warszawa, Poland, pp. 144–153 (2005)

3. Kanemune, S., Nakatani, T., Mitarai, R., Fukui, S., Kuno, Y.: Dolittle — Experiences in Teaching Programming at K12 Schools. In: Proc. of the Second International Conference on Creating, Connecting and Collaborating through Computing (C5), pp. 177–184. IEEE, Kyoto, Japan (2004)
4. Dolittle Programming Language, http://dolittle.eplang.jp/
5. MYUROBO Controller Board (Japanese), http://www.geocities.jp/shuinoue/myurobo/
6. MYU BASIC COMPILER (Japanese), http://www.geocities.jp/shuinoue/myurobo/myubasic.html
7. Martin, F.: Real Robots Don't Drive Straight. In: Proceedings of the AAAI Spring Symposium on Robots and Robot Venues: Resources for AI Education, Stanford, CA (March 2007)
8. Martin, F., Mikhak, B., Resnick, M., Silverman, B., Berg, R.: To Mindstorms and Beyond: Evolution of a Construction Kit for Magical Machines. In: Robots for Kids. Morgan Kaufman, San Francisco (2000)

Proposal for Teaching Manufacturing and Control Programming Using Autonomous Mobile Robots with an Arm

Shuji Kurebayashi[1], Hiroyuki Aoki[2], Toshiyuki Kamada[3], Susumu Kanemune[4], and Yasushi Kuno[5]

[1] Shizuoka University
eskureb@ipc.shizuoka.ac.jp
[2] Korea University
hiroyuki.aoki@inc.korea.ac.kr
[3] Aichi University of Education
tkamada@acm.org
[4] Hitotsubashi University
kanemune@acm.org
[5] University of Tsukuba
kuno@gssm.otsuka.tsukuba.ac.jp

Abstract. We propose a technology education curriculum for lower secondary school students using an autonomous mobile robot with an arm. The purpose of our curriculum is to teach the concept of systems that work with mechanics, electricity and computers. For this purpose, we have developed a control board and a computer language for an autonomous mobile robot with an arm. The benefit of this kind of robot is that students have to seriously think about the program for controlling the arm to lift and carry objects. This kind of serious thought is not necessary in programming simple mobile robots without arms[1]. In this paper, we will report a test conducted to evaluate our teaching materials and lessons in lower secondary school. As a result, our technology education curriculum satisfies requirements for students that have more incentives to learn the concept of systems.

1 Introduction

In today's information society, we are living with lots of embedded computers, such as those within refrigerators, cars, and so on. To foster zest for living in this information society, it is important to understand models of how embedded computers control machines.

However, in Japanese "Technology and Home Economics" subject, mechanics and computers are treated separately; mechanics controlled by embedded computers are not taught. Therefore, students cannot get the idea of systems with embedded computers, in spite of widespread technology which we use everyday in our life. The downside of the fact is that they will not become citizens who understand the risks of technology and cannot evaluate the technological products correctly.

In Japanese lower secondary schools, robot contests are quite popular (used in more than 3,000 schools) in the manufacturing lessons of "Technology and Home Economics" curriculum. In the robot contests, students compete with each other to test their skills of controlling their hand-made robots. However, those robots are not autonomous robots; they are controlled by humans through remote controllers. Therefore, from such contests, students learn much about mechanics, but almost nothing about computer controlled mechanics. We believe that the heart of today's embedded systems is computer controlled automatism, and students should definitely learn such concepts. To enable such learning, (1) appropriate material and (2) an effective curriculum are neccesary.

In this paper, we present an autonomous tri-axial robot (a mobile robot with an arm) that we have developed as teaching material. Tri-axial means three motors, two of which are used to drive wheels to move the robot around, and one of which is used to lift the arm to carry things. Such robots can do some useful work (e.g. carrying things and so) and are attractive for students. We also present a curriculum we have developed which effectively make use of such robots. Additionally, results of two experimental classes, one for lower secondary school students and another for teachers, are reported. Finally, we discuss the effectiveness of those curricula and teaching materials for students to learn the computer controlled mechanics.

2 Overview of Our Hybrid Lessons

Our goal is to make the students comprehend the model in which mechanics are controlled by embedded computers (and programs running on them). However, such complex models cannot be taught in a single step. Therefore, we propose a step-by-step style of lessons:

(1) Manufacturing the robots
    In the first step, students assemble mechanical parts of the robot car (body, gearwheels, motors, arms, and so on). They also learn wiring of electric parts so that they can understand what electrical parts (CPU board, power supply, motors, sensors and so on) their robots have, along with their connecting topologies.
(2) Primitive programming experiences
    In the second step, students experience primitive programming. With this lesson, students understand that every action of a computer is controlled through programs, and programs work in a concise step-by-step manner.
(3) Programming to control robots
    As the third step, students finally craft programs and download those programs to the robot car, which operates autonomously under program control.

Through these lessons, students can grab practical models of computer controlled mechanics along with collaboration among hardware and software. This goal has been difficult to achieve in traditional lessons in Japan in which mechanics and computers were taught separately.

3 Design of Teaching Materials

To carry out our lessons effectively, appropriate teaching materials are necessary. The requirements for the teaching materials are as follows:

- The material should support learning of how the mechanics work. Therefore, instead of being complete products, assembly kits, with which students compose various parts as gearwheels, arms, etc. together, are desirable.
- The material should support learning of computer hardware. Through wiring, and soldering to put the electric parts on a circuit board, students can understand how the electrical hardware such as CPUs, sensors and electric power supplies make the mechanics work.
- The material should support learning of embedded software with minimal effort. Spending lots of time learning programming language syntax or complex libraries is undesirable; the majority of time should be used to actually experience robot control. Therefore, easy-to-learn programming languages and/or environments with Japanese language support are necessary.
- The materials should be moderately priced, so that each of the students can have their own robot. To achieve this goal in practice, price of materials should be around ¥3,000 (about €20) or so.

There was no teaching material which satisfies all of the above conditions. Therefore, we have developed (1) electrical board with a CPU to control robot cars, and (2) an educational programming system which runs cooperatively on the electrical board and on a personal computer.

3.1 Control Board

For the purpose of controlling robots, a programming facility is required for the control board. Our control board uses a PIC (CPU, program/data memory and external interface packaged on a chip). Within the PIC, there is a small byte code interpreter, and students' programs are transferred from outside and stored as byte code programs. Some of the byte code operations put a signal on the external interface through which motor rotation is controlled.

In our curriculum, students put electrical parts on the control board and connect them through soldering and wiring. Through those experiences, students get a general idea of electrical circuitry and operation of the control board. The circuit board we developed is shown in Fig.1.

As described earlier, our robots are tri-axial; two motors are used to control two wheels (to move the robot car around), and one motor is used to raise/lower arms. Therefore, our control board is capable of controlling three DC motors, and also has four input ports to connect various sensors/switches. The sensors include light sensor and touch switch (collision detector).

We use PIC16F630[2] as the micro controller on the board. This PIC has FLASH memory, where we record our firmware. The firmware is responsible for receiving the byte code program from the host computer and running (interpreting) the program. The maximum length of the byte code programs is 127 bytes.

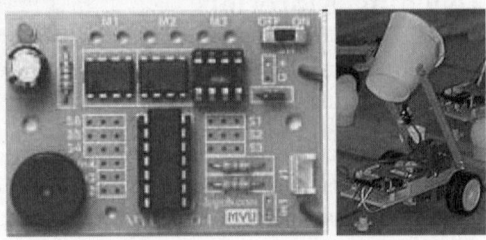

Fig. 1. The control board and student's work

Most of the byte code operations occupy 2 bytes (operation code and argument). Byte code programs are transferred to the board from the host computer using an RS232C cable and interface.

Aside from the control board, the mechanics of the robot car is built using standard parts, such as a general purpose frame, gearwheels, wheels and so on. The work of a student is shown in Fig.1.

3.2 Programming Language "Dolittle"

We adopted "Dolittle"[3] as a programming language and environment. Dolittle is an object-oriented educational programming language with compact syntax, and students can write programs using Japanese characters. Dolittle has turtle graphics (inherited from LOGO). Turtle graphics are well suited to primitive programming experiences because students can see the result of their programs on the screen.

```
ROBO= MYU! "com1" create.                                      // (1)
ROBO: sendProgram= [! beginRobot                               // (2)
  powerOnStart                                                 // (3)
  [!                                                           // (4)
    [! 2senserNo ifLow ] then [! rightForward ]                // (5)
      else [! leftForward ] execute                            // (6)
    [! 1senserNo ifHigh ] then [! getBall ] execute            // (7)
  ]repeat                                                      // (8)
endRobot].                                                     // (9)
ROBO: getBall= [!                                              //(10)
  10 stop                                                      //(11)
  [! 4senserNo ifLow] whileRepeat [! motorRight ] execute      //(12)
  10 motorLeft                                                 //(13)
  10 back                                                      //(14)
].                                                             //(15)
ROBO! sendProgram.                                             //(16)
```

Fig. 2. An example control program

Additionally, we have implemented a simple robot language translator written in Dolittle. With this translator, students can write their robot control programs using Dolittle syntax. However, those robot control programs are translated to byte code and transferred to the robot car.

Dolittle also has the facility to read/write RS232C communication ports. This facility is used to control communication between the host computer and PIC monitor and to transfer byte code programs.

Fig.2 shows a sample program for controlling a robot:

- (1) makes a robot object which will communicate through the port "com1".
- (2)–(9) defines a method "sendProgram".
- (2), (9) "beginRobot" and "endRobot" delimit the beginning and end of the robot control program.
- (3) specifies that the program of the robot starts soon after the power switch is turned on.
- (4)–(8) repeats infinitely.
- (5), (6) if the left sensor (sensor 2) touches a wall (or object), the robot moves to the right, otherwise to the left.
- (7) if the center sensor (sensor 1) touches an object, the robot calls up method "getBall".
- (10)–(15) defines method "getBall" : The robot stops, moves the shovel up to the limit, then goes back.
- (16) transfers compiled byte codes to the robot.

Adopting Dolittle[3] made it possible for lower secondary school students to learn this primitive program easily in a short period. This was essential to the success of our curriculum because we cannot invest many hours for teaching programming alone.

4 Experimental Classes for Teachers

To assess the usefulness and practicality of our materials and curriculum, we have given two workshops, or experimental classes, for teachers. One was given in August 2006 for five teachers at Fukuyama city in Hiroshima prefecture; another was in November 2006 for eight teachers at Fujieda city in Shizuoka prefecture.

In the workshop, teachers first manufactured mobile robots with an arm, then controlled them with their programs. The major goals of the lessons, when applied to students, are as follows:

- Students can learn widely about mechanics, electricity and computers.
- Students can learn the outline of systems in which mechanics are controlled by electricity and computers.

We asked the teachers to asses whether our materials and curriculum meet the above goals, and to give us feedback as to what portion of the materials and curriculum need to be revised (where it is too difficult for students or has other problems). Kurebayashi took charge of two workshops.

Table 1. Schedule of the workshop

description	#hours
robot manufacturing	3
robot programming	3

Table 2. Q1 and Q2: You find it difficult for students to learn

	Difficult				Easy
	5	4	3	2	1
Q1. robot manufacturing	0	2	6	5	0
Q2. robot programming	0	1	5	6	1

Table 3. Q3–Q6: The effect expected from our teaching material and curriculum

	Agree				Disagree
	5	4	3	2	1
Q3. Good for students to study informatics and computers	6	7	0	0	0
Q4. Good for students to study technology and manufacturing	6	6	1	0	0
Q5. You would like to perform robot contest in class	5	7	1	0	0
Q6. Good for students to foster creativity and invention skills	6	7	0	0	0

Table 1 shows the contents of the workshops.

After the classes, we conducted a questionnaire survey to evaluate our materials. In the questionnaire, teachers answered each question choosing from a five level scale (5: strongly agree 4: agree 3: not sure 2: disagree 1: strongly disagree). The questions and the numbers for each choice are shown in Table 2 and Table 3.

In total, we think that subjective evaluations from teachers have confirmed that our teaching materials and curriculum are effective for use in classes, both for teaching manufacturing and teaching computers in a unified manner, and also will have the effect of developing students' creativity.

5 Experimental Classes for Lower Secondary School Students

To evaluate the effectiveness and practicality of our materials and curriculum with actual students, we conducted experimental classes in Hanashi lower secondary school (3rd grade, 123 students), Shizuoka prefecture, Japan. The lesson started with each student creating a robot and then composing a program for the robot. At the end of the lessons, a robot contest was held. Mr. Akiyama took charge of these lessons.

Table 4. Contents and schedule of the classes

contents	#hours
Let's learn about computer controls	1
Let's try making a program	4
Let's manufacture a robot	10
Create a program for robot control	3
Robot contest	3

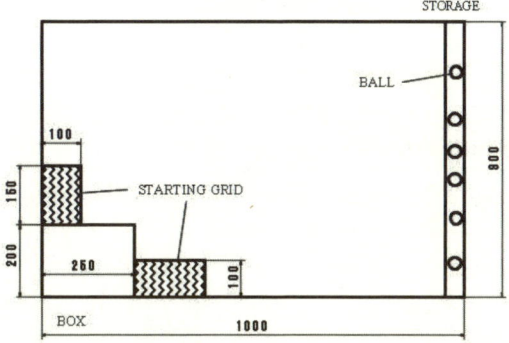

Rule of the Programming Robot Contest:

1. The robot must start from the starting grid
2. Pick up the ball on the storage
3. Carry it into the box

Fig. 3. The field layout and rules of the contest

5.1 Contents of the Classes

The contents and the number of hours for the classes are shown in Table 4. After the overview, students practiced simple graphics programming using Dolittle. Then, students manufactured their own robots.

At the end of the arm of the robot, a paper cup with its bottom cut out and an elastic band is fastened; when the robot puts the cup over an ping-pong ball and raises the arm, the ball enters the cup and can be carried by the robot. Students can freely elaborate and/or enhance the mechanism at will.

For robot control programming and the final contest, the task of picking up ping-pong balls and carrying them was chosen. The layout of the field and the rules are shown in Fig.3. Scenes from the lessons are shown in Fig.4.

5.2 The Result of the Lessons

All 123 students were able to complete their robots and control programs on time. Also, there was no problem in learning the basics of programming. We think that the choice of Dolittle programming language and associated robot programming system contributed to this. Students were modifying and enhancing the sample program at will; after trying their programs on the robot, they could change the program to suit their intentions. As a result, the final robot contest was held successfully.

Fig. 4. A student working on his task and Students programming their robot

5.3 Questionnaire to the Students

After completing the lessons, we gave a questionnaire to the students. The goal of the questionnaire was to evaluate the following points:

- Students' willingness to learn
- Ease/difficulty level of our materials

The questionnaire was composed of 5 closed questions and a text description. The selective questions were answered with a 5-level scale (5: Strongly agree, 4: Agree, 3: Not sure, 2: Disagree, 1: Strongly disagree). The content of selective questions and numbers of students with percentages those who answered positively (choice 5 and 4) are shown in Table 5.

The result suggests that students perceived both manufacturing and programming as "hard fun" [4]. Therefore, the difficulty of our materials and curriculum seems to be appropriate for lower secondary school students. Moreover, the ratio of answers "I would like to continue the lessons" was very high; these lessons raised students' willingness to learn considerably.

We also requested students to describe freely at which points they felt difficulty. Multiple answers were allowed. The purpose of this question was to investigate what is the hard point for the students and what aspect of the classes were useful to them, from their own viewpoint. All students described something, resulting in 243 answers in total. We categorized the answers, whose summary is shown in Fig.5.

Table 5. Results of the enquiry

description	#students	%positive
1. Manufacturing robots were difficult.	88	71.5
2. Manufacturing robots were enjoyable.	115	93.0
3. Programming robots were difficult.	87	70.1
4. Programming robots were enjoyable.	91	74.0
5. I am willing to continue this lessons	96	78.0

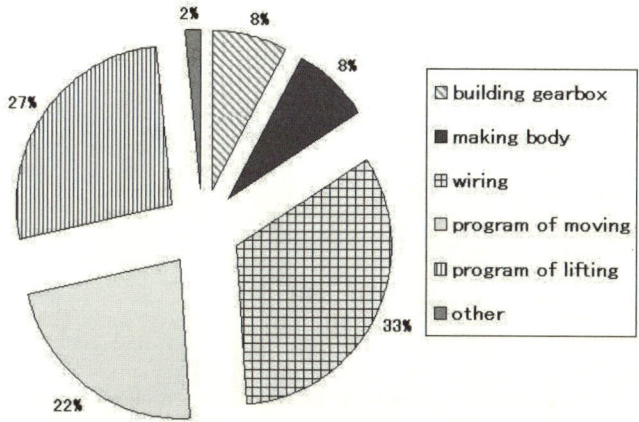

Fig. 5. Summary of "difficult points"

From the above summary, we can point out that students learned a lot about mechanics, electricity and computer programming. In other words, we think that our original goal of teaching students a combined system of mechanics and computer control was successfully achieved. Moreover, the ratio of answers concerning computer programming is very high (49% in total), indicating that students put lots of effort into computer programmings. This is an accurate reflection of today's embedded system or computer-controlled devices.

5.4 Study on Level of Understanding Embedded Systems

The original motivation for our curriculum is to develop students' understanding of embedded systems in which computers control mechanics, because such systems are widely used, and today's citizens should understand the principles and risks of such technology. To assess this kind of understanding, we made another question to the students. The question concerns the mechanism of elevators, which are representative of computer controlled mechanics and which are also familiar to the students. We showed them the picture of Fig.6 and asked the following questions:

Q1. Do you understand the meaning of the phrase "errors in control panel program?"
Q2. Please explain the role of the control panel.

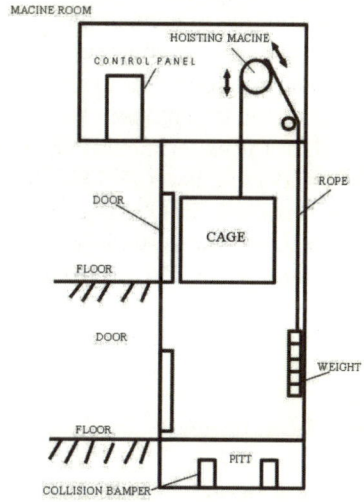

Fig. 6. Mechanism of elevators

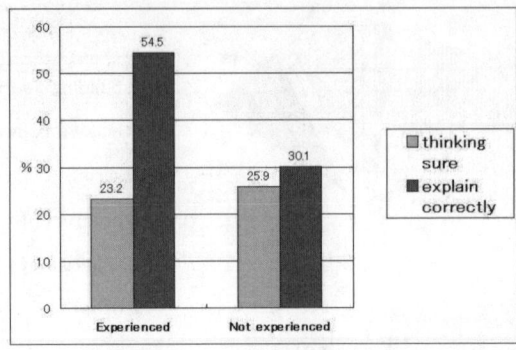

Fig. 7. The result of questionnaire on elevators

For Q1, we asked students to choose one from "Yes," "Not sure," or "No." For Q2, we checked if the student could choose at least one part shown in Fig.6 and explain its role correctly.

As a control group, we made the same questionnaire to students of another public lower secondary school in the same city. This school does no teaching about embedded systems at all. The number of students was 111. Fig.7 shows the ratio of students who chose "Yes" for Q1 and could correctly answer Q2 for two schools. Additionally, we asked the students to raise their hand if they thought that they understand the mechanism of the elevators, but no students raised their hands.

As a result, the ratio of students who think they can understand the meaning of the phrase "errors in the program of control panel" is almost the same, but there is a large difference among the two groups in the ratio of students who can write the role of control panel correctly.

In the control group (no embedded-system learning), there was a strong correlation in understanding the role of the control panel and understanding the meaning of the phrase "errors in the control panel program." On the other hand, in the experimental group (which experienced our curriculum), even when the students answered "No" in Q1, lots of them could write the role of control panel correctly in Q2. This means that there are many students who understand the principle of systems with computer controlled mechanics, even if they do not comprehend the somewhat difficult concept of "errors in the control panel program." The result confirms the effectiveness of our materials and of the curriculum in enhancing understanding of the principle of embedded systems.

6 Discussion

We have developed teaching materials which can motivate students and which support students to understand the principle of embedded systems. Students did not feel much difficulty in manufacturing the robots and controlling them, as the robot consisted of processable materials such as plastic and brass, and programming was easy to learn.

In the class, students handled lots of parts, such as motors, sensor switches and control boards. Through these experiences, they could understand the principle of systems in which motors move a robot and computers control motors referring to signals from sensors. As a result, students thought "It's difficult but fun." and teachers thought "It's suitable for our classes".

The robot contest was effective for learning. Students could refine their control programs according to their intention, meaning that they could have concrete understanding of computer controlled mechanics.

The elevator questionnaire revealed that students who experienced our curriculum could answer properly, compared to the control group. This also indicates the effectiveness of our materials and teaching methods.

7 Related Works

LEGO Mind-storms [5] can control a tri-axial robot which is constructed by LEGO blocks. The robot can be programmed by a graphical language. The CPU and other parts are packaged, so we can't see the electrical parts inside the block. These features are suitable for novices. But we think that in a technology class, students should have the experience of seeing and constructing electronic circuits in order to understanding systems, and they should have the experience of programming and debugging by coding.

Cricket [6] can control a tri-axial robot also. It can be controlled by a graphical language. It is useful for scientific education, but it is too expensive for students. So we didn't use it in our classes.

8 Conclusion

We developed autonomous mobile robots with an arm and conducted experimental lessons. The robot can be used for robot contests in classes. Students can learn the concept of systems by technology education and information education.

There are many system products, but they are a black box for many users. Users cannot understand what they are and how they work. To understand their principles, users should understand principles of software and hardware.

But not so many lower secondary school and higher secondary school students want to become specialists. Therefore teaching materials and concepts which students can be interested in are needed.

Our teaching materials for autonomous mobile robots with an arm and control programs are useful for hardware and software system education. By the experience of manufacturing robots and control programming, We can expect that students began to know the systems by analogy. Thus we are convinced of the effect to learn the concept of systems that work with mechanics, electricity and computers by using our teaching materials in Information and Technology education.

References

1. Kurebayashi, S., Kamada, T., Kanemune, S.: Learning Computer Program with Autonomous Robots. In: Mittermeir, R.T. (ed.) ISSEP 2006. LNCS, vol. 4226, pp. 138–149. Springer, Heidelberg (2006)
2. Microchip Coop.: PIC16F630 Datasheet (2007),
   http://ww1.microchip.com/downloads/en/DeviceDoc/40039E.pdf
3. Kanemune, S., Kuno, Y.: Dolittle: An Object-Oriented Language for K12 Education. In: EuroLogo 2005, Warzawa, Poland, pp. 144–153 (2005)
4. Papert, S.: The Children's Machine. Basic Books (1993)
5. Resnick, M.: Behavior Construction Kits. Communications of the ACM 36(7), 64–71 (1993)
6. Martin, F., Mikhak, B., Resnick, M., Silverman, B., Berg, R.: To Mindstorms and Beyond:Evolution of a Construction Kit for Magical Machines. In: Robots for kids. Morgan Kaufman, San Francisco (2000)

Design Disciplines and Non-specific Transfer

David Ginat

CS Group, Science Education Department
Te-Aviv University
Tel-Aviv 69978, Israel
ginat@post.tau.ac.il

Abstract. Computer science educators expect their students to develop a scientific design discipline with programs and proofs. Established acquisition of a scientific discipline encapsulates rich cognitive representation, which is reflected by competent non-specific transfer. Do computer science graduates demonstrate non-specific transfer of fundamental design notions? The study presented here reveals some undesired findings. Computer science graduates, who are engaged in teaching, showed rather limited competence with task representation and the heuristic of decomposition and (re-)composition, as well as with progression through ordered design stages. Many followed a rather unordered and unconvincing solution plan, which yielded only partial outcomes, and no conviction of exploitation. We describe our findings and offer suggestions for explicitly elaborating (sometime implicit) design notions.

1 Introduction

Design is a fundamental skill in computer science, repeatedly required in the development of computer programs (algorithms) and proofs. A design process is composed of a series of stages – task analysis, solution planning, plan-execution, solution evaluation (and verification), and the consideration of alternative solutions.

The design process may involve various problem-solving heuristics, among them analogy (between the given task and other, familiar tasks), selection of a suitable representation, task de-composition and re-composition, based on the chosen representation, and more. The design also involves the utilization of concrete resources, such as programming language constructs, data structures, design patterns (e.g., [1,8,17]), proof schemes, and computational models components.

Learning and acquisition of the design stages, heuristics, and resources involve transfer [4,19,22]. The resources are explicitly studied in various curriculum courses, and are acquired through repeated, focused practice, which involves specific transfer (e.g., the learning of loop constructs). The design stages and design heuristics are studied more implicitly, through solution-process illuminations. Their acquisition is expected to develop gradually, into a scientific discipline, with accumulated experiences of non-specific transfer. The main difference between the two kinds of transfers is that specific transfer is simpler to teach, observe, and expect. Non-specific transfer is subtler, in terms of its development, practice, and application.

Although it is subtler, non-specific transfer is essential for competent problem solving in any domain [4,5,15,19,21], including that of computer science. Students should develop competence in utilizing and employing fundamental ideas in diverse contexts within a domain [4,22], and demonstrate a scientific discipline that encapsulates proficient expression of essential skills, including the skill of design.

A variety of studies illuminated novice difficulties with concrete resource transfer of language constructs (e.g., [7,13,23]) and design patterns [18]. Novices demonstrate limited comprehension and utilization of concrete constructs like loops and recursion, and inadequate utilization of programming templates and schemes.

Very little was studied with respect to students' demonstration of non-specific transfer of heuristics and disciplined design progression. One partial exception is [24], which specifically examined novice difficulties with formulating proper goals and plans during the program-design stages of planning and execution.

All the above studies focused on the design of computer programs. No studies were conducted, to the best of our knowledge, with student difficulties in designing suitable proofs in computer science. (Studies of proof comprehension and construction were conducted in the domain of mathematics education.) However, proof design is essential in computer science. Moreover, leading computer scientists, including Hoar [16], Dijkstra [6], and Gries [14] argue that program design should be done hand-in-hand with proving, or convincing its correctness.

Computer science educators expect their students to develop a scientific design discipline, be it with programs or proofs, by the end of their studies. Established acquisition of a scientific discipline and scientific notions encapsulates rich internal (cognitive) representation, which is reflected by competent non-specific transfer [15]. Is it really the case with design in computer science? Do computer science graduates demonstrate non-specific transfer of fundamental design notions? Do they demonstrate suitable heuristic invocations and a scientific design discipline? The objective of this study is to examine this aspect, with computer science graduates who completed their studies and are currently engaged in teaching.

In the next section we describe our study, with a rather less common tool of an a-typical task, and display our findings. In the section that follows, we discuss our findings, and offer suggestions for explicitly elaborating sometimes-implicit design elements, in order to enhance students' scientific design disciplines.

2 Design Disciplines

The population of our study included 33 computer science graduates, who teach in college or high-school (some teach mathematics). We posed them a single task, which did not directly involve computer-program design or proof design. Rather, they were asked to generate and write on a paper a complete set of entities. For this, they had to plan and apply a convincing, systematic scheme, thus demonstrating a scientific discipline and embedding notions of both program and proof design. In order to examine non-specific transfer, we chose a task with elementary Geometry elements. The participants were given 90 minutes for solving the Polygon task described below. They were requested to describe their debates, diverse attempts, and decisions made during their solution progress, in addition to the final answer.

Polygons. Given a 3×3 grid of nine dots, as displayed in Figure-1 below, were the distance between every two horizontally adjacent points is 1 (cm) and the distance between every two vertically adjacent points is 1 (cm), generate and display on paper <u>all</u> the different simple (non self-intersecting) polygons with area 2 (cm²), such that their vertices are grid points. We consider all the different orientations (rotation, reflection) of a polygon as the same polygon.

Fig. 1. The grid of nine dots

<u>Note</u>: We are not strict about avoiding redundant polygons in your answer, since our focus is not on no-redundancies, but on the complete set of different polygons.

<u>Example</u>: One obvious polygon is the rectangle below, in Figure-2. (Recall that any rotation or reflection of this polygon is not considered a different polygon.)

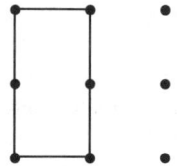

Fig. 2. A rectangle of area 2, whose four vertices are grid points

At a first glance, one may get the impression that non-trivial geometrical insight is required here. But, due to the grid size, the area calculation of any polygon placed on the grid points is straightforward, and different orientations are rather easy to check. The challenge is to select and utilize task characteristics with which it will be appropriate to reach a feeling of exploitation in generating <u>all</u> the relevant polygons. Complete generation of all the polygons will be derived from an illuminating task representation and a convincing applied plan.

In the beginning of the solution process, it is natural to start with some arbitrary, straightforward polygons, as shown in Figure-3 below. One may rather quickly identify a large triangle, a hexagon, and a quadrilateral as those in the figure. It may initially seem that the total number of polygons is rather small, perhaps even less than 10; but, it actually is more than 20. After gaining some initial "feeling" of the task, one should seek an illuminating perspective and yield an ordered generation plan.

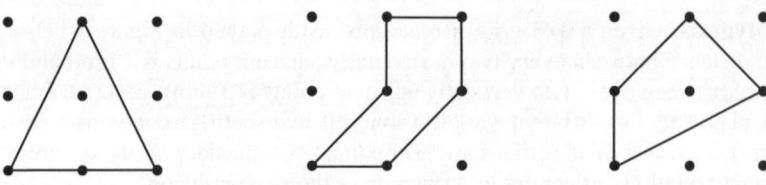

Fig. 3. Three rather straightforward polygons

Some problem solvers may start from the range of elements (polygons); whereas others may start from a suitable domain representation (grid parts). In the former case, one may try to yield polygons by: their number of sides, or by their side lengths, or by the number of points on their exterior (interior), or by their sub-components. In the latter case, one may start from the grid and represent it in various ways, by parts which may be assembled and yield polygons. The notion of a suitable perspective plays an important role here, as well as the heuristic of decomposition and (re-) composition. It is probably natural for one to try different perspectives before devising an ordered systematic plan. One should carefully examine the domain, the range, and their inter-relations.

We observed the participants during their solution process, and collected their written comments and solutions. In what follows, we classify and characterize the participants' solutions, while referring to the above elements and the design stages indicated in the Introduction (task analysis, solution planning, plan-execution, and solution evaluation). The classification is divided into five groups, of different design disciplines. They are described below, from the less disciplined to the more disciplined.

Design-Discipline 1: Unordered Progress + Local Restructuring

Nine participants demonstrated a very limited design discipline. After getting some initial feeling of the task, by generating a few straightforward polygons, they did not try to carefully analyze the task and yield an ordered polygon-generation plan. Rather, they continued looking for additional polygons, by locally changing lines and parts of the already generated polygons. Most of them generated between 12 to 16 polygons, and obviously did not reach any feeling of exploitation, as they did not employ any systematic theme.

The better ones among these participants applied some partially-ordered progression after noticing that some polygon parts are actually basic 1×1 (base, height) isosceles right triangles, of area 0.5, obtained from connecting 3 nearby grid dots, as displayed in Figure-4 below. After observing one or more such triangles in a generated polygon, they decomposed the polygon, and restructured it "locally" by rotating or reflecting such triangles for obtaining new polygons, as also shown in Figure-4.

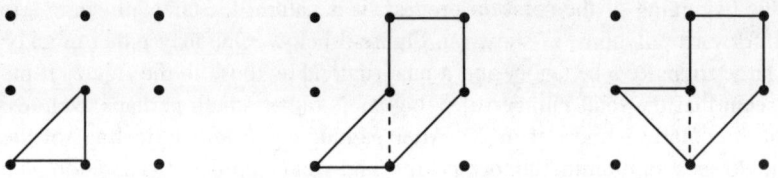

Fig. 4. A basic right triangle, as a polygon part, and reflected

All in all, these participants did not perform any ordered task analysis, and their progress looked like a series of patches. They generated the rather straightforward polygons, and then upon wondering whether they are done or not, they "discovered", a few times, one or two additional polygons. These discoveries were sometimes rather arbitrary, or due to a "local recognition" of polygon parts that may be rotated or reflected.

Design-Discipline 2: Partial Decomposition and Re-Composition
Ten participants demonstrated a somewhat better design discipline. After generating a few straightforward polygons, they observed that these polygons may be decomposed into parts, which may be re-composed in diverse ways and yield new polygons. Most of them identified the 1×2 (base, height) right triangle as such a part (the rectangle in Figure-2 and the triangle in Figure-3 may be viewed as a composition of two such 1×2 triangles; the quadrilateral in Figure-3 includes such a triangle as well).

Additional observed parts were: a 1×1 square, a 1×1 parallelogram, and a 2×1 isosceles right triangle, of area 1 (all these can be extracted from the polygons in Figure-3). Some participants also observed as parts 1×1 isosceles right triangles (of area 0.5), as the one in Figure-4.

After identifying the above polygon parts, these participants tried to systematically compose all the area 2 polygons that may be obtained from the various compositions of these parts. Some participants followed a very thorough generation scheme, of "going through" all the possible combinations, and some were less systematic. They yielded polygons like the left polygon in Figure-5 below. Those that observed as parts the 1×1 isosceles right triangles also added polygons such as the two right polygons in Figure-5.

All in all, these participants generated between 12 to 19 polygons, and some were rather fond of their observations and polygon generation. However, although they decomposed polygons into parts, their observations were rather limited and only partially illuminating. Most of the above parts are rather large, and therefore yield limited compositions. The participants tried to overcome this limitation by compositions that include overlapping of sub-parts. But, a systematic scheme of such compositions is not simple to yield, and therefore degrade the feeling of exploitation in the process of polygon generation. In addition, the above parts were yielded from the rather straightforward polygons, and not from a thorough analysis of all the possible parts that may be used in composing polygons. Some polygons were missing.

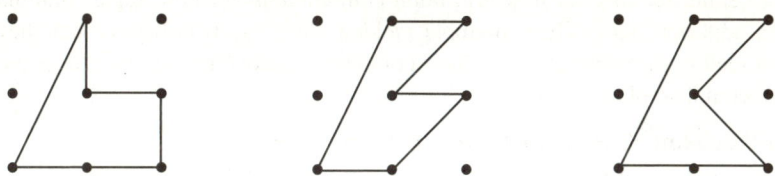

Fig. 5. Polygons composed of a triangle and a square, or only right triangles

Design-Discipline 3: Inconvenient Representation
Six participants sought characteristics that did not involve polygon decomposition. Some recalled Pick's theorem [20], which provides an elegant formula for the area

of lattice polygons (the area equals I+B/2-1, where I is the number lattice (grid) points inside the polygon and B is the number of the boundary lattice points). They noticed that in the given task, I may either be 0 or 1 and B may be 6 or 4, accordingly. Following this observation, they sought a systematic way for generating polygons, but obtained only partial progress. (Though, others may yield an ordered way.) However, some of them yielded the kite polygon (in Figure 6), upon generating polygons with an inner point. This polygon was not often reached by the other participants.

Some participants tried to generate polygons by their number of sides. They started with triangles, continued with quadrilaterals, and then pentagons and hexagons. Others looked at the grid squares, and noticed that a square may be fully inside a polygon, or fully outside, or may be divided into a part that is inside and a part that is outside. Some tried to follow some systematic ways with angles between adjacent sides. Unfortunately, all these approaches yielded only limited progress. The number of polygons generated by these participants diverted from 12 to 17.

All in all, these participants turned to various representations, or perspectives, which were related to polygon characteristics; but were not illuminating enough for them to yield thorough, systematic progress.

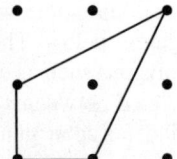

Fig. 6. A kite polygon, not often reached by the participants

Design-Discipline 4: Combined Approaches

Three participants felt that the initial approach they followed led them to unexploited outcomes, and decided to continue with another approach, which will hopefully "complete the picture". They started with the partial decomposition approach (design-discipline 2) and felt that they were still missing some polygons. At this point they turned to either looking for new grid point combinations, or new angle combinations between adjacent sides. Their attempts yielded close to 20 polygons, but they still lacked a feeling of exploitation, as their combined approaches did not encapsulate an ordered, complete plan.

Design-Discipline 5: Suitable Representation

Five participants started in a way different from all the previous participants. They examined the grid, and analyzed different shapes that may be obtained from connecting its points by lines. They particularly looked for small, "atomic" shapes from which the different polygons may be composed. They identified two shapes: the 1×1 isosceles right triangle (of figure-4), and the 1×1 obtuse triangle in Figure-7 below.

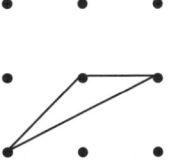

Fig. 7. An "atomic" obtuse triangle

A short analysis shows that any polygon may be composed from (a combination of) the above two atomic triangles. Some polygons may be composed from 4 atomic right triangles, some – from 3 atomic right triangles and one atomic obtuse triangle, and some – from 2 atomic right triangles and 2 atomic obtuse triangles. The latter observation, of {4,0} {3,1} and {2,2} combinations of the atomic triangles may serve as an upper-level decomposition of the task into three sub-tasks. (One may also specifically distinguish the case of a 1×1 square, which is composed of two 1×1 isosceles right triangles.)

Each sub-task may then be further divided into sub-tasks, in planning the systematic generation of polygons. The case of {4,0} (four atomic right triangles, and no atomic obtuse triangle) may be divided into sub-cases by the number of occupied grid squares – first two squares (1 polygon, the 1×2 rectangle), then all the polygons that are laid on three squares, and then all the polygons that (partly) occupy each of the four squares. The case of {3,1} may be divided into two sub-cases – the case where the atomic obtuse triangle occupies two grid squares together with an atomic right triangle (and they form a 1×2 right triangle), and the case where the obtuse triangle occupies two grid squares by itself and all the three atomic right triangles are in the other two squares. The latter case yields the 3 polygons in Figure 8 below. The case of {2,2} yields the remaining polygons – the kite, a parallelogram, and the 2×2 isosceles triangle of Figure 3.

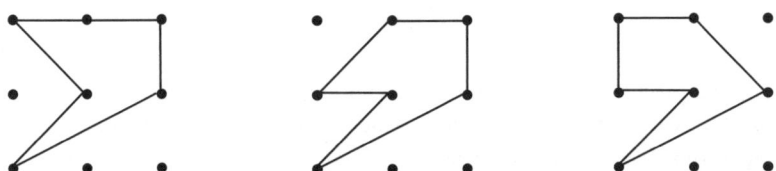

Fig. 8. The atomic obtuse triangle is separate, on two grid squares

The participants in this group employed the above plan or a variant of this plan. They started with different ways to divide the grid by lines, before reaching the ordered plan. Some distinguished a-priori the cases of a 1×1 square and a 1×2 right triangle. Two of these participants validated their solution by employing a systematic examination of the complementing areas of the grid; i.e., the areas that are not occupied by the polygons.

Some of the participant answers (here, and in the other groups) included redundancies, as the same polygon may be generated in more than one way (e.g., the 1×2 rectangle may be obtained from two 1×1 squares or two 1×2 right triangles) or may be generated twice, in different orientations. However, we were aware of this potential difficulty a-priori, and therefore indicated in the note of the task definition that we are not strict about no-redundancies.

All in all, the participants in this group demonstrated a scientific discipline in all the stages of the design process. They conducted a thorough task analysis; chose a suitable representation, based on atomic triangle shapes; and devised and implemented an ordered plan of systematic polygon generation. They obtained a feeling of exploitation in their generation scheme, as their plan combined hand-in-hand the design and its correctness features, of thorough case analysis.

3 Discussion and Conclusion

The findings in the previous section reveal five different design disciplines, of which only one was appropriate. Unfortunately, a vast majority of the participants demonstrated the less suitable disciplines. One may try to relate the cause of these findings to the a-typical task posed to the participants. We believe that this is not the case.

The Polygons task posed to the participants was indeed different and not analogous to tasks they have encountered during their computer science studies. However, this is a task suitable for examining non-specific transfer of design elements. Although the participants were neither required to develop a computer program (algorithm) nor to explicitly prove their answer, they had to employ fundamental feature of program and proof design.

In solving the task one needs to conduct careful and thorough task analysis, and seek a suitable representation, which will yield a systematic and complete solution scheme. This may be obtained by carefully examining both the domain features (grid lines and points) and the range features (of the polygons). Such an examination is required in the design of programs and proofs. Failure to carefully look at both the domain and the range may result in incomplete outcomes.

The task does not involve an "Aha" illumination. Rather, it requires careful decomposition into cases and sub-cases. However, proper decomposition may only be yielded from a representation that encapsulates atomic parts. This, again, is the case in program and proof design. Failure to reach atomic features may result in a cumbersome design, with overlapping objects, which will in turn yield partial outcomes due to overlooked cases (as happened here).

The Polygons task may be viewed from diverse angles, and thus may elicit creative observations [12]. Yet, one should seek the angle that "illuminates the picture" and allows clear and ordered progress that leads to a feeling of exploitation, in the sense of handling all the possible cases. Again – a fundamental theme in program and proof design. When one does not follow a convincing plan, one may yield only partial outcomes and lack the feeling of exploitation (as happened here).

The findings in this study reveal several difficulties with respect to the process of design and the above fundamental notions. We describe them below.

- **Task (domain-range) analysis.** In four out of the five groups (of the previous section), the task analysis was not thorough. Participants mostly analyzed the task range – the polygons, and often not thoroughly. Many of them studied only the straightforward polygons, and some less obvious polygons which they observed during trial-&-error attempts. The vast majority did not carefully analyze the domain – the grid, in particular with respect to grid lines and atomic grid shapes.

- **Resources and Heuristics.** The resources required in this task involved elementary-school Geometry, in the form of basic geometrical conceptions and triangle (area) calculations. The main heuristics required to solve the task were two common computer science and problem solving heuristics – object and case decomposition & re-composition, and suitable task representation. Most of the participants employed these heuristics only in a limited way.

- **Decomposition & re-composition.** The task involved two kinds of decompositions & re-compositions – object (polygon) decomposition into parts and case decomposition (by polygon characteristics), where each case involved a different set of the parts assembly, or composition. Unfortunately, the participants in the first four groups did not perform complete and ordered object decomposition and did not thoroughly yield the various cases of part compositions.

- **Representation.** Proper object decomposition is tied to careful domain analysis, and both involve the recognition of atomic parts. In this task there were two atomic parts – a right triangle and an obtuse triangle, which could be recognized by proper domain (grid lines) analysis. Yet, only the participants in the fifth groups clearly recognized these parts. The other participants recognized only one of the parts (the right triangle) or none. Failure to recognize the second atomic part yielded incomplete outcomes, as well as cumbersome plan-execution, since larger, overlapping parts were chosen instead.

- **Planning and plan-execution.** The participants in the first group devised no plan. They advanced through trial-&-error attempts, and showed no systematic progression. Their local progress at times reminded in some sense the "patching advancement" that is observed with novice designers [11]. The participants in the second group did devise and follow a plan, but this plan yielded only a partial outcome, as it was based on incomplete task analysis and heuristic employment. The participants in the third and the fourth groups did not follow, or execute a consistent plan, but rather changed their plan upon reaching points of no-progress. Only the participants in the fifth group employed and followed an ordered plan.

- **Correctness, exploitation.** The limited task analysis and heuristic employment of the participants in the first four groups caused them a feeling of possibly-incomplete outcomes. They did not reach a feeling of exploitation, in the sense of generating a complete output set, as there were no solid observations which could support convincing correctness argumentation. The only participants that reached a feeling of exploitation and argued correctness were those in the fifth group, who recognized a suitable representation and devised an ordered plan, based on a thorough case analysis. They devised and executed a plan together with its supporting correctness argumentation.

The above difficulties illuminate problematic expressions of non-specific transfer of heuristics and disciplined design. Non-specific transfer involves rather different domains and situations. Computer science graduates should acquire a rich scientific perspective that may be suitable for not only solving tasks similar to those posed to them during their studies, but also to tasks like Polygons, which require the same fundamental notions as the more standard computer science tasks.

The teaching of program and proof design should aim for competence in employing non-specific transfer as the one that was required here. Computer science teachers should broaden their students' perception and application of the fundamental design notions indicated above. These notions are often not explicitly underlined and elaborated, possibly because textbooks and tutors expect students to assimilate them with practice and experience. Yet, the above findings reveal that this is not the case. We believe that one may not expect implicit acquisition of these notions. Textbooks and tutors should explicitly underline and elaborate the essential design notions examined above. In particular, they should explicitly illuminate and underline the notions of:

- Task analysis, with particular emphasis on thorough examination of the domain elements, the range elements, and their inter-relations.
- Representation, which illuminates the key task objects and cases.
- Atomic elements, in particular with respect to decomposition and re-composition of the task objects and cases.
- Exploitation, in the sense that all the possible domain-range relations are considered and handled. The above three notions are essential for reaching a feeling of exploitation.

No less important is the illumination of characteristics of improper design. Students may significantly learn from wrong [3,10,12,25], and should be aware of the undesired outcomes yielded from:

- Partial domain-range examination.
- Trial-&-error progression, with repeated patching, due to an unordered progression plan.
- Incomplete task decomposition, which may result in overlooking relevant cases.
- Case redundancies, in the sense that the same cases may be handled more than once, due to cumbersome decomposition and re-composition.
- Absent correctness conviction, due to the lack of exploitation.

Textbooks and tutors should repeatedly underline the above elements during the design processes of both computer programs and proofs. In addition, occasional utilization of non-standard, colorful tasks like the one presented here may offer a refreshing enhancement to the standard way of teaching [2]. Tasks likes Polygons, may serve as stimulating and inspiring means for pointing to students both the right and the wrong. Due to their colorful characteristics, they raise motivation, enhance intuition, and their lesson may be better remembered [9]. In addition, their non-standard features yield practice of non-specific transfer, which should be enhanced in the teaching of any domain [4,15,19]. The embedment of tasks like Polygons, for underlining the right and the wrong in students' design disciplines, may develop their scientific monitoring and control competence [21] as well as their scientific perspectives and beliefs.

References

1. Astrachan, O., Berry, G., Cox, L., Mitchener, G.: Design Patterns: an Essential Component of CS Curricula. In: Proceedings of the 29th SIGCSE Symposium, pp. 153–160. ACM Press, New York (1998)
2. Bergin, J., Kelemen, C., McNally, M., Naps, T., Goldweber, M., Power, C., Hartley, S.: Non-Programming Resources for an Introduction to CS: A Collection of Resources for the First Year Courses in Computer Science. SIGCSE Bulletin 33(2), 89–95 (2001)
3. Borasi, R.: Reconceiving Mathematics Instruction: A Focus on Errors. Ablex Pub, Greenwich (1996)
4. Bruner, J.S.: The Process of Education. Harvard University Press (1960)
5. Collins, A., Brown, J.S., Newman, S.E.: Cognitive Apprenticeship: Teaching the Crafts of Reading, Writing and Mathematics. In: Resnick, L.B. (ed.) Knowing, Learning, and Instruction: Essays in Honor of Robert Glaser, pp. 453–494. Lawrence Erlbaum Associates, Hillsdale (1989)
6. Dijkstra, E.W.: A Discipline of Programming. Prentice-Hall, Englewood Cliffs (1976)
7. Ebrahimi, A.: Novice Programmer Errors: Language Constructs and Plan Composition. International Journal of Human-Computer Studies 41(4), 457–480 (1994)
8. Gama, E., Helm, R., Johnson, R., Vlissides, J.: Design Patterns: Elements of Reusable Object-Oriented Software. Addison-Wesley, Reading (1995)
9. Ginat, D.: Loop Invariants, Exploration of Regularities, and Mathematical Games. Int. J. of Mathematical Education in Science and Technology 32 (2001)
10. Ginat, D.: The Greedy Trap and Learning from Mistakes. In: Proceedings of the 34th SIGCSE Symposium, pp. 11–15. ACM Press, New York (2003)
11. Ginat, D.: Hasty Design, Futile Patching, and the Elaboration of Rigor. In: Proceedings of the 12th ITiCSE Conference, pp. 161–165. ACM Press, New York (2007)
12. Ginat, D.: Learning from Wrong and Creative Algorithm Design. In: Proceedings of the 39th SIGCSE Symposium. ACM Press, New York (2008)
13. Gotschi, T., Sanders, I., Galpin, V.: Mental Models of Recursion. In: Proceedings of the 34th SIGCSE Symposium, pp. 346–350. ACM Press, New York (2003)
14. Gries, D.: The Science of Programming. Springer, Heidelberg (1981)
15. Hiebert, J., Carpenter, T.P.: Learning and Teaching with Understanding. In: Grouws, D.A. (ed.) Handbook of Research on Mathematics Teaching and Learning, pp. 65–97. Macmillan, Basingstoke (1992)
16. Hoare, T.: An Axiomatic Basis for Computer Programming. Communications of the ACM 12, 576–583 (1969)
17. Linn, M.C., Clancy, M.J.: The Case for Case Studies of Programming Problems. Communications of the ACM 35(3), 121–132 (1992)
18. Linn, M.C., Clancy, M.J.: Patterns and Pedagogy. In: Proceedings of the 30th SIGCSE Symposium, pp. 37–42. ACM Press, New York (1999)
19. Mayer, R.E., Wittrock, M.C.: Problem Solving Transfer. In: Berliner, D.C., Calfee, R.C. (eds.) Handbook of Educational Psychology, pp. 47–62. Macmillan, Basingstoke (1996)
20. Pick, G.: Geometrisches zur Zahlenlehre. Lotos, Naturwissen, Zeitschrift. Sitzungber 19, 311–319 (1899)
21. Schoenfeld, A.: Learning to Think Mathematically: Problem Solving, Metacognition, and Sense Making in Mathematics. In: Grouws, D.A. (ed.) Handbook of Research on Mathematics Teaching and Learning, pp. 334–370. Macmillan, Basingstoke (1992)

22. Schwill, A.: Fundamental Ideas of Computer Science. Bulletin of the European Association for Theoretical Computer Science 53, 274–295 (1994)
23. Sleeman, D., Putnam, R.T., Baxter, J., Kuspa, L.: Pascal and High-School Students: a Study of Errors. Journal of Educational Computing Research 2(1), 57–73 (1986)
24. Spohrer, J.G., Soloway, E., Pope, E.: A Goal/Plan Analysis of Buggy Pascal Programs. In: Soloway, E., Spohrer, J.G. (eds.) Studying the Novice Programmer, pp. 355–400. Lawrence Erlbaum, Mahwah (1989)
25. Yerushalmi, E., Polingher, C.: Guiding Students to Learn from Mistakes. Physics Education 41, 532–538 (2006)

Like a (School of) Fish in Water
(or *ICT-Enhanced Skills* in Action)

Evgenia Sendova[1], Eliza Stefanova[2], Nikolina Nikolova[3], and Eugenia Kovatcheva[2]

[1] Institute of Mathematics and Informatics, Bulgarian Academy of Sciences,
Acad. G. Bontchev 8, 1113 Sofia, Bulgaria
jenny@math.bas.bg
[2] Faculty of Mathematics and Informatics, Sofia University, James Bourchier 5,
1164 Sofia, Bulgaria
{eliza,epk}@fmi.uni-sofia.bg
[3] National High School of Mathematics and Sciences "Acad. L. Chakalov" 52, Bigla Str.,
1164 Sofia, Bulgaria
nnikolova@npmg.org

> *Swimming: from the outside looking in, you can't understand it; from the inside looking out, you can't explain it.*
> Author Unknown

Abstract. The paper presents pilot experiences related to an educational methodology developed within the European *Innovative Teacher (I*Teach)* project for building ICT-enhanced skills [1]. The methodology is presented in the context of a workshop for teachers in mathematics and informatics with a special focus on enhancing presentation skills. The authors share their experience in treating the very workshop as a project with specific stages - analyzing the audience's interests, developing a presentation scenario around a leading metaphor in harmony with the setting, distributing different roles among the presenters, involving the audience in an active reasoning and sharing. Thus the workshop has demonstrated at a meta-level how the collective intelligence of teachers could be harnessed in action. The main message is: such an approach makes teachers feel like co-creators of the *I*Teach* project´s ideas and teachers need only a bit of praise or encouragement to recognize themselves as *innovative teachers*.

Keywords: Teacher education, ICT-enhanced skills, active learning methods.

1 Introduction

A broad range of new skills needed for teachers in the knowledge-based and life-long learning society have been identified in studies within the EC program *Education & Training 2010* [2]. An important part of these skills refers to the competences and abilities of teachers and trainers to design, develop, conduct, facilitate and assess teaching and learning processes aimed at acquisition of productive *soft skills* enhanced by Information and Communication Technologies (ICT). These skills include:

knowledge presentation, working on projects, problem solving, and communication skills [3]. In response to the demand of enhancing the ICT skills with such soft skills the Leonardo da Vinci *Innovative Teacher (I*Teach)* project has been launched with the participation of Bulgarian mathematics and informatics educators [4]. The focus of this project is on developing a practical methodology and supporting tools for building *ICT-enhanced skills* – a concept coined to denote the synergy between soft skills and ICT skills. The preliminary study within the project is oriented to the elaboration of this concept. Through the collaborative effort of partners from seven European countries (Bulgaria, Germany, Italy, Lithuania, the Netherlands, Poland, and Romania) the skills for

- searching and selecting information
- presenting information
- working on a project
- working in a team

are identified as the *ICT-enhanced skills* for which there was a biggest need in the countries involved [5]. In what follows we try to give an idea of how to implement the *I*Teach* methodology in the context of building presentation skills. The particular event discussed herein is a workshop organized as a satellite event of the *Annual Spring Conference of the Union of the Bulgarian Mathematicians*, Varna, 2007. This workshop is a meeting of math researchers and teachers of highly achieving students in mathematics and informatics.

2 *How to Make a Good Presentation* – Easier Said than Done

As discussed by Syslo and Kwiatkowska in [6], changes in mathematics education may be expected according to the model for ICT development when the first stage (*Discovering ICT tools*) and the second stage (*Learning How to Use ICT Tools*) are passed, and the third stage (*Understanding How and When to Use ICT Tools*) is reached. Thanks to numerous training courses in ICT for mathematics teachers in Bulgaria the first two stages have been passed successfully. Now has come the most difficult and important one – understanding *How* and *When* to use ICT tools so as to achieve particular educational goals. A series of sample educational scenarios have been designed and offered in [7] in support of this third stage. An *I*Teach* scenario according to the project framework represents a composition of tasks (implemented by active learning methods) leading to an educational goal by covering intermediate objectives (*milestones*). The metaphor behind such a scenario is a *journey* (the process) traced by *milestones* leading to the final goal [4]. It was important for the *I*Teach* research team to convince the ICT teachers with whom we worked that their (the teachers') own presentation skills and the presentation skills they were expected to develop in their students should be far beyond the technical skills of using PowerPoint. Thus the teachers should realize the very preparation of a series of slides is just one part of a very complex project in which the objective of communication is not the transmission of information but the reception of it. Of course, guidelines on how to make a good presentation and how to avoid bad ones could be found on numerous sites of Internet and in many textbooks on ICT today. The real problems now are how to implement this advice and, even more difficult, how to teach what *good presentation skills* mean. This was the gauntlet the authors of this paper took up when deciding to organize a workshop on *I*Teach* methodology for building ICT-enhanced skills.

2.1 Preparing – Some Necessary Conditions

We had made PowerPoint presentations on the *I*Teach* methodology at longer previous workshops [4] but we were not sure how to make best use of them. Following the custom of some presenters we might have just as well reduced the number of slides... Really? We knew that our whole preparation and presentation at the workshop should be geared not to us, the lecturers, but to the audience. Our main objective was to make our message understood and remembered. (Easier said than done.) As the ancient Greek aphorism goes *You could not step twice into the same river*. This time the "waters" (the concrete conditions) were really very different: the workshop was held at the biggest sea resort in Bulgaria and we decided that it would be a good idea to center it around the Chinese proverb: *Give a man a fish and you feed him for a day. Teach a man to fish and you feed him for a lifetime*. We had quoted this proverb on many occasions but this time we decided to check it in practice and discuss the matter with an expert in fishing. We talked with him about his skills and asked his permission to take pictures of him in action letting him know that they would be used in our workshop. He was very cooperative and sympathetic with the teacher's labor. The scenario was becoming clearer in our heads: the next thing we did was to buy two toy fishing rods.

2.2 Refining the Idea of How to Start

We kept looking for the most appropriate opening (as a very essential part of the scenario) – probably one in the style of showing that we were not scared to be an object of laughter; we hoped to prevent the teachers from following the man who had decided *not to go into the water until he learned to swim*. It would have been nice to be original and many of our trainees expected us to be so (at a previous *I*Teach* training session immediately after the New Year we, the lecturers, appeared with funny hats in harmony with the season [4]). But to invite the audience in the swimming pool in bathing suits and funny hats would have been too crazy even for us. Still we needed something that would give a special flavor to our workshop and we found it – *to catch our audience with fish bites*. The chef from our hotel was gained for the cause – he prepared small fish sandwiches. Thus the opening was ideally tuned to the circumstances – noon time, the audience had sacrificed their lunch to attend the seminar and deserved to be awarded in a cocktail style. The educational role of the fish bites was still to be seen...

2.3 Analyzing the Audience

We knew in advance that most of our audience would be mathematics and informatics teachers. In addition, as a satellite event of the conference there was a section of high school students at which they were expected to present their projects in mathematics and informatics at a very high performance level [8]. Thus the workshop title *The innovative teacher* had to attract both young and very experienced colleagues who were eager to keep up with the most modern tendencies of applying ICT in mathematics education. What would be most interesting for them, something we could help them with? The original plan was to orient the workshop towards written presentations of teachers' good practices, e.g. *How to write an article for a math journal?* But after some preliminary discussions we realized that teachers were lacking a real motivation for submitting articles to journals. At the same time there was a serious interest in the oral presentations of projects – most of the teachers were working with their students on research projects and teachers' success depended to a certain extent on the presentation skills of their students Furthermore, the teachers themselves were in the role of presenters in their everyday activities. Depending on their presentation skills the attention and the interest of their students would be held or lost. But how could we be sure that we know better than our audience? And even if we did, should we follow the traditional style of preaching the rules (taught by many of the teachers themselves) by means of professionally made slides? It was clear that we should not deliver a lecture but rather rediscover the ideas together and present at a meta-level the *I*Teach* methodology for building ICT-enhanced skills (with a focus on the oral presentations skills). Our message would be: *If you want to learn to swim jump into the water with us,* quite in harmony with the active learning methods [7].

2.4 Balancing the Realization – Some Sufficient Conditions

Our rich teaching experience and the fact that we would present as a team made us confident in tuning dynamically our presentation to the audience during the workshop. Thus, with the idea of balancing between the *careful planning* and *divine inspiration* we felt ready for the start.

The mini-sandwiches were accepted with pleasant surprise but it was obvious that their quantity would not replace a proper lunch. The first slide appeared as a background of this somewhat unexpected opening (Fig. 1)

What? – No title and authors? Every guide for a good presentation says that it is important to start properly – with introducing ourselves and the theme of the talk. Not necessarily! In fact, many of the participants knew us for various reasons and we decided to leave this part for the end. The first idea to be conveyed by the slide was that the presenters and the audience should be like a *school of fish* – enjoying the water together! Another message would be revealed later on.

Fig. 1. A school of fish

Since there were several parallel sessions at the conference a very important problem for the participants seemed to be the factors influencing the choice of what to attend. This was the topic of brainstorming we organized with our audience (Fig. 2). We gave them some time for reflections and the teachers began offering their suggestions which we started filling in the blank slide in real time (Fig. 3).

At the beginning the teachers were slightly hesitant, just like students in a classroom, but gradually they became very active and it was clear that another slide would be needed to reflect all their ideas.

We chose the factors that were the most representative ones and showed our audience with pride and joy the next slide (Fig. 4).

These were in fact the same ideas which the teachers themselves had suggested (but with slightly different phrasing).

It became clear that the audience and the presenters were interweaving their roles and everybody was expecting with genuine interest the contribution of the others.

Although our team felt fairly self-confident in improvising thanks to our long practice in working jointly on projects and presenting together as lecturers in teacher training courses we had carefully distributed our roles in the work-

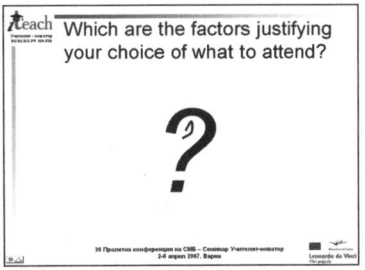

Fig. 2. Factors according to the audience

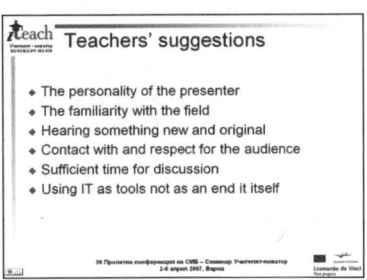

Fig. 3. What the teachers suggested

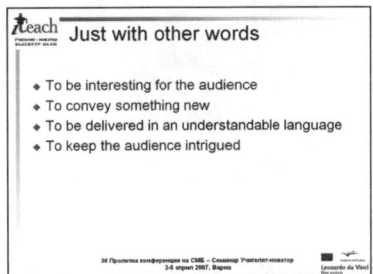

Fig. 4. Authors' suggestions

shop. The captain of the presenting team had the role of challenging the well-established rules for a *good presentation* and would provoke her co-presenters in the hope of encouraging the audience to express their own view and opinion rather than to receive passively information. The youngest member of our team in turn stayed among the audience (thus making the argument with the rest of us more natural since the audience didn't know at the time that she was one of the presenters). With such an approach we hoped to demonstrate skills for working in a team in addition to the other ICT-enhanced skills (such as skills for planning, looking for information from different sources, and working on a project). Our audience gradually realized the message that a good presentation is like a good performance – *the viewer expects to be surprised*. But to feel free to improvise it is crucial to know your partners and to tune the distribution of the roles according to the potential and interests of all the team members. Our youngest colleague shared her experience as a teacher in the *National High School of Mathematics and Sciences* whose students can bring many surprises for which there is no recipe. Thus the next question to the teachers came naturally: *How do you build ICT-enhanced skills in your school practice?*

There were several enthusiasts ready to share their good practices – Boryana Kuyumdzieva who was the first one in Bulgaria to introduce graphic calculators in mathematics classes, Katya Stoyanova who had organized a mathematical theater, Steliana Kokinova who had participated in a team competition for teachers developing a set a problems on a given mathematical theme. Our role was to give comments where appropriate, to extract the most essential things from all the examples, to help these teachers realize what was innovative in their experience and how it could be implemented by others. The important message we would like to convey was that the teachers were co-creators of the *I*Teach* project ideas (metaphorically they were swimming *against tides of trouble the world knows very little about* and they needed only a bit of praise or encouragement to recognize themselves as *innovative teachers*).

The next step in our presentation scenario was to summarize what was the most valuable in teachers' good practices in the form of a challenge – we offered them to participate in a competition for interpreting in educational context three slides with pictures (Fig. 5).

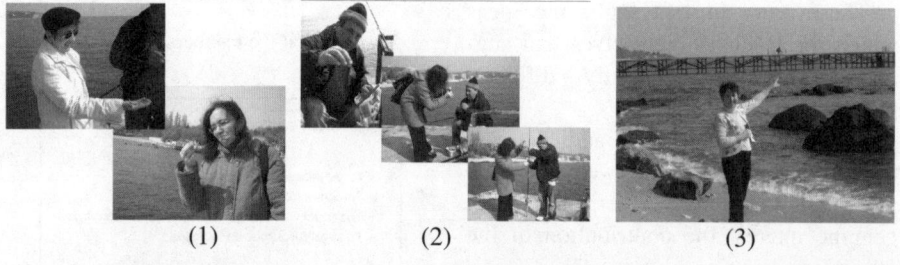

Fig. 5. The challenge

A few-minute silence of surprise followed, but then a lot of ideas were thrown in the air as follows:
  About Fig 5 (1)
    Is this the golden fish? Students have more than three wishes.
    Raising funds for education.
    Is this the bait (for the student) or the catch (of the teacher)?
  About Fig 5 (2)
    Are we (the teachers) expected to learn this as well?
    Consultations with the expert...
    A lesson on catching whales.
    ICT teacher training for 5-8 grade
  About Fig 5 (3)
    The hypotenuse is not always the shortest path.
    Imagine that this is plus infinity...
    The finger shows which way the "educational wind" blows.

A colleague of ours, Prof. Neli Maneva, gave the following interpretation of the whole challenge: *The road to the useful knowledge requires sharing, attention and illustrative examples. After the training, the trainer is free and satisfied but someone has to do the real work.*

Of course, our original interpretation was inspired by the Chinese proverb about the fishing quoted above and the Zen koan: *I'm pointing at the moon, and you're looking at my finger* (the *moon* been replaced by the *sun* this time) and we were trying to express the current situation with the teacher education – we, the teachers' educators are talking about *what we expect to* see *one day*, and the teachers are interested in *what they are going to do on Monday*. But we were open to the interpretations given by the participants with such a sense of humor and wisdom.

Thus we reached the moment of demonstrating the *collective intelligence* in action. This intelligence was illustrated by Cornu [9] interestingly enough in terms of "fish"– when facing a big challenge a school of small fish would take the form of a much bigger fish as a self-defense (Fig.6).

This originally hidden message had to be experienced to be captured!

The final goal of our *journey* (the project development process) was rediscovered with the joint efforts of the audience and the presenters (Fig.7).

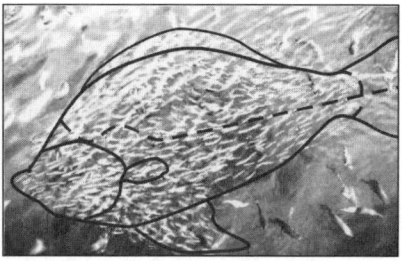

Fig. 6. Collective intelligence

The audience had realized that this presentation could be considered as a product of a whole project with a carefully planned scenario (containing a challenge for the audience), carried out by a team (including the fisherman, the chef, the presenters in different roles, and the audience itself).

The methods, strategies and approaches included various means and technologies. The information search combined with the knowledge of experts in different fields reflected our experience in project work

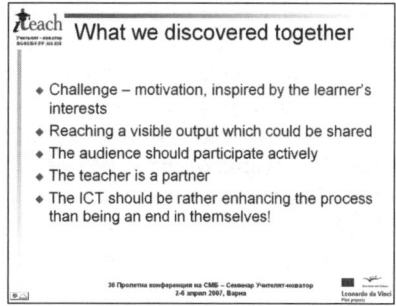

Fig. 7. The joint product

which justified our choice to treat the workshop as a project itself (the team had to generate the theme of the workshop and the way of presenting it in a fixed short time and to find an original and appropriate way to implement it). The participants confirmed our belief that the innovative teaching methods are often forgotten ones (possibly enhanced by the new technologies). And in harmony with the whole presentation idea, the introduction of the presenters was left for the (happy) end. We had special awards for the most active participants – the two toy fishing rods were delivered to the best catchers of ideas (Fig. 8).

Fig. 8. The opening and the closing ceremony

The chef and the fisherman also received certificates for valuable contributions to the workshop. As for us, the biggest reward was the impression of one of the innovative teachers (Boryana Kuyumdzieva from *Baba Tonka Mathematical High School* in Rousse) who shared after the event that she felt fully satisfied with the setting, the support and the hope for the future conveyed by the workshop. The genuine novelty for her was the quality of communication of ideas since: ***Everything could be said and heard but what really matters is to experience it!***

3 Reflections

After coming back to the hotel we smoothly passed to the next phase of our project – the reflection. Why did the teachers so greatly appreciate this style of interaction? One possible explanation is it gives people the feeling of achieving something that is already within them and only needs a little encouragement to be seen and harnessed into action. In other words, an *innovative teacher* in terms of the project *I*Teach* could be any one of them, provided they *look at where our fingers were pointing, not at out fingers* (the latter being very often the case with the teacher training courses). To be *innovative* the teachers should experience as intellectually rewarding and enjoyable what they are doing and learning by means of ICT; they shouldn't think only of how to remember all the technical details and make those as a teaching objective. Within the whole *I*Teach* project (of which this workshop was only a milestone) we tried to demonstrate to the teachers involved that the ICT are simply a means for accomplishing a concrete goal and that they could enhance important soft skills which are not included in the current curriculum. Of course, the evaluation of the soft skills (such as skills for searching for relevant information, working in a team, working on a project, presenting your results in written and oral form) is very difficult and there are not sufficiently refined tools for it. But the challenge should be faced and the *gauntlet should be taken*. One way to show this was not to be afraid to risk being laughed at. This helped our audience to share freely their own experience, their problems and opinion. The teachers felt proud not only with their own ideas but were able to enjoy and appreciate the ideas of the others – something which is very important for their students as well. They caught our message that information should not be searched on the Internet only – there are plenty of sources and experts around us. Furthermore, the rules for a "good presentation" could be extracted jointly with the audience rather than being listed on a slide as a set of axioms. Besides, these rules are a good basis to start with but if you want to reach a particular audience, your work starts with them since *divine inspiration* is based on a solid preparation. The initial fish bites (no matter how tasty and well prepared) were seen now as a metaphor for the need of teaching students how to fish as opposed to feeding them with *bites* of knowledge. The participants ended the workshop even hungrier - not only for a proper lunch but for knowledge to be gained thanks to their personal experience and ideas. As for us, we tried to to look at our workshop scenario with new eyes and present it as a roadmap (in a suitable form, of course) (Fig. 9).

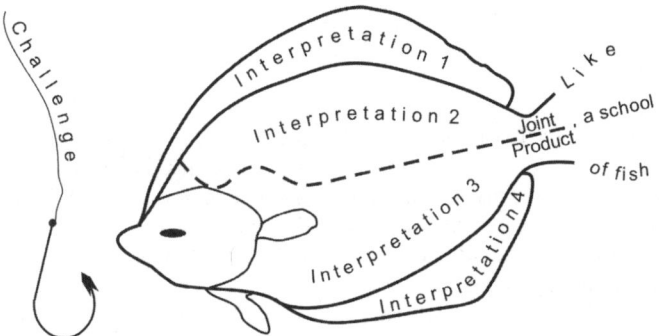

Fig. 9. Scenario roadmap

The tail of the fish illustrates the idea that educational strategies in the spirit of the *I*Teach* project could prepare teachers for their changing role of partners in a creative process [10]. Furthermore, such a partnership could be further supported and maintained in the context of specially designed web-based collaborative environments [11-12] and virtual centers for facilitating teacher's professional development [13-18].

4 Conclusion

The audience became aware of the fact that their observations and experience were the basis of our research and that we treat them as fellow researchers instead of as a *reality check* for researchers.

The *I*Teach* workshop was a demonstration on a meta-level of how the collective intelligence of innovative teachers could be harnessed in action. Pedagogical patterns with similar ideas could be found in [19]. In our approach we tried to demonstrate all the stages of an oral presentation tuned to a given audience – a careful analysis of the audience's interests and problems, making the best possible use of the particular setting, developing a scenario around a leading metaphor, distributing specific roles among the presenters, involving the audience in brainstorming and sharing of good practices, making them aware that the *innovative ideas* were things they had already probably done or were ready to do, and that all this was just the beginning – the real cooperation was to start then.

Our real reward was when already back at work we received a lot of e-mails and letters with questions and requests for further courses and materials. Some teachers invited us to attend their schools and observe project presentations of their students. When visiting these schools we were convinced that as far as their presentation skills were concerned the students felt like *a school of fish in water*.

Acknowledgements. This research has been partially supported by the Leonardo da Vinci project *Innovative teacher* (*I*Teach*), BG-05/PP/166038. We would like to thank our reviewers for their helpful comments and suggestions. Special thanks go to Andy Kositsky for his thorough reading of the text, witty remarks and language editing.

References

1. Leonardo da Vinci I*Teach (Innovative Teacher) Project, http://i-teach.fmi.uni-sofia.bg
2. European Commission Progress reports of the European Commission's working groups Improving education of teachers and trainers and ICT in education and training (2003)
3. Sendova, E.: Handling the Diversity of Learners' Interests by Putting Informatics Content in Various Contexts. In: Mittermeir, R.T. (ed.) ISSEP 2006. LNCS, vol. 4226, p. 80. Springer, Heidelberg (2006)
4. Stefanova, E., Sendova, E., Nikolova, I., Nikolova, N.: When I*Teach means I*Learn: developing and implementing an innovative methodology for building ICT-enhanced skills. In: Benzie, D., Iding, M. (eds.) Joint IFIP Conference: WG3.1 Secondary Education, WG3.5 Primary Education: Informatics, Mathematics, and ICT: a 'golden triangle' IMICT 2007 Proceeding, CCIS, Northeastern University, Boston, MA (2007)
5. Forcheri, P., Molfino, M.T., Diepen, N., Stefanova, E., Sendova, E.: Giving Teachers a Hand(book) to Develop ICT-enhanced skills. In: Proceedings of 3rd Balkan conference in Informatics BCI2007 Research in informatics and information society technologies, Demetra, vol. 2, pp. 301–312 (2007)
6. Syslo, M., Kwaitkowska, A.B.: Contribution of Informatics Education to Mathematics Education in Schools. In: Mittermeir, R.T. (ed.) ISSEP 2006. LNCS, vol. 4226, p. 219. Springer, Heidelberg (2006)
7. Stefanova, E., Sendova, E., Deepen, N.v., Forcheri, P., Dodero, G., Miranowicz, M., Brut, M., et al.: Innovative Teacher - Methodological Handbook on ICT-enhanced skills. In: Faleza-Office 2000, Sofia (2007)
8. Dimitrova, N., Georgiev, V., Mogensen, A., Muskarov, O., Sendova, E., Ulovec, A.: Meeting in mathematics, Demetra, Sofia (in press, 2008)
9. Cornu, B.: Conference talk. In: ISSEP2006 Informatics at Secondary School: Evolution and Perspectives (2006)
10. Kovatcheva, E.: Tuning the ICT instruments for harmony in mathematics and arts. In: Benzie, D., Iding, M. (eds.) Joint IFIP Conference: WG3.1 Secondary Education, WG3.5 Primary Education: Informatics, Mathematics, and ICT: a 'golden triangle' IMICT 2007 Proceeding, CCIS, Northeastern University, Boston, MA (2007)
11. Gachev, G., Nikolova, I.: Web-based Collaborative Environments to Support Learning Activities. In: Proceedings of the 2nd international conference ISSEP2006, Informatics at Secondary School: Evolution and Perspectives (2006)

12. Nikolova, N.: IDWBL Methodology at the National High School of Mathematics and Science. In: Proceedings of 3rd Balkan conference in Informatics BCI2007 Research in informatics and information society technologies, Demetra, vol. 2, pp. 263–270 (2007)
13. Dodero, G., Ratcheva, D., Stefanova, E., Miranowicz, M., Vertan, C., Musankoviene, V.: The Virtual Training Center: A Support Tool for Teachers Community. In: Proceedings of 3rd Balkan conference in Informatics BCI2007 Research in informatics and information society technologies, Demetra, vol. 2, pp. 349–362 (2007)
14. Ratcheva, D., Stefanova, E., Nikolova, I.: A Virtual Teacher Community to Facilitate Professional Development. In: Proceedings of the Second International conference ISSEP2006 Informatics at Secondary School: Evolution and Perspectives, pp. 297–305 (2006)
15. Miranowicz, M., Burewicz, A., Dodero, G., Stefanova, E., Ratcheva, D.: Virtual Training Centers of the I*Teach Project - Continuous learning. In: Proceedings ot the 13th International Conference on Technology Support Learning & Training - Online Educa Berlin, November 28-30, 2007, pp. 435–441 (2007)
16. Nikolova, N., Miranowicz, M.: I*Teach Methodology in School Practice. In: Proceedings of 3rd Balkan conference in Informatics BCI2007 Research in informatics and information society technologies, Demetra, vol. 1, pp. 296–387 (2007)
17. Nikolov, R.: Towards web 2.0 schools: rethinking the teachers' professional development. In: Benzie, D., Iding, M. (eds.) Joint IFIP Conference: WG3.1 Secondary Education, WG3.5 Primary Education: Informatics, Mathematics, and ICT: a 'golden triangle' IMICT 2007 Proceeding, CCIS, Northeastern University, Boston, MA (2007)
18. Stefanov, K., Naskonova, I., Nikolov, R.: ICT-enhanced teacher training for lifelong competence development. In: Benzie, D., Iding, M. (eds.) Joint IFIP Conference: WG3.1 Secondary Education, WG3.5 Primary Education: Informatics, Mathematics, and ICT: a 'golden triangle' IMICT 2007 Proceeding, CCIS, Northeastern University, Boston, MA (2007)
19. The Pedagogical Pattern Project, http://www.pedagogicalpatterns.org

Duality Reconstruction – Teaching Digital Artifacts from a Socio-technical Perspective

Carsten Schulte

Computer Science Education
Freie Universität Berlin
Takustr. 9
14195 Berlin
schulte@inf.fu-berlin.de

Abstract. This paper presents a duality perspective for teaching everyday software products. The concept includes didactical lenses as a means to teach students conceptual models of such digital artifacts. The duality of structure and function is proposed as a didactic category to educationally reconstruct digital artifacts from different perspectives (lenses). A comparison of teaching concepts for word processors serves to illustrate the proposed concept of duality reconstruction.

1 Introduction

It is very common for today's students to have daily contact with computers and applications (in short: with ICT). Consequently, the need and perspective on teaching ICT and computer science at school is changing. In this paper, a socio-technical perspective on Informatics (CS) education is used to develop a concept for teaching ICT as part of CS education. The concept is outlined using word processors as main example.

In 7, the concept of educational lenses for the deconstruction of Informatics Systems (=IS) in specific application areas (contexts) was introduced. These lenses were proposed to combine technical and social aspects. Using the socio-technical perspective while at the same time acknowledging the idea of the dual nature of digital artifacts, we can now refine the concept: Educational lenses enable a perspective which makes the dual nature of specific parts of an IS visible. This process is called duality reconstruction. Its purpose is twofold: on the one hand, didactic filters (lenses) highlight the important parts of IS; they enable to teach the important parts of todays IS without being overwhelmed by their manifold aspects, features and parts. They reduce complexity without cutting off important issues. On the other hand, duality reconstruction unfolds an educational perspective which acknowledges the dual nature of these important parts and issues of IS.

The other aim of this paper is to give a more precise definition of educational lenses and show how to use them for a didactic reconstruction of digital artifacts.

The chosen example is a topic that is usually considered as not very relevant for CS education, because (presumably) only some aspects of CS are incorporated:

teaching the use and understanding of word processors. This topic is often considered as being redundant, as presumably every child is able to learn how to use word processors without help, and also using word processors is not really associated with other CS-related tasks (whereas e. g. the use of spreadsheets is considered as more related to programming). However, from the socio-technical perspective, duality Reconstruction can be used to develop courses in which the use of word processors is taught in a way that reveals many important insights about CS.

The paper is structured as follows: First students' current experiences with ICT are described, and some didactical conclusions drawn. In the next section, concepts from literature for teaching word processors are discussed. On this basis, the new concept will be outlined and described. The paper ends with some concluding remarks.

2 Educational Relevance of Computer Usage in Everyday Life

Today, computers and ICT are simply an ordinary part of the everyday lives of our students – with some important implications for teaching the science behind these artifacts. Before discussing these implications, today's experiences with ICT are shortly outlined.

For the study KIM 2005 in Germany 9, a representative sample of 1.203 children between 6 and 13 years were asked about their experiences with media and computers: 47% own cell phones (71% at the age of 12-13); 76% use a computer (52% for children between 6 and 7 years old; over 90% of children between 12 and 13); the rate of computer usage is 26% every day; 56% once or more per week, 18% more seldom (everyday usage: 14% of age 6-7, 36% of age 12-13); How to use a computer was most often learned from the father (62%) or mother (37%), and then from friends (24%). At school, 20% learned something about computer usage. In case of usage problems, children ask peers in the same ratio.

Alan Mitchel 10 reports results from studies with secondary school students in the UK: 55% say the experience of ICT in school "has put me off"; 68% would only take CS, if they wanted a career in computing. 54% think it is more of a skill than a career; juniors mostly think CS is 1) the science needed to produce computers, 2) similar to ICT, and 3) understanding the ways computers operate; seniors compare CS to 1) technological studies or engineering, 2) ICT and 3) math; many think CS is boring.

In our group, we qualitatively surveyed effects of computer usage in everyday life. The main results are (see e.g. 11): University Students outside CS (such as psychology majors) conceptualize CS as science that is focused on computers; experts are seen as a kind of professional users whose job it is to solve usage problems and irrational computer errors. The job is focused on technical aspects, it is not creative. Majors in different CS-related subjects focus on CS without drawing connections to contexts. Both groups only seldom differentiate between ICT-courses and CS-courses at school.

From these empirical results we can draw some conclusions: Students do not differentiate between teaching ICT and/or CS at school. Therefore, teaching ICT should aim at supporting viable mental models of CS too (see [CB06] for a discussion of effects of ICT on CS). Although ICT and CS are often mistaken seen as the same;

CS-issues (in a more correct meaning) are seen as irrelevant and detached from ICT-experiences in everyday life.

In summary, the educational question is how to relate ICT and CS, so that

- learning ICT becomes valid and meaningful for students (given that many learn computer usage outside school),
- learning ICT does not have negative effects for the learnability of CS,
- learning CS becomes meaningful and valid from a ICT literacy perspective.

Fortunately, there are some didactical concepts we can discuss in the next section.

3 Concepts for Teaching Word Processors

In this section three different concepts for teaching word processors are compared, before presenting the socio technical approach.

3.1 Object-Oriented Analysis of Word Processors

Hubwieser uses the idea of object-oriented modeling to combine ICT and CS: "our novice courses start in grade 6 with the elaboration of the basic concepts ("object", "attribute", "method" and "class" in the context of vector graphics. In a second step we develop the models by introducing the concept of aggregation (e.g. paragraphs containing characters) in the context of text processing." (5, p. 106). A character *object* has several *attributes* (see Figure 1).

Character
Symbol
Font
Size
Color
...

Fig. 1. Attributes of a character in a word processor in lower secondary CS courses at school according to Hubwieser

The educational aim of this approach is – as Hubwieser (5, p. 104) states – „to give every child a fair chance to master the challenges of the information society" and" to prevent them from building wrong "self-made" mental models of these technologies or from using an inappropriate vocabulary to describe them".

3.2 Teaching with a Conceptual Model of Word Processors

Ben-Ari and Yeshno propose conceptual models to provide „a link between the target system and the user's mental model" (1, p. 1338), because a „user who must build a mental model directly from the behavior of the target system is very likely to be mystified" (1, p. 1343) and develops an inefficient or inappropriate mental model.

They suggest that WYSIWYG software cannot be understood completely from usage experiences; hence the internal data structure is (at least partially) hidden. A conceptual model should be taught that allows the user to understand the internal data structures and operations on that structure.

Interestingly, Ben-Ari and Yeshno discuss the model given above (see Figure 1) as such an inappropriate model (p. 1341). To prevent learners from conceptualizing font "as a[n] attribute of the characters forming the WYSIWYG text" (p. 1341), they propose a block model as conceptual model for teaching word processors. A block is a sequence of characters for which certain attributes are valid (font, language, etc.), certain operations open a new block, and moving the cursor can have the effect to enter another block, so that typing a character has a different effect.

| A line of text containing several blocks affecting the | layout of the text. |

Fig. 2. Example of a block according to the block model proposed by Ben-Ari and Yeshno

From the results of a comparative study (block model vs. 'activity based teaching') the authors conclude that conceptual models "enable the students to develop viable mental models of applications, improving their performance on tasks and quite likely decreasing their anxiety. [...] We also believe that once users learn to interpret system behavior in terms of conceptual models, it will significantly change their approach to learning software artifacts" (1, p. 1347).

3.3 Strategic Knowledge vs. Command Knowledge

Bhavnani et. al. 2 state that inefficient teaching relies on command knowledge: Such concepts propose to demonstrate the given commands of an artefact like a word processor, and then focus on practicing. They propose teaching strategic knowledge, by exploring alternative methods for solving complex tasks, discussing and demonstrating efficient methods and generalizing them to strategies which then can be practiced in similar complex tasks. The Strategies are shown in Figure 3.

Iteration	1.	Reuse and modify groups of objects
	2.	Check original before making copies
	3.	Handle exceptions before/after modifications of groups
Propagation	1.	Make dependencies known to the computer
	2.	Exploit dependencies to generate variations
Organization	1.	Make organizations known to the computer
	2.	Generate new representations from existing ones
Visualization	1.	View relevant information, do not view irrelevant information
	2.	View parts of spread-out information to fit on the screen

Fig. 3. Strategic knowledge for using word processors (or spreadsheets), 2

The authors conducted a study in which teaching strategic knowledge was compared to teaching command knowledge. However, it is not clear whether the results are due to the different teaching methods used (in addition to the changed content of teaching).

The authors summarize their findings as follows: Teaching strategic knowledge "(1) enables students to learn efficient strategies; (2) benefits student populations with either technical or non-technical backgrounds; (3) does not require extra time compared to the traditional approach focused on command knowledge; (4) does not harm the acquisition of command knowledge; (5) has the potential of enabling the transfer of strategic knowledge across different applications." (2, p. 236).

3.4 Discussion of Concepts

The three approaches to teaching software artifacts (word processors) are quite similar. All aim at giving the learner some additional knowledge that goes beyond teaching commands. The empirical results of the second and third approach suggest that such additional skills do not lead to lower command knowledge – but at the same time not to higher command knowledge, either.

The approaches differ in suggesting different conceptual models: An OO model, a block model and a strategy model. In terms of mental models we can distinguish structural and functional (mental) models, applying the terms Mann (8, p. 12 and p.15) used for distinguishing models of programming languages: A functional model describes operational rules; that is a relationship between goals and a sequence of (usage) actions to achieve the goal. A structural model describes the general structure and state of a system, and how this state is altered by specific operations. The focus of a functional model is on steps to reach a goal; the focus of a structural model is on predicting effects of operations. Both models lead to inferences about the other model: When learning a functional model, the learner is likely to build (or: infer) a structural model, too – and vice versa.

The first two models here are structural, the third is functional. Note that all three approaches focus on one side only – hoping the learners will implicitly gain a sufficient model of the other side, too. According to diSessa 4, functional models should be taught first, as they "provide a way in", followed and deepened by structural knowledge (4, p. 114). The first two approaches therefore seem to rely on some prior knowledge in using word processors. They aim at deepening this knowledge.

Interestingly, the same is true for the third approach. The approach to teach strategy knowledge by means of function aims at teaching advanced knowledge based on function; but without structure, strategies remain black boxes. It is an interesting question whether functional knowledge taught can lead to appropriate structural knowledge. It might be that by analyzing structure, different, or additional strategies can be obtained.

In summary three questions remain unanswered:

1. How to assess the completeness and richness of aspects used for teaching?
2. How to find a proper sequencing of teaching structural and/or functional aspects?
3. How to combine structural and functional models?

Implicitly, and that is why this discussion is relevant for CS education research: a certain level of usage skills is not possible without computer science knowledge.

In the following section, the socio-technical perspective is presented, which builds a framework from which the three questions may be answered.

4 Dual Nature of Digital Artifacts

In this section the socio-technical perspective (see 7) is refined according to the dual nature of digital artifacts. In that approach, educational lenses were proposed as an organizing principle for the integrated teaching of technical and social aspects of informatics systems. Each lens highlights one educationally relevant dimension of a sociotechnical informatics system. The lenses (see left column in the following table) are: 1. Automation, 2. Interaction, 3. Information processing, 4. Networking, 5. Standardization and 6. Societal and ethical aspects.

Table 1. Overview of structural and functional aspects of educational lenses

Educational Lenses	Structure (the 'technical' aspect as it would be called by the traditional Engineer)	Function (the 'social' aspect as it would be called and considered as being not important by the typical engineer)
Automation	What is the data structure that allows which kinds of operations? What is the structure (algorithm) of the prototypical (important) explicit and implicit operation(s)?	What process is (partially) automated, and for what purpose?
Interaction	What is the structure of the explicit operations?	What is the effect/purpose of the interaction (gui/use) metaphor? Check use strategies.
Information processing	What is the structure of the implicit operations and data visualization?	What is the effect/purpose of these implicit operations and data visualization?
Networking (Cooperation)	Are there any networking/cooperation facilities? If so, how do they operate?	How can people cooperate using the artifact? How is cooperation organized-/affected by embedding the artifact within an application context?
Norm, regulation and law (Standardization)	Which structural aspects (operations, data structure) are due to regulation (standardization), and/or lead to regulation?	What is the purpose or rational of certain regulations? What is the effect of these regulations?
Societal and ethical aspects	Analyze the structural development path of the artifacts: which structures are fundamental/important and are affecting larger structures (e.g. other artifacts)?	Analyze the functional development path: which functions are fundamental/important (e.g. other artifacts)?

From the sociotechnical point of view they build a sequence from the most inner ('technical') part of the system to the most outer parts, which are the social parts or the social surrounding of the technical part. The system perspective alone fails in bringing together social and technical aspects. Instead it reinforces their separation; but based on the perspective of dual nature of digital artifacts, each part of the system has a dual nature; and therefore each lens points to structural and functional aspects.

Structure can roughly be interpreted as focusing on the classical 'technical' aspect, whereas function focuses on the classical social aspect. This is the core idea of using the dual nature approach developed for the philosophical discussion of technical artifacts 6 for the educational discussion of digital artifacts.

We can think of data structure and operations on this structure as the structural aspect of digital artifacts; and their functional aspect is connected to the goals one wants to achieve with a certain artifact. It is determined by (and determining) the surrounding social context.

Acknowledging this idea of the dual nature of digital artifacts, educational lenses have to be reorganized. That is, instead of conceptualizing the lenses as highlighting either structural ('technical') or functional ('social') aspects, each lens now highlights one relevant aspect of a digital artifact in its dual nature.

For example, the lens Standardization (norms regulation and law) now highlights social processes of regulation and legislations connected with digital artifacts, as well as 'technical' processes of standardization. There is an ongoing debate about standardization of file formats for text processing. From the engineering point of view, file formats of e.g microsoft word and openoffice are changed to use xml-based solutions. However, the driving force for this change is the discussion about the necessity of having product-independent formats for storing text documents. So both sides are needed to understand the change from .doc to .docx.

Table 1 gives a short characterization of the dual nature of each lens.

In the description of lenses some concepts were used which need to be explained: The difference of explicit and implicit operations, and development paths.

Explicit operations are those whose effects are easy to assess, as e.g., in WYSIWIG software, their results are explicit. Usually these results give visual feedback whether the user is one step closer to his (usage) goal, or not. Therefore, explicit operations are often executed without delay and allow the user to obtain the impression of directly writing on a piece of paper, i.e., to directly interact with some material provided by the digital artifacts. In addition, user actions often trigger operations not directly visible, these are implicit operations. Such operations are needed to prepare the data: to store it in suitable data structures, to define additional data in order to enable other explicit operations in later steps. One example is to format headings by using pre-defined style sheets (Heading1, Heading2 ...), so that later a table of contents can be computed automatically.

The difficulty with the distinction between explicit and implicit operations is that there are many cases in which the distinction is based on the knowledge of the user. E.g. for a skilled user it is obvious to use pre-defined style sheets like Heading1 when starting a new chapter. However, there are cases where operations remain implicit (for example that typing a character in a word processor implicitly stores a code, and triggers an operation to layout the character with a given font). Implicit operations might be regarded as triggered side effects; however, they often allow additional function, as they automate information processing.

Thinking of development paths sometimes helps to uncover such implicit operations (or, to be precise: to find ways to teach such implicit operations).

In the case of word processors, the development path goes back to writing texts on paper or with typewriters. From the typewriter era we have inherited concepts like tab stops and carriage return.

5 Example: Duality Reconstruction of the Word Processor

In this section, the duality reconstruction is demonstrated using the WYSIWYG word processor as example. This example was chosen because text processing is usually be seen as easy to learn, and furthermore because it is seen as learnable by focusing on the functional aspect only. Learning text processing in this point of view means learning to use this type of digital artifact – and not to learn its structure. So when the duality reconstruction of this example demonstrates how function and structure are interwoven, and how both are needed to understand and being able to use even such a 'trivial' application, then the approach is likely to be useful with more complicated (= more 'technical') digital artifacts as well.

The second purpose of this section is to check whether the lenses really are applicable to digital artifacts. Remember, initially they were suggested to analyze the social surroundings of a technical system. Interestingly, automation, the first, most concrete lens and societal and ethical aspects, the last and most abstract lens, are closely connected. Therefore these two lenses will be discussed initially, followed by a brief discussion of the remaining lenses. Figure 4 gives an overview about the key aspects discussed as results of the duality reconstruction of the word processor.

The answer to the question what is automated (first lens) by word processors seems trivial: the mechanics of writing. Instead of laboriously producing marks on a sheet of paper with a feather or a pencil, the word processor – like the typewriter – produces these markings; and in addition to the typewriter with its fixed fonts we can easily change the font of our text from e.g. Arial to Times New Roman. Of course, word processors have many useful additional features like spell checking, support for including tables, etc. – but the improvement of what we call mechanics of writing is the major feature.

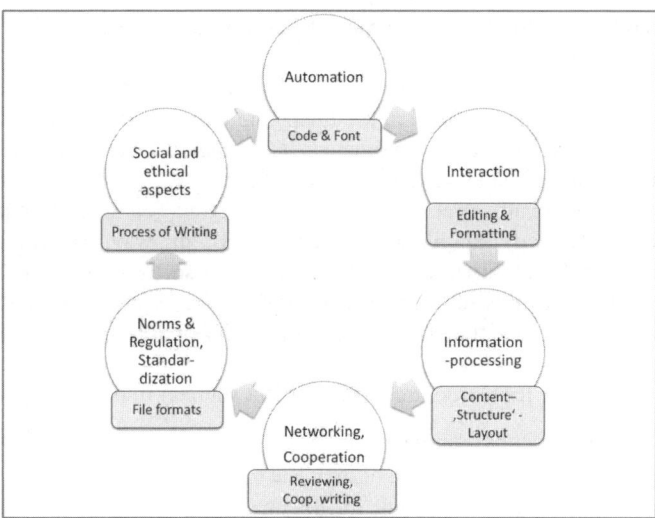

Fig. 4. Assigned to lenses keywords resulting from duality reconstruction

This feature is more important than it may seem, building the foundation for many additional features. Therefore, we have to analyze the structural aspect of this feature, how can it be, that it is now so easy to change the layout of the text, say by changing the visual representation of characters from 'Arial' to 'Times New Roman'? It is, because word processors (or the computer) changed the nature of the written language. For centuries, written language was defined as (more or less) permanent markings in a material. Materials like stones, parchment, papyrus, or paper can be used to be marked with written characters. The important thing is that a character is a visible marking on the material – if the marking is changed, the written text is changed, too. Therefore a character was regarded as a unity of layout (glyph) and meaning as a member of the alphabet of the language. With the introduction of computers, characters lost this unity – they are now separated in a visual marking (given by the fonts) and an underlying data structure (given by code, like e.g. Unicode).

When the user types in a text, patterns of code are stored and in modern word processors they are immediately visually presented in the actual chosen font. This produces the illusion that typing a text in a word processor can be compared to typing text with a typewriter.

It is important to note that this structural feature (dividing character in code and font) is the foundation for many features of word processors. It is the reason why a word processor can assign a different font to a given text without destroying it – the used codes of the characters stay the same.

While supporting the mechanics of producing a marking on a material may seem to be trivial, the structure behind this function immediately leads to several additional functions: Regardless of the chosen font, a computer can search for a pattern of codes. When a finished text is finally printed on paper, without additional effort we can save a 'copy' on our hard disk (that is, in reality we save a pattern of codes and some additional information from which the word processor can produce a copy). It is easy to change the text, to e.g. swap, add, and delete sentences, because these changes are changes of code, and after that the new pattern of code is visually designed and arranged in the used font.

Before discussing why this seemingly trivial feature - automation of the mechanics of writing - has important societal and ethical implications, let us summarize briefly what a word processor basically automates: It changes the act of writing characters from producing a fixed visual pattern on a material into storing the code of the character, which is automatically presented in a visual layout (on screen or paper) given other (usually predefined) data like the chosen font. By the way, the article about TeX in Wikipedia (http://en.wikipedia.org/wiki/TeX) has a section about the hyphenation and justification algorithms used in TeX to produce the layout of a paragraph which gives a good impression of the algorithmic complexity of automatically producing the visual layout of text.

Overall, the code & font structure has important societal impacts:

- Writing texts: copying texts and plagiarism,
- The electronic dissemination of texts via e.g. mail, www changes dramatically.
- Using written text: searching for documents; dissemination of text via electronic books (and their extra value compared to paper-based books)

- Overall: it changes a fundamental defining feature of written language as some fixed (permanent) visual pattern on a material. This feature has the impact that written language was, as the writing process itself, sequential. Now it is possible (or at least easier) to write iteratively. Interestingly, texts in the WWW are often not sequential any more like we were used to from book pages.

Based on this discussion of word processors from the above outlined socio-technical perspective, the following sections present results from educational lenses applied to word processors.

SECOND LENS: INTERACTION

Word processors can be seen as the prototypical application based on the principle of WYSIWYG. Bravo for the XeroX Alto System seems to be the first WYSIWYG editor. It uses a combination of mouse input and textual commands.

Table 2. Excerpt from Bravo's user manual explaining the command ‚Paragraph Append', p. 21 (http://www.bitsavers.org/pdf/xerox/alto/BravoCourse.pdf)

> "To begin typing this additional text, select the last paragraph of the memo *as a paragraph*-- cursor on the left margin, arrow pointing to the right, push the **Yellow** mouse button. The cursor will indicate a paragraph selection by changing its shape to a paragraph symbol. With the paragraph selected, give an append command. That is, type:
> **a**"

There are some functional issues connected to this

1. The user directly changes the layout without having to remember commands (in the example above, the Bravo Editor, a mixture of commands and direct manipulation was used)
2. The user directly sees the result, as it will be printed on paper.
3. The way automation is used changes. Instead of typing in text, giving layout commands, 'compiling' the input for processing, and then receiving the output (the I-P-O model), the interactive model aims at hiding the processing in order to give the user the illusion of directly typing characters as fonts on a simulated piece of paper.
4. Formatting of the layout of the text now comes more into focus, which then creates the need for the corresponding function to effectively change the layout (e.g. style sheets).

These functional issues are reflected in (more precisely: enabled by) the structure.

In addition to storing the characters or a text as code together with information how they are to be formatted, types of layout (style sheets) are saved. Changing the layout direction at a single place (changing the style sheet) thus can affect several pieces of text.

THIRD LENS: INFORMATION PROCESSING

The division of a text document in content, layout and formation leads way to enable more advanced functionalities we analyze as information processing. Note that we changed the usual content-layout-structure into content-layout-formation in order to avoid confusion with the concept structure as part of the duality of digital artifacts.

The interesting aspect is that in addition to code and fonts (roughly: content and layout) additional information about the formation of the text is given. Information about division of a text in sections, subsection and according headings and subheadings can be used to generate an outline-view which supports thinking about the theme. It also allows changing the outline.

A typical general feature of information processing of digital artifacts is the ability to (automatically) produce different views on the information. These different views highlight different aspects, show central issues, abnormalities, or relations between different parts. Word processors also allow different views on texts. For example the outline view, showing the outline of the text.

FORTH LENS: NETWORKING

For collaboration, there are sometimes functions like comments and change tracking, and for combining and comparing documents. Structurally, adding information about changes and comments, and allowing different views (i.e. hide and show) seems quite easy.

In addition, it seems that a new generation of web-based word processors is currently developed (or popularized), allowing multiple users synchronous writing in the same document.

Fifths and sixth lenses were already briefly discussed above. (For standardization, the pressure on using interchangeable file formats was discussed)

6 Discussion

In summary, the process described is not only analytic but also reconstructive. For instance development path and interactions with usage contexts are added as enrichment of the teaching content. The purpose is to make investigation of structure meaningful, relevant and useful to the learner. The duality reconstruction connects 'technology' (in is isolated, single-sided meaning) with individual and social experiences and practices. Thereby it opens a path to explore the science behind the many digital artifacts.

In addition, taking into account function in the didactic reconstruction is a first step to support students' prior knowledge from everyday experiences. Therefore, explication of usage contexts is valuable. Putting the discussion of structure (or function) in classroom in context supports this enrichment, so that function becomes understandable through structure, and structure becomes meaningful through function.

Lenses support a didactic reconstruction of the duality of digital artifacts: The complexity and amount of functionalities and 'technical' ideas involved in today's typical digital artifacts is thus reduced and focused on specific issues – but without isolating and de-contextualizing them.

While the initially discussed examples of teaching word processors tend to focus on structure or function, duality reconstruction reveals their interrelation, and in addition enriches teaching aspects to include more abstract, more general and contextual information.

References

1. Ben-Ari, M., Yeshno, T.: Conceptual models of software artifacts. Interacting with Computers 18(6), 1336–1350 (2006)
2. Bhavnani, S.K., Reif, F., John, B.E.: Beyond command knowledge: identifying and teaching strategic knowledge for using complex computer applications. In: Proceedings of the SIGCHI Conference on Human Factors in Computing Systems, CHI 2001, Seattle, Washington, United States, pp. 229–236. ACM, New York (2001)
3. Clark, M.A.C., Boyle, R.D.: Computer Science in English High Schools: We Lost the S, Now the C Is Going. In: Mittermeir, R.T. (ed.) ISSEP 2006. LNCS, vol. 4226, pp. 83–93. Springer, Heidelberg (2006)
4. di Sessa, A.: Changing Minds: Computers, Learning, and Literacy. MIT Press, Cambridge (2001)
5. Hubwieser, P.: Functions, Objects and States: Teaching Informatics in Secondary Schools. In: Mittermeir, R.T. (ed.) ISSEP 2006. LNCS, vol. 4226, pp. 104–116. Springer, Heidelberg (2006)
6. Kroes, P.: Technological Explanations: The relation between Structure and Function of Technological Objects in: Techné. Journal of the Society for Philosophy and Technology 3(3) (1998)
7. Magenheim, J., Schulte, C.: Social, ethical and technical issues in informatics—An integrated approach. In: Education and Information Technologies, Oktober 2006, vol. 11(3-4). Springer, Netherlands (2006)
8. Mann, L.M.: The Implications of Functional and Structural Knowledge Representations for Novice Programmers. Doctoral Thesis. UMI Order Number: UMI Order No. GAX92-28760. University of California at Berkeley (1992)
9. Medienpädagogischer Forschungsverbund Südwest: KIM-Studie 2005: Kinder und Medien, Computer und Internet (2005)
10. Mitchell, A.: Computing science: What do pupils think? (2006) (accessed December 2007), http://www.ics.heacademy.ac.uk/studentretention/workshops/pres/Alison20Mitchell.ppt
11. Schulte, C., Knobelsdorf, M.: Attitudes towards computer science—computing experiences as a starting point and barrier to computer science. In: Proceedings of the third international workshop on Computing education research, Atlanta, Georgia, USA, pp. 27–38 (2007), http://doi.acm.org/10.1145/1288580.1288585

What's My Challenge?
The Forgotten Part of Problem Solving in Computer Science Education

Ralf Romeike

University of Potsdam
Department of Computer Science
A.-Bebel-Str. 89
14482 Potsdam, Germany
romeike@cs.uni-potsdam.de

Abstract. In this paper we present a teaching framework that extends the traditional problem solving method in computer science education in order to increase student motivation. It replaces problems by so-called challenges and in particular emphasizes the learning situation and inspiration of the students. Furthermore it combines several pedagogical principles and applies them in a process of how students learn in a motivating and self-regulated way. In order to justify the necessity of a new concept, problems in the traditional problem solving approaches in general high school education are highlighted. Implications from research addressing similar issues are summarized. In order for addressing students' motivation changes are necessary; challenges can provide a basis to start from.

1 Introduction

The core of computer science is all about problem solving: In software companies customers usually have problems which programmers need to find a solution for. Detailed models have been developed for finding the best methods to solve these problems most efficiently. Some of these models, together with the general problem solving approach, have found their way into computer science education. But is it really all about problem solving? In a literature review about introductory programming it looks like it does – problems seem to be everywhere: in the textbooks and tasks as well as in the results of the courses. This paper considers the question, whether learning in computer science[1] possibly happens differently: motivated by personal challenges and creativity. Taking these factors into account, one of the major problems in computer science may be solved: the decreasing interest and success of our students.

---

[1] We refer to computer science in general even if illustrating the issue with examples from programming in particular. The use of problem solving tasks is common but not unique to teaching programming. Many concerns we bring up in this paper can be generalized to other topics in teaching general computer science as well.

2 Ways of Learning Computer Science

2.1 How Learning Computer Science Has Changed

Children today grow up in a different environment than they did 10 years ago and a lot different than 20 years ago: Today computer technology is a part of their life. Since young students more frequently use videogames, programmable mobile phones, notebook computers and such, the use of technology becomes more and more normal. People who are currently teaching grew up differently: If technology was available at all, it was something special, something "fragile" and something you needed to put a lot of thought and study in before you could use it efficiently. Also, you needed to use it efficiently as technology was expensive and not that powerful. Things have changed. Using computers today is generally easy and something most students can do. Modern operating systems strive for being intuitive to understand (and are improving in that). Hence the instructors' efforts towards teaching usability of technology can be diminished. Fortunately, this implies that computer science education in schools can focus on matters that are essential to computer science instead of training computer use. Also programming languages are progressing that way and are increasingly used by non-computer scientists. People are getting to know the computer as a new medium for expressing themselves, as a tool, which is supporting them not only in work they need to do, but also for fun and in their hobbies [1].

Hence, what are the essential matters computer science education can now concentrate on? One of the most common answers to this question would be problem solving. This makes sense because by solving problems with the computer students can learn important strategies that are typical for computer science. On the other hand this approach labels computer science as just "dealing with problems". It is questionable, whether this view brings up the right motivation for today's learners (cp. [1]). In addition we are still teaching computer science in the way we learned it: getting excited about solving problems by manipulating invisible data structures, computations and "Hello World" programs as the peak of interactivity. So how can we better engage our students?

As educational research points out, learning is not just a rational act; it happens also in emotional connections (e.g. [2, 3]). This means that not only facts need to be learned in order to become a good rational problem solver. It is also about how a student feels about what is learned and which meaning the facts to be learned have for the student.

Altering the image we, as educators, have of computers may help in following the change of technology usage in society: Computers are a part of life. They represent fun, enjoyment, personal fulfillment and quality of life. This view brings up a lot of motivation for using the computer. This can be seen when watching students using the computers out of the lesson context. Why does that need to be different within the lesson?

2.2 How Computer Science Concepts Are Learned Outside of the Lesson – A Problem Solving Approach

In an interview we asked a committed student about how his interest in computer science started [4]. His computing experiences started with gaming, which is typical for many students' way of getting into computer science [5]. Through the interest in gaming the student became familiar with his computer, started to improve little things and finally got interested in the internet and web design. He discovered that there are preconfigured modules he could use for achieving potential goals – as setting up a homepage or an internet forum. By administrating the forum for his school class, the student learned how he could be a designer for computer software. He learned to handle problems which he encountered when doing so and each problem was perceived as a challenge that he wanted to overcome in order to achieve what he wanted to do. When the student wished to do things he could not achieve with modifying other software, he learned basic programming concepts and started to write programs for his needs. He perceives programming as interesting because without a lot of effort he can achieve a lot. Furthermore, he states that programming for him is a creative task. It is motivating for him that in the end he always will come up with a product; with something "in his hand". As this example shows, getting involved with meaningful tasks can greatly motivate students for learning programming. Similar experiences where students learn self-motivated are reported in papers about computer clubhouses in the U.S. (e.g. [6-8]) and the application of games in programming courses [9, 10].

These experiences can be generalized in the following steps:

1. The student gets to know a few examples of what a software/system/ programming language is capable off.
2. The student, step by step, learns the fundamental principles of a tool and what can be done with it.
3. The student becomes familiar and comfortable with the (programming) environment.
4. The student generates ideas, e.g. what else can be done or what could be done better or what he would like to have.
5. The student adjusts example programs for his purpose or builds new ones from scratch.
6. The student implements, tests, analyzes, improves and presents his product.

In computer clubhouses similar steps are reflected in the underlying principles for engaging with learning: imagine, create, play, share, reflect, imagine and so on [11].

As we consider these steps essential for a natural motivated way of learning programming, they can be a basis for a checklist for computer science lessons. Psychology research shows that intrinsic motivation declines with the age of the student, starting from grade three. Furthermore extrinsic motivation is negatively correlated with academic outcomes [12]. Hence, as educators we have to consider how we can more intrinsically motivate our students. The possibility of creatively challenging the students is quite unique for computer science classes and returns motivation to the students. Later in this paper we will refer to the above mentioned steps for consideration in a challenging teaching framework.

2.3 How Computer Science Concepts within the Class Room Are Learned – Another Problem Solving Approach

In high school the first contact with computers generally follows a similar schema: As every student needs to be able to use a computer and software, general recipes of how to operate standard software are taught in a procedural way. At this point already the "problem solving" starts: Assignments such as "Create a tabular CV with the following requirements" or "Create a spreadsheet that looks like the given example and calculates the average gas consumption of a car" are common. We find this troublesome for the following reasons: Creating a CV may make sense, but at the time the task is assigned the students usually are still quite far away from applying for a job. Furthermore a tabular CV does not really allow including a possibly creative personal touch (what actually is often wanted by the employees). Also typically the students are still quite far away from driving a car and becoming interested in the gas mileage of a car.

As the problem with the procedural methodology was already acknowledged in computer science education, it is postulated to emphasize concepts instead of step-by-step instruction (e.g. [13]). However, somehow this does not seem to be successful. In many schools step-by-step instruction is still taught and also many school books more or less match the "How to" methodology. A reason for this could be that the approach and the tasks stayed the same as before. If a change in methodology is wanted, new teaching concepts also need to be put into action with new kinds of tasks. This can be difficult if the traditional problem solving approach is kept.

As seen, both approaches involve problem solving, but they are very different in their origin and motivation of the students. One reason for this could be that the school-teaching problem solving approach is derived from the science of computer science: Problems of a "customer" (the teacher) are solved – as it is the task of a computer scientist. Maybe, at least for the beginning, a different approach would be more appropriate. Investigating what is happening in the classrooms we found many issues with the problem of problem solving.

3 Problems of the Problem Solving Approach in Practice

3.1 Problems Often Are Not Problems (but Tasks)

A problem can be defined as an obstacle that stands between a person and a desired goal, objective or purpose (cp. [14-16]). It should contain a certain difficulty and something to solve, not just to do. The emphasis lies here in the unknown way of how the desired goal can be achieved and stands in contrast to the understanding of "something to be done". It may be arguable what is unknown. Unfortunately the unknown often is interpreted as not knowing the recipe. But this is just a task. The Compact Oxford English Dictionary defines a task as "a piece of work to be done" [17]. As soon as the recipe is found, the problem becomes trivial and is solved in a few steps. Typically in programming courses the problem then only consists of the implementation of code. Students in such situations do not need to reflect about their actions and do not need to think about the concept of a problem. Instead they research how they can quickly move from the point of origin to the problem's "solution".

An example from a school book illustrates this problem [18]: Given is a program which adds two times (minutes and seconds). The given problem, which actually just is a task, is: "Extend the program in a way that days can be input and handled". A typical student approach would be to copy the other lines of code and to adjust the converting factor. This indeed is a solution for the given problem. However, the learning outcome is questionable. The student refreshed his mathematical knowledge about converting days into hours, but he did not learn or reinforce anything about computer science concepts. This leads to another problem as discussed in the next section.

3.2 Problems Often Are Not Computer Science Problems but Math Problems

At the beginning, computers were used for what they could do best: to compute. This fact has a tremendous impact on computer science education even today: computer science teachers love numbers. A vast amount of problems assigned are derived from mathematics. As mathematics is quite important and necessary for computer science this may be understandable and there should be nothing wrong with it. However, keeping in mind that we want to teach the students something about computer science, the question needs to be raised: Is this goal actually achieved? We think that in computer science students should learn about solving problems that are typical for computer science with methods derived from computer science. If they do not, then teaching this subject is not necessary. Many examples illustrate this problem, e.g. the following example from a schoolbook [18]: Given is a python program which adds two fractions. Task: "Extend the program that it realizes subtraction, multiplication and division." A commonly used task in many programming courses is the GCD: "Realize a program that finds the Greatest Common Divisor". These examples have in common that the students need to find and solve the mathematical equation for a given problem and implement it in code. There is no genuine algorithmic problem solving involved.

Also, in computer science education research it happens that mathematical problem solving is equated with algorithmic problem solving as demonstrated in a paper called "Misleading Intuition in Algorithmic Problem Solving" [19]. The author demonstrates how intuition can be an obstacle when searching for a problem's solution: "A long railway is divided into many equal sections. The distance between every two adjacent sections is 1. N wagons are placed in N different sections which are not necessarily consecutive. How can the railroad workers move all the wagons to one of the sections such that the sum of all movements is minimal?" Problems in this task (average or median?) are of mathematical nature, not derived from computer science. As reported in the study, students chose the wrong mathematical solution. They were not using a wrong algorithm.

Problematic as well is the motivational factor of mathematics. Mathematics does not have the highest popularity among students. Despite the importance of mathematics, perhaps other problems – closer to computer science – would motivate the students better. Looking at the programs which learners code when they are not in a lesson context or learning autodidactic, programs related to mathematics can rarely be found. This is probably because the students want to learn about programming and not about mathematics. Indeed, mathematical problems have the advantage that they are well-defined. This actually is atypical for computer science and comes with the disadvantage that they generally only have one valid solution and they are remote from the learners' reality.

3.3 Problems Often Are Not Problems to the Student

Educational research tells us that students perform better and are more motivated if a task is meaningful to them (e.g. [20]). This view can be transferred to problem solving. A problem is relevant and meaningful to a student if it comes out of his or her reality, if he or she actually considers it as an obstacle and if he or she really wants to achieve the required goal. If the problem is not apparently a problem to the student because it is given to him or her by the teacher and additionally is just a task (as the teacher knows the solution for it), in our opinion it does not fulfill the requirements of a problem in this understanding as there is no internal motivation to solve it. These factors also typically appear in the problem solving scenarios described above.

4 Approaches for Overcoming the Problems of Problem Solving

4.1 Problem Solving and Problem Finding in Computer Science Education

Problem solving skills are considered essential in computer science lessons. Nevertheless a number of problems with the problem solving approach in the context of programming have been reported. Researchers in computer science tried to overcome them in various ways and found that highly intrinsically motivated students performed better [21]; many students did not have a general interest in programming per se [22, 23] but motivation could be raised by using meaningful tasks and exercises [24-26] and by assigning personally challenging tasks, e.g. competitions [27].

A few researchers extend their view on another often overlooked part of problem solving, which actually plays an important role in computer science: problem finding, problem posing or problem management. They found that problem solving skills alone are not enough. It is necessary to include realistic problem finding with it: Kaasbøll [28] could improve the failure rate in introductory programming courses by teaching problem defining skills. The problems were new and partly unknown and were motivating for and of interest to the students. As well, the students were required to keep them realizable and manageable during the course. Sutinen and Tarhio [29] also emphasize the importance of open problems. They report increased student motivation by applying creative methods for problem management, which includes identification and specification of problems and training at the attitudinal level. Eastman [30] reports success with a method emphasizing problem identification. Reed [31] takes into account that education research has shown that an effective technique for developing problem solving and critical-thinking skills is to expose students early and often to "ill-defined" problems in their field. He successfully integrated ill-defined problems in a CS1 course.

In summary, even if programming is not meeting the students' motivation per se, motivation and achievements can be raised by introducing open situations and letting the students define problems to be solved themselves instead of assigning definite problems.

4.2 An Overlooked Aspect

Authors considering problem finding as important already pointed out the necessity of considering personal aspects of the students. Also contextualization, personalization, and choice can have beneficial effects on motivation and achievements [32]. Students are individuals, coming with their own ideas, wishes and needs. These can be utilized in a way that students are encouraged to develop their own goals in the lesson context. When working on realizing these goals they will encounter problems they enjoy facing – and solving. Thus the teacher needs to influence the learning situation in such a way that students are inspired to develop their own ideas and find their own challenges. This way they will solve problems that are meaningful to them.

Several pedagogical concepts from educational sciences and computer science education share these thoughts and consider the students perspectives and needs. The situated learning theory suggests incorporating the learning situation and the context of learning. Discovery learning values that learning happens with a positive attitude and is most effective when ones own questions and problems are mastered. This way experiences are gained and a broader view of the field is adopted. Also the theory of constructionism emphasizes that learning happens especially felicitously when the learner is consciously engaged in constructing a public entity [20].

Considering the essential ideas of these learning theories reveals that two more student-oriented aspects need to be regarded: The learning situation and the generation of ideas. Both are important to be considered in the process before the phases of problem finding and problem solving begin.

The learning situation: The situation in which a student learns and in which he is supposed to solve problems needs to be prepared and designed for activating and inspiring the students' ideas. In the computer science classroom this means on one hand to provide the right IT and software for classroom use. On the other hand, it is fundamental to prepare the learning situation by helping the students to get attitudinal readiness, problem sensitivity, understanding of underlying principles and concepts and awareness of the possibilities.

Inspiring ideas: Being allowed to realize ones own ideas is very motivating to students. However, especially in a new surrounding with new tools or with new learned concepts it is not easy to generate new ideas. Therefore, the teacher should support students in finding new ideas and inspire them. This can happen with inspiring examples, creativity techniques (e.g. brainstorming), discussions, suggesting analogies and modifications.

5 The Challenge Cycle of Computer Science Education

We consolidated the factors found in the literature and our research in a teaching framework. It substitutes "traditional" problem solving tasks with challenges[2]. As a challenge we consider a problem that is relevant to the student, which has an open ending and which preferably is chosen by the student himself. Thus the students are encouraged to be creative and solve challenges that are meaningful to them. In the

---

[2] A challenge can be defined as "an interesting or difficult problem or task" [16] and "something needing great mental or physical effort in order to be done successfully" [14].

challenges students can follow their own interests. They are guarded by the frame of the lesson context and thus learn individually the content of the lesson on a theme or a derivation of the theme they determine themselves. It is intended to support the key factors found for addressing students' interests: Motivation, meaningful and personally challenging tasks, relevance, creativity, applicability, contribution of ideas, experimentation and IT support for creativity which is found in programming environments.

The sequence is described by a cycle (cp. Fig. 1) that is iterated through several times in a lesson unit. It starts with each learning situation where new concepts are taught. In a challenge phase the teacher clarifies the situation and prepares the students to come up with ideas and to find their challenge. The challenge is then solved, implemented and presented by a student. A first walk through the cycle will be illustrated. A framework similar to the Challenge Cycle we used in conducting a lesson for introducing an 11th grade class to programming in a creative way (cp. [33]). In order to support the creative participation of the students we found that it is beneficial to embed every teaching phase in such a motivating teaching framework. This can be done with regard to the Challenge Cycle which will be described as follows.

Challenge Phase
The situation in which a learner finds himself when entering the Challenge Cycle is based on the prior experience, knowledge, the learning situation and comfort level of the student. Thus the preparation of the situation by the teacher has an important

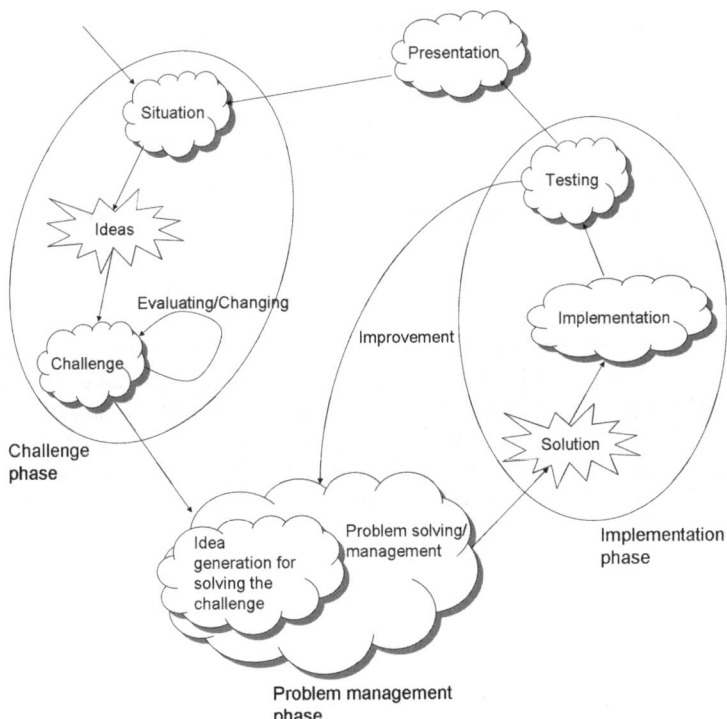

Fig. 1. The Challenge Cycle

impact on the motivation of the student to engage with the learning content. Therefore, the teacher needs to assure that the knowledge and concepts which are needed to solve a desired challenge are well introduced or can be discovered by the learners themselves. Also, in the beginning the field of the challenge needs to be limited to certain constraints so that the students do not get "lost" in the space of possibilities and choose a challenge that is manageable in the time given. We observed that students come up with a lot of ideas after a new "playground of possibilities" is discovered. Then, out of these ideas, they choose a challenge which they want to put into practice. Finding the challenge also involves evaluating the challenge in the context of time, knowledge, expected difficulty, and, if needed, changing/accommodating the challenge. Typical characteristics of these challenges are – in contrast to many problem solving tasks – openness in possible elaboration, relevance, originality, and the identification of the students with the task.

In the lesson unit conducted the students did not have any prior experience in programming. Thus it was fundamental to provide the necessary motivation by making them comfortable with the use of the programming environment and show them a few basic examples of what it is capable of. Out of this, a task was assigned to create a short movie reflecting a scene of their everyday life, a vacation, or a scene out of their favorite movie. In the subsequent runs, through the cycle challenges such as animating their name, letting self designed balls fly over the screen, or the programming of games have been encouraged.

Problem Management Phase
After finding their challenges the problem management phase starts with generating ideas for solving the challenge. This phase involves problem solving strategies with the added bonus that the students are highly motivated for solving their personal challenge. As for the introduction of programming, the ideas of the students have been quite straight forward. Besides applying brainstorming of possible solutions no further creativity techniques have been applied. Anyhow, for application in more advanced challenges the emphasis of more creativity techniques for idea generation is intended.

Implementation Phase
Once a strategy and solution for the challenge is found the result can be implemented and tested. This gives students the possibility to test the solution right away. If new problems are encountered they need to be solved. Often potential for improving the product is found and solved within the time available. In the conducted lesson unit the open-ended tasks allowed improvements e.g. in game features, usability and appearance. After the students finished their mini-project, time is provided by the teacher to present the outcomes to the class. Questions, encountered problems and their solutions are discussed with all students. Learning from the problem solving and being inspired by the ideas of the others, the students are now ready for learning the next concept. The situation is prepared for it.

6 Implications

Applying a New Perspective of IT and Programming
If the students come to computer science courses with the view of computer technology as a tool for enhancing quality of life and personal expression as well as the belief

that they can do great things with computers, then this view is something that should be encouraged and should not be taken away from them. This outlook may maintain the students' motivation for deep engagement in the field. Even for those students who come with a different perspective, being challenged will be a good starting point for entering the field. Chances are that this will help them to persist in difficult times and when encountering bigger problems.

With this new outlook, a new teaching concept becomes necessary. This has already been experienced with the transition of changing from software-use oriented teaching towards teaching fundamental concepts: The goal can rarely be achieved if the method and tasks stay the same. The Challenge Cycle has potential as a substitute for the traditional problem solving method, at least in introductory courses. In our future research we will address this question in detail.

Difference between Computer Science and Computer Science Education
The learning of computer science happens differently in school settings than in university and in professional settings. Different is the motivation: A university student chose to get involved with the subject with respect to his later career. Thus he may tolerate solving "other's" problems as he may expect the same as he enters the workforce. The educational objectives in high school are different. The motivation and personal factors of the students need to be considered in a special way. As students are used to solving tasks given by the teacher, solving their own problems will open for them a new horizon. After having experienced this, they will have the self-confidence to and feel capable of "if they choose so" solving other people problems. Perhaps it will be a challenge to them.

Teaching Computer Science in University
Nevertheless, even if the learning settings in general school and university are quite different, challenging the students may help to overcome common problems in university courses as well. Several approaches to enhance the learning experience in programming courses share basic ideas of the challenge cycle. Especially for non-majors and introductory courses this may be an approach worth trying.

7 Discussion

We presented a teaching concept that extends the traditional problem solving approach in computer science education. It replaces problems by so-called challenges and in particular emphasizes the learning situation and inspiration of the students. Furthermore it combines several pedagogical principles and applies them in a process of how students learn in a motivating and self-regulated way.

The approach of motivating students in computer science with tasks that are interesting to them is not unique. Some already have been mentioned, others employ motivators like game programming (e.g. [9]) or real life contexts [34]. The Challenge Cycle approach aims at taping students' motivation earlier - through leaving them choices, by contextualization and by personalization.

Another kind of challenge is described in a study by Long [10] where challenges and competitions were used in programming games. Intrinsic motivation and learning effectiveness improved. From our point of view a challenge does not necessarily need to involve a competition – students can be motivated by the context and ideas. This possibility of creatively challenging the students is quite unique to computer science classes and brings back the motivation to the students.

It has been demonstrated that the approach may work especially well in programming topics, but we believe challenging the students will be beneficial in other contexts as well. We are currently applying this approach in computer science classes in a high school setting and investigate the effective impact on motivation and learning success. First experiences are promising.

References

1. Guzdial, M., Soloway, E.: Teaching the Nintendo Generation to Program. Commun. ACM 45(4), 17–21 (2002)
2. Lewis, T., Petrina, S., Hile, A.M.: Problem Posing-Adding a Creative Increment to Technological Problem Solving. Journal of Industrial Teacher Education 36(1), 5–35 (1998)
3. Hascher, T.: Emotions in Everyday School-Life: Effects and Forms of Regulation (in German). Zeitschrift für Pädagogik 51(5), 610–625 (2005)
4. Romeike, R.: Creative Students - What Can We Learn from Them for Teaching Computer Science? In: 6th Baltic Sea Conference on Computing Education Research, Koli Calling, Uppsala University, Uppsala, Sweden (2006)
5. Knobelsdorf, M., Schulte, C.: Computer Biographies - a Biographical Research Perspective on Computer Usage and Attitudes toward Informatics. In: 5th Baltic Sea Conference on Computer Science Education, Koli (2005)
6. Resnick, M.: Rethinking Learning in the Digital Age. In: Kirkman, G. (ed.) The Global Information Technology Report: Readiness for the Networked World, pp. 32–37. Oxford University Press, Oxford (2002)
7. Resnick, M., Rusk, N., Cooke, S.: The Computer Clubhouse: Technological Fluency in the Inner City. In: High Technology and Low-Income Communities, pp. 266–286 (1998)
8. Peppler, K.A., Kafai, Y.B.: Creative Coding: Programming for Personal Expression (2005)
9. Korte, L., Anderson, S., Pain, H., Good, J.: Learning by Game-Building: A Novel Approach to Theoretical Computer Science Education. In: 12th Annual SIGCSE Conference on Innovation and Technology in CSE, pp. 53–57. ACM Press, Dundee, Scotland (2007)
10. Long, J.: Just for Fun: Using Programming Games in Software Programming Training and Education. Journal of Information Technology Education 6, 279–290 (2007)
11. Resnick, M.: Sowing the Seeds for a More Creative Society. In: Learning & Leading with Technology, International Society for Technology in Education (ISTE) (2007)
12. Lepper, M.R., Corpus, J.H., Iyengar, S.S.: Intrinsic and Extrinsic Motivational Orientations in the Classroom: Age Differences and Academic Correlates. Journal of Educational Psychology 97(2), 184–196 (2005)
13. Schwill, A.: Fundamental Ideas - Rethinking Computer Science Education. Learning and Leading with Technology 25(1), 28–31 (1997)
14. Cambridge Dictionary of American English Online (accessed December 14, 2007), http://dictionary.cambridge.org/Default.asp?dict=A
15. 1828 Edition of Webster's American Dictionary of the English Language (accessed December 14, 2007), http://1828.mshaffer.com
16. Wordsmyth Educational Dictionary-Thesaurus (accessed December 14, 2007)
17. Compact Oxford English Dictionary (accessed December 14, 2007), http://www.askoxford.com

18. Fothe, M.: Problem Solving with Python (in German). ThILLM, Bad Berka (2002)
19. Ginat, D.: Misleading Intuition in Algorithmic Problem Solving. In: 32nd SIGCSE Technical Symposium on CSE, pp. 21–25. ACM Press, Charlotte, USA (2001)
20. Papert, S.: Mindstorms: Children, Computers, and Powerful Ideas. Basic Books, NY (1980)
21. Bergin, S., Reilly, R.: The Influence of Motivation and Comfort-Level on Learning to Program. In: PPIG 17, University of Sussex, Brighton UK, pp. 293–304 (2005)
22. Curzon, P., Rix, J.: Why Do Students Take Programming Modules? In: 6th annual conference on the teaching and computing and the 3rd annual conference on integrating technology into CSE: Changing the delivery of Computer Science Education. ITICSE 1998, Dublin, Ireland, pp. 59–63 (1998)
23. Mamone, S.: Empirical Study of Motivation in an Entry Level Programming Course. ACM SIGPLAN Notices 27(3), 54–60 (1992)
24. Scragg, G., Smith, J.: A Study of Barriers to Women in Undergraduate Computer Science. In: 29th SIGCSE Technical Symposium on CSE, Atlanta, United States, pp. 82–86 (1998)
25. Feldgen, M., Clua, O.: New Motivations Are Required for Freshman Introductory Programming. In: 33rd ASSE/IEEE Frontiers in Education Conf., Boulder, pp. T3C–T24 (2003)
26. Rich, L., Perry, H., Guzdial, M.: A Cs1 Course Designed to Address Interests of Women. In: 35th SIGCSE Technical Symposium on Computer Science Education, pp. 190–194. ACM Press, Norfolk, Virginia, USA (2004)
27. Lawrence, R.: Teaching Data Structures Using Competitive Games. IEEE Transactions on Education 47(4), 459–466 (2004)
28. Kaasbøll, J.J.: Teaching Critical Thinking and Problem Defining Skills. Education and Information Technologies 3(2), 101–117 (1998)
29. Sutinen, E., Tarhio, J.: Teaching to Identify Problems in a Creative Way. In: 31st Frontiers in Education Conference. IEEE Computer Society, Los Alamitos (2001)
30. Eastman, E.G.: Fact-Based Problem Identification Precedes Problem Solving. J. Comput. Small Coll. 19(2), 18–29 (2003)
31. Reed, D.: The Use of Ill-Defined Problems for Developing Problem-Solving and Empirical Skills in CS1. J. Comput. Small Coll. 18(1), 121–133 (2002)
32. Cordova, D., Lepper, M.: Intrinsic Motivation and the Process of Learning: Beneficial Effects of Contextualization, Personalization, and Choice. Journal of Educational Psychology 88(4), 715–730 (1996)
33. Romeike, R.: Applying Creativity in CS High School Education - Criteria, Teaching Example and Evaluation. In: 7th Baltic Sea Conf. on Comp., Ed Research, Koli Calling (2007)
34. Hill, A.M.: Problem Solving in Real-Life Contexts: An Alternative for Design in Technology Education. International Journal of Technology and Design Education 5(3), 1–18 (1998)

Bringing Abstract Concepts Alive.
How to Base Learning Success on the Principles of Playing, Curiosity and In-Classroom Differentiation

Peter Gruber

Paris Lodron Universität Salzburg, Austria
Peter.Gruber@sbg.ac.at

Abstract. This article addresses the question which goals a valuable and sustainable learning process should aim at. Meaningful learning activities, emotional commitment and meeting individual needs are identified as core principles. According to these principles, several theories that support the construction of such lesson sequences are discussed. In particular, the importance of knowledge as compared to pure information retrieving is highlighted. From this perspective, the concept of In-Classroom Differentiation is derived. Finally, a concrete example demonstrates how this concept translates from theory into practice. Thus, this article addresses both, the theoretical foundation and the practical implementation.

Keywords: individualization, motivation, in-classroom differentiation, curiosity, learning activities.

1 Introduction

When talking about education, teachers, psychologists and educational scientists alike share a wide range of common goals. They all emphasize the importance of sustainable learning, pointing out the indisputable fact that students' knowledge should extend considerably beyond the next examination date. They also declare the principle to secure significant learning successes for at least most of the students, and thus they demand to meet each student's individual needs. And last but not least, everybody wants to promote a high level of learning, not only in terms of technical skills, but also in the realms of personal and social learning ([2], [13]).

All of these aims can hardly be dismissed, and at least I for myself can fully agree with the notion that every teacher should try to achieve these goals. Of course there will always be shortcomings of various kinds in our classrooms - education is a highly human-centered activity, and human beings are anything but perfect. I think this is a fact we should appreciate rather than bemoan, but anyway, this is the reality we have to face.

Nevertheless, such ideal goals can serve as a guideline for planning, conducting and evaluating lessons. They can do a great job as benchmarks for teaching quality and help to establish and continuously reassert the qualities we want our schools to stand for.

But my personal experiences - and, unfortunately, also lots of serious studies - tell us that there is a huge gap between theoretical postulations and practical outcomes. And this is not a gap due to the simple fact that these theories tend not to translate directly into practice. It looks as if there were completely different theories at work in our schools ([7], [8]).

Sometimes it is claimed that practice does not need elaborate theories in order to work. I think this is a huge and dangerous, though common, misconception. Every practitioner - experienced as he might be - has at least an implicit theory in his mind he refers to. And this theory largely commands his actions - sometimes even interfering with the intentions he explicitly aspires [6].

Just to give an example, every teacher wants his students to develop profound knowledge and applicable skills which help students not only to master the next exam, but prove helpful in many other fields (that's the intention teachers aspire). In practice, students are frequently asked to simply reproduce facts everybody could easily look up in a dictionary; and this just once for an exam. Evidently, the underlying theory is that learning pure information by heart directly translates into applicable knowledge - a theory most of us are likely to have serious doubts about. To sum it up: what teachers do in practice contradicts what they aim at in theory. (This phenomenon cannot be observed with teachers only, of course.)

So in this paper, we want to develop a very concrete, very detailed plan of lesson which can be directly transferred into practice. But we also want to establish clear ties between theoretical assumptions and concrete actions. In fact, this article should convince the reader that the methods proposed here are indeed suitable for bringing the ideas we value in theory alive in practice.

2 Theoretical Foundations

2.1 Basic Ideas of In-Classroom Differentiation

Following Herber [11], Herber/Vasarhelyi [9] and Herber/Vasarhelyi [10], the basic assumption of In-Classroom Differentiation is that it is neither possible nor adorable to trim the plurality of individual personalities to fit a single, specific norm. This acknowledges the fact that students come into the classroom from many individual and thus different backgrounds - and this fact prevails no matter how many different types of schools may exist. As this statement cannot sensibly be declined, many teaching methods conclude trying to detect some "average" student learner that serves as a model. All lessons are designed for the needs and preconditions of that model. The hope is obviously that all students resemble more or less that model, and therefore all students will more a less profit from lessons that are designed according to that model.

I have the feeling that this is a very vague hope. It certainly does not support goals like "motivation of students", "meeting students' individual needs" or "high level of learning" to a degree worth mentioning.

Furthermore, it promotes a very pessimistic and depreciative perception of students as persons. They are only inclined to learning if each and every step of the learning process is planned, supervised and continuously graded.

I think - and psychology tells us (Tolman [17], Schneider/Schmalt [14], Herber [12], Weiner [18]) - that the opposite is true. It is not possible to teach people directly. Human beings decide for themselves if and what they want to learn. Persons like teachers can only facilitate this process - which does not mean that their influence would be negligible. We can provide a setting and offer helpful hints which raise the probability that successful learning processes will be taking place.

The basic concept of In-Classroom Differentiation is simple. Students are presented a pool of possible tasks (learning activities), ranging from very easy examples to more difficult challenges. Sometimes it is even possible to address a thematic complex in two or more different ways.

Roughly, examples can be separated into a group F of fundamental learning activities and a group A of additional learning activities, which are more difficult and/or more complex and require an above-average performance.

A set of tasks should be defined as the "learning criterion", meaning the very basic foundations about a topic each student should make sure to know about - or otherwise, to seek help immediately if he or she has problems with this part.

Furthermore, an "explorative path" of examples can be proposed (and should be proposed, especially if the concept is new to students), which can help students to structure their work and assure them they are on the right way. This learning path should start with very easy questions, making sure each student can experience success and gets immediate, positive feedback. Consequently, more demanding examples may be proposed, but should always be followed by one or more easy ones in order to reduce the risk of frustration. Each path should end with some easy (criterion) questions in order to guarantee final success. This complies with well established psychological theories of learning and motivation, like Atkinson's concept of a " middle degree of activation".

Students can always choose for themselves which task they want to address next - if they want the thrill out of more demanding tasks (where you don't know the outcome in advance), or whether they prefer more encouragement through easier examples.

This concept is well documented and was empirically examined and found to work well in practice (Herber/Vasarhelyi [9], Herber/Vasarhelyi [10]). Yet it has not been applied specifically to the teaching of Computer Science so far.

Obviously, this approach relies strongly on the intrinsic motivation of students. Apart from acknowledging that such a motivation exists (that students accept the notion of schools as places where they can and should learn something), many elements of this theory are designed to encourage such intrinsic motivation.

Learning activities should have ties to a person's previous experiences, the existent knowledge base, the everyday life he or she lives etc. - in other words: learning activities should have some "personal importance" or some "emotional meaning". We tend to forget things, no matter how easy they may be, if we do not assign them any emotional meaning. If students can choose questions with different thematic priorities, we increase the chance that some of them will be meaningful to students' minds.

Also, people who are motivated by their individual performance and successes can be actually discouraged if they are constantly told what to do when and in which way. So we may assume that in some conventional settings of school learning, those students who would be willing to learn without any further incentive loose this inclination, whereas other students are not really motivated by a monotone and strict learning plan.

2.2 On the Importance of Playing for Learning Activities

Why do children play? Probably, that's a question typical for scientists; many other people would simply state, "Well, they just do it." According to my opinion, questioning what looks trivial or self-evident at first glance is a promising starting point for more detailed, new and revealing insights.

Psychology would teach us that children play in order to prepare for their later life. Through playing, they can gain and try out skills and abilities which would be way too dangerous to apply directly in practice. Playing is interpreted as a training field for skills and techniques that prove essential to the adult (Gould/Gould [5], Gonzalez/Moll/Amanti [4], Spitzer [16]).

That's doubtlessly true - and it also sounds sensible - but it is only part of the truth. It does not really explain why children play, as it focuses on the evolutionary aspect - the species as an abstract entity has an advantage from the playing of children. But that's not what motivates children to play.

They simply play because it is fun. In that sense, playing is a massive expression of intrinsic motivation - and in turn the conclusive proof for its existence.

There are many hints that learning through playing encourages high learning success. Most species loose their inclination to play once they grow older - humans don't. That's one main reason why humans can easily learn new things throughout their entire lifetime.

Let's summarize at this point: playing teaches and trains new skills and techniques in a highly efficient way – however, we do not play because we urgently want to learn something, but because it is fun.

Of course, the way we play changes over time - and many games we play happen entirely in our fantasy, they are plays of our minds. But the principle remains the same.

We should import this powerful learning tool (playing) into our classrooms. I sometimes get the impression that every joke, every smile inside a school is somehow misplaced, not to say subversive. Learning - according to the historical significance of the topics and the gravity of life in general - has to take place in a serious and decent atmosphere.

I would suggest, learning should take place in an environment that promotes learning successes in every possible way. And so we ought to appreciate it whenever children have fun in lessons and can experience a playful encounter with new topics - it is very likely that they will make significant learning progresses this way.

2.3 The Curiosity Hypotheses

Much research was done on intrinsic motivation - much of it under the label of curiosity behavior; a term that is largely synonymous to intrinsic motivation as it describes a behavior that occurs without an obvious need to trigger it nor will an evident benefit to hope for. It is performed for the sheer fun of it.

Curiosity - the need to explore unknown things and new environments - is a behavior as ubiquitous and elementary as eating and drinking. And it is clear that curiosity teaches individuals new things and widens theirs view of the world (Schneider/Schmalt [14]).

You may guess what comes next - we should welcome curiosity behavior of students as it is likely to support their learning efforts. And curiosity is something we can expect from every student, because it is a general characteristic of individuals (not only humans).

But curiosity can only express itself if there are sufficient opportunities - meaning a large enough number of learning activities students are interested in. As we cannot assume that all students are interested in the same question at the same time, this demands measures of In-Classroom Differentiation - in the sense described above.

2.4 Fundamental Ideas – Knowledge vs. Information

According to Bruner 1974, fundamental ideas can help to structure the abundance of topics that might be implied by terms like "mathematics", "computer science" and the like (Schubert/Schwill [15], Fuchs [3]).

We will only state here that recursion constitutes a fundamental idea in computer science. I think this is a reasonable fact for anybody familiar with the field.

If learning activities are centered around fundamental ideas, this is also a good precondition for knowledge being generated rather than simplistic information. We are often told that we live in a "knowledge society" nowadays, and this self-description of our society carries along lots of promises and misleading concepts, with terms often ill-defined that show an indistinctive use. In particular, the terms "information" and "knowledge" are often used synonymously. In opposition to this trend, I think a clear distinction is necessary.

"Information" - the way I see it - stands simply for chunks of facts. They are at most loosely interlinked, very mobile, general, ubiquitous, show a considerable loss of value over time, are no scarce resource and are easily accessible. Think of the Internet, and everybody would subscribe to the fact that we live in an "Information Society" today. Tools like the Internet confront us with an unstructured plenty of information.

Knowledge, on the contrary, is the ability to work with information, to make use of them and to derive benefits from them. Knowledge is generated "out of the right questions", it aims at structuring a flood of information. Knowledge provides a system of coordinates to navigate the unstructured plenty of information. Knowledge is a scarce resource, but contrary to information, it usually does not loose its value over time.

Learning tasks in the sense of In-Classroom Differentiation - with their emphasis on optimal activation, playful learning and encouraging curiosity - provide an excellent basis for creating knowledge.

3 A Concrete Example for a Learning Sequence

We finally present a detailed concept for a learning sequence that puts our theoretical considerations and demands into practice. However, this plan should be considered a suggestion which is still open to changes in order to satisfy specific needs or requirements. But it should do a good job in giving a lively impression on what this may look like in reality.

3.1 Steps of the Learning Sequence

The steps as they are presented here should be seen as an "explorative path" as described above. Order and other details might be adapted, as well as there may be included other activities students think of during the lessons.

- Information about the upcoming topics and activities (from the teacher). This information is a crucial point of the concept. It gives students an overview about what they can expect and may also help them to organize their work. It is easier to learn something if one knows what to learn about, because one can focus the attention on this aspect. It is also important for assigning value and meaning to learning activities. Students should be assured at this point that they are not just supposed to play around, but while they are encouraged to have fun with their activities, they are about to learn some important and outstanding concepts. This information part should not exceed some 5-10 minutes - students should get a first impression, but do not need to understand details at this point.
- Presentation of the problem "The Towers of Hanoi". We have a tower of a given number of disks with different diameters. The disks are stapled one on top of the other such that the diameters continuously decrease from bottom to top. Furthermore, there are three possible construction sites. The task is to move the tower from site 1 to site 2, obeying two rules: first, always move only one disk at a time, and second, when placing one disk on top of another make sure that diameters always decrease from bottom to top. The game is illustrated by a set of small wooden (or other material) disks which serve as a realistic model.
- Try for solutions of the problem using the haptic disk model. The more disks one uses, the more challenging the task becomes. The solutions should be documented in an informal way such that they are replicable by the students. Students may choose whether to work alone or in groups on the problem.
- Some solutions should be documented in a way such that they are reproducable by others. Students can also try to aim at a general solution principle that works for any given number of stones.
- One of the solutions found before (remember that it is almost sure that everybody will find a solution for at least two disks!) should be modified as follows:
  1. Place one additional disk on bottom of the starting tower.
  2. Move the tower from site 1 to site 3, using the solution found before.
  3. Move the last disk (from the bottom) from site 1 to site 2.
  4. Move the tower from site 3 to site 2, using the solution found before.
  5. Look what happened.
     It's easy to discover: once we know how to move n-1 disks from one site to another, it is very simple to move n disks from one site to another.
- A prototype-solution is presented. Such a solution can be derived by students in individual ways, or they might refer to a given suggestion provided by the teacher. Being able to demonstrate such a prototype solution using the disk model could be one criterion task of the learning sequence.
- Similar problems are proposed or invented by students themselves (n!, Binomial Coefficient, Fibonacci Numbers, Growth Functions, Interest Calculations etc. - depending on the previous knowledge of students). Students should document/explain

in some informal way how the concept of recursion is applied to the new problems. In other words: how the idea is transferred from the tower-game to similar fields.
- One (or more) of the previous problems is formalized such that it can be modeled as a computer program. This implies the definition of variables, the introduction of formal equations, a formal way to describe how disks are moved from one site to another etc. Once again, some prototype solutions for specific problems can be provided.
- Develop an algorithm that solves one of the problems given.
- Implement the algorithm.
- Test the outcome of the program by comparing results to previously found solutions.

During all these activities, students may help each other when they face difficulties or ask the teacher for assistance. The teacher acts as a facilitator of the learning process (which assigns an important function to the role of the teacher!), but it is not necessary that he initiates or supervises every single step.

Also consider the fact that it is guaranteed that every student achieves the most important, fundamental learning goals (e.g. prototype solutions). On top of that, individual priorities can be built.

For grading purposes (a reality no learning paper should ignore) students can be asked to present their solutions of previously defined criterion tasks. It is also possible to require students to solve examples similar to those criterion tasks on their own; this can take on the form of a very "traditional" test. The important thing here is that such grading measures must not interfere with the learning process itself, but constitute a clearly separate (though associated) activity.

3.2 Links Between Theory and Practice

I would like to pick out some points which illustrate how theoretical considerations translate into practical actions.
- The model disks introduce a playful element into the learning sequence.
- The game might appeal to students' curiosity ("I want to know how that works!").
- Students are aware that they learn about a powerful and complex concept, which can provide a meaning for the activities extending beyond the walls of the classroom.
- All proposed learning activities follow the guidelines of In-Classroom Differentiation; the sequence itself is an example for an explorative path.
- Students can choose tasks that go along with their interests and abilities and thus encourage their motivation and promote experiences of success.
- Once the learning sequence is completed, students are likely to have developed knowledge about the concept of recursion rather than having assembled some isolated chunks of information. Otherwise, they would not have been able to work on problems this way.
- Different levels of abstraction are integrated in the learning sequence: disks as a haptic model belong to the descriptive-concrete level; an informal (verbal) description of solution processes constitutes a symbolic representation, and a computer program that calculates a solution is itself a prototype of a formal-abstract representation of a problem.

4 Conclusion

We have discussed some theoretical requirements for a sustainable learning process. We have examined several theories which might help in trying to establish such learning processes. As a consequence, we arrived at the concept of In-Classroom Differentiation.

We've also put this theory into practice, and shown how it might work. Let us finally repeat that learning sequences like the one presented here address both aspects: they encourage motivation among the students and welcome joy and fun during the learning process, but they also put great emphasis on high-raking, sustainable learning successes.

Remark

One might argue that it is quite a lot of work for a teacher to prepare such a learning sequence. Thus, it would be a great thing to develop learning materials for this type of learning processes which are easily available for teachers. They are not more complicated or more expensive than other learning materials. So I'm pretty confident that they will be available once the demand is there. This article intends to create demand...

References

1. Bruner, J.S.: Entwurf einer Unterrichtstheorie. Cornelsen Verlag, Berlin (1974)
2. Fuchs, K., Landerer, C.: Das mühsame Ringen um ein Kompetenzmodell. CD Austria 3/2005 (Folge), pp. 11–14 (2005)
3. Fuchs, K.: Schulinformatik, quo vadis? CD Austria 10/2003, pp. 18–19 (2003)
4. Gonzalez, N., Moll, L.C., Amanti, C.: Funds of Knowledge. Lawrence Erlbaum Associates, Mawhaw (2005)
5. Gould, J.L., Gould, C.G.: Bewusstsein bei Tieren. Spektrum Akademischer Verlag, Heidelberg (1997)
6. Grell, J., Grell, M.: Unterrichtsrezepte. Beltz, Weinheim (1999)
7. Grell, J.: Techniken des Lehrerverhaltens. Beltz, Weinheim (2001)
8. Haider, G., Reiter, C. (eds.): PISA 2003 – Ergebnisse im Überblick. Leykam, Graz (2004)
9. Herber, H.J., Vasarhelyi, E.: Das Unterrichtsmodell, Innere Differenzierung einschließlich Analogiebildung. Salzburger Beiträge zur Erziehungswissenschaft, Jg. 6 Nr. 2, pp. 5–20 (2002)
10. Herber, H.J., Vasarhelyi, E.: Kompetenzstreben und Kompetenzerwerb. Salzburger Beiträge zur Erziehungswissenschaft, Jg. 8 Nr. 2, pp. 5–34 (2004)
11. Herber, H.J.: Innere Differenzierung im Unterricht. Kohlhammer, Stuttgart (1997)
12. Herber, H.J.: Motivationspsychologie: eine Einführung. Kohlhammer, Stuttgart (1976)
13. Hubwieser, P.: Didaktik der Informatik. Grundlagen, Konzepte, Beispiele. 2. Springer, München (2003)
14. Schneider, K., Schmalt, H.-D.: Motivation. Kohlhammer, Stuttgart (1981)
15. Schubert, S., Schwill, A.: Didaktik der Informatik. Spektrum Akademischer Verlag, Heidelberg (2004)
16. Spitzer, M.: Geist im Netz. Spektrum Akademischer Verlag, Heidelberg (1996)
17. Tolman, E.C.: Ein kognitives Motivationsmodell. In: Thomae, H. (ed.) Die Motivation menschlichen Handelns, pp. 448–462. Kiepenheuer & Witsch, Köln (1966)
18. Weiner, B.: Motivationspsychologie. Beltz Psychologie Verlags Union, Weinheim (1994)

Analysis of Learning Objectives in Object Oriented Programming

Peter Hubwieser

Technische Universität München
Fakultät für Informatik
Boltzmannstr. 3, 85748 Garching
Peter.Hubwieser@in.tum.de

Abstract. The paper presents an analysis of the learning objectives that have to be achieved in order to learn Object Oriented Programming. By using the prerequisite relation between these objectives we develop a sequence of concepts for a textbook. The article is closed by some considerations concerning the electronic management of learning objectives using ontologies.

1 Introduction

As already pointed out in [4] and [6] it seems to be an extraordinary challenge to teach Object Oriented Programming (shortened OOP) in a beginners course. On the occasion of designing the new mandatory subject "Informatics" for Bavarian secondary schools (as described also in [4] and [6]) we had to master exactly this challenge. The most difficult task was to write a suitable textbook [7], because we had to arrange all concepts of the curriculum in a sequence that could be followed by the practically teaching persons in their everyday teaching lessons. This task was made even more challenging by the guidelines we had set up with the preceding two textbooks of this series [3, 5]: the book should consist of relatively small lessons that do not contain more than 2-3 pages of information presentation, followed by at least two pages of interesting exercises that are connected with the everyday experience of the students. This demanded to break down the whole curriculum into many learning objectives, which turned out to be heavily interconnected in many respects. It also turned out that the basic subject areas "Algorithms", "State Modelling", "Object Oriented Modelling" (shortly OOM) and "OOP" are intervowen so strongly that we were forced to apply a spiral approach that covers these areas repeatedly and alternatively.

This paper might be regarded as a continuation of [4] and [6], where I described the course of lessons of our newly designed mandatory subject on informatics in Bavaria, in terms of content focussing on the state aspect of object oriented programming.

In this paper I want to concentrate my explanations on the logical and didactical interconnections of the subject areas of Algorithms, state modelling, OOM and OOP. I will show that these interconnections lead to circular dependencies in certain aspects and propose a possible teaching sequence in order to resolve these dependencies. The paper shall not only present a particular learning approach for OOP but also suggest a methodology to elaborate such new learning approaches for difficult, complex or complicated subject areas.

2 Learning Objectives

In order to describe the learning process that was suggested by our new curriculum we used the concept of learning objectives. Concerning the generality of these objectives we distinguish (following [1]):

- *global* objectives: "Complex, multifaced learning outcomes that require substantial time and instruction to accomplish";
- *educational* objectives: derived from global objectives by breaking "them down into a more focused, delimited form";
- *instructional* objectives, with the purpose "to focus teaching and testing on narrow, day-to-day slices of learning in fairly specific content areas".

The following considerations will be restricted to the third type (instructional objectives). While the global objectives of our course of lessons are mostly fixed by legal prescriptions (like the Bavarian Law of Education), we have described some of our educational objectives in [6].

Also following [1] we regard learning objectives as a combination of a certain *type of knowledge* and an *observable behavior* (called cognitive process) concerning this type of knowledge, forming the two dimensions of their revision of Bloom's taxonomy:

Knowledge dimension, partitioned into
    A. *factual*,
    B. *conceptual*,
    C. *procedural* and
    D. *metacognitive* knowledge,
Cognitive process dimension, partitioned into the behavior types
    1. *remember*,
    2. *understand*,
    3. *apply*,
    4. *analyze*,
    5. *evaluate* and
    6. *create*.

In [6] I have already pointed out why it is so difficult for students to understand even simple OO-programs: firstly because the learning objectives easily reach the most difficult category (D6) of the taxonomy (*creating meta-cognitive knowledge* e.g. by learning different programming strategies) in this taxonomy. Secondly because there is a big number of objectives that has to be reached before the first program can be really understood.

Of course I am aware of the fact that modern constructivistic learning and teaching approaches do not worship the concept of observable learning objectives very much. One of the reasons might be found in the suspicion that by elaborating a sequence of such objectives the teachers might be tempted to restrict the learning process of their students exactly on this sequence (see [2]). As we have pointed out in many publications (eg. [6]), we definitely encourage our informatics teachers to follow constructivistic approaches, because in our opinion these are well suited to the demands of the subject of informatics in secondary schools. Therefore, we do not propose to partition every teaching lesson by a sequence of learning objectives. However we suppose that under certain specific circumstances learning objectives are very useful, e.g. in order to:

- identify (one or more) possible learning paths trough a specific subject area that is very complicated, very broad or very difficult,
- arrange a set of concepts sequentially forced by certain circumstances, e.g. by the urge of writing a textbook (as in our case),
- design an examination which has to take into consideration which learning progress the students have made up to its point of time,
- evaluate learning processes in detail,
- compare two similar courses of lessons, e.g. similar modules of Bachelor degrees from different universities,
- design an E-Learning system, particularly to define the possible sequences of learning objects that will be offered to the user,
- describe the context of usage of any teaching material (media, examples of lessons, examinations etc.).

Hence, despite all reservations against the usage of learning objectives that arise out of constructivism, apparently there still is a strong need for learning objectives under certain circumstances. Without the usage of learning objectives the didactical research and practice would fall back to mysticism in these cases.

As a compromise for the practicing teacher we propose to elaborate only some few very important learning objectives in order to describe and evaluate processes during longer periods of time, but not to use such objectives to plan the course of a single lesson.

3 Connecting Instructional Objectives

When talking about instructional objectives during the following considerations, I will often list only the pure *concepts* that represent the knowledge part of the objectives, thus apparently belonging to the type *conceptual*. Concerning the *cognitive process* dimension the students mostly will have to achieve at least the stage of the second category *understand*, while later in the course they might have to *apply* the concepts. By listing a pure concept like *class* I want to address the instructional objective "*understand* the *conceptual* knowledge *class*", thus belonging to the category B2 of the taxonomy described above.

Apparently it is not possible to arrange the instructional objectives in any arbitrary order, because some of them have to be achieved before certain others can be reached. For example one has to *understand* the concept of *object* (O1) before one is able to *understand* the concept of *class* (O2). This connection can be described by a *prerequisite relation* on the set of learning objectives, in this case between O1 and O2: "O1 *is prerequisite of* O2", meaning that "O1 has to be achieved before O2" (see [8]). More precise considerations show that there are (at least) two different types of prerequisite relations:

1. "Hard" prerequisite (P1) forced by a substantial or logical dependency: concept2 contained in objective O2 *is based on* concept1 contained in objective O1. This means that it is not possible to understand concept2 without having understood concept1.
2. "Soft" prerequisite (P2) suggested by didactical deliberation: It is necessary to reach objective O1 in order to apply teaching or working methods that support didactical principles. Therefore it is not *necessary* to reach O1 before objective O2, but it is *advisable* in order to ease or to improve the learning process towards O2.

Let us assume that our overall educational objective is "creating object oriented programs that implement given algorithms". In the first step we search instructional objectives out of OOP that necessarily have to be (at least) understood in order to achieve this and try to arrange them in a possible learning sequence. In the second step we detect that there are some objectives out of other subject areas ("Algorithms", "state modelling" and "OOM") that are connected with some of the objectives out of OOP by prerequisite relations P1 respectively P2. Fig. 1 shows the simplified result of these considerations.

Most of the relations of type P2 shown in Fig. 1 result from the desire of implementing and simulating theoretical concepts by programs as soon as possible.

4 Resolving Circular Dependencies

If we want to respect not only the hard prerequisite of type P1 but also the soft type P2, we often get circular dependencies. Fortunately there are some strategies to resolve these.

Short cycles formed by one single connection of type P1 and an opposite one of type P2 can be solved by arranging the connected objectives very close together in a single lesson, starting with the predecessor objective regarding P1. By this way the second objective didactically supports the achieved one first.

Longer cycles over more than two objectives (e.g. O1, O2, O3,..) might be solved by applying a spiral teaching approach: the same concept (contained e.g. in O1) is treated repeatedly at different levels. The first level is determined by a propaedeutic approach, where the students only get a rough idea of the concept, knowing some applications but not really understanding it. Nevertheless O1 might serve already at this stage as precondition for O2 as demanded by P1 or P2. At the one or more following teaching levels the students might achieve deeper understanding of the concept and finally will be enabled to apply it on their own.

In our exemplary OOP course we might teach the concept of the assignment statement at a first propaedeutic level by explaining its pure effect on the value of the assigned attribute, followed later by teaching its full state semantics.

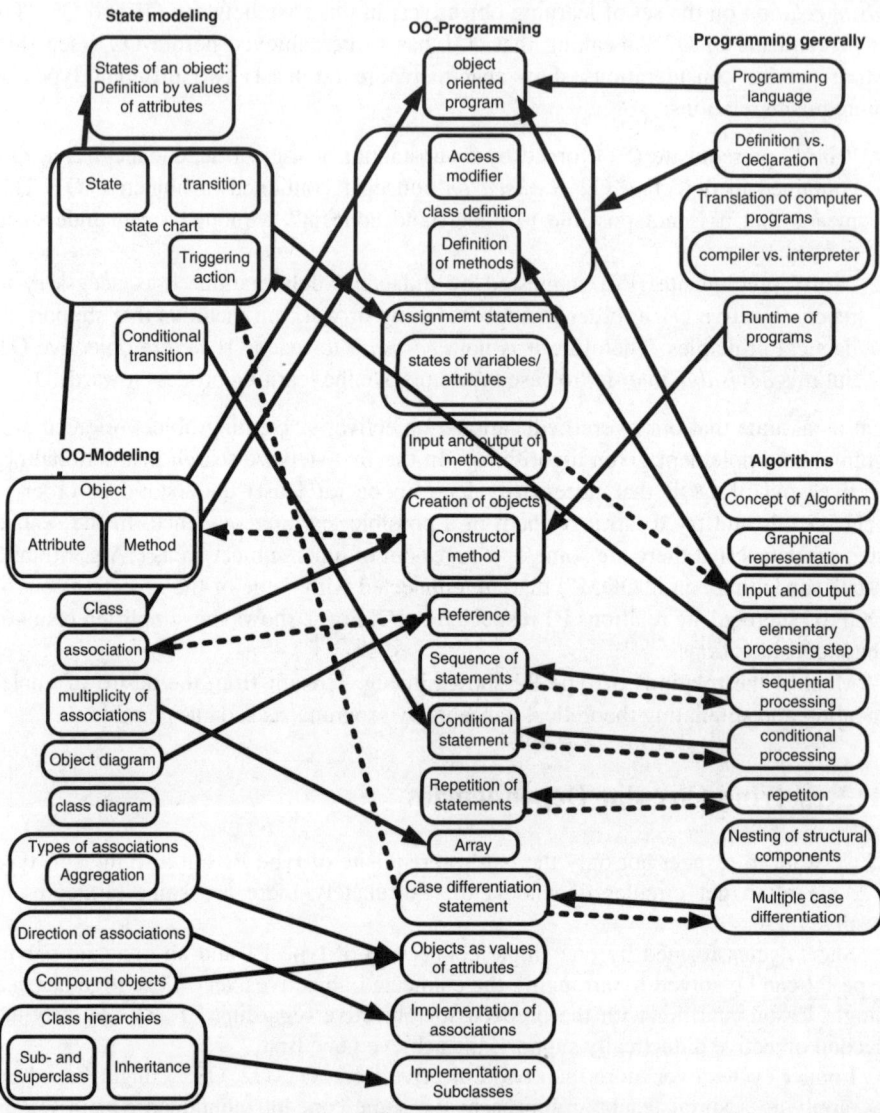

Fig. 1. Prerequisite relations P1 (unbroken arrows) and P2 (dotted arrows) on the learning objectives of OOP

All in all we came to the following sequence of concepts (restricted to the names of the concepts), which simultaneously forms the list of contents of our textbook [7].

Analysis of Learning Objectives in Object Oriented Programming 147

Table 1. List of contents of our textbook as a result of the learning process analysis

Chapter	Covered concepts
I Objects and States	
1 Objects and Classes	*repetition:* object, class, attribute, method, class card, object card,
2 Algorithms and Methods	algorithm
3 Structure of Algorithms	graphical representation of algorithms structural components of algorithms: sequence, conditional statement, repetition, nesting components input and output of algorithms
4 States of Objects	state, transition, state diagram, real and program objects
5 Diagrams and Associations	object diagram, association, class diagram, multiplicity of associations
II Algorithms and Programs	
1 Definition of Classes	programming language, object oriented program class definition: definition and declaration, signature of methods, access modifier attribute declaration, definition of methods
2 Assignment of Values	assignment statement, ring exchange, assignment in constructor methods encapsulation equality
3 Communication with Methods	input, output, side effects, local and global variables/attributes
4 Creation and Removal of Objects	creating objects at runtime constructor method reference removal of objects
5 Implementation of Algorithms	structure elements in programming languages: sequence, conditional statement, repetition
6 Arrays	index, array
III State Modelling	
1 Finite Automatons	triggered action, finite automaton, state chart implementation of automatons
2 Multiple Case Differentiation	case differentiation in programming languages case differentiation in state charts
3 Conditional Transitions	conditional transition, complete state modelling states of variables, states of models implementation of conditional transitions
4 States of Programs	translation of computer programs: compiler vs. interpreter, execution of programs course of events of a program

Table 1. (*continued*)

IV Interaction	
1 Aggregation and References	compound objects: creation of objects as values of attributes
2 Working with References	identity and equality multiple referencing access to objects of foreign classes
3 Communication between Objects	types of associations, multiplicity, direction implementation of associations: local or global attribute, association class
4 Sequence Charts	calling of methods, sequence charts
V Generalization	
1 Specialization	sub- and superclass, specialization, inheritance implementation of specialization overriding of methods
2 Generalization	generalization, class hierarchies
3 Polymorphism	polymorphism calling methods of foreign classes abstract classes

5 Representation of Didactical Knowledge

As I pointed out above in section 2, there are many cases in which a learning objective analysis is helpful or even necessary. Currently we are working intensively on elaborating this methodology mainly for the following application areas:

- evaluation of Informatics courses at secondary schools and university level (see [9],
- description of education modules (e.g. out of courses of study that lead to Bachelor degrees) by learning objectives,
- description of learning objects in E-Learning systems by metadata that support reuse and flexible learning paths, chosen as far as possible by the learner himself,
- design of a Learning Content Management System (LCMS) that is able to manage learning and teaching media, tools and material of any kind.

Unfortunately in most cases it is not easy to manage the instructional objectives once they are found, mainly out of two reasons:

- there are huge numbers of objectives and/or,
- there are many relations between these objectives.

In fact we found that often it is almost impossible to manage the elaborated objective structures without electronic support. For that purpose we adapted some concepts of the Semantic Web research, particularly the concept of ontology. Our vision is to construct a LCMS that is based on a editable ontology, which means that the classes and property types defined by the ontology might be changed without reprogramming the LCMS. As already published by Alexander Staller (a former member of my team, see [8]), we used the Web Ontology Language OWL and tried to implement a first, very simple experimental learning system in 2006, which was elaborated within a student's thesis. This attempt showed that all necessary software tools and programming languages already existed at that time, but they were still not in a development stage that made them really useful in practice. Nevertheless we produced some really helpful ideas to solve some of the major obstacles, which were partly already published in [8]:

1. The metadata of learning objects have to contain information about prerequisite relation to other learning objects. For this purpose every learning object should be described by at least one instructional objective that is supported by this object. Thus this way the possible sequences of learning objects are determined by the prerequisite relations between the associated learning objectives.
2. In order to connect pure subject domain knowledge with additional didactical information about the learning process, we found that the subject domain knowledge can be represented by the first three categories (*factual, conceptual* and *procedural*) of the knowledge dimension following Anderson and Krathwohl [1]. In this way we should be able to "plug in" any ontology that describes subject domain knowledge in our ontology for learning objectives.
3. In most cases concepts are represented by classes. This seems to be suitable at the first glance, because concepts are abstractions of individuals (e.g. the statement x := 5 is abstracted to the assignment concept) and because the subconcept relation ("is_a") might easily be defined by a subset relation: A is subconcept of B if all individuals of A are individuals of B, too. On the other hand there are many concepts that have values of some attributes, e.g. the assignment concept might be described by an attribute "typically used in the programming style" with the value "imperative". This dilemma could be solved by treating concepts simultaneously as classes and as individuals. From a pure technical point of view with every new concept C there is generated a new class C as well as a new individual ConceptC (of the class "Concept").
4. A concept is characterized by a definition. But what to do if there are concurring, inconsistent definitions by different authors (e.g. A1, A2) for a certain concept? The solution is to create a separated subject domain ontology for every of the concurring publications. Then the two definitions might be accessed by A1.concept1 or A2.concept1, respectively. The user could decide which of the two definitions he wants to follow at every time he needs the concept simply by including one or more of these ontologies into his system.

6 Conclusion and Further Work

As these considerations showed, the analysis of learning objectives might still be very helpful in certain cases. We used this technique to design a sequence of concepts for a new textbook that covers OOM and OOP, using the prerequisite relations between instructional objectives.

Moreover we are working towards an evaluation project that is based on learning objective analysis. It will investigate the learning processes within our newly designed subject of informatics at some crucial points. At the last phase of this project we plan to evaluate the new subject in a representative scale.

Concerning the development of software systems we aim to construct an ontology based LCMS that allows the teachers of the new subject of informatics to exchange teaching materials of any kind in order to share their experiences.

The most crucial challenge in all these research plans is the ability to manage the huge number and complex structure of learning objectives by electronic means. This is in the current focus of our research efforts.

References

1. Anderson, L.W., Krathwohl, D.R. (eds.): A Taxonomy for Learning, Teaching, and Assessing: A Revision of Bloom's Taxonomy of Educational Objectives. Longman, New York (2001)
2. Duffy, T.M., Jonassen, D.H. (eds.): Constructivism and the Technology of Instruction: A Conversation. Lawrence Erlbaum, Hillsdale (1992)
3. Frey, E., Hubwieser, P., Winhard, F.: Informatik 1. Objekte, Strukturen, Algorithmen. Klett, Stuttgart (2004)
4. Hubwieser, P.: Functions, Objects and States - Teaching Informatics in Secondary Schools (ISSEP 2006, Vilnius, Litauen). In: Mittermeir, R.T. (ed.) ISSEP 2006. LNCS, vol. 4226, pp. 104–116. Springer, Heidelberg (2006)
5. Hubwieser, P., Schneider, M., Spohrer, M., Voß, S.: Informatik 2. Tabellenkalkulationssysteme, Datenbanken. Klett, Stuttgart (2007)
6. Hubwieser, P.: A smooth way towards object oriented programming in secondary schools. In: Benzie, D., Iding, M. (eds.) Informatics, Mathematics and ICT: a 'golden triangle'. IFIP WG 3.1 & 3.5 Working Conference CD proceedings, IFIP & College of Computer and Information Science Northeastern University Boston, Massachusetts, USA (2007)
7. Hubwieser, P., Steinert, M., Spohrer, M., Voß, S.: Informatik 3. ALgorithmen, Objektorientierte Programmierung, Zustandsmodellierung. Klett, Stuttgart (to appear, 2008)
8. Staller, A.: Merging domain knowledge and task analysis in an ontology. In: Méndez-Vilas, A., Solano Martín, A., Mesa González, J.A., Mesa González, J. (eds.) Current Developments in Technology-Assisted Education, Badajoz, Spain. Technological Science Education, Collaborative Learning, Knowledge Management. FORMATEX, vol. II, pp. 1585–1589 (2006)
9. Steinert, M.: Functional modelling and the graph of learning objectives. In: Benzie, D., Iding, M. (eds.) Informatics, Mathematics and ICT: a 'golden triangle'. IFIP WG 3.1 & 3.5 Working Conference CD proceedings, IFIP & College of Computer and Information Science Northeastern University Boston, Massachusetts, USA (2007)

To Have or to Be? Possessing Data Versus Being in a State – Two Different Intuitive Concepts Used in Informatics

Michael Weigend

Institut für Didaktik der Mathematik und der Informatik
Westfälische Wilhelms-Universität Münster
Fliednerstraße 21, 48149 Münster, Germany
michael.weigend@uni-muenster.de

Abstract. In computer programming it is sometimes helpful to start with the definition of a state transition diagram (finite state automaton), which describes on a rather abstract level but in an intuitive way how the system is supposed to react to events in certain situations. The reaction is dependent on the internal state of the running program. The concept of being in a state differs fundamentally from the concept of data storage or data possession usually associated to variables or object attributes. Thus there are certain cognitive difficulties to overcome, when creating a program on the basis of a state transition diagram.

1 To Have or to Be?

Fischbein [4] and diSessa [2,3] assume the existence of intuitions or intuitive models – pieces of subjectively certain knowledge about the world, which are based upon experience in everyday live. People use intuitive models, when they try to understand, explain or create computer programs [13]. Two intuitions, which are relevant in the field of informatics, are the concepts of having something and being in a state.

In many cases people think of variables as containers for data. Using this intuition a statement like x = 1000 is interpreted as "The variable x gets the value 1000" or "1000 is stored in the variable x". These and other phrases like "data input" or "data transport" assume that data are quasi-material entities that can be moved and stored in containers.

By contrast, a state is an immaterial concept. It is a meaningful Gestalt associated to some activity and a few other states, which can directly be reached. To *be* sick is something different than to *have* a body temperature of 39°C and headache. When you are sick, you are supposed not to work, but stay at home, consult the doctor and take some medication. Typical connected states are "healthy" or "dead". States are usually identified by significant names. A process can be in states like "sleeping" or "active". But for the state of a running program after the execution of an assignment like x = 1234 there exists no specific word.

In his last major work Erich Fromm [5] uses the antithetical concepts "to have" and "to be" to discuss two fundamental human orientations – so called modes of existence.

The having mode, which predominates in modern societies, roots in the biological urge for survival. Humans are predisposed to collect and possess things. On the other hand human nature includes the desire to *be* a genuine subject – regardless of property –, expressed in sharing, giving and cooperating with others.

2 Finite State Automata and Modelling

In theoretical computer science finite state automata are used to define a formal language, which is considered as a set of words over an alphabet of characters. The language L(A) of an automaton A is defined as the set of all the strings (sequences of terminal symbols), which are accepted by A. An automaton is said to accept a string, if and only if processing a sequence of symbols leads from the initial state to a final state. Extended definitions include transducers, which are finite state automatons that yield output which is dependent on the present state (Moore automaton) or the input and the present state (Mealy automaton). In the educational programming system Kara [1] the state transition concept is applied to define the activity of a virtual beetle moving and interacting with its environment on the screen.

Finite state automata can be used to describe the behaviour of computer programs or individual objects within an object oriented system. In German informatics didactics Hubwieser [8] has coined the term "state-oriented modelling" for software development based upon an analysis of state transitions.

Finite state automata are visualized by state transition diagrams. They consist of circles representing states and arrows representing state transitions triggered by events (called input) that are described by annotations. In a Mealy automaton a possible activity triggered by the input is annotated behind the input separated by a slash. The basic idea of state transition diagrams is to represent a change of state by a motion from one place to another. There exist games, in which a player's state is indicated by a figure standing on a certain place. The concept of motion seems to be intuitive for human beings, possibly because we are mobile creatures and a good understanding of space and motion has been an evolutionary advantage. In arithmetic teaching the concept of "motion along a line" is commonly deployed as a "grounding metaphor" [9]. For instance the addition of a (positive) number is represented by moving to the right for a certain number of steps while subtraction is moving to the left.

The use of the state concept sometimes helps to model relevant aspects of a complex problem to make it tractable. It can be considered as a facet of this "universally applicable skill", Jeanette Wing calls "computational thinking" [14].

2.1 The Vending Machine – A Bad Example for a Finite State Automaton?

Textbooks in the field of theoretical computer science sometimes use a model of a vending machine to illustrate the syntax of state transition diagrams. Figure 1 shows on the left hand side a deterministic automaton, which is in some respect a minimal model of a vending machine. It sells two different drinks (not more) and accepts two different coins (not more). Although it is a highly reduced model, it is quite complicated and not intuitive. It does not capture the "idea" of a vending machine. Note that most of the states represent the chosen drink and the coins, which already have been inserted into the machine. They are encodings of tuples (*drink, paid money*) and therefore correspond to the concept of having something and not of being in a state. There is no simple holistic state description for s_2 which might express a fundamental difference to state s_4.

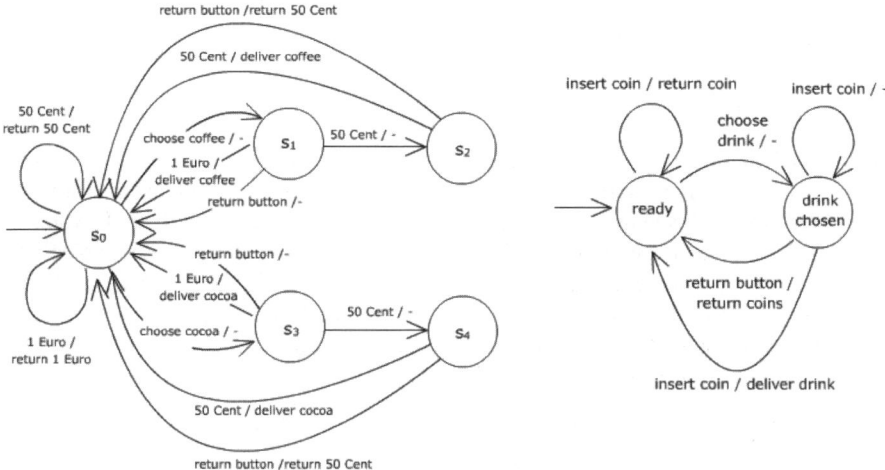

Fig. 1. Deterministic and non-deterministic finite state automata modelling a vending machine

The automaton on the right sight of Fig. 1 is nondeterministic. It distinguishes only between two states, in which the vending machine behaves fundamentally differently. In the first state called "ready" it does not accept any coins. When the customer has chosen a drink, the automaton switches to the second state. Then it takes coins until the required sum is completed and the drink can be delivered or the customer decides to abort the vending process by pressing the return-button. Obviously this automaton is an incomplete model of a vending machine. It is an abstraction and focuses on the basic idea of the behaviour of the machine. The chosen drink and the money – the "having" aspects – are completely ignored. When writing a program on the basis of this state transition diagram, these aspects have (additionally) to be considered, using variables that contain values, thus applying the notion of data possession instead of being in a state.

3 Intuitive Automata and Software Development

Simple finite state automata, which are intuitive models that focus on (holistic) states which are abstract from data, can be of help during a software development. Since they represent certain knowledge they serve as solid rocks in an ocean of uncertainty with regard to functionality and structure, which is typical at the beginning of a software project. In this section I discuss two classroom projects based on finite state automata. In the first example the design of an abstract state transition diagram is major part of the task and the implementation is quite easy. In the second – more complex – project two automata are given in order to clarify some functionality of the goal system.

3.1 How to Make Your Friend Wash Up the Dishes

Some sociologically inspired models are basically (nondeterministic) finite state automata. The Forming-Storming-Norming-Performing model of group development [12] and the No-Lose conflict resolution method [6] are examples.

The first classroom example focuses on the effect of verbal messages. Imagine two friends, Tom and Jenny. Jenny tries to convince Tom to wash up after lunch. According to communication theory [6, 10] it would be a bad idea to say "You never wash up after lunch!" This is a "You-message", which implies a negative statement about Tom. The natural reaction to this is to become angry and to reject any request for help. It would be cleverer to use just an open request ("Please help me …") or to say something nice first, "I am really happy that you are my friend, Tom" and then add some "I-message" with an implicit request: "I am so tired, I think I am not able to wash up today." In general, the response to a request depends on the mood of the receiver.

A classroom project includes two tasks:

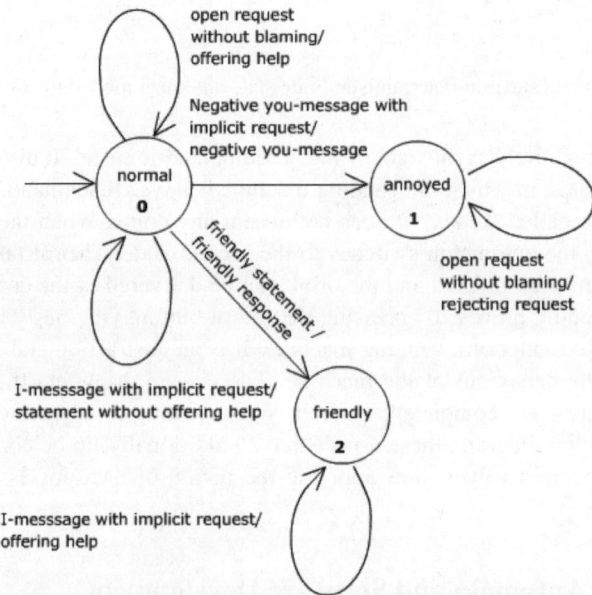

Fig. 2. State transition diagram modelling responses to different kinds of requests

Develop a state transition diagram with three states, which models Tom's reactions to different kinds of requests.

Create a Scratch program to visualize possible dialogs between Tom and Jenny based upon the state transition diagram.

Fig. 2 shows a simple solution for the first task.

Scratch (http://scratch.mit.edu/) is a programming environment that was developed by the Lifelong Kindergarten group at the MIT Media Lab. It supports the very quick creation of interactive visual animations. One major feature is sprites - visual elements on the screen, which have a look (defined by a so called costume) and behaviour. The latter is defined by scripts (event handlers) that the developer can put together using given blocks of program code. It is important to note that the scripts are textual and therefore comparable to conventional programs written in languages like Java or Python.

In the Scratch application corresponding to the automaton the user can determine Jenny's behaviour manually by keystrokes. In contrast, Tom's answers are generated automatically according to the state transition diagram. For instance, when the 1-key is hit, Jenny says, "You NEVER wash up after lunch". Tom answers "You're always blaming me for something!" and switches to state 1 (fig. 3).

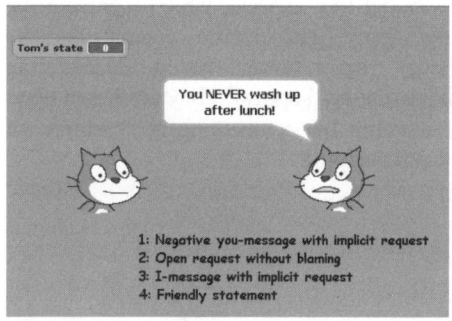 

Fig. 3. Screenshots from a visualization of the automaton in fig. 2

The scripts associated to the sprite visualising Tom are event handlers that are triggered by messages sent by the sprite representing Jenny. In Scratch syntax the script processing Jenny's message would look like this:

```
When I receive negative you-message
set state to 1
switch to costume angry
say "You are always blaming me …" for 2 secs
```

What cognitive activities are required to create a program on the basis of a finite state automaton? The first difficulty is to find a representation for a move from one state to another. The Gestalt of a state as a condition associated with meaning and a potential of activities gets lost in the program. Its coherent knowledge is split and diffuses into separated parts of the formal text. The identification of the current state is represented by a global variable called *state*. This is necessary because all event handlers require a mechanism to test whether the current state is 0, 1 or 2. These tests are allocated to if-statements spread all over the program text. In Scratch the values of variables have to be numbers. The values just serve as IDs and nothing else. The meaning of a state – for example Tom being angry – is reflected by several features. Tom's present mood is visualised by a certain look (angry face), which is implemented in Scratch by the choice of a certain "costume". Note that an atomic action, a move from one state to another, has been replaced by a more complex operation, in this case changing the value of a variable and switching to another costume showing a different facial expression. More problems will be discussed later in the context of a second example.

3.2 Modeling a Hybrid Electrical Vehicle

A hybrid electrical vehicle (HEV) is a car, which has a conventional combustion engine and an electric motor [12]. A battery that is recharged by a generator powers the electric motor. The generator is driven by the movement of the car during deceleration (while using the brake) or by the combustion engine, when it is working. A simple speed control system using a brake and a gas pedal can be defined like this: When the brake pedal is pressed, the car is decelerating until it stands still or the brake is released. When the gas pedal is pressed, the car accelerates. This very concise verbal explanation can be formalized and stated more precisely by two simple and easy to understand automata like in fig. 4. They model two aspects, which represent the basic idea of the whole system: The energy supply (gas, electric or none) and the propulsion (accelerating and consuming energy from a storage system, decelerating and charging the battery and rolling without any energy supply). They are based upon a "being concept". Each state is not just a value but a meaningful condition of existence associated with activity the system can perform.

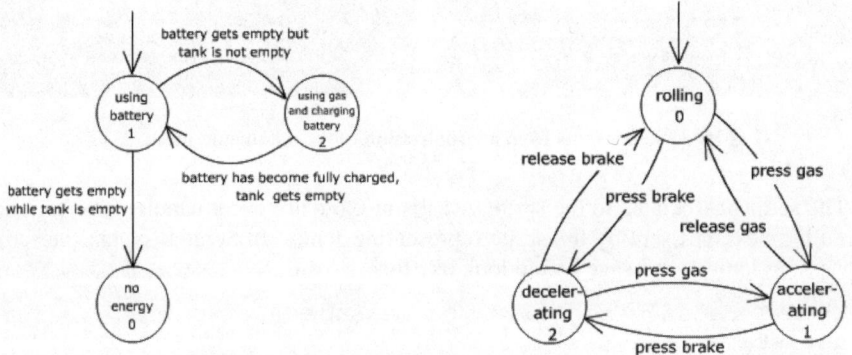

Fig. 4. Two state transition diagrams for the energy control system and the speed control system of a hybrid electrical vehicle

When the propulsion system is in the state of rolling it means that the engine does not require any energy and the speed of the car is slowly decreasing. We have a clear concept about that from every-day life. Rolling is associated with relaxing and using no energy. Imagine sitting on a bicycle just letting it roll. It is relaxing and good when you are quick enough, exhausted and not in a hurry.

These finite state automata can be used as a basis for the development of a visual simulation program showing a hybrid car on the screen that can be controlled by pressing on keys. Fig. 5 shows a screenshot from an implementation with Scratch. When the green flag is clicked, the program starts. The car has got a limited amount of energy (stored in gas and battery), the player drives the car along the road trying to get as far as possible. The present content of the gas tank and the battery, the speed and the distance already covered are displayed on top of the screen. The down-arrow (placed on the left) indicates that the car is decelerating. Since the advantage of hybrid cars is best shown in a stop-and-go traffic, zebra crossings and a traffic light are added. They force the driver to stop, when the light is red. During the deceleration the battery is recharged.

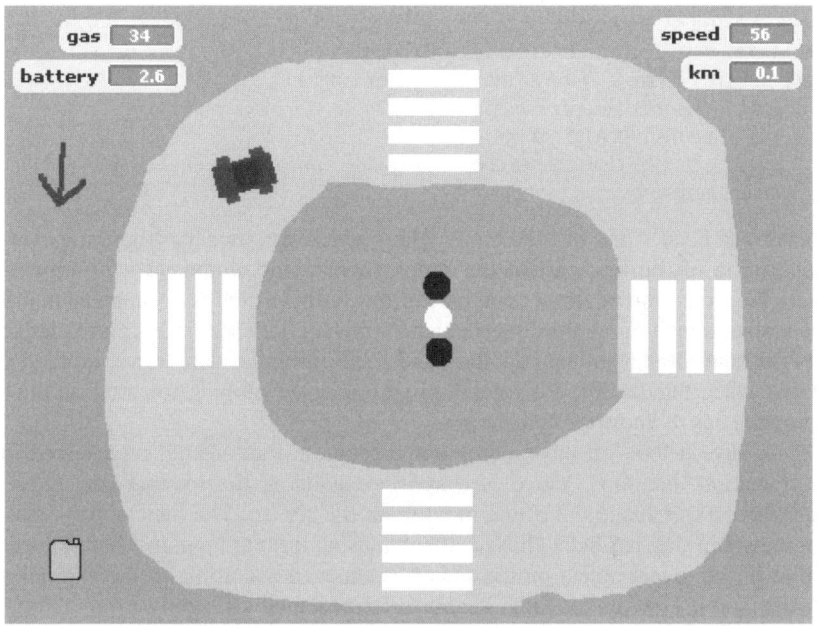

Fig. 5. Screenshot from a Scratch program modeling an HEV

What cognitive activities take place on the way from the (given) automata to the Scratch program? Roughly speaking the task is to transfer a system definition based upon meaningful states to a system definition based upon data possession and data manipulation. Since the state transition diagrams are very abstract – their purpose is to represent an idea on a qualitative level – they do not contain all the information that is needed to implement the simulator. In particular the visualisation of the car moving on the screen is completely omitted in the state transition diagrams. Nevertheless they provide some hints.

First of all it is a good idea to create a sprite for each of the two automata. Their current states are identified by variables and visualized by costumes. For example, if the car consumes gas because the combustion engine is running, the corresponding sprite is switched to a costume that displays a canister in the lower left corner. But additional sprites for the visualisation of a moving car and for environment-related elements like a traffic light are needed.

A major difficulty is to implement the triggering of moves to other states and activity. In the state transition diagram potential activities and moves are directly associated to states. They are part of the meaning of a state. But only when a certain event takes place, the state transition is actually performed. There are several different triggering mechanisms, which can be used in a Scratch program. One of them is the concept of event handlers – scripts, which are run, when a certain event occurs. Let us have a look at the script belonging to the propulsion sprite, which is started when the space-key (representing the brake) is pressed:

```
when space-key pressed
set acceleration to 2
switch to costume decelerating
wait until not (key space pressed?)
if not (key up-arrow pressed?)
    set acceleration to 0
    switch to costume rolling
stop script
```

Beside the header line of the eventhandler, which specifies the triggering event for the execution of the first part of the script, there is the command *wait until* ... . It triggers the execution of the second part of the script, which is an implementation of another state transition. A third mechanism, which is not used in this particular script, is a permanent loop, testing a condition and performing the state transition (and some activity), when the condition is true. A programmer developing software on the basis of automata has to know these techniques.

Let us have a look on those parts of the program that are not represented in the state transition diagrams. There is a sprite visualising the moving car. Its scripts (event handlers) manage the actual moving on the screen. The main script is started, when the green flag has been clicked. It contains an infinite loop, in which the current position of the visual object on the screen is changed according to the current speed and orientation. This functionality cannot be represented efficiently by an automaton, since it is data-oriented. A slight change of the position of the car does not lead to a fundamentally different state (unless it leaves the road and experiences an accident). Nevertheless the implementation of data-related functionality might be *inspired* by an automaton. For example the concept of acceleration (one of the states of the propulsion automaton) includes the notion that there is an entity that moves with a certain speed. This speed is increased by a certain value in each time interval. Note that these thoughts are about data processing and are therefore based upon a having-concept, but the *reason* to think about these quantitative aspects is rooted in a the holistic concept of *being* accelerated.

4 Psychological Reality of State-Oriented Thinking

Holland et al. [7] observed in university classes on programming that students often believe that an object may have just one attribute. This might indicate a tendency to associate the (one and only) current attribute value to a holistic state. In autumn 2007 I had the opportunity to collect some more specific evidence that in certain contexts people tend to think of states opposed to variables with content, when they interpret computer programs. 26 German high school students (18 female, 8 male) in the age of 16 and 17, who attended a class on informatics in grade 11, were asked to explain the execution of a Scratch program with one variable. They were familiar both with state transition diagrams and variables. The Scratch application contained one sprite visualising a cat reacting to key strokes by thinking or saying something. The following listing shows an abridged version of the scripts (the originally German parts have been translated to English):

```
when green flag clicked
    think "I have nothing to do" for 2 sec
    set activity to 0
stop script
when a key pressed
    if activity = 0
        set activity to 1
        say "Thank you for the job" for 2 sec
    else
        say "Sorry, I have no time"
stop script
when b key pressed
    if activity = 1
        say "I have finished the job" for 2 sec
    set activity to 0
stop script
```

The students were asked to answer questions like this:
What happens, when the user clicks the a-key for the first time?
What happens, when the user clicks the a-key a second time after 5 seconds?

The scripts use one variable named *activity*. It may contain either 1 or 0, thus indicating, whether the cat is active - and therefore not available for some new job - or not. Therefore this variable is clearly representing a state. But the question is, whether or not the students use the concept of "being in a state" in their verbal explanations. The major results of the language analysis are displayed in table 1. The majority (15 out of 26) used state-related phrases like "The sprite switches to state 1" or "the cat is in state 0" instead of data-related phrases like "The variable activity is set to the value 1" or "activity equals 0". Three students used both state-related and data-related phrases, but 12 persons described the Scratch application exclusively as an automaton moving from state to state. Some students' descriptions included improper phrases like "the state is set to 1", which are disregarded in table 1.

Table 1. Language analysis of high school students' explanations

Phrase	Number of Students	Average Frequency (standard deviation)
use of state related phrases	15	4.7 (3.8)
use of data related phrases	9	5.6 (1.8)
use of state related *and* data related phrases	3	3.6 (3.0)

5 Conclusions

Since small state transition diagrams are easy to understand and represent intuitive knowledge, they are useful for developing a complex system. Informatics education should lead to awareness of the underlying concept of "being in a state", in contrast to "having data". A finite state automaton may serve as an anticipatory intuition [4]. In this case it represents a preliminary global view, which precedes the development of all the details of software. The competence of creating a computer program on the basis of a state transition diagram includes the ability to use programming language constructs

- to represent meaningful states by variables and object attributes storing data,
- to trigger activity
- to merge several automata into one system.

The structure of a computer program might be very different from automata used during the process of software development. And it might be difficult to see which parts of a program represent a certain state resp. its meaning. But even then intuitive state transition diagrams are useful for checking the logical correctness of complex – and therefore not intuitive – programs.

References

1. Brändle, M., Hartmann, W., Nievergelt, J., Reichert, R.: Kara: Ein theoriebasierter Ansatz für Lernumgebungen zu fundamentalen Konzepten der Informatik. In: Proceedings INFOS, pp. 201–210 (2003)
2. di Sessa, A.A.: Knowledge in Pieces. In: Forman, G., Pufall, P.B. (eds.) Constructivism in the Computer Age, pp. 49–70. Lawrence Erlbaum, Hillsdale (1988)
3. di Sessa, A.A.: Changing Minds. In: Computers, Learning, and Literacy. MIT Press, Cambridge (2001)
4. Fischbein, E.: Intuition in Science and Mathematics. Reidel, Dordrecht, Boston, Lancaster, Tokio (1987)
5. Fromm, E.: To have or to be? Harper and Row, NewYork (1976)
6. Gordon, T.: Parent Effectiveness Training: The Proven Program for Raising Responsible Children. Three Rivers Press (2000)
7. Holland, S., Griffiths, R., Woodman, M.: Avoiding Object Misconceptions. In: Proceedings ACM SIGCSE, pp. 131–134 (1997)
8. Hubwieser, P.: Didaktik der Informatik. Springer, Berlin, Heidelberg, New York (2004)
9. Lakoff, G., Núnez, R.E.: The Metaphorical Structure of Mathematics: Sketching Out Cognitive Foundations for a Mind-Based Mathematics. In: English, L.D. (ed.) Mathematical Reasoning. Analogies, Metaphors, and Images, pp. 21–92. Lawrence Erlbaum, Mahwah (1997)
10. Schulz von Thun, F.: Miteinander reden. Störungen und Klärungen. Rowohlt, Reinbek bei Hamburg (1981)
11. Toyota Motor Corporatiom: Toyota Hybrid System THS II. Tokyo (2003)
12. Tuckman, B.: Developmental sequence in small groups. Psychological Bulletin 63, 384–399 (1965)
13. Weigend, M.: Intuitive Modelle der Informatik. Universitätsverlag Potsdam, Potsdam (2007)
14. Wing, J.M.: Computational Thinking. Communications of the ACM 49(3), 33–35 (2006)

Understanding Object Oriented Programming Concepts in an Advanced Programming Course

Tamar Benaya and Ela Zur

The Open University of Israel, Computer Science Department
108 Ravutzky st. Raanana, Israel 43107
{tamar,ela}@openu.ac.il

Abstract. Teaching Object Oriented Programming (OOP) is a difficult task, both for teachers who have to find the best way to illustrate the concepts and for students who have to understand them. Although the OOP paradigm and its concepts reflect the "real world", it has been shown that students find hard to understand and internalize the OOP concepts such as encapsulation, inheritance and polymorphism. This paper describes difficulties in understanding OOP in an Advanced Java course given at the Computer Science Department of the Open University of Israel. We present a typical question which focuses on several aspects of OOP. We discuss the students' answers and point out typical hardships in grasping the topic.

Keywords: Object Oriented Programming, Inheritance, Encapsulation, Polymorphism.

1 Background

The Open University of Israel (OUI) is a distance learning university which offers a variety of undergraduate programs and several graduate programs [1]. Our university is similar to other universities in its pursuit of excellence and its commitment to superior scientific and scholastic standards. It is an accredited university regulated by the Council of Higher Learning of the state of Israel. The OUI differs in that it is open to all those who wish to study a single course or a number of courses, or to pursue a full program of study towards a degree. Enrolment does not require matriculation or any other certificate from an educational institution. Though applicants are not required to provide a proof of prior scholastic achievements, their academic achievements are the key to their success at OUI. Students who study at the OUI can transfer credits from the OUI to other major universities in the country.

The teaching methods practiced at the OUI combine traditional distance education based on written materials which are sent to the students at their homes and web-based teaching [2]. The course materials are based on books especially adapted to self-study. Each course includes an optional face-to-face component in the form of small group tutorials led by tutors. However, this component does not constitute the core of the course. Students who wish to study on their own can do so with utmost success due to the distance learning method practiced at the OUI. The tutorial sessions are held at the OUI study centers dispersed throughout the country. Students must submit assignments, exercises or other types of tasks during the semester. They receive a grade and feedback on each assignment. Students must also pass the final examinations, held at study centers near their homes.

All the courses at the OUI have course websites which provide an interactive learning environment. The websites provide for continuous contact with faculty and fellow students. They include a discussion group and supplementary course materials such as lecture notes and sample exams and a fully integrated assignment submission system. Each course has a course coordinator who is responsible for the academic and administrative planning and the implementation of all course activities, including the web-based ones. The coordinators and tutors are those who provide the contact between the student and the OUI.

One of the advanced elective courses in the Computer Science Department at our university is "Advanced Programming with Java". The course is usually taken towards the end of the undergraduate degree. The prerequisites of the course include: "Introduction to Computer Science" (CS1), "Data Structures and Introduction to Algorithms" and at least one additional intermediate programming course. Until two years ago our CS1 course was based on procedural programming using Pascal or C++ (the procedural facet of the language), but recently the CS1 course was replaced by an OOP course with Java. To date, most of the students in the "Advanced Programming with Java" course took the previous version of the CS1 course which used Pascal or C++, that was the course offered at the time they started their studies.

The aim of the "Advanced Programming with Java" course is to acquaint students with advanced programming principles as recommended in CC2001 [3]. The course is based on the textbook: "Java How to Program" by Deitel & Deitel [4]. The topics of the course include: OOP; Graphical user interface; Multi-threaded programming and Client/Server systems. Similar to other courses at the OUI, the textbook is supplemented by a study guide, which highlights major topics of the course and provides additional examples to those presented in the textbook. The Integrated Development Environment (IDE) supplied with the course material is the NetBeans IDE. The students are free to use any other IDE they wish and many of them choose to use Eclipse. The students are required to hand in at least 4 out of 6 exercises covering the course material and to take a final exam at the end of the semester.

One of the major topics in the course is OOP. Being an advanced course, most of the students have a good amount of programming experience but one must recall that this is their first in depth exposure to OOP. Although the OOP paradigm and its concepts reflect the "real world", it has been shown that students find it hard to understand and internalize OOP concepts such as encapsulation, inheritance and polymorphism [5], [6], [7], [8], [9], [10]. Teaching OOP is a difficult task, both for the teacher who has to find the best way to illustrate the concepts and for students who have to understand them [11]. "In procedural programs, program flow is rather simple: you start with the main program and continue from there, invoking subprograms with parameters as necessary. In the OOP paradigm, there are many classes rather than a single program, and program flow must consider aspects such as: objects are allocated and constructed; their references are assigned to variables in objects of other classes; methods are invoked on objects including an implicit "this" parameter" [9].

Most of the research dealing with the comprehension of OOP concepts refers to novice students. These papers discuss difficulties concerning basic programming principles such as: program flow and parameter passing together with OOP concepts such as: object vs. class, object construction, simple classes vs. composite classes [5], [6], [7], [9]. Our research deals with students in an advanced programming course who are introduced to OOP for the first time.

2 The Research

We conducted a research in order to better identify common OOP pitfalls in an advanced programming course. The students in the course have a good programming background but this is their first exposure to OOP. The difficulties we expect the students to encounter are not those encountered by novice programmers, but difficulties that are more specifically related to OOP concepts.

2.1 Research Questions

The research questions were:

1. To what extent do students understand the underlying process which takes place when creating an object, specifically the chain of constructor calls?
2. To what extent do students understand that methods defined in the superclass can be invoked from the subclass?
3. To what extent do students understand the encapsulation concept, specifically, that private data members defined in the superclass cannot be directly accessed from the subclass?
4. To what extent do students understand polymorphism and the relationship between superclass and subclass objects?

2.2 Research Population

The research population was composed of 39 students who took the final exam in the course "Advanced Programming with Java" in the spring semester of the year 2006.

2.3 Research Instruments

The research instrument was the final exam which was composed of three questions covering the course material. One of the questions on the exam emphasizes several aspects of OOP. The question was composed of several sections, each emphasizing a unique OO concept. We present here the question taken from the final exam.

The Question. The question presented a program followed by 6 sections. The program was composed of two classes: Class 'A' with a single 'int' attribute and Class 'B' which extended 'A' and added a String attribute and a "getter" method for that attribute.

```java
public class A{
    private int n=0;
    public A(){
        this.n=0;
        System.out.println("A constructor1");
    }
    public A(int n){
        this.n=n;
        System.out.println("A constructor2");
    }
    public String toString(){
        return ""+n;
    }
}
public class B extends A{
    private String text;
    public B(int n, String text){
        super(n);
        this.text=text;
        System.out.println("B constructor1");
    }
    public B(String text){
        this.text=text;
        System.out.println("B constructor2");
    }
    public String getText(){
        return text;
    }
}
```

a. What will be printed as a result of the execution of the following statement?
   `B b=new B("bbb");`

   Correct answer:
   ```
   A constructor1
   B constructor2
   ```

b. Given 'b' from the previous section, is the following statement valid? If yes, what will be printed? If not, explain what is wrong.
   `System.out.println("b= "+b);`

   Correct answer:
   The statement is valid. The output will be: b= 0

c. Override the method 'toString' in class 'B' so that it returns the value of the attribute n concatenated with the attribute text.

Correct answer:
```
public String toString(){
    return super.toString()+text;
}
```

d. Is the following code valid? If yes, what will the last line print? If it is not valid, write which statement causes the problem and explain why.
   1. A x1 = new A(5);
   2. B x2 = new B(7,"bbb");
   3. x1 = x2;
   4. System.out.println(x1.getText());

   Correct answer:
   The code is not valid. Line 4 causes a compile time error: cannot use superclass reference in order to invoke methods defined in subclass. That is, the method 'getText' cannot be access using a reference of type 'A'.

e. Assuming that the 'toString' method from section (c) was added correctly, is the following code valid? If yes, what will the last line print? If it is not valid, write which statement causes the problem and explain why.
   1. A x1 = new A(3);
   2. B x2 = new B(4,"xxx");
   3. x1 = x2;
   4. System.out.println(x1.toString());

   Correct answer:
   The code is valid. The output will be: 4xxx

f. Assuming that the 'toString' method from section (c) was added correctly, is the following code valid? If yes, what will the last line print? If it is not valid, write which statement causes the problem and explain why.
   1. A x1 = new A();
   2. B x2 = new B("bbb");
   3. x2 = x1;
   4. System.out.println(x2.getText());

   Correct answer:
   The code is not valid. Line 3 causes a compile time error: a reference of type 'B' cannot refer to an object of type 'A'. A subclass reference type cannot refer to a superclass object.

3 Results

In this section we present the mean score achieved by the students on each of the sections of the question and discuss these results.

The overall mean score of all the sections was 79 (out of 100), STDEV=3.937. Table 1 presents the mean score (out of 100) for each of the six sections of the question. Each section was worth a maximum of 3 points, and the students received either full points or no points for each section. We checked the correlation between the answers to the different sections and found that there is a significant, although weak, correlation between the answers to the following sections: sections d and b (r=0.4202, p=0.0077), sections f and a (r=0.3276, p=0.0418), sections f and b (r=0.4774, p=0.0021) and sections f and e (r=0.3276, p=0.0418).

Table 1. Mean score and STDEV for each section

Section	Mean Score	STDEV
a	74 %	1.327
b	87 %	1.016
c	82 %	1.166
d	82 %	1.166
e	74 %	1.327
f	74 %	1.327

From analyzing the students' answers we can detect the following areas in which students exhibited difficulty:

Section (a). In section (a) the students are required to exhibit understanding of the underlying process which takes place when creating an object. The constructor invoked by the object 'b' created in this section does not include an explicit invocation of the superclass's constructor. The students need to understand that part of the creation process includes an invocation of the superclass's constructor even when it is not explicitly written in the code. In this case the no-parameter constructor of the superclass 'A' is the one that is invoked.

From table 1 we can see that 26% of the students did not thoroughly understand the process of the chain invocation of constructors. These students provided only the output produced by the constructor defined in class 'B' – the one which was explicitly invoked. Their output indicates that they did not understand that part of the initialization process includes an invocation of the superclass's constructor.

Section (b). In section (b) the students are required to display the output produced by printing the object 'b'. In this section, the students need to understand that any object can be printed using the 'toString' method inherited from the superclass.

From table 1 we can see that only 13% of the students did not answer correctly. Three students thought that an object cannot be printed by simply naming it in an output statement. One student thought that the object cannot be printed because its class does not define its own 'toString' method. One student did not answer this section.

Section (c). In section (c) the students are required to override the 'toString' method so that it returns the value of the attribute "n" followed by the attribute "text". The students were expected to invoke the superclass's 'toString' method and to concatenate "text" to its' returned value.

From table 1 we can see that 18% of the students did not invoke the superclass's 'toString' method. These students tried to directly access the inherited attribute "n". They wrote the following code:

```
public String toString(){
   return "" + n + text;
}
```

These students mistakenly think that the private data member 'n' defined in the superclass can be accessed directly.

Section (d). Section (d) presents code which declares and creates two objects one of type 'A' and one of type 'B'. Then, the object of type 'B' is referred to by a reference of type 'A', that is, a super-class reference refers to a sub-class object. Following that, there is an attempt to use this superclass reference in order to invoke the method ' getText', which is defined in the subclass.

From table 1 we can see that 18% did not answer correctly. All of these students but one thought that the subclass method can be invoked using a superclass reference. They did not understand that the only way to invoke the 'getText' method is by explicitly casting the superclass reference back to the subclass. One student mistakenly thought that the assignment of a subclass object to a superclass reference is illegal.

Section (e). Section (e) presents code which is similar to the code in section (d), it declares and creates two objects one of type 'A' and one of type 'B'. Then, the object of type 'B' is referred to by a variable of type 'A'. Following that, the 'toString' method of this object is invoked. The students are required to identify which 'toString' method is invoked, the one defined in class 'A' or the one defined in class 'B'. This is the classical case where the object reference is declared as a reference of the superclass type, but it refers to an object of the subclass type.

From table 1 we can see that 26% of the students did not answer correctly. All of these students but one invoked the 'toString' method defined in class 'A'. They did not understand the concept of dynamic binding which takes place during run time. One student, the same one from the previous section, thought that the assignment of a subclass object to a superclass reference is illegal.

Section (f). Section (f) presents code that declares and creates two objects one of type 'A' and one of type 'B'. Then, the object of type 'A' is referred to by a variable of type 'B'. Following that, the 'getText' method of this object is invoked.

From table 1 we can see that 26% of the students did not answer correctly. Half of these students thought that it is legal to assign a superclass object to a subclass reference. The other half thought that casting the superclass object to the subclass will solve the problem in the assignment statement. They did not understand that casting an object to its subclass is not possible if the object is not actually a subclass object.

4 Discussion

The question we analyzed included six sections, each dealing with a different aspect of OOP:

- Section (a) deals with object creation and the sequence of constructor calls.
- Section (b) deals with the 'toString' method inherited from its superclass.
- Section (c) deals with private data members in the context of inheritance.
- Section (d) deals with accessing subclass methods using a superclass reference.
- Section (e) deals with dynamic binding.
- Section (f) deals with assignment of a superclass object to a subclass reference.

Section (a) refers to the first research question which deals with how students understand the underlying process which takes place when creating an object. We found that about one fourth of the students did not thoroughly understand the process of the chain invocation of constructors which takes place when objects are created. They did not know that, when the constructor does not explicitly invoke a superclass constructor, the no-parameter constructor of the superclass is automatically invoked.

Section (b) refers to the second research question. From table 1 we can see that a high percentage of the students (87%) understood how an object is printed using its 'toString' method even though it was not invoked explicitly and it also was not defined explicitly in the class. They understood that the 'toString' method inherited from the superclass is the one that is executed.

Section (c) refers to the third research question which deals with the subclass's access to private data members defined in the superclass. About a fifth of the students tried to access private data members defined in the superclass instead of using a superclass method which returns the required value.

Sections (d), (e) and (f) refer to the fourth research question which deals with polymorphism and the relationship between superclass and subclass objects. The first part of section (d) and (e) includes an assignment of a subclass object to a superclass reference and all the students but one understood that this assignment is legal. The second part of (d) and (e) uses this superclass reference in two different ways: section (d) invokes a method defined solely in the subclass, while section (e) invokes a method which was overridden in the subclass and the students are required to exhibit understanding of the dynamic binding concept by identifying the method invoked. From the results shown in table 1we can see that there was a difference in the success rate of the two sections. More students (82%) understood the fact that methods defined solely in the subclass are only accessible through a subclass reference, while only (74%) of the students understood the dynamic binding concept

Section (f) deals with assignment of a superclass object to a subclass reference. About a fourth of the students (26%) did not answer correctly. Half of them thought that the assignment is legal and the other half thought that explicitly casting the superclass object to its subclass will solve the problem. They did not understand that casting an object to its subclass is not possible if the object is not actually referencing a subclass object.

5 Conclusions

To conclude, it is apparent from the above results that the students have a good understanding of the following concepts:

- That the 'toString' method is inherited from the superclass and that it is invoked automatically when printing objects.
- The encapsulation concept, specifically, that private data members defined in the superclass cannot be accessed from the subclass.
- That superclass variables may refer to subclass objects and that the subclass cannot be accessed via the superclass reference. This is one part of the concept of polymorphism.

On the other hand, the students had more difficulty with understanding the following concepts:

- The process of object creation involving the invocation of superclass constructors.
- The dynamic binding that takes place when invoking methods using superclass references.
- That subclass variables cannot refer to superclass objects and that down casting the object will not necessarily solve the problem.

Overall the above results are relatively good, although we expect advanced students to exhibit a better understanding of these concepts. We pointed out specific areas of difficulty which educators must be aware of so that they can plan the learning process accordingly.

As a result of this study, we plan to change the way we teach OOP in the course "Advanced programming with Java". We will put more emphasis both in the lectures and in the exercises on the issues found to be most difficult to comprehend. We will focus on presenting concrete examples and we will consider introducing software tools aimed at helping students to understand what is happening during program execution. Many educators believe that there is a need to support the learning of OOP concepts using software tools [9], [12], [13], [14], [15]. There are three different types of OO software tools: a micro world (such as Karel J Robot), developments environments (such as BlueJ and MiniJava) and class libraries (such as Objectdraw). Several visual environments for teaching elementary OOP have been developed [16], [17], [18], [19]. Numerous visualization tools are already available [19], [20] for introductory programming courses. These tools, if used effectively, are capable of clarifying difficult concepts. Our course is an advanced course. Therefore, we think that a visualization tool can be added as an extra aid but it is not a candidate for the main integrated development environment (IDE) used in the course. We believe that it is important to expose the students to one of the standard IDEs used in industry. We will examine several visual tools and decide which to adopt. We will examine students' perceptions of these concepts, in order to see if the change improves their understanding.

References

1. The Open University of Israel website, http://www.openu.ac.il
2. Benaya, T., Zur, E.: Website Usage in a Computer Science Course Given in a Distance Learning Environment. European Journal of Open, Distance and E-Learning (2007/I)
3. Joint IEEE Computing Society/ACM Task Force on Computing Curricula. Computing Curricula 2001 Final Report (2001), http://www.acm.org/education/curric_vols/cc2001.pdf
4. Deitel, H.M., Deitel, P.J.: Java How to Program for Program, 6th edn. Pearson Education, London (2005)
5. Teif, M., Hazzan, O.: Partonomy and Taxonomy in Object-Oriented Thinking: Junior High School Students' Perception of Object Oriented Basic Concepts. ACM SIGCSE Bulletin 38(4), 55–60 (2006)
6. Holland, S., Griffiths, R., Woodman, M.: Avoiding Object Misconceptions. In: Proceedings of the 28th SIGCSE, pp. 131–134 (1997)

7. Ragonis, N., Ben-Ari, M.: A Long-Term Investigation of the Comprehension of OOP Concepts by Novices. Computer Science Education 5(3), 203–221 (2005)
8. Fleury, A.E.: Encapsulation and Reuse as Viewed by Java Students. ACM SIGCSE Bulletin 33(1), 189–193 (2001)
9. Ragonis, N., Ben-Ari, M.: On Understanding the Statics and Dynamics of Object-Oriented Programs. In: ACM SIGCSE, pp. 226–230 (2005)
10. Georgantaki, R., Psaromiligkos, Y., Retalis, S., Dendrinos, V., Adamopoulos, D.: Developing a Blended Learning Strategy for Teaching Object-Oriented Programming Using the 'Model First' Approach. In: Proceedings of Informatics Education Europe II – IEEII, pp. 87–96 (2007)
11. Milne, J., Rowe, G.: Difficulties in Learning and Teaching Programming – Views of Students and Tutors. Education and Information Technologies 7(1), 55–66 (2002)
12. Murray, K.A., Heines, J.M., Kolling, M., Moore, T., Wagner, P.j., Schaller, N.C., Trono, J.A.: Experiences with IDEs and Java Teaching: What Works and What Doesn't. ACM SIGCSE Bulletin 35(3), 215–216 (2003)
13. Lahtinen, E.: Integrating the Use of Visualizations to Teaching Programming. Methods, Materials and Tools for Programming Education, pp. 7–13 (2006), http://www.mmt2006.net
14. Roberts, E.: An Overview of MiniJava. ACM SIGCSE Bulletin 33(1), 1–5 (2001)
15. Bergin, J., Bruce, K., Kolling, M.: Objects-Early Tools – A Demonstration. ACM SIGCSE Bulletin 37(1), 390–391 (2005)
16. Ben-Ari, M., Myller, N., Sutinen, E., Tarhio, J.: Perspectives on Program Animation with Jeliot. In: Proceeding of the Software Visualization International Seminar, Germany, pp. 31–45 (2002)
17. Goldman, K.J.: A Concepts-first Introduction to Computer Science. In: Proceedings of the 35th SIGCSE Technical Symposium on Computer Science Education, Virginia, pp. 432–436 (2004)
18. Hendrix, T.D., Cross, J.H., Barowski, L.A.: An Extensible Framework for Providing Dynamic Data Structure Visualizations in a Lightweight IDE. In: Proceedings of the 35th SIGCSE Technical Symposium on Computer Science Education, Virginia, pp. 387–391 (2004)
19. Myller, N., Bednarik, R.: Methodologies for Studies of Program Visualization. Methods, Materials and Tools for Programming Education, pp. 37–42 (2006), http://www.mmt2006.net
20. Lahtinen, E., Jarvinen, H.M., Melakoski-Vistbacka, S.: Targeting Program Visualizations. In: Proceedings of the 12th ITiCSE, pp. 256–260 (2007)

Spiral Teaching of Programming to 10–11 Year-Old Pupils After Passed First Training (Based on the Language C++)

Biserka Boncheva Yovcheva

Shumen
University of Shumen "EPISKOP Konstantin Preslavski"
Faculty of Mathematics and Informatics
Department "Computer informatics"
Biserka Boncheva Yovcheva
bissy_y@yahoo.com

Abstract. The article presents a unique approach of teaching programming to 10 – 11 year old pupils. Based on the idea that teaching pupils of writing algorithms must start right after teaching the first elements of the programming language and develop with time, one and the same problem is considered many times but each time with adding of new knowledge. According to the described methodology a textbook is issued on the basis of which an experimental four-year training of pupils is organized. This article gives the curriculum of the second year of training based on the approach described.

Keywords: education, informatics, didactics.

1 Introduction

A common approach in creating a new concept or a system of concepts is by repeatedly returning to it at different stages of the process of teaching. Unfortunately it is hard to find a systematic theoretical description of the problems arising from of applying this concept. The idea of applying the spiral approach in the lead-off teaching of programming is exposed in several consecutive articles by this author. In [3] the basic ideas connected with this approach were described and in [4] – its elements. The ideas of the spiral approach during the first year of teaching programming to 10-11 year old pupils in extracurricular or out-of-school learning are presented in the designated materials. It must be pointed out that there is no such discipline "Programming" in the official curriculum for this age group. The objectives of such kind of education are:

- Digestion of the basic elements of a programming language as well as basic algorithmic constructions at early age, so that the later training could be concentrated on serious algorithmic problems.
- Developing of the logical and abstract thinking of the trainees.

– Preparing of the trainees for competitors of programming in the terminology of the international competitions of informatics. [5]

It becomes evident that only pupils with proven abilities in the field of mathematics and initial computer training can participate in this training. The main problems regarding the teaching of programming to little pupils are exposed in detail in [6];

The approach presented in this article has been experimented for 10 years in the Private School of Mathematics and Informatics A&B in Shumen [7] with more than 500 pupils. The results achieved gave us reasons to assume that the experiments are successful. As a result of the training using the approach described, the pupils show one of the best results at the national and international competitions of informatics. As examples, the achievements of Rostislav Rusev can be pointed out: two silver and one gold medal (first place) from the Balcan Olympiad of Programming, two silver and two gold medals from the International Olympiad of Programming; of Rumen Hristov; a gold medal from the First Balcan Olympiad of Programming and some other examples of pupils that won prize places at all national competitions in the last 6 years [1].

The basic concepts and a curriculum for the second year of training, based on the discussed spiral approach, will be presented in this article. For this purpose we need to specify the knowledge acquired by the pupils up to the moment.

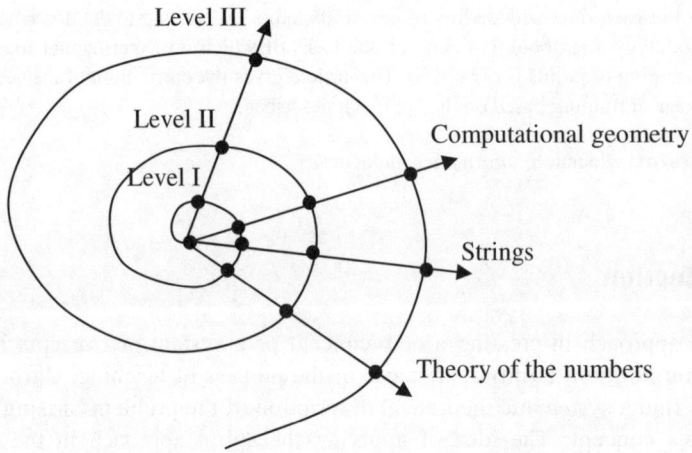

Fig. 1. Scheme of the spiral approach

The teaching during the first year is described in detail in [2], [3], [4] and [6] and on the basis of these articles a textbook is created which has been used for two years now for training of pupils in the above mentioned School A&B as well as in other extracurricular forms in the country.

In short, all the operators of the language constructions are already known: conditional operators and operators for cycle, the pupils also know the standard scalar data types: numerical types and the type char; from the basic algorithms they know, finding an optimal element from a given succession, counting of elements with certain properties, basic algorithms from theory of numbers, processing of textual information; the pupils know some basic concepts in the field of computer geometry.

2 Basic Concepts of the Curriculum of the Second Year of Training

During the second year of training the teacher should emphasize on the means of the programming language for working with different complex data types: arrays, records, strings, as well as basic algorithms which are applied to these structures. Again, it is necessary to pay attention to the presentation of the data in the computer memory as at this stage the binary presentation of the numbers should be introduced. Knowledge in the field of the theory of numbers is expanded again. At this stage it is good for the pupils to get acquainted with some basic techniques of programming like using recursion and eventually dynamic programming. Yet, regarding the latter, only an idea is given through some elementary examples on the basis of the principles of the spiral approach. Getting acquainted with these techniques will continue in the next years of training. To fulfill these purposes the curriculum for the second year of training is offered during 72 school hours (see Table 1).

Here is the continuing of the spiral when the last few consecutive rounds will still be separate language constructions that are expected for teaching (fig. 1)

The consecutive full rounds of the spiral correspond to the learning of the following language constructions:

Level I. Subprograms. Functions with parameters, return value.
Level II. Arrays. Representation of the arrays in the memory of the computer.
Level III. Recursion.
Level IV. Structures.

All the illustrations of the approach in hand that we are going to offer in this article are based on the programming language C++, but they could be realized on a different programming language with the same success:

- Each area of algorithmisation (geometry, divisibility, optimization, processing of textual information, processing of images, etc) is presented by one thread;
- The common points of the spiral with the threads correspond to the level of knowledge of the relevant area of algorithmisation based on the language constructions learned up to the moment.

Within the described curriculum we examine different threads, crossing the described "twists" of the spiral:

- Algorithms, connected with iterrating, processing and searching of an optimal element in a given structure;
- Working with text information.
- Theory of numbers.
- Computer geometry.

Table 1. Curriculum for the second year of teaching programming for 10-11 year-old pupils for 72 school hours

№	Theme	Number of hours
1.	Functions. The concept of function. Kinds of functions depending on the returned result. Functions with parameters, handed over by value.	4
2.	Divisibility of the numbers. Algorithm of Euclid (with subtraction, with division, binary algorithm), least common multiple, solving Diofant equation of first degree, operations with noncanceling fractions.	4
3.	One-dimensional arrays. Basic problems – searching of an element, counting of elements with a determined property, finding an optimal element, polynomial methods of sorting.	6
4.	Concept of complexity of algorithms. Evaluation of complexity of the algorithms for working with arrays.	2
5.	Strings. Presenting of strings as an array of symbols. Tools for work with strings, offered by the library `string.h` (`cstring`).	6
6.	Divisibility. Simple numbers. The sieve of Eratostenes.	4
7.	Strings. Presenting the strings with the standard data type `string`. Means of the programming language for working with quantities of the data type `string` and their application to solving problems for processing of text.	4
8.	Searching of a substring by pattern. The idea of lexical and syntactical analysis (check if a given string responds to given requirements – identifying of numbers, successions of lower and upper case letters and so on.)	4
9.	Rectangles with sides parallel to the coordinate axes. Belonging of points to a rectangle. Common points of two and more rectangles. Number of points with integer coordinates that belong to a rectangle.	4
10.	Counting systems.	4
11.	Two-dimensional arrays. Processing of table information.	6
12.	Recursion. Forward and backward run of the recursion.	4
13.	Structures. Declarations of quantities of type structure.	4
14	Long numbers. Simple realizations – adding, subtraction and multiplying by a one-digital number.	6
15.	Concept of dynamic programming. One-dimensional problem for counting of elements according to certain properties and finding an optimal result.	6
16.	Square nets. Labyrinths. Regions.	4

For each one of the threads we can point to knowledge that is assumed to be learned between two full turns of the spiral. The only thread for which new knowledge is taught only once is the one, presenting the computer geometry. More theorizing is not acceptable because of the age specifics and insufficient theoretical training of the trainees.

3 Illustration of the Spiral Approach through the Theme "Theory of Numbers"

Later we will point out the illustration of the theme "Theory of numbers" (Fig. 2).

We will also point out the amount of knowledge in a certain area as points of the thread in the chronological way in which they should be taught. (Fig. 2) The points in which the thread crosses the spiral are also marked.

It must be noted that each new knowledge is given right after the language constructions learned up to that moment in order to allow its interpretation. We will offer some example problems that can be solved at each one of the stages of the training on the theme discussed.

3.1 Level I

As we can see from Fig. 2, the knowledge connected with the divisibility of numbers, finding of common dividers, the least common multiple, etc., is improved. At this stage it is required from the pupils to be able to apply their knowledge of the previous year for realization of some auxiliary functions, by means of which the solution of the problem becomes more reliable and the probability of making a mistake much less probable. Example of problems that can be solved at this stage:

Problem 1. Row
*The numbers in a row are calculated in this way: each succeeding number is calculated from the previous one by adding to it the number of its dividers. Let's name the first number of that row with a. For example, if $a=6$, the next number is 6+4=10, because 6 has 4 dividers – 1, 2, 3 and 6. Write a program **ROW.CPP**, that reads from the standard input the first number of the row and an integer N and output the Nth number of the row.*

    Input:
    From the first row of the standard input two integers are entered – the first element of the row and N.
    Output:
    On the standard output print the Nth element of the row.
    Limitations:
    $0 < a \leq 10000$
    $0 < N \leq 100$
    Example:
    Input
    7 3
    Output
    12

Problem 2. Palindromes

Write a program **PALINDROM.EXE**, that inputs from the standard input two integers: *m* and *n* and outputs all palindromes in the interval *[m, n]*.

> **Input**
> 110 150
> **Output**
> 111
> 121
> 131
> 141

Problem 3. LCM

Write a program **LCM.EXE**, that inputs from the standard input three integers *m, n* and *k* and outputs all the pairs of numbers in the interval *[m, n]*, having a common multiplier that is less or equals k..

> **Input**
> 11 27 8
> **Output.**
> 11 22
> 12 24
> 13 26
> 16 24
> 18 27

We can point out some more examples here but the amount of material does not allow it.

3.2 Level II

At this stage the pupils have already a powerful tool for data processing: arrays and together with them the standard algorithms for statistical processing, searching, etc. Here are some example problems that can be solved at this stage:

Problem 4. Number

а) Write a subprogram that calculates the number of the different digits of a given integer.
б) Using the subprogram from a) write a program **DIF.CPP**, that fills in from the standard input an array with integers with *n* elements ($1 \leq n \leq 100$) and outputs those of them which have three different digits.

Problem 5. Competition

Write a program **COMP.CPP** that inputs the points *n* competitors (*n* <= 25) obtained in a tournament consisting of at most three rounds coded into a 3-digit number. The code is set up in such a way that each digit represents the number of points the competitor obtained in a particular round. (For example the number 1 means that the *competitor has had 0 points at the first two stages and 1 at the third. 165 means 1 point at the first stage, 6, at the second and 5 at the third.) We assume that the competitors are identified by the order of the input of their results – the first value in the input is the result of the first competitor, the second is of the second competitor etc.*

a) output the numbers of the competitors with equal results from each stage. (For example , 555, or 0, or 111, etc
b) transform the results of all the competitors as you replace the entered number with the sum of the points from the three stages;
c) print the number of the competitor with the highest result.

It is obvious from the curriculum that it is expected that the theme "Counting systems" must be taught. For acquainting of these pupils with this theme they do not have to know arrays and functions. That theme is put off in time, because it is pretty abstract and hard to be understood by pupils (10-12 year-old). The algorithmic knowledge accumulated up to that moment and the new stage of developing of their logical thinking allows them to learn the new material efficiently enough. The problems that should be solved in connection with that theme should aim at the rearranging of numbers from one counting system into another and the other way round.

3.3 Level III

Here the tasks of dividing a number into its digits, divisibility and counting systems are rather aiming at illustrating the most elementary application of the recursion – forward and backward run. A double effect is achieved. On the one hand, the pupils think over, from another point of view, algorithms already known, and on the other hand they learn better the method "recursion" as another means of solving problems.

It should be noted that at this stage we do not pay serious attention to the inefficiency of the recursion in most cases.

3.4 Level IV

After introducing structures as a tool of presenting objects composed of many components, the theme of numbers and their representation in the computer memory becomes again an interesting object of learning. In most cases we have to use integers, which cannot be presented by the standard numerical types of the programming language. Then some own tools for their processing must be added – presenting them mostly as an integer that means the number of the digits and an array of the digits; realizing of the basic operations with them. At this age the realizing of the operation "multiplying" of two multi-digital numbers is not recommended, neither any operations for dividing.

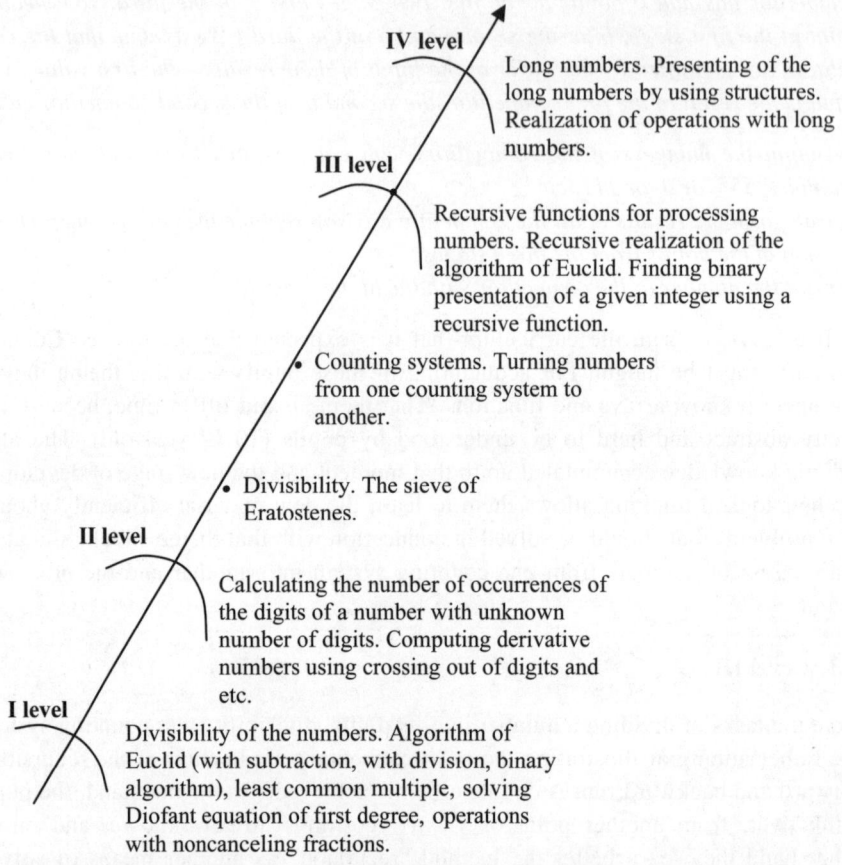

Fig. 2. The theme "Theory of the numbers", realized with the spiral approach

The other threads of the spiral can be presented in a similar way: i.e. the different levels of algorithmisation, described above.

4 Conclusion

The described spiral approach gives an effective methodology of teaching programming to little pupils (10-11 year-old). The basic concept of it is that the teacher should not try to present the theme in discussion in detail but just the part of it which at this stage is most accessible to the pupils. In this way the training of the pupils at an early age turns from a practically impossible task into a pleasant occupation both for them and their teachers.

References

1. National web portal for competitions in informatics, http://infoman.musala.com/
2. Yovtcheva, B., Ivanova, I.: First steps in C/C++. KLMN Sofia (2006)
3. Yovcheva, B.: Spiral teaching programming to 10 – 11 year old pupils (based on the language C++). Mathematics and mathematical education, Sofia (2007)
4. Yovcheva, B., Mollov, A.: The idea for realization of spiral approach in the early training programming – V Balkan congress, June 22-24, Stara Zagora, The Education, The Balkans, Europe (2007)
5. Web site of International Olympiad of Informatics, http://olympiads.win.tue.nl/ioi/
6. Mollov, A., Yovtcheva, B.: Main problems connected with developing programming program of studies for 10 – 11 year old children (based on the C++ language), collection. In: Covering and value of teaching. Reports from the third autumn scientific conference of the faculty of preschool and primary school education – University of Sofia, Veda Slovena –GZ Sofia (2005)
7. Private School of Mathematics and Informatics A&B in Shumen, http://ab-bg.com

Multi-facet Problem Comprehension: Utilizing an Algorithmic Idea in Different Contexts

Bruria Haberman[1], Orna Muller[2], and Haim Averbuch[3]

[1] Computer Science Department, Holon Institute of Technology, and
Davidson Institute of Science Education, The Weizmann Institute of Science,
Rehovot 76100, Israel
bruria.haberman@weizmann.ac.il
[2] Science Education Department, School of Education, Tel-Aviv University, and
Software Engineering Department, Ort Braude College of Engineering, Karmiel, Israel
ornamu@post.tau.ac.il
[3] Computer Science Group, Science Education Department, School of Education
Tel-Aviv University, Israel
haimav@zahav.net.il

Abstract. Instructional design has a significant influence on the construction of knowledge, especially for novices. Specifically, the way the instruction of algorithmic problem solving is designed has a significant effect on the development of the student's capabilities to analyze and solve problems. We present a pedagogical approach regarding teaching algorithmic problem solving, which is based on the assimilation of a new concept by demonstrating its different facets through a variety of relevant examples. The approach aims to support multi-facet problem comprehension, as well as to enhance the student's ability to utilize algorithmic ideas in different contexts. The approach was introduced to computer science teachers through a workshop activity aimed at discussing the topic of evaluating the complexity level of problems and their challenging characteristics. We think that an activity of this kind is beneficial for raising teachers' awareness of the way they select problems in order to develop students' problem-solving skills.

Keywords: Algorithmic problem solving, Instructional design.

1 Introduction

Teaching *Fundamentals of Computer Science* (CS) is considered a first step towards acquiring computational thinking [15] and specifically, algorithmic thinking; it involves acquaintance with basic algorithmic concepts, principles, and algorithmic problem-solving methods. The way instruction of algorithmic problem solving is designed has a significant effect on the development of the student's capabilities and skills needed to analyze and solve problems. Therefore, establishing a collaborative community of teachers, which discusses and shares pedagogical aspects of algorithmic problem-solving instruction, is important for significantly enhancing the teaching of computer science to novices.

Several studies demonstrated that experts construct in their memory a dynamic structure of cognitive schemas related to different types of problems and their solutions [1, 4, 10, 14]. These structures are updated and enriched while the experts gain problem-solving experience. Specifically, CS experts and experienced programmers' knowledge structures include schemas for solving algorithmic problems. Experts use their cognitive schemas to solve analogical problems and perform the necessary adaptations to previously known solutions. In contrast, novices have difficulties in matching a familiar solution to a new, though similar, problem that presents some new constraints. Usually, the novice's main difficulty lies in recognizing a problem's type, and the structural similarities between analogical problems; this may result from relatively undeveloped abstraction and generalization abilities. In addition, even when a problem's type is correctly recognized, novices often fail to adapt familiar (and suitable) solutions to construct the required solution for the new problem. Teachers' awareness of students' difficulties and frequent mistakes is of major importance in order to minimize this phenomenon.

Instructional design has a profound and persistent influence on constructing knowledge, especially for novices. Assimilation of a CS concept, idea, or principle should be accompanied by a demonstration of its different facets through a variety of relevant examples. A suitable sequence of problems may enhance one's ability to identify the problem's type, to utilize a familiar solution, and to better modify a solution according to a problem's constraints [6]. Organizing the problems presented around examples, along with non-examples, demonstrates when and how to use a familiar solution and when not to. In addition, it is important to present problem-solving processes besides the "final school solutions" (which are the final products of experts' problem-solving processes), and to discuss the considerations and decisions that an expert performs throughout the entire problem-solving process.

This paper presents a method for teaching problem solving a centered around concept or idea that is related to a basic algorithmic problem and its solution. The method can be used by teachers to choose and arrange examples of problems in a way that benefits and supports constructing students' knowledge schemas, enhances their problem-solving abilities, and reduces common mistakes. This method is based on presenting a series of apparently similar problems that gradually change, while focusing on different facets of the concept or idea presented. In section 2 the method is demonstrated by teaching the concept of *extreme value computation*. We chose this example since it is a common problem, recurring in a wide range of contexts. In section 3, we discuss cognitive and pedagogical aspects of instructional design aimed at supporting the construction of knowledge. Section 4 demonstrates an in-service workshop activity that engages CS teachers in a discussion related to the design of algorithmic problem-solving sessions. One specific goal of the workshop was to examine how the teachers evaluate a problem's level of complexity, as well as to predict the difficulties students may encounter when dealing with the problem. Section 5 generalizes the method demonstrated in section 2 and presents pedagogical guidelines for pattern-oriented instruction.

2 (Gradual) Presentation of Problems Centered around a Concept

This section presents a pedagogical approach for teaching problem solving, centered around an algorithmic idea that recurs in various contexts. In this approach, a series of apparently similar problems, which consist of a gradually mutated base problem, is presented. Solving the problems involves focusing on different facets of the concept presented. Beyond understanding the algorithmic idea presented, one main goal of the pedagogical method is that students will acquire the ability: (1) to analyze a problem, (2) to identify its type (i.e., the relevant basic algorithmic problem), (3) to recognize its unique requirements, and (4) to adapt the algorithmic idea to the problem's constraints. Various aspects of a problem are discussed: the initial state of the problem, the target state, the special case it demonstrates, and the algorithmic problem-solving principle it illuminates.

The first problem presented to the students, centered around a concept, matches its general case; thus, its solution is associated with a general algorithmic idea. As such, the problem actually serves as a prototype of a large set of similar problems. The gradual change in the problems presented encourages the students to carefully examine how the general algorithmic idea is utilized in order to solve a specific problem of that prototype. In some cases, there is a need to integrate several algorithmic ideas to construct a solution. In other cases, a seemingly small modification in a problem's requirements may cause a significant change in the solution, up to the point where the classic algorithmic idea stops being relevant (when the "new" problem is actually of a different prototype).

2.1 A Sequence of Problems Centered around the Concept of "Extreme Value"

Without the loss of generality, this method is demonstrated through the concept of *extreme value computation* and similarly, it can be employed to teach other concepts or ideas as well. The algorithmic idea upon which the concept of *extreme value* is based relates to the concept of *loop invariant*. An invariant is an assertion that we presume is maintained during each stage of the algorithm's execution. For example, in the case of computing the maximum value, we presume that a variable called Max holds at any stage (iteration) the maximum value related to the values manipulated until that moment. As a result, the algorithmic idea is based on comparing each (next) element to Max and updating Max whenever necessary.

Example 1 – The initial Problem

The opening problem is an elementary problem that involves finding the maximal value in a set. Its solution constitutes the basis for solving various similar problems. Note that the problem's presentation does not include special assumptions regarding the values of the set:

Develop an algorithm that obtains a set of N values and returns the maximal value of the set.

When one presents a concept, an opening example has an important role in its assimilation. The decision to begin with this example derives from three main reasons:

(a) A conventional approach for presenting the general concept of finding the maximum consists of gradually presenting solutions from specific examples (as a dependent on the length of the set). We first presented the concept of the solution for N=2 for which there is no immediate need for an auxiliary variable, Max, a need that is already evident for the solution of N=3. From here on, the transition to finding the maximum in a set of N>3 values while using Max initialized as the first value of the set, is most natural.

(b) The problem in this example and the general idea for its solution (which is appropriate for any set of values) actually creates the basic schema for finding the maximum.

(c) Another reason for beginning with this example is supported by the research of Samurcay (1989), who claims that novices encounter difficulties in initiating variables, and that they would prefer to initialize a variable with an input value instead of using the assignment operator [13].

The general algorithmic idea is that the value of an auxiliary variable Max is initialized to the value of the first element in the set, and at each iteration of the computation an element in the set, starting from the second, is compared to Max and Max is updated when a larger value is encountered.

Example 2 – I am a Simple Case

Develop an algorithm that obtains a set of N positive values and returns the maximal value of the set.

The general algorithmic idea presented in the opening problem is also appropriate for solving this problem. However, since the input set in this problem has a lower bound value (zero), it is possible to use this lower bound to initiate Max. This change necessitates other accommodations when using the solution of the first problem to solve the current problem, namely, comparing to Max all the set's elements. Presentation of this modified solution to the students demonstrates that it is not necessary to use the general algorithmic idea as it is, but rather, that it can be adjusted to the characteristics of the given problem.

Example 3 – Am I as Simple?

Develop an algorithm that obtains a set of N negative values and returns the maximal value of the set.

Presenting this example immediately after the previous one shows that despite the great similarity between the problems, the solution presented in example 2 cannot be used for solving this problem (since a lower bound does not exist), and that the appropriate solution is the one presented in example 1. However, since students tend to adopt a general case also for cases for which it should not be used [9], they tend to initiate Max with a very small negative number.

Example 4 – I Need Special Treatment!

Develop an algorithm that obtains a set of N natural numbers and returns the maximal value of the sum of the digits of each number of the set.

This problem consists of (a) the main task of calculating the maximum, and (b) the secondary task of handling each element, which requires using additional algorithmic ideas – breaking the number into digits and calculating their sum. As a result, the complexity level of this solution increases relatively to the previous solutions.

Example 5 – If they ask about me, does It Mean that I Exist?

Develop an algorithm that obtains a set of N integer values, and finds the maximal even value of the set.

This case involves finding a maximal value that satisfies a certain condition. In fact, we need to find the maximum among all the even numbers that occur in a given set. However, it is possible that there are no even numbers in the set. A typical mistake made by students is not considering such a possibility. Their solutions assume that there is at least one even number in the set. Accordingly, this example calls for a discussion of the set's characteristics and considering different representative input examples.

One possible solution to the problem consists of combining two algorithmic ideas utilized in a serial manner: first locating the first even value, if it exists (a search algorithm), and then using the general algorithm to find the maximum. An alternative solution interweaves these two algorithmic ideas while using a flag indicating whether there is at least one even value in the set.

Example 6 – I also Demand Special Treatment!

Develop an algorithm that obtains a set of N integral values and finds the maximal prime number of the set.

This example combines characteristics found in examples 4 and 5: there is no certainty that in the given set there is a value that satisfies the condition, and also, one must handle the primality test. The outline of the solution is similar to that of the previous example, but since a primality test may be considered more challenging than calculating the sum of the digits of a number, in general, the complexity of the solution increases.

Example 7 - A Story

A bus departing from City A to City B stops on its way at N bus stops, including the first station and the final one. Passengers can get on and off the bus at the intermediate bus stops. At the first bus stop, the passengers only get on the bus, and at the final stop, all the passengers get off. Assumption: the bus can hold 50 passengers at most. Develop an algorithm that obtains as an input the number of ascending passengers at the first bus stop and the number of passengers that go on and off the bus in each intermediate stop, and returns the maximal number of passengers that were on the bus at any given moment during the drive.

The complexity level of this example increases relatively to the previous examples, since its solution deals with a dynamically generated set; the values of the set are created through an operation involving "accumulation by compensation" of the input data. Another source of possible difficulty is the realization that it is necessary to initialize the sum that represents an element of the dynamically generated set.

The following examples demonstrate how a small modification of the problem results in a significant modification of the algorithm.

Example 8 – It is not what It Looks Like!

Develop an algorithm that obtains a set of N real numbers and returns the maximal value of the numbers bigger or equal to the set's average.

Mathematical knowledge and tools are part of the training necessary for Computer Science graduates [2]; it is important that students acquire those tools and use them for analyzing and solving problems. This example demonstrates the importance of analyzing a problem mathematically. Analysis of the problem reveals that there is actually no need to calculate the average, since the search for the maximum among numbers bigger or equal to the average is equivalent to searching for the maximum of the complete set. Accordingly, the simple solution of the problem is the one presented in example 1.

Students often propose a solution that first calculates the average and then searches for the maximum among numbers larger than or equal to the average. This idea for solving the problem necessitates going over the input set twice. The reason why students propose such a complicated solution probably stems from their desire to translate the question "as is" to a programmed solution without first analyzing it mathematically. Needless to say, those students who adopt this idea for a solution will find it impossible to implement before they have learned arrays. On the other hand, students who did learn arrays are used to going over the set of values stored in the arrays several times; thus, they may not recognize the simple idea underlying the problem's solution. A possible explanation is that students tend to refer to seemingly similar examples and to use tools that are appropriate for a certain task yet irrelevant in a different context [9].

Example 9 – It is what It Looks Like!

Develop an algorithm that obtains a set of N real numbers and returns the maximal value among numbers smaller than the set's average.

The difference between this problem's phrasing and the previous one is minimal, yet the solution is significantly different. In this example we cannot avoid calculating the average before looking for the required maximal value. The complexity of this problem is especially high. Max must be initialized with the first value of the set, which is smaller than the average, or alternatively, with a lower bound (which is the minimal value of the set). Furthermore, the requirement to find a maximum smaller than the average requires referring to a case where such a value does not exist (in a case where all the values in the set are identical).

Example 10 – Where Is the Algorithm?

Develop an algorithm that obtains a set of integer numbers within the range of 21 to 30 (inclusive), which includes at least 10 different numbers and returns the maximal value of the set.

A mathematical analysis of the starting point of the problem reveals that any number from 21 to 30 (inclusive) occurs in the set. Based on the data that the set includes at least 10 numbers, it can be immediately concluded that the maximum value is 30 (hence, there is no need to scan the set). Again, presenting such a problem may demonstrate that the use of a familiar algorithmic idea should not be immediate, but rather, it should be preceded by appropriate mathematical analysis.

Example 11 – Why am I here at All?

A group of people is defined as "homogeneous" if the age range of its members does not exceed 5 years. Develop an algorithm that gets as input the age of a group of students and returns 'true" if it is homogenous and 'false" if it is not.

This example is unique among the problems we presented, since here finding the maximum (and similarly the minimum) is not a goal in itself but a means to achieve a different goal – to test homogeneity. The outcome of a mathematical analysis is that the group is homogeneous if the gap between the maximum age and the minimum age of the group members does not exceed 5 years. Accordingly, a solution is based on finding the maximum and minimum of the set through one scan over the list (by interweaving both algorithms); and even better than that, stop searching whenever an undesirable case is detected, meaning that the difference between the actual extreme values (computed at a certain point) turns greater than 5. In our experience, students find it difficult to come up with the idea to search for extreme values, since there is no explicit reference (or hint) for that in the problem's phrasing; as a result, students tend to solve the problem inefficiently by testing the condition on each of the possible pairs.

2.2 A Concise View of the Problems

The sequence of problems presented in section 2.1 serve as examples of designing instruction around a concept. Note that the problems and the order of their presentation are merely suggestions. The examples demonstrate how we can utilize a problem whose solution requires using a basic algorithmic idea, and owing to modifications of the starting point or the goal, we have to make adjustments to the basic algorithm in order to solve a given problem.

Sometimes the idea of the problem's solution is identical to the previous example of a problem, and sometimes the modification of the problem requires formulating a different solution – either a trivial one or a more complicated one, for example, by combining algorithmic solutions to additional tasks. Table 1 describes the characteristics of the problems, their similarity and dissimilarities, and ideas for their solution. The examples demonstrate important concepts and strategies that should be considered when analyzing a problem, such as the following: (1) Do the values of the set have unique characteristics (a starting point); does the maximal value satisfy a certain condition (goal), and does the relation between the starting point and the goal inevitably ensure the existence of a maximal value? (2) Is there a simple solution to the problem? (3) Can finding the maximum simplify the solution even when finding out that it is not a goal in itself?

Table 1. Description of problems

Prob. #	Description of the problem		Idea for a solution
	Starting point	Goal	
1	A set of real numbers	Finding the maximum in the set	Initialize Max as the first value, scan, compare, and update Max.
2	Positive numbers (a lower bounded set)	Finding the maximum in the set	Initialization as either the first value, or a random value lower than the range.
3	Negative numbers (an upper bounded set)	Finding the maximum in the set	Initialization as a first value (no lower bound).
4	A set of integers	Finding the maximum in a new set generated from the given set	Equivalent to problem 1, but the complexity is increased since each number's sum of its digits needs to be computed.
5, 6	A set of integers	Finding the maximum of a subset that satisfies a condition	Possibly no value that satisfies the condition exists in the set; thus, the algorithm includes a search for an even number (Problem 5), Similarly, in problem 6 a primality test is included.
7	A dynamically created set	Finding the maximum of a dynamically created set	Initializing two variables, handling each element through accumulation by compensation.
8	A set of integers	Finding the maximum of a subset that satisfies a condition	Satisfying the condition of a subset is not a component of this solution. Converting the problem to a simpler one: finding the maximum of the whole set.
9	A set of integers	Finding the maximum of a subset that satisfies a condition	The solution requires two scans over the set (by using an array). Satisfying a condition is a vital component of the problem. In contrast to problem 8, it is possible that no value that satisfies the condition exists.
10	A set of integers	Finding the maximum of the set	A trivial solution: defining the set allows one to immediately recognize the maximum.
11	A set of integers	Checking homogeneity	Finding the maximum and minimum and calculating the difference between them. No need to compare all pairs.

3 Cognitive Aspects of Problem-Solving and Instructional Design

Presentation of a variety of problems that deal with different aspects of the same idea (a concept, a principle, or an algorithm) in diverse contexts has a significant implication with regard to its comprehension and assimilation and thus it supports one's ability to apply the idea in new situations [11]. The approach of teaching problem solving around a topic is supported by cognitive theories. According to Schema Theory, the process of problem solving in different areas of our life is based on the existence of general solutions to different problems stored in our memory. Schemes exist for solving everyday problems or problems that occur in our professional life. This is especially prominent in the area of solving algorithmic problems in Computer Science, where the experienced solver stores schemas for solving different recurring algorithmic problems. Proficiency is expressed by the number of schemes retained by the solver and the level of their richness. According to the model of the schema theory, a rich schema is one whose components are interconnected as a "knowledge chunk", linked to various examples of its uses, to other schemes, to typical errors, to references of its application, and more. From a cognitive perspective, the goal is to enhance the formation of cognitive schemas [12] that are related to algorithmic problem prototypes and their solutions.

A well-organized set of problems, referring to the selection of problems, their ordering, and their presentation in proximity in time was found to influence the way students cope with problem solving in that area [5]. Presenting examples at gradually increasing levels of difficulty may raise the confidence and the ability of the student to try and solve problems. The cognitive theory thus strengthens the perception of the significant effect of instructional design on the efficiency of learning and the development of proficiency in problem solving.

4 A Teachers' Workshop on Instructional Design

Training teachers to work according to this approach is required; an in-service teachers' training that focuses on the aspects of developing students' problem-solving skills is of outmost importance. A 56-hour workshop was conducted for CS teachers who teach *Fundamentals of Computer Science* in high school. Fifteen teachers attended the workshop. The workshop referred to the difficulties that novices experience in solving algorithmic problems and discussed the ways instructional design may handle these difficulties. One specific workshop activity was designed to stimulate a discussion related to evaluating the complexity level of problems and their challenging aspects. We think that activities of this kind are vital for increasing teachers' awareness of the way they select problems in order to develop critical thinking and effective problem-solving skills among their students [6].

The set of example problems presented in section 2 was presented to the workshop participants. The teachers were asked to rank this collection of problems according to the order of presentation they would recommend. Note that the task of grading was not a goal in itself but a means of encouraging a comprehensive discussion among the workshop participants regarding the different aspects of teaching problem solving around a concept; this goal was indeed achieved. Each teacher presented a grading vector having the following format: the number of the example and its recommended place in the sequence of examples presented. After the grading suggestions were collected, a discussion was held regarding the considerations needed to be taken when constructing a set of problems developed around a concept/idea.

Figure 1 illustrates how teachers graded the set of problems (according to the average taken for each problem). The findings show that teachers tended to grade the problems similarly to the order that the problems were presented above. Differences were found with regard to two cases: (a) the opening problem and (b) changing the order of consecutive problems in some pairs.

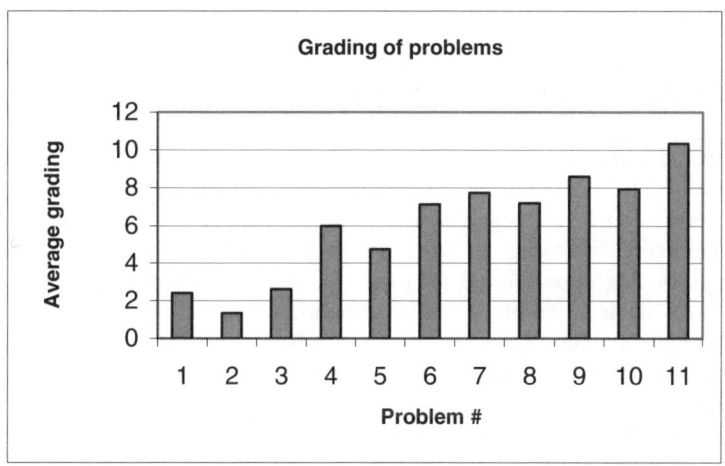

Example #	1	2	3	4	5	6	7	8	9	10	11
Teachers' grading*	2	1	3	5	4	6	8	7	10	9	11

* According to an average grading for each example, the number represents the recommended location of the problem in the set of problems (1- the first problem).

Fig. 1. Grading the examples by the teachers (N=15)

(a) Questions were raised with regard to the opening example: Should it follow the general case or should it refer to a simple limited case? The majority of the teachers preferred example 2 as an initial example, since from their own experience, students tend to initialize variables with zeroing (contrary to the outcome of the study done by Samurcay (1989), which shows that students prefer to initialize with an input [13]). The teachers thought that it is better to begin with a problem having a more tangible solution that is natural for the students, and only later to confront them with solutions that demonstrate the limitations of initializing a special constant value (note that examples 2 and 3 were similarly ranked).

(b) Another controversy was related to the level of complexity of pairs of consecutive problems ((4, 5), (7, 8), (9, 10)). For example, a difference shown in the teachers' ranking refers to the order of presenting problems 4 and 5. Since a maximum that satisfies a condition is not necessarily found in a set, our intention was to present to the students an example that requires testing the existence of a maximum in the context of a given problem. Such a test adds another dimension to the complexity of the problem, and we recommend that example 4 be presented before example 5. It seems that teachers' priority of factors that determine the level of complexity of a problem was different. Most teachers preferred to present example 5 before example 4, explaining their preference in relation to the extent of the complexity of handling each element. Specifically, according to the teachers' view, example 5 is simpler since testing duality is easier than calculating the sum of digits in a number.

5 Concluding Remarks and Recommendations

In this paper, dealing with teaching algorithmic problem solving, we elaborated on the importance of selecting appropriate problems introduced to students. The pedagogical approach presented here integrates several goals, mainly the assimilation of a new concept in Computer Science and improving students' problem-solving skills. It focuses on promoting opportunities to present various aspects of algorithmic problem-solving issues such as problem analysis, identifying constraints in a problem, and adjusting a known solution to satisfy these constraints. The approach was introduced to teachers through a workshop activity aimed at discussing the topic of evaluating the complexity level of problems and their challenging characteristics. We think that an activity of this kind is highly recommended for raising teachers' awareness of the way they select problems in order to develop essential problem-solving skills for students.

The idea of "teaching around a concept" is further developed through the pedagogical approach of Pattern Oriented Instruction [7]. According to this approach, a set of basic algorithmic patterns, introduced in the *Fundamentals of Computer Science* course, was defined [2] and patterns are taught according to similar guidelines; these guidelines include presenting a variety of problems centered around a pattern; the patterns' components are discussed as well as the ideas that are captured in a pattern the instruction points to similarities between problems and patterns. Various links are drawn between different aspects of a pattern and its use in typical applications. Special cases of using a pattern are introduced in different contexts, as well as examples of common misuses and frequently encountered difficulties with problems associated with each pattern. Adjusting patterns according to various constraints is emphasized. Different solutions to a problem are evaluated with regard to efficiency, style, and the tradeoffs between them. In addition, compound problems are analyzed with respect to the ways several sub-tasks are related to one another. This approach was found beneficial in improving students' problem-solving skills [8].

We hope that the approach presented here will assist teachers in designing instructional activities, specifically, in constructing sets of problems aimed at refining and assimilating different aspects of particular topics that they plan to introduce to their students.

References

1. Fleury, A.E.: Encapsulation and reuse as viewed by Java students. In: Proceedings of the 31th SIGCSE Technical Symposium on CS Education, pp. 189–193 (2001)
2. Ginat, D., Haberman, B., Cohen, D., Catz, D., Muller, O., Menashe, E.: Patterns in computer science. Tel- Aviv University (in Hebrew) (2001)
3. Hoare, C.A.R., Jones, C.B.: Essays in Computing Science. Prentice-Hall International, Englewood Cliffs (1989)
4. Linn, M.C., Clancy, M.J.: The case for case studies of programming problems. Communications of the ACM 35(3), 121–132 (1992)
5. Marshall, S.P.: Schemas in problem solving. Cambridge University Press, New York (1995)
6. Muller, O., Haberman, B., Averbuch, H.: (An almost) pedagogical pattern for pattern-based problem-solving instruction. In: Proceedings of ITiCSE 2004, Leeds, UK, pp. 102–106 (2004)
7. Muller, O.: Pattern oriented instruction and the enhancement of analogical reasoning. In: Proceedings of the 1st International Computing Education Research (ICER) Workshop, pp. 57–67 (2005)
8. Muller, O.: The effect of pattern-oriented instruction in computer-science on algorithmic problem-solving skills. Doctoral dissertation, Tel-Aviv University, Israel (2007)
9. Perkins, D.N., Martin, F.: Fragile knowledge and neglected strategies in novice programmers. In: Soloway, E., Iyengar, S. (eds.) Empirical Studies of Programmers, pp. 213–229. Albex Publishing Corporation, Norwood, New Jersey (1986)
10. Rist, R.S.: Schema creation in programming. Cognitive Science 13, 389–414 (1989)
11. Robins, A.: Transfer in cognition. Connection Science 8(2), 185–203 (1996)
12. Robins, S., Mayer, R.E.: Schema training in analogical reasoning. Journal of educational Psychology 85(3), 529–538 (1993)
13. Samurcay, R.: The concept of variable in programming: its meaning and use in problem-solving by novice programmers. In: Soloway, E., Spohrer, J.C. (eds.) Studying the Novice Programmer. Lawrence Erlbaum Associates, Hillsdale (1989)
14. Soloway, E.: From problems to programs via plans: the content and structure of knowledge for introductory lisp programming. J. Educational Computing Research 1(2), 157–172 (1985)
15. Wing, J.M.: Computational thinking. Communication of the ACM 49(3), 33–35 (2006)

VIPER, a Student-Friendly Visual Interpreter of Pascal

Michał Adamaszek[1], Piotr Chrząstowski-Wachtel[2], and Anna Niewiarowska[2]

[1] Institute of Mathematics
[2] Institute of Informatics
University of Warsaw
ul. Banacha 2, 02-097 Warsaw, Poland
{aszek,pch,annan}@mimuw.edu.pl

Abstract. We introduce VIPER, a visual interpreter of Pascal, designed to help both the teachers and the students of an introductory programming course. The main innovation of VIPER is the ability to display typically encountered data structures (e.g. trees, lists) in an intuitive way. This, and other usability improvements, have been designed specifically to meet the needs of future users. The interpreter is aimed mostly at *small scale* programming exercises, and lets the user edit and run portions of code step-by-step with all the needed values being displayed in a suitable manner.

1 Introduction

Teaching programming can be challenging. Beginners do not always imagine the state and flow of the program properly. The teachers have several aids at their disposal, from the traditional blackboard where pointers may be drawn as arrows to premade interactive presentations of selected algorithms. Unfortunately, when students want to run a program on their own, try to understand its behaviour, or create and debug a new program, all they are left with is the compiler and a (usually quite obscure and unfriendly) debugger.

Experience also shows that the teacher's job is to form a correct mental model of the control flow, memory state, and their interaction. There are quite a few matters which are not at all obvious for novices with no such model in their heads. Typical areas of misunderstanding are the proper usage of arrays, the meaning of pointers, passing of arguments to functions etc.

We believe that Pascal is the right language for an introductory programming course: it emanates all the features of the imperative paradigm, yet its syntax is fairly simple and straightforward. VIPER (**VI**sual **P**ascal Interpret**ER**) is a graphical tool designed to support students in the learning process. It is a visual interpreter of a slightly adjusted version of a subset of Pascal. VIPER demonstrates the execution of the program and displays the contents of the memory in an intuitive way. The focus of VIPER is not on teaching the concepts of imperative programming, but on explaining the behaviour of algorithms. VIPER is a tool both for the teacher and for the student who wants to learn and experiment with the code on his/her own. Our experiences with VIPER as a tool for the students of an introductory programming course, together with these students' opinions, are given in section 6.

The idea of a visual interpreter is not new. The closest relatives of VIPER are VIP (for C++, [1,2]) and The Teaching Machine (for C++ and Java, [3,4]). They both visualize the memory state during execution. The Teaching Machine is a very well developed software, with such features as micro-steps in expression evaluation and multiple views of the memory. Other environments, like Turbo Pascal, offered a basic view of the variables' values as well. VIPER includes some brand new ideas, that will be discussed in section 3.

2 Motivation

What should we expect from a visual interpreter? It should be able to execute any correct program[1], displaying the memory state. Typical data pieces should be presented in the way we are accustomed to: simple variables as memory slots, arrays as rows of values, pointers as arrows, records (objects) as boxes containing the fields and so on. Clearly not everything can and should be displayed: an attempt to present the contents of a complicated data structure, linked from records with multiple fields and nested arrays etc. would inevitably cause a terrible mess on the screen. Luckily, in a typical learning environment one does not need such monsters.[2] In the design process we focused on what experience says about the real needs of our target users — the teachers and the students.

A typical visual interpreter has all the features described above. We want more. Suppose, for instance, that we are trying to understand the binary search algorithm:

```
{ input: a[1..N], x }
left := 0; right := N + 1;
repeat
   mid := (left + right) div 2;
   if x < a[mid] then
      right := mid
   else left := mid;
until right = left + 1
found :=  x = a[left]
```

A typical visual interpreter will give us a display that looks more or less like the one in the left part of Fig.1. To check, which part of the array is being searched, we need to perform a few tedious and error-prone steps. Would it not be better if the memory state was displayed as in the right part of Fig.1? This

---

[1] There is a difference between a general-use interpreter and a presentation engine, which can only be used to prepare visualisations of predefined (and unmodifiable) pieces of code.
[2] In either case we want the interpreter to execute such a program, even if too compound data is not displayed.

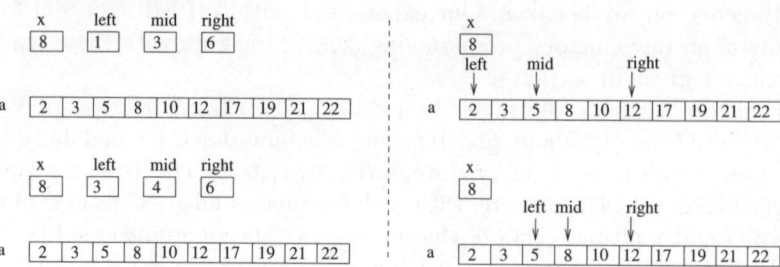

Fig. 1. One step of the binary search algorithm displayed in a traditional way (left) and with VIPER enhancements (right)

presentation is easier to follow. Another example of this sort is depicted in Fig. 2: both sides show the same data structure, but the presentation on the right is far more convincing and intuitive. For a general-purpose interpreter a binary tree is just a bunch of records linked with pointers with no special meaning. We want this sort of data structures (trees, linked lists) to be displayed the way we are all accustomed to, since otherwise they become counter-intuitive and clumsy.

Observations of this sort motivated us to come up with a new visual interpreter. Some other observations have lead to new extra features, which may seem to be of little importance, but as we anticipated, they would have impact on the usability and user-friendliness, particularly in the learning environment. These are described in the next section. Later we shall give two step-by-step examples of interaction with VIPER.

Let us outline the most important missing features of the existing debuggers or interpreters that we think would let the students better understand how programs work. Our experience makes evidence that there are some basic problems the students face when they make first steps in programming. Even later, when they learn about more advanced topics, they lack sufficiently friendly programming environments to visualize the concepts and to make learning programming in small scale attractive and neat.

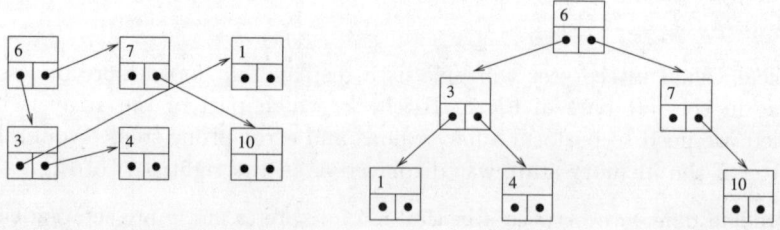

Fig. 2. A mysterious data structure that turns out to be a binary tree when laid out in the common way

Among others we consider the following features of greatest importance:

Array indices. It may be quite hard to follow many array indices at a time. When we explain algorithms on a blackboard, the most usual way to represent indices is to draw arrows pointing to specific array cells. It seems a natural idea to use the same visualization concept in the tool.

Stack operations. When explaining recursion, the visualization of the activation records is a great advantage and a big step towards understanding the recursion implementation.

Linked lists. The list data structure is not easy to visualize. Again, when drawing on a blackboard or explaining the algorithmic concepts in a book, the best way to explain the list operations is to visualize the pointer values as arrows pointing to specific records.

Rooted trees. Algorithms on trees are much better understood, if a tree is represented by means of graphical visualisation of its nodes and edges. The crucial moment is to observe how the tree structure changes after certain operations (like rotations).

Another disadvantage of the existing visualization environments is the difficulty to initialize data — especially when we talk about lists or trees. Our tool is equipped with a user-friendly initialization procedure, allowing to assign the desired values quickly, and — moreover — to keep the chosen values for consecutive runs. Initializing data visually by pointing at the appropriate data structure fields and inserting the requested values (or choosing them by one of the standard ways) saves a lot of time and allows the student to concentrate on the important aspects of programming.

3 System Overview

Figure 3 contains the screenshot of VIPER's main window. The left panel contains the code of the executed program (1) and two consoles, one acting as standard output (2) and one for the auxiliary messages (3). The display with the memory state uses most of the window (5). The presentation of selected variables can be turned on and off (4) and the whole window can be resized (8), so that only the important elements are visible. The currently executed line of code is highlighted. The interpreter works in three modes: editing, compilation and execution. In the execution mode VIPER covers the functionality of a reasonable debugger with run, stop, step and step over commands (6), breakpoints and speed control (7). The main display presents the values of global variables and the call stack (9). Complex nested types will never be displayed. However, from our perspective the ability to handle nested types in a graphical way is of little importance.

What mattered to us a lot more was to increase the efficiency of the learning process. To this end we introduced the following features:

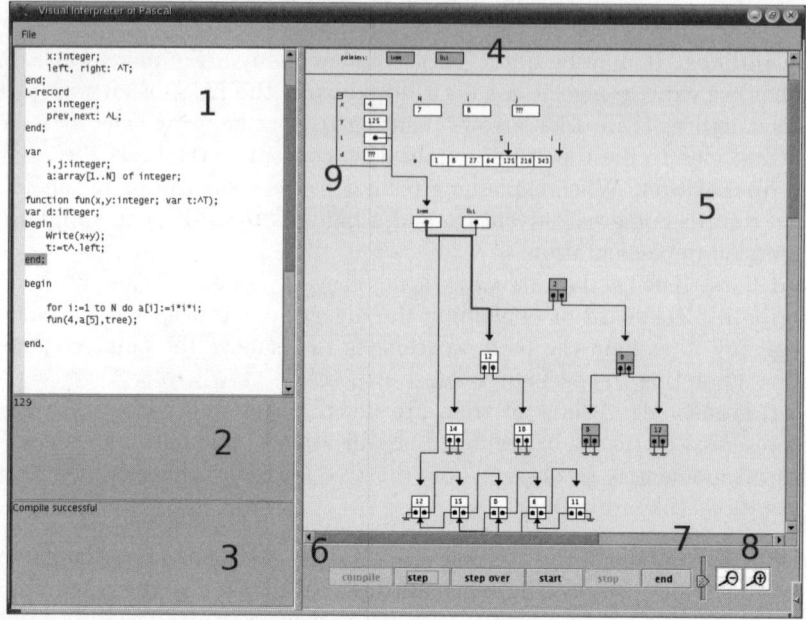

Fig. 3. The layout of VIPER

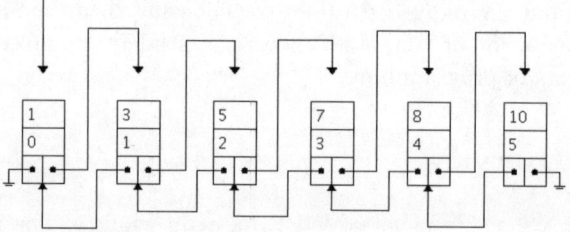

Fig. 4. The visualisation of a linked list. A screenshot from VIPER.

Innovative animation.

– The array indices are pointing to the appropriate elements of arrays, as suggested in figure 1. They start being displayed as arrows once the variable is used as an array index.
– The call stack with local variables and parameters is available: by default only the top frame is visible, but any frame can be unwinded and displayed by just one mouse click, together with its entry point in the code.
– The display of any variable can be switched on and off, so that the uninteresting variables (if there are any in a particular example) do not obscure the view.
– Simple and bidirectional linked lists, as well as binary trees are treated specially: the order of the displayed entries is always preserved, even when a new element is entered into the structure or during other manipulations (see

figures 2 and 4). These data structures cover most of the students' needs when it comes to implementing algorithms.

VIPER uses the "best-effort" strategy to visualize and animate lists and trees appropriately. Of course all assumptions concerning the layout are void if the user manipulates the pointers in some arbitrary, unreasonable way (still a sudden decoupling of the view may also be a very clear indicator of errors in the program).

Initialization. During experimentation a user may often wish to test his/her program against different data sets, or to test different versions of one program against one data set. Providing initial data for an algorithm can be a very tedious thing to do. For instance, if one wants to test an algorithm that searches a value in a linked list, then the code needed to create the initial list may easily grow longer than the code of the actual algorithm. To make the initialization easier we enable the initial data to be parameters of the program, just as if the program was a procedure. That means we extend the Pascal syntax to allow constructions like:

```
program Merge(x: integer; list: ^TList);
```

We assume the type TList to be defined later in the program. When the program is started, the user will be prompted to provide the values of the variables declared in the header. The types of variables initializable in this way are primitives (integers, reals and booleans), arrays of primitives, lists and trees. All of them can be given values with an intuitive initialization interface, which enables "shaping" lists and trees and, besides straightforward data input, provides some predefined initialization patterns for various data types (like increasing, consecutive, constant, random, etc.). What we believe to be especially useful in a learning environment is the possibility to fill a variable with the value from the previous program run (which can be altered before it is approved for use). This feature can be used even after modifying the program code.

Of course the extended header is not obligatory. One may use traditional, non-parametrized header and not be prompted for any initial data at all.

Runtime features. VIPER performs some runtime checks to detect common mistakes a student should learn to avoid:

- accessing an array index out of range, even though in some low-level languages (like C) this would not necessarily cause a runtime error.
- reading from a non-initialized variable.
- memory leaks. With an algorithm resembling the mark-and-sweep technique VIPER finds unreachable objects. They are marked appropriately so that the user is notified that such a problem appears (these are the shaded tree nodes on the screenshot in Fig.3). Even in the era of automatic garbage collection programmers should understand when their objects become unreachable.

When designing the conveniences described in this section we kept in mind the needs of a novice programmer. The initialization schemes are especially useful for testing and presentation of algorithms that operate on more complex inputs. Now we turn to some examples of VIPER in action.

4 Example: Longest Common Subsequence (LCS)

Let us see how to solve the Longest Common Subsequence problem with VIPER. We begin with declaring what input the program should expect. This amounts to using an appropriate header. The variables of the header will be initialized by VIPER with the help of a user-friendly interface.

```
program LCS(n,m:integer;
            A:array[1..n] of Integer;
            B:array[1..m] of Integer);
```

When the program is run, the user will be prompted to provide initial values for n, m, A and B, as shown in Fig.5. At this point the user may choose to use the values from the previous program run, to enter new values manually or to use one of the predefined schemes.

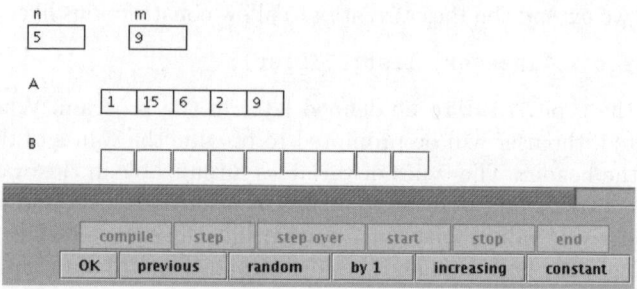

Fig. 5. Initializing the LCS algorithm

The given LCS problem will be solved by a dynamic algorithm (see [7]). It utilizes an auxiliary array T, where T[i,j] is the length of the longest common subsequence of the sequences A[1..i] and B[1..j]. Then the 0-th row and column are set to 0, and each subsequent entry depends on at most three of its neighbours: to the left, up, and to the up-left:

```
for i:=1 to n do
 for j:=1 to m do
 begin
   if A[i]=B[j] then
     T[i,j]:=T[i-1,j-1]+1
   else T[i,j]:=T[i-1,j-1];

   if (T[i-1,j]>T[i,j]) then T[i,j]:=T[i-1,j];

   if (T[i,j-1]>T[i,j]) then T[i,j]:=T[i,j-1];
 end;
```

Figure 6 demonstrates the display at some point during the program execution. The interpreter keeps track of all expressions that are being used as array indices and relocates the labeled arrows whenever the expressions' values change.

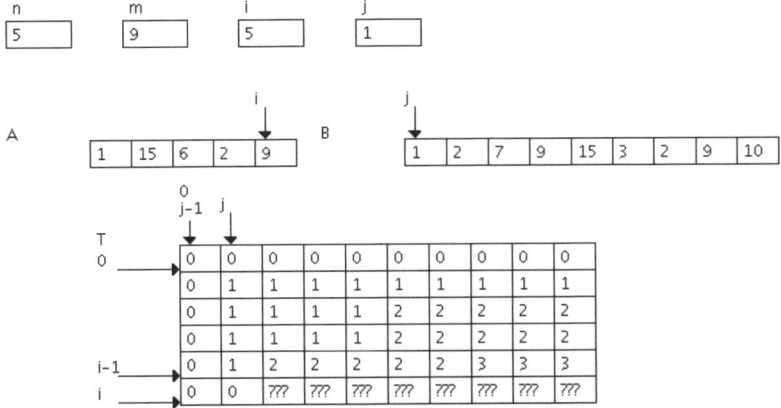

Fig. 6. In the main loop of the LCS program. Here the LCS of A and B is $[1, 15, 2, 9]$. Observe that both pointers `j-1` and `j` as well as `i-1` and `i` are displayed, because all of them were used as array indices in the code.

The final answer (`T[n,m]`) is printed to the console upon the completion of the program. This example shows how the use of enhanced array indices improves the clarity of an algorithm.

5 Another Example: Binary Search Tree

Our next instructive task is to insert the elements of a given array into a (possibly already non-empty) binary search tree. We assume the processed elements are integers. Once again we begin with declaring all the necessary input variables:

```
program bstInsert(
    N: integer;
    a: array[1..N] of integer;
    root: ^Tree);

type Tree = record
    w: integer;
    left, right: ^Tree;
end
```

After the compilation the user will be asked to define, among other variables, the initial binary tree referenced by the pointer `root`. There is a dedicated visual interface which allows shaping a binary tree easily. All it takes is to simply wind or unwind the chosen nodes to obtain the desired shape, which can be filled in with data (in our case the x fields). Here again we may benefit from certain initialization schemes.

It should be mentioned here that the recognition of records forming the nodes of binary trees is syntax-based: the last two fields of the record should be appropriately named pointers of the tree's type, as in the above example. If not, then such data structure will be considered "random" and will not be laid out in a tree-like fashion. A similar remark applies to the lists. Except for this requirement the nodes may contain an arbitrary set of fields with any contents (the structure of a binary search tree is just being used as an example here).

Inserting a single value is fairly simple. The function `insert` returns the pointer to the currently processed tree or to the new node:

```
function insert(t: ^Tree; x: integer):^Tree;
begin
   if t=nil then insert:=new_node(x)
   else begin
      if t^.w>x then
         t^.left := insert(t^.left, x)
      else if t^.w<x then
         t^.right := insert(t^.right, x);
      insert := t;
   end
end;
```

Now the main loop is very short:

```
var i: integer;

begin
   for i:=1 to N do
      root := insert(root, a[i]);
end.
```

In this example we may observe how a student might deal with an error situation. Suppose the provided definition of new_node was a bit untidy:

```
function new_node(x:integer):^Tree;
begin
   new(new_node);
   new_node^.w:=x;
end;
```

This sort of unintended omission is actually pretty frequent. It may cause the program to fail due to an attempt to read from an uninitialized variable (`left` or `right`) when traversing the tree. Uninitialized variables are marked appropriately, so this problem can be detected very soon. To fix it we need to interrupt the execution, add the missing lines:

```
   new_node^.left:=nil;
   new_node^.right:=nil;
```

and restart the interpreter. Now the ability to restart the program with the

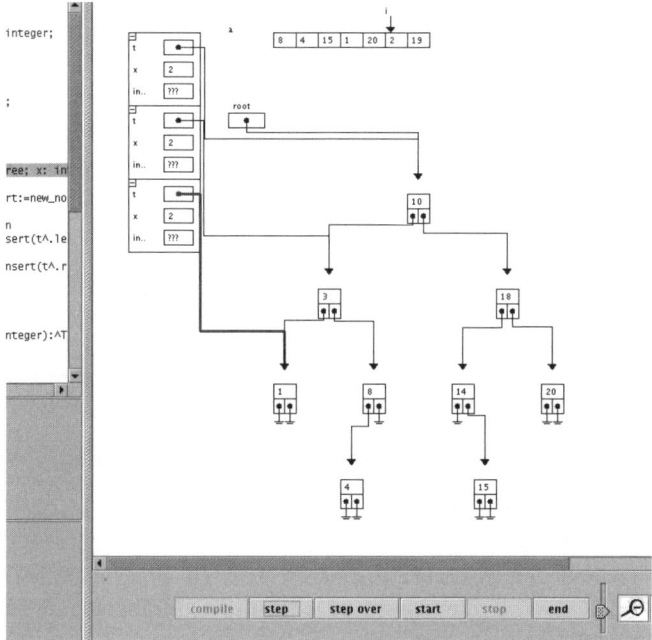

Fig. 7. The tree has been successfully expanded

previous initial data proves extremely useful — just imagine that we wanted to restart the program multiple times with the same data set, which is quite a typical thing to do when testing or experimenting.

The corrected program will now continue, creating a structure shown in Fig.7. The screenshot in this figure demonstrates also the visualization of the unwinded call stack. The thick arrow is a pointer whose beginning was clicked with a mouse. This helps conveniently track a pointer in a dense maze of arrows.

6 The Usage and Perspectives of VIPER

VIPER was designed to be part of the Open Studies in Computer Science platform ([5]), a comprehensive collection of course material for students of computer science in Poland. We have used VIPER for 2 years at the University of Warsaw during the introductory programming course for the first-year students. Our students, who come to study computer science at the Department of Informatics, have quite a wide scale of programming skills at the entrance. There are finalists of the IOI as well as absolute beginners among them. We made a poll about the usability of VIPER and got a warm feedback, especially from the beginners group. In fact this was the target group of our project.

We quote here a few opinions of the students, that concern mainly the new VIPER features:

- "I was especially happy to be given a tool that enables me to see step by step, how my program works. It made me understand the whole process of programming."
- "The most useful option in VIPER is the visualization of lists, arrays and so on. A nice feature is the possibility to adjust the execution speed."
- "The possibility to input data in an easy way (for instance the array or list elements, including the list or tree extensions) was a great advantage of this tool."
- "Using VIPER during the lectures was especially instructive, when the details of the recursion and the tree algorithms were illustrated. Tree visualization is the main advantage of VIPER for me."

The students complained about the limitations of VIPER. In particular they mentioned:

- lack of nested procedures (more generally: VIPER does not cover all of the Free Pascal syntax),
- not enough standard initialization patterns (like non-decreasing values in an array),
- "The generated pictures were not clever enough when complex algorithms were tested. The program should be a bit more intelligent, and see more of the user's needs."

Having in mind the students' comments, we plan to extend VIPER with some more functionalities. In particular we plan to allow nesting procedures and introduce other data structures like trees of arbitrary degree, stacks, queues and so on. The next step might be to enable meta-programming of visual presentations. The creator of a presentation (or simply: a teacher) might then annotate the program with markers indicating default initial values, breakpoints, extra display options etc.

It would also be very valuable to allow younger pupils (such as in secondary schools) benefit from VIPER at their lessons of informatics.

VIPER was written entirely in Java and thus remains compatible with all platforms equipped with the Java Virtual Machine (another advantage of this is easy internationalization). It is available both as a stand-alone program with the ability to read/save programs from/to files and as a Web applet. The latter version is especially useful to prepare course material for students. In this form VIPER was integrated with the site [5]. The solutions to some exercises are accompanied by visualisations prepared in VIPER. The relevant code of the solution is pre-loaded by the applet, but then the students can experiment with it in whatever way they like.

More information about VIPER, with a detailed user manual, syntax definition, on-line applet and numerous examples (including the ones from this paper) can be found at the website [6].

Acknowledgements. This work was partially supported by the EU European Social Fund. VIPER relies on the modified version of the parser generator

Coco/R by H. Mössenböck, M. Loberbauer and A. Woss from the University of Linz. We would also like to thank Daria Walukiewicz-Chrząszcz, Jacek Chrząszcz and Wiesław Bartkowski whose ideas shaped some of the features of VIPER. Robert Gontarczuk, Paweł Laskowski, Michał Oniszczuk, Adam Panasiuk and the referees provided us with helpful comments.

References

1. The VIP Interpreter, http://www.cs.tut.fi/~vip/en/
2. Virtanen, A., Lahtinen, E., Jarvinen, H.-M.: VIP, a Visual Interpreter for Learning Introductory Programming with C++. In: Proceedings of The Fifth Koli Calling Conference on Computer Science Education, Koli, Finland, November 17-20 (2005)
3. The Teaching Machine, http://www.teachingmachine.org/
4. Norvell, T., Bruce-Lockhart, M.: Teaching Computer Programming with Program Animation. In: Canadian Conference on Electrical and Computer Engineering, Calgary, Alberta (2004)
5. Open Studies in Computer Science, http://wazniak.mimuw.edu.pl
6. VIPER Website, http://viper.mimuw.edu.pl
7. Cormen, T.H., Leiserson, C.E., Rivest, R.L., Stein, C.: Introduction to Algorithms. MIT Press, Cambridge (2001)

Analysis of Students' Developed Programs at the Maturity Exams in Information Technologies

Jonas Blonskis[1] and Valentina Dagienė[2]

[1] Kaunas University of Technology
Sukilėlių str. 112–34, Kaunas, LT-49240 Lithuania
jonas.blonskis@ktu.lt
[2] Vilnius University, Faculty of Mathematics and Informatics
Naugarduko str. 24, Vilnius, LT-03225, Lithuania
dagiene@ktl.mii.lt

Abstract. Two models of the maturity exams in information technologies have been developed in Lithuania. The first one is intended to evaluate the students' skills for using information and communication technologies (ICT). Another is focused on programming skills and is intended to promote the professional studies (informatics) in higher education. The first national exam in information technologies (programming) was launched in 2006. The exam consists of a set of tests (questions of IT and questions of programming) and two practical programming tasks. The goal of practical tasks is to create programs for given tasks. Developing programs is one of the most important parts of the exam and also one of the most difficult tasks for students. The paper deals with solutions of practical tasks – students' developed programs during the national exams in information technologies (programming) in 2006 and 2007.

Keywords: programming, teaching informatics, writing programs, data structures, algorithms.

1 Introduction

In Lithuania, informatics was incorporated into the optional maturity exams' block of science. Informatics as a separate subject was taught many years in comprehensive schools. To establish the maturity exam in informatics was quite natural. Discussion on maturity of informatics exams have been presented in the second ISSEP conference [2].

Since the content of informatics teaching has turned more to information technology it was decided to develop two types of exams [3]. The first one is focused on the user and is intended to evaluate students' ICT skills. Another one is focused on programming skills and is intended to evaluate the professional interest of students in computing.

The main goal of the national exam in IT (programming) is to encourage students to take interest in programming. The demand for programmers is considerable. Programming as a creative process is being comprehended by learning to write programs from one's as early as possible youth upwards. Algorithmic and structural thinking skills greatly influence the conception of the exact sciences, and not only.

The results of the national exam are being recognized when choosing studies of informatics or informatics-related specialities at Lithuanian universities. Those, who pass the national exam in IT (programming) successfully, have wider possibilities to become students of their desired direction of studies, *i.e.* informatics. At the same time it is a check weather a student has the aptitude for studying informatics: there are quite many first year students who quit their studies since they find programming too hard to understand and an uninviting occupation for themselves.

2 Structure and Content of the Exams

It makes a little confusion that both maturity exams are called IT (due to the subject´s name – informatics was renamed in 2002 to information technology including programming as well). However both types of exams are strongly differentiated by their level: the school exam is based on ICT skills and the national exam is based on programming skills.

The content of the school exam in IT is based on the general curriculum of IT for grades 11-12. When developing the content, the recommendations of world experts were taken into consideration [1, 2]. The national IT (programming) exam is based on the optional module of the advanced course named "Basic of programming" [4]. The curriculum of this module consists of: 1) introduction – basic elements of programming; 2) data structures; 3) developing algorithms; 4) testing and debugging programs.

In spring of 2005, the pilot national IT (programming) exam was completed [2]. After the analysis of the pilot exam and evaluation of the remarks provided by teachers and students it was decided to establish the national exam in IT (programming) since 2006.

The national exam in IT (programming) consists of two parts: the larger part (75%) is allocated to programming, while the remaining part (25%) concerns the issues of computer literacy. The programming part consists of test (25%) and two practical tasks (50%). The aim of the programming test is to examine the level of students' knowledge and understanding of the tools required in programming (elements of programming language, data types and structures, control structures, basic algorithms).

The national exam in IT (programming) focus on: the knowledge and understanding – 30%, the skills – 30%, and the problem solving – 40%. The problems are oriented towards the selection of data structures and application of basic algorithms to work with the created data structures.

Further, we will deal just with the practical tasks of the national exam in IT (programming): their aims, complexity, and evaluation. Solutions developed by students and the problems with them are discussed. The national exam curriculum and tasks are prepared in the National examination centre of the Republic of Lithuania (URL: http://www.nec.lt) [5].

The main attention is being paid to the abilities to choose the proper data types and data structures (Fig. 1.), also to the implementation of the algorithms and developing the programs (Table 1.).

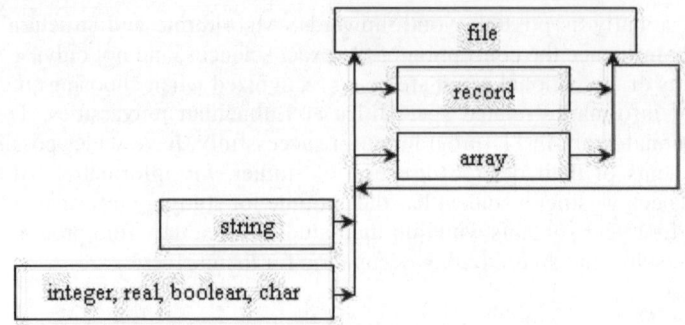

Fig. 1. Relations of data structures used in practical tasks

Table 1. Requirements for practical tasks (evaluation criteria)

Elements of program	Scores (percentage)
1. Analysis and development of data structures	20
2. Algorithms of data processing	40
3. Control structures	10
4. Programming tools and environments	10
5. Programming technology	10
6. Testing and debugging	5
7. Programming style	5

3 Concepts of Solving Practical Tasks – Writing Programs

The practical part of the national exam in IT (programming) consists of two tasks – students have to write programs for the given problems. The practical tasks constitute 50% of all points. The main aim is to examine the students' ability to master independently the stages of programming activities, *i.e.* to move from the formulation of the task to the final result. The number of students' who attempted to solve each task and the statistics of their achievements is provided in Table 2 (for the year 2006 and 2007).

The first tasks are easier. Therefore, the bigger number of students have attempted to solve them. It should be pointed out that when performing the examination at the second time (in 2007) the number of students who didn't try to solve any of the two tasks has significantly decreased: from 9 % (in 2006) to 1 % (in 2007).

Table 2. Statistical data on solving tasks in 2006 and 2007

Number of students	Task	Number of students who tried to solve	have got all scores	have got zero score
1164 in 2006	The first task	997 (86%)	8	167
	The second task	869 (75%)	8	295
	The first + the second task	1159 (99.5%)	12	109
876 in 2007	The first task	766 (87%)	102	110
	The second task	600 (68%)	114	114
	The first + the second task	803 (92%)	65	9

The first tasks are intended to examine the students' abilities to write programs of the difficulty described in educational standards. The abilities of students to use the array data type for work with integers, to realize the algorithms for work with data structures as well as the abilities to manage with input and output in text files are being examined.

The second tasks are intended to examine the students' understanding and abilities of implementation of the record data type. The core of the task is to develop the appropriate structures of record together with arrays. The abilities to input data from text file into arrays containing elements of record type, to perform operations by implementing the analyzed algorithms, and to present the results in a text file are being examined. The operations are to be performed just with the numerical values. The curriculum doesn't suppose operations with character strings, only reading and derivation of such strings are being applied.

4 Analysis of the First Tasks

The main aim of first tasks is to show the abilities to develop array data types, input data from a text file into an array, implement basic algorithms, and output the results in a text file. Besides, the student's ability to distinguish the separate operations and to write the procedures and functions for them is being examined.

4.1 The National Exam in IT (Programming) in 2006

Calculation of the resistance in the electrical wiring. Write the program which calculates the total resistance in the circuit, if the circuit consists of one or more coherently connected parts; each part of the circuit consists of two or more parallelly connected resistors whose resistance are known.

In the task mathematical formulas for calculation of the resultant resistances in the system of coherently and parallelly interconnected resistances were provided. Example of input file (the chart of the electrical circuit and the data file) is shown in Fig. 2.

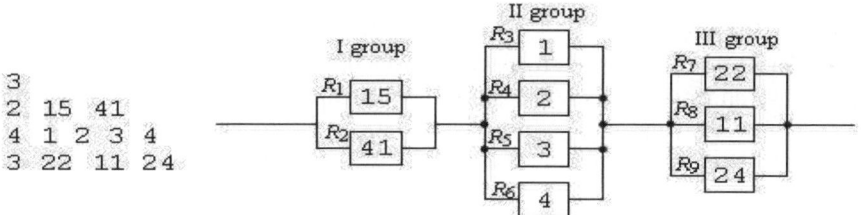

Fig. 2. Electrical wiring example

The main aim of the task is to select the proper data structures. There were no limitations considering the structure of program, data types, and algorithm of the task (the way of solution): students could choose the most appropriate measures for themselves.

Students have chosen very different data structures (Table 3). Certainly, not only the size of the program but also its complexity depended on this.

Table 3. The examples of data types used by students in their programs

number of resistors	2		4			3				
resistors	15	41	1	2	3	4	22	11	24	
number of resistors	2		4			3				
resistors	15	41	1	2	3	4	22	11	24	
resistors of group	R1		R2			R3				
number of resistors	2		4			3				
resistors and resistors of group	15	41	1	2	3	4	22	11	24	R1 R2 R3	
conduction of groups	L1	L2	L3							
numbers of resistors and resistors	2 / 4 / 3	15 / 1 / 22	41 / 2 / 11	3 / 24	4					

| record date type | ```TResistors = array [1..50] of real;`
`TGroup = record    NResistors : integer;    // Number of resistors`
`       Resistors : TResistors; // Resistors of one group`
`       RR : real;              // Conduction of group`
`end;`
`TAllGroups = array [1..100] of TGroup;``` |
|---|---|

To store the data the following data types were used:

- The set of variables;
- One-dimensional arrays (one, two or even three arrays);
- Two-dimensional array (separately or combined along with one or two one-dimensional ones);
- Arrays of record types (the records with the fields of array type were implemented).

A quarter of the programs was randomly selected for the analysis (Table 4).

The complexity of the program was seriously influenced by its structure, number of the procedures implemented and their rationality. It is obvious that there are three parts that can be pointed out when performing the task: data input (from file), calculations, and output of the results (in the file). There were student programs in which the

Table 4. Selection of data structures

Used data structures	Selected by evaluators	
	Number of programs	Size (bytes)
1. Variables	32	473–1675
2. One-dimensional array	129	574–3123
3. Two-dimensional array	48	600–2767
4. Record	64	632–2883
5. Non-working programs	38	86–1882

mentioned parts were realized by separate procedures or blocks in the main program; however, there were also programs where all calculations were performed during the data input. The essential differences noticed in the programs rest upon the selection of data structures.

It was hard to evaluate the solutions of this task since students have applied nearly everything what was possible.

The task, however, has certain advantages: students can independently choose their way of writing the program by applying what they know and understand best. The disadvantage is that such freedom enabled less-skillful students to choose more complicated and confused ways to solve the problem. They didn't manage to assess the chosen ways of solving, to understand their complexity. Some students made quite plenty of the mistakes while performing the mathematical operations.

After analyzing and evaluating the solutions of the task it is possible to assume that when formulating the tasks the measures for their solution should be pointed out. The measures that are not foreseen in the module should be restricted. It is presumable that students will better reflect on their programs and will write them in more simple ways, thus avoiding the majority of the mistakes. It will be possible to evaluate programs written by students who have less practical experience.

4.2 The National Exam in IT (Programming) in 2007

Mushrooms. *In July, each day after returning home from a forest Peter writes down how many ceps, chanterelles, and champignons he has picked up. Sometimes Peter goes to the forest several times a day. Write the program which: 1) calculates the number of mushrooms picked up each day of mushrooming according to their sort; 2) finds the day that was the most successful for mushrooming and estimate the number of the mushrooms picked up that day.*

Requirements:

- Use just one-dimensional arrays of integers.
- Use a function to obtain the number of the day that was the most successful.
- Write the procedure to output the list of mushrooms picked up depending on the days in the file.

These exact requirements were intended to examine the abilities of students to write and apply procedures and functions as well as data structures (array).

It was prescribed to apply just one-dimensional arrays of integers. The solution would appear to be more simple if the application of two-dimensional arrays or arrays with records were allowed. However, that was not provided in educational standards. Besides, that would determine unequal conditions for the evaluation. Programmers must be capable to follow predescribed requirements.

The results of the evaluation are presented in Fig. 3.

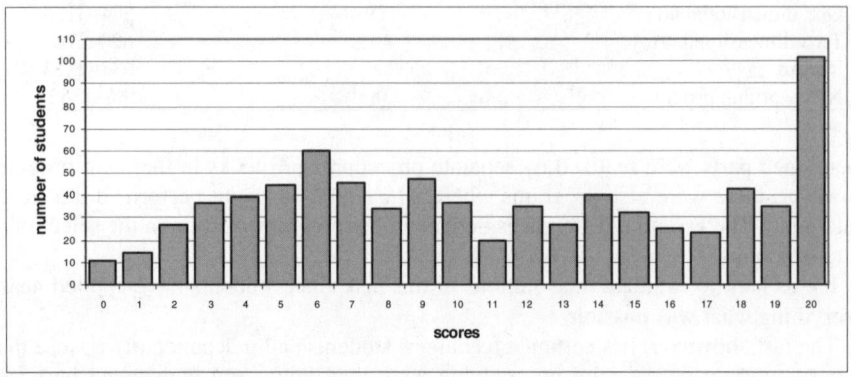

Fig. 3. Evaluation of the first task (the national exam in IT, programming, 2007)

The task has clearly distinguished students who are able to reflect and do not follow merely the standard solutions, who are open for creativity. By implementing the numbers of the days used as an index value (subscript) of the array the program of the task turns to be simple and short, it doesn't require complex operations for data processing.

5 Analysis of the Second Task

The task is intended to examine the students' practical skills to apply the record data structure. Record is a sufficiently complex, but at the same time quite flexible data structure. Students have to show their abilities to analyze the task by creating a reasoned data structure and by appreciating that not only the size of the program, but also its complexity depends on it. The task clearly distinguishes students' abilities to reflect.

5.1 The National Exam in IT (Programming) in 2006

The Journey. Make a timetable for the bus running between Vilnius and Klaipėda. You know the distances between the stops, the time of departure from Vilnius (hours and minutes) and the average speed of the bus. The bus arrives to Klaipėda on the same day. Write the program to calculate the time of bus arrival to stops. The calculation must be performed in one minute accuracy. Consider that the bus doesn't spend time in the stops.

Requirements:

- Store the data and the results in arrays of record type elements.
- Create and apply the data input procedure from the file to the array

- Create and apply the procedure for the calculation.
- Create and apply the procedure to output the results to a file.
- Apply the function which calculates the time (in minutes) spent by the bus to travel the indicated distance:

```
function Time (distance, speed : real) : integer;
begin
    Time := Trunc (distance / speed * 60);
end;
```

The requirements help to make clear the students' abilities to apply procedures and functions, their skills to structure programs and to develop data structures. When performing the calculation real numbers must be converted to integers. It is possible to apply function Round or Trunc. In FreePascal, Delphi, and Lazarus function Trunc doesn't work correctly. This was discovered just after the exam was over.

There are at least two ways of solving the given problem.

The 1st way. The distance from Vilnius to the stop is being calculated. That is a simple algorithm for the accumulation of the sum of the distances between individual stop. Then, with the help of the function Time, the time (in minutes) spent by bus to travel from Vilnius to the particular stop is being calculated. By converting the time of the departure to minutes we obtain the time of the arrival to the stop. Now we just need to transform the obtained result in hours and minutes.

The 2nd way. The time spent to travel between adjacent stops is being calculated. Then the obtained time is being added to the time spent on travelling to the previous stop. However, this way of calculating causes the appearance of too many errors: each time of departure to the stops was calculated by converting the obtained minutes to integer number. Besides, the programs written in such a way were bigger in size and contained much more mistakes. Especially, when hours and minutes were being calculated separately and summed up separately. This way of solving the task is irrational. It demonstrates that students who have chosen it didn't spend too much time for thinking on the other, simpler solutions.

Such type of tasks is inappropriate for exams since it is hard to unambiguously evaluate issues related to the application of real numbers. Nevertheless, this task has helped a lot to examine the students' abilities to create data structures of record type. One, two, three, and even four records of different structure were applied in the programs. It was nice to notice which structure for storage of the data and the results obtained was created.

Both ways of solving the task were nearly equally popular among the students. The results of the evaluation are provided in Fig. 4.

5.2 The National Exam in IT (Programming) in 2007

Mushrooms, again. *A club of mushrooming enthusiasts was established. Each participant after returning from a forest writes down the number of ceps, chanterelles, and champignons he has picked up. Write the program which: 1) calculates how many ceps, chanterelles, and champignons separately were picked up by each mushrooming enthusiast during the season, and 2) finds which of the participants was the most successful one and how many mushrooms he has picked up.*

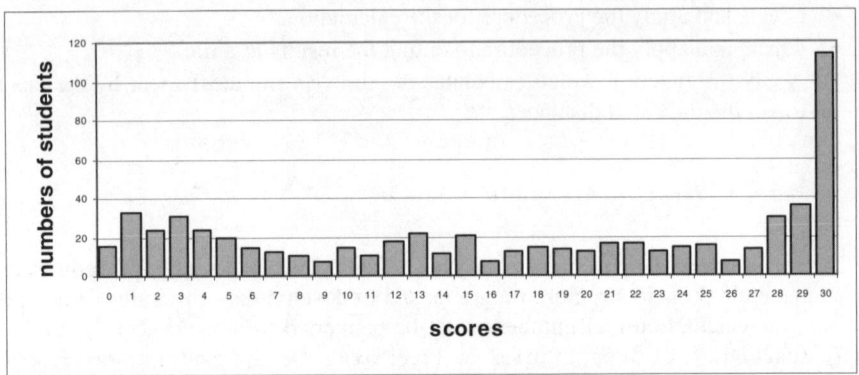

Fig. 4. Evaluation of the second task (the national exam in IT, programming, 2006)

Requirements:
- To process the data and the results use variables of record type and arrays with record typed elements.
- Write the procedure to input the data from file. It is not necessary to stick to the initial form of the data.
- Write the procedure for output, printing the results (who has how many mushrooms picked up and what sort they were).
- Write the function to find the best participant (the one who has picked up the largest number of mushrooms).

The point in this task is to choose the appropriate data structure, *i.e.* what kind of record and how many of them have to be created. The variety of possible solutions is wide; however, the most reasonable one is to perform a part of the operation (summation) during the process of input reading from file. The results of the evaluation are provided in Fig. 5.

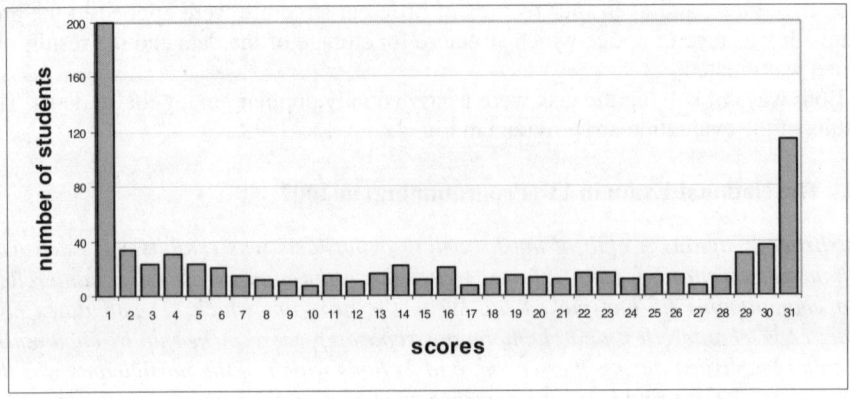

Fig. 5. Evaluation of the second task (the national exam in IT, programming, 2007)

6 Comparison of the Tasks

When comparing the tasks of both years (Table 5) one can observe that the tasks of the year 2006 not sufficiently verified the practical skills and abilities of students: just knowledge of algorithms provided in educational standards was partially examined. Both tasks were structured insufficiently. Students have applied data structures irrationally; they have employed even such structures that are not provided in the curriculum and that were off the purpose (e.g., two-dimensional array).

In 2007 the implementation of data structures was restricted. The tasks contained more possibilities to realize the algorithms. For example, by applying data as index there was no need left for sorting, the search operations became simpler, and the deleting appeared to be unnecessary for the formation of the new data lists (in second task). The tasks covered the entire curriculum and students have reached better results. It was determined not only by analysis and conclusions made from the tasks of the previous year, but also by the greater attention paid to creativity rather than to standard repetition of operations during the pilot exam.

Table 5. Comparison of the tasks according to the requirements

Tasks	2006		2007	
	first	second	first	second
The total points	17	33	20	30
Writing and using procedures and functions	+	+	+	+
Text files, data input and output	+	+	+	+
Array and variables of arrays	+	+	+	+
Record and variables of record		+		+
Algorithms of sum, product, quantity, average	+	+	+	+
Search for the maximum (minimum) value	+	+	+	+
Search for the values of the defined property			+	
To form new data list			+	+
Data sorting			+	

The difficulty of the task is expressed by the percent relation between the sum of the points obtained by all students and the sum of theoretically possible points to obtain (Table 6). According to the statistical theory of tests the tasks of approx. 50 % of complexity are considered to be the most suitable ones (too easy > 80% and too hard < 20 %).

Table 6. Comparison of the tasks according to the statistical exponents

Task	Difficulty	Resolution	Correlation
2006 first	48.32	91.34	0.88
second	38.09	85.52	0.93
2007 first	49.24	68.65	0.81
second	39.88	85.62	0.90

Resolution of the task shows how the particular task discerns the best and the worst students. If a task is easy its resolution appears to be low. Similar resolution can be obtained through tasks that remained unsolved by the majority of the students. A negative value of resolution demonstrates that students whose solutions were worse (considering the whole task of the exam) have obtained more points for the task than students whose solutions appear to be better. That is a feature of a poor task.

According to the statistical theory of tests the resolution of suitable tasks has to be 40–50 and the resolution of the especially apt tasks exceeds 60. Due to various educational and psychological goals some of the especially hard problems/questions (or especially easy ones) are being presented in the task, although their resolution is not the optimal one.

Correlation of the task is the coefficient of the correlation between the points for the separate task and the points for all tasks. As we see the tasks of the national exam in IT (programming) were quite competently developed both in 2006 and in 2007 (Table 6).

7 Conclusions

In Lithuania, two kinds of maturity exams on information technology (programming) are introduced: the school exam and the national exam. The school exam consists of a general curriculum of the IT course. The national exam in IT (programming) have been prepared according to the advanced module of programming.

Obviously, the most important part of the exam in IT (programming) is developing of the appropriate tasks that would examine the students' abilities and clearly discern them. The evaluation of the programs is also closely related to the issue.

The analysis of the national exams performed in the recent two years have shown that when developing problems the following rules must be respected: 1) the practical tasks with the real numbers should be withdrawn since operations accelerate the errors of calculating; 2) the practical tasks in which the obtained results do not depend on the chosen way of solution should be selected; 3) the conditions of practical tasks must contain certain limitations for using data types and control structures that increase programs complexity and size but have no influence upon the results.

It was noticed that the complexity of programs depends on the complexity of the chosen data types. Students seldom think about this when choosing the data types. This means that teachers should pay more attention to the selection of data structures when they teach programming.

References

1. Anderson, J., Weert, T.: Information and Communication Technology in Education. A Curriculum for Schools and Programme of Teacher Development. Division of Higher Education, UNESCO (2002)
2. Blonskis, J., Dagienė, V.: Evolution of Informatics Maturity Exams and Challenge for Learning Programming. In: Mittermeir, R.T. (ed.) ISSEP 2006. LNCS, vol. 4226, pp. 220–229. Springer, Heidelberg (2006)

3. Dagiene, V.: Alternation of concepts of Informatics maturity exam (in Lithuanian). Informacijos mokslai, Vilnius 16, 39–47 (2001)
4. General Curriculum for General Education School in Lithuania and General Education Standards for Grades XI-XII. Ministry of Education and Science of the Republic of Lithuania, Vilnius (2002)
5. Information technologies. Tasks of national maturity exam in 2007 National examination centre of the Republic of Lithuania (in Lithuanian) (2007), http://www.nec.lt

Creating and Testing Textbooks for Secondary Schools
An Example: Programming in LOGO

Karin Freiermuth, Juraj Hromkovič, and Björn Steffen

Information Technology and Education
Department of Computer Science
ETH Zürich, Switzerland

Abstract. The main goal of this paper is to present our approach for writing textbooks that are self-contained and available for individual learning. These texts are written in the language of the corresponding pupils and are not restricted by any length limitations. This allows us to write as clearly and thoroughly as possible. Minimizing the time for mastering the subject instead of minimizing the presentation length is the main goal. The detailed lecture notes provide a safety net for the teacher and the pupils alike. They do not restrict teachers in their interaction with the class or in the freedom of choosing alternative ways in approaching the subject. On the contrary, the freedom of designing the content of the lesson increases because pupils have the certainty to be able to learn from the lecture notes if something was not fully understood.

Here some general rules for writing learning aids are presented and then applied for an introductory course about programming in LOGO. Finally, we summarize our teaching experience in different classes with the produced learning aids.

1 General Concepts and Basic Rules

We are missing textbooks for teaching fundamental concepts of informatics in german that would at least partially satisfy the following requirements:

- The main focus is on presenting the programming skills and fundamental concepts and ideas of information processing instead of reducing the computer science education to computer driving license and product knowledge.
- The texts are suitable for learning autonomously for pupils in the corresponding age.
- They systematically build the foundation of concepts following the historical roots of informatics in a similar way as other natural sciences do.

We do not discuss the misleading concepts of computer science education that were broadcasted in many countries as the consequences of the emphasis created by the fast development of information technologies. First, we present some guidelines we use when creating learning aids.

1. **Mastering the Topic to be Teached.** At the beginning it is important not to think about the didactical methods to be used, but to check your own knowledge. Is my understanding of the subject deep enough? Do I see the topic in the correct context of my scientific discipline? Do I know the history of the development of the basic concepts of the subject I want to teach? Do I understand why the concepts were developed in the way they did and not in another one? There is always something that still has to be discovered. Study the appropriate literature and discuss the open questions with colleagues.

2. **Which Notions and Concepts are Known?** A careful formation of concepts is crucial for the success in teaching. A clear picture about the previous experience of the class has to be established and written down. The main point is not to think about skills and methods only, but mainly about concept formation in the sense of building new notions (terminology). Which notions and concepts are already known and how deeply are they understood? Which terms are unknown or only partially understood? One fixes the current state of the knowledge and thinks about questions and tasks suitable for checking the previous experience. This is not a black and white game. For instance, one can ask to which extent are the pupils able to correctly and transparently describe their course of action in a natural language (without programming).

3. **Learning Objectives.** What do I want to achieve? Again, thinking in the black-and-white-manner and stating that the pupils learn something that was unknown before, has to be avoided. Deepen the understanding of basic concepts, extend the applicability of different methods and develop various skills. All this has to be explicitly formulated.

4. **Recurrent Theme.** The chosen learning objectives need to be arranged in a linear sequence. The order of introducing new notions and concepts has to be defined. Usually several suitable orderings exist. This part of your work is more or less based on your experience. A good idea is to discuss your concept with colleagues and test it in classes.

5. **High Willingness to Revise.** The next steps go into the details. Here, you might recognize that some of your educational strategies are not optimal or even do not work. Be prepared and willing for frequent revising and change the work you have done in 1.–4. if necessary.

6. **How to Explain?** Do not yet think about the choice of your didactical method. Formulate all explanations in detail. Use the language which is already understood by the class. Do not use terms or words that have not been carefully introduced before. Check and verify your explanations.

7. **Interaction between the Teacher and the Class.** For each learning step, think about the possibility to communicate with the class. Which questions and tasks are suitable for checking and deepening the understanding of the class for the just introduced subject? What kind of misinterpretations can occur and how to deal with them? The interaction with the class has to be planed and written down.

8. **Exercises and Solution Proposals.** Think about exercises for individual work. Solving these exercises has to guarantee to master the subject introduced to a reasonable extent. The number of exercises has to be larger than needed in average. For those exercises that essentially check or deepen the understanding of introduced notions and concepts, provide a detailed description of the ways how to solve them. Successful work with the formulated exercises must give the pupil a guarantee of being successful in the examination. A variety of tasks has to assure the ability of the class to apply the acquired knowledge in different situations. The tasks for the exam are formulated in harmony with the exercises and the learning objectives.

9. **The choice of the Didactic Methods.** Now decide about the didactical methods for each part of teaching. Think about those parts of the education process which require a strong control and which parts can be developed by the class on their own. As soon as you have taken this decision you can adopt the texts in an appropriate way.

10. **Summaries.** At the end of each teaching unit write a summary. The summary repeats the learning objectives and the knowledge of the unit in the acquired language of the class.

There are many principles and small hints that should be considered during the whole work on a textbook. Here we list some of them:

- It is worthwhile to ask the class to keep a dictionary of the notions and concepts introduced until now. If a notion or a concept is too complex record the expected depth of its understanding.
- Use pictures where they can be helpful. The meaning of these figures has to be carefully explained. Ask the class to develop similar graphical representations.
- Never use words whose meaning is not completely clear to everyone in the class.
- All written tasks need to have a clear and unambiguous interpretation. Omit long sentences whenever possible. The tasks should be clearly structured.
- No long sequences of explanations without intermediate questions and tasks are allowed.
- The most efficient way to teach is to connect the new knowledge with the previous experience. Try to use analogies whenever possible.
- Essential things have to be clearly highlighted. Posing appropriate questions and tasks can be helpful for this purpose.
- A good motivation must always be given. It is not necessary to always search for applications. The aim to discover something essential or to learn to understand something complex can be even more exciting.
- For each small part of your work with the class, plan the interaction (communication) with the pupils.

2 The Concept of Our Textbooks

To support and encourage teaching of computer science in german speaking countries, we decided to develop several modules, each dedicated to another topic. These modules have to be as independent and self-contained as possible. There is no restriction given on the number of pages and so we use as much space as we need to explain everything carefully, to train and to verify the acquired knowledge.

The style of these modules is close to "ETH-Leitprogramme" [1], which is an improvement of the Personalized System of Instruction (PSI), also known as Keller Plan. The main idea, however, is not to create texts for learning autonomously. The texts may be used in this way, but the main purpose is to provide complete information about the topic, and so to assure as many high-quality iterations of the subject as the individuals of the class need or wish. In addition to detailed explanations, the text contains numerous questions, tasks and exercises which are placed exactly where we recommend to apply them. At the end of every lesson the module contains also questions and exercises to check the understanding of the lesson. Furthermore, the textbooks contain hints for teaching persons. These hints are based on our experience and call attention to possible troubles and misinterpretations usually occurring when teaching some more complex matters. Proposals to overcome these difficulties are given too.

Each module is divided into lessons. One lesson is usually for 2–4 hours of teaching and is devoted to one or more new concepts or methods.

3 Introduction to Programming with LOGO

Here we present the concept of the module for an introductory course on programming. The first six of the fourteen lessons can be used in primary schools and the last four lessons are a challenge for the final classes at secondary schools.

3.1 Basic Idea

The idea of this module is not to completely replace a programming course in a high-level language. It is left up to the teacher to decide after which lesson she or he switches to a higher programming language.

The reasons for choosing LOGO for an introductory programming course are the following:

1. One can start with this language already in the third class of the basic school. Drawing pictures is exciting for pupils. They immediately see the actions of the turtle and can easily revise their instructions if something has gone wrong.

2. One can learn programming by starting with five instructions only and working totally with about fifteen instructions that are sufficient for programming any complex behavior of the turtle. Our philosophy is to follow the history of programming, and so to derive all complex instructions as programs consisting of a very small set of basic instructions.

3. The most fundamental concepts such as
   - modular design (programs, subprograms)
   - loops
   - parameters and variable
   - branching of programs, conditional loops
   - recursion
   - descriptional and computational complexity

   can be successfully taught with LOGO.
4. LOGO can be used to build bridges between teaching mathematics and computer science. Teaching elementary geometry in LOGO is a well known example [2,3], but one can support teaching of trigonometry, function analysis and vector geometry as well.
5. Proper teaching of LOGO circumvents the gender problem in programming courses. Programming is a systematic work. Too many ad-hoc decisions and too much improvisation may be dangerous. If programming is correctly taught in a systematic way, girls and young women like it and are often more successful than their male classmates.

Note that LOGO is a programming language developed solely for educational purposes [4] and is used for introductory courses in programming for pupils in more than 40 languages.

3.2 Organization of the Module

To understand the concept of our module properly, we present it lesson by lesson and explain the goals of each one.

Lesson 1 – Programs as Sequences of Instructions

Following the strategy to work with as few simple computer instructions as possible, only four instructions fd, bk, rt and lt for the movement of the turtle are introduced. The enclosed exercises are devoted to pupils of basic school and focus mainly on viewing the movement direction from the point of view of the turtle. Another aim is to learn to see programs as sequences of simple instructions that are unambiguously interpretable by the computer.

Lesson 2 – Repeat-Loops

The aim is to learn to work with loops with a constant number of repetitions, and to put one loop into another. An essential point is that one does not need the concept of variables for this purpose. The exercises focus on recognizing how to partition the picture into repetitions of the same figure and what needs to be done between drawing recurring figures.

Lesson 3 – Modularity

Modular design is one of the fundamental concepts of engineering. Here, one has to learn to use it by giving names to programs and then using the given names as new instructions. The importance of this design method for the transparent and systematic development of computer programs and their verification is explained. The notions of the main program and subprograms are introduced and the pupils learn to represent the program structure in a graphical way.

Lesson 4 – Drawing Circles and Regular Polygons

There is no new programming concept introduced in this lesson. A bridge is built to elementary geometry and working with repeat-loops and subprograms is trained. Using colors is introduced and time for creating own fantasy pictures is provided.

Lesson 5 – The Concept of Parameters

Parameters are introduced as variables whose values do not change during the execution of a program. The general concept of variables is still unknown. Our experience shows that children in the third and fourth classes can master the work with parameters, but only few are able to understand the concept of a variable. The values are assigned to the parameters exclusively as program inputs. In this way the pupils design programs for a class of pictures instead of having one specific program for each potential figure. Here we teach that the computer assigns a register (memory unit) to each parameter and saves its actual value in the assigned register. This enables to parametrize the size of figures drawn, as well as the number of repetitions.

Lesson 6 – Parameters and Subprograms

In this lesson we teach how to pass the values of the parameters of the main program to the subprograms. The pupils learn how to use a subprogram several times with different values of its parameters in one execution of the main program. With Lesson 6 the part of this course for the basic school finishes.

Lesson 7 – Optimizing Program Length and Computational Complexity

This lesson does not introduce any new programming concepts. It is about measuring the "quality" of programs by quantitative measures as descriptional complexity (the number of instructions) and as computational complexity (the number of instructions executed). While the length of a program is a constant, the computational complexity is a function of the program parameters. One learns to measure both. An interesting attraction is to organize competitions in writing the shortest program or the most efficient program for a given task.

Lesson 8 – The Concept of Variables

A good recommendation is not to start with the concept of variables to early. We do it by introducing the instruction make and taking care that we explain the execution of the instruction make on the level of computer registers. The pupils are motivated to work with variables by writing programs for drawing classes of figures and really complex figures.

Lesson 9 – Local and Global Variables
The understanding of variables is deepened by dealing with information transfer between (global) variables of the main program and the (local) variables of its subprograms. Everything is again explained and trained on the level of computer registers.

Lesson 10 – Branching of Programs and While-Loops
This lesson is devoted to the introduction of the instructions if and while. The pupils learn to use conditions not only for drawing pictures, but also for programming methods for solving mathematical problems.

Lesson 11 – First Bridge between Programming and Mathematics: Geometry and Equations
In this lesson no new programming paradigm is presented. The aim is to apply the acquired knowledge and skills to develop graphical solutions to several tasks of elementary geometry (constructions of triangles, intersection of geometric objects). Furthermore methods for solving simple equations are implemented. Using while-loops one can also find approximate roots of polynomials.

Lesson 12 – Recursion
Recursion is the most complex programming concept of this course and so we devote it a lot of space. Again we take care of showing all important details about the execution of recursive calls on the level of the computer registers. Starting with infinite recursion depth we continue with programs using only one recursive call. By now we defined the recursion depth and present the pushdown principle of executing a recursive program. Rewriting recursive programs to while-loops and vice versa is also trained. After that recursive programs with a few recursive calls are introduced and analyzed. The working of the copies of the variables is explained into detail. Graphical representations of the execution of recursive programs are developed and applied.

Lesson 13 – Second Bridge between Programming and Mathematics: Trigonometric Functions
The pupils learn to implement different methods for solving trigonometric tasks. After the introduction of the instructions sin and cos, they also learn to develop programs that approximately compute the functions arcsin and arccos.

Lesson 14 – Third Bridge between Programming and Mathematics: Vector Geometry
One develops programs for working with vectors in a graphical way without using the powerful operations working with the values of coordinates. Hence, by drawing a line between two points it is required to compute the corresponding angle and its length first. This essentially supports the understanding of methods for solving different tasks in the two-dimensional (and partially in the three-dimensional) space.

3.3 How We Introduce New Concepts

To demonstrate our approach to introducing new programming concepts, we show how we stepwise motivate, illustrate and teach the concept of the variable.

1. **Basic Commands.** First the LOGO module introduces a few basic commands. Some of the most important commands of the programming language LOGO are shortly explained here:

   fd 100. The command fd moves the turtle a certain amount of steps forward, e. g. fd 100 moves the turtle 100 steps forward.

   rt 90. There are two ways of turning the turtle: Right turn (rt) and left turn (lt). The command rt 90 executes a 90 degree right turn.

   repeat 4 [fd 100 rt 90]. The command repeat is followed by an integer which indicates how many times in a row the commands in the brackets are executed. The repeat command above draws a square of length 100.

2. **Named Programs.** After doing some exercises, where the pupils always use the same programs, it is easy to motivate the need to give the programs unique names to later call them. It also shows how to structure programs into subprograms.

   Instead of writing repeat 4 [fd 100 rt 90] the pupils can now give this program the name Square100 such that later on, they can just write Square100 to draw a square of size 100×100. For drawing a square of size 50×50, they need to write another program called Square50 for example.

3. **Programs with Parameters.** With named programs the pupils are able to write more complex programs without rewriting commands over and over again. We introduce a further concept to make programming more convenient, namely parameters. The need of parameters is depicted by a concrete example:

   ```
   to Square50
   repeat 4 [fd 50 rt 90]
   end

   to Square100
   repeat 4 [fd 100 rt 90]
   end

   to Square200
   repeat 4 [fd 200 rt 90]
   end
   ```

   With the knowledge the pupils have gained up to that point they are forced to rewrite a new program for every size of the square to be drawn. By doing so, the idea of introducing parameters, which lets us call the same programs with different values, becomes obvious. We introduce parameters for the size of the square and write the following program by replacing the concrete size of the square in the program above by the parameter SIZE.

```
to Square :SIZE
repeat 4 [fd :SIZE rt 90]
end
```

Not only the concept of the parameter and its usage is explained, but also the relationship with the memory is illustrated. The computer memory can be considered as composed of a set of registers. In each of these registers exactly one number can be placed. Each unassigned register contains the value 0. Furthermore, every register can be named.

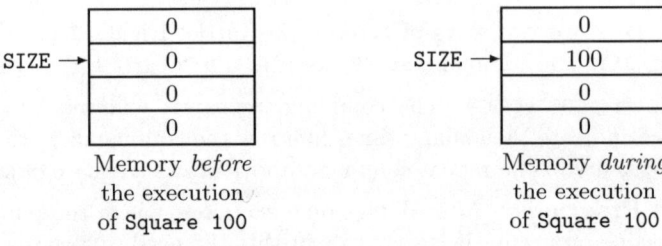

Memory *before* the execution of Square 100

Memory *during* the execution of Square 100

There exists a register with the name SIZE representing the parameter of the program above. Since no value has been placed up to that point, the register contains the value 0. As soon as the program has been called with Square 100, the number 100 is placed into the register with the name SIZE. During program execution the register is accessed every time the value of the parameter SIZE is needed.

4. **Variables.** Finally, to motivate the introduction of variables, we discuss with the pupils the following problem: We would like to draw an arbitrary number of squares with growing sizes as shown in the following picture. The number of squares should be configurable by the parameter N.

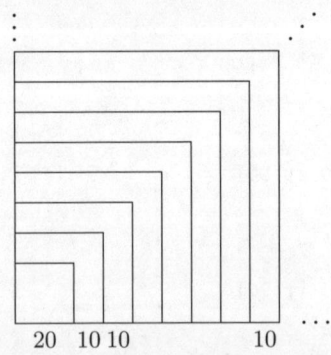

Without the concept of the variable this problem is not solvable.

We explain now the variable as a generalization of the parameter. This means that in contrast to the parameter, the value of a variable may be changed during program execution. What we want to achieve is something like the following:

```
to ManySquares :SIZE :N
Square :SIZE
Increase the value of :SIZE by 10
Square :SIZE
Increase the value of :SIZE by 10
  ⋮
Square :SIZE
Increase the value of :SIZE by 10
end
```
} N-times

The pupils see that the following lines
```
Square :SIZE
Increase the value of :SIZE by 10
```
are repeated N times.

Using the newly introduced `make` command, the pupils learn to rewrite the program to:
```
to ManySquares :SIZE :N
repeat :N [Square :SIZE make "SIZE :SIZE + 10]
end
```

As with parameters the concept of the variable is explained on the level of registers. To train this, there are also several exercises where the pupils need to specify the contents of variables at different stages of the program execution.

4 Observations and Considerations

In this section we present how we teach LOGO with our module. The following suggestions have been developed during numerous lessons at a variety of secondary schools in Switzerland.

4.1 Using the Module in Classes

As already mentioned, our module about programming in LOGO discussed in section 3 does contain all information, theory and exercises to learn individually. This is very important because it allows the pupils to iterate through the material as often as needed to understand the introduced programming concept.

None the less, teaching of programming can be even more improved by the following guidelines:

– The more difficult topics of programming, like variables and recursion, are best introduced with a short presentation by the teacher. By carefully motivating and introducing the new concepts, the class will much better understand them. Furthermore an additional iteration of the topic is achieved.

- Even though the pupils work mostly on their own, a certain control is often helpful. By letting the pupils present some of their solutions to the teacher, their understanding of the new concepts can be controlled and additionally it shows emerging problems as early as possible. Also hints and further explanations can be given to the students to guide them or to even improve their programs.
- If a pupil wrote a good program, let him or her present that solution to the entire class. By discussing the structure of the program and the approach taken, the students learn by good examples. Also this brings more interaction and variation to the class.
- The previous experience in programming of the individual pupils is often very diverged. Since all the details of each lesson are clearly written down, its possible that every student works in his own speed. For the very experienced pupils additional exercises or puzzles can be provided.

4.2 Experiences Made with the Teaching Material

The pupils who worked with the module were between 15 and 19 years old. In some schools we acted as teachers, in others we did only support their ordinary teacher. We present the experience we made during the lessons at these schools.

At the schools where we did not teach ourselves, the concerning teacher did usually neither have any experiences with LOGO nor with this special way of teaching. We only provided the teaching material and an introduction including tips and advices we have collected during our own teaching with the module. Additionally we would have had provided support in case of problems or when further information was needed. However, this was actually never used. The fact that in most cases the teachers could use the teaching material without any additional support shows that the material is convenient for teachers and does not contain any gaps or obscurities.

The following list summarizes knowledge we have gained while teaching programming with the module:

- As long as the students are motivated to work with the module they make progress. It has been shown that motivation is sustainable during at most 6 lessons. We therefore recommend having a break after the first six lessons. The best solution might even be to teach lessons 1 to 6 at the beginning of secondary school and the rest at the end of secondary school (age 16 to 19).
- We observed differences in the way female and male pupils work with the learning material. Female students basically read the text without skipping any sections. They usually solve all the prescribed exercises carefully. Male students, on the other hand, often use the trial-and-error method by skipping reading parts and exercises. As soon as they realize that something is missing they go back in the module. However, both ways of learning are possible and the material is suitable for both.

– Especially in lesson 4 (Drawing Circles and Regular Polygons) and lesson 12 (Recursion) the students become very creative. They individually start drawing new figures, which are not part of the module. We consider it as important not to prevent the students from creating invented figures but to give them the freedom to design fancy graphics. By getting the chance to include own ideas the students are more motivated during the learning process.

 – During periods when students work individually they set their own work pace and work independent of their colleges. It is interesting that students who have realized that they work slower than others don't get affected by their faster colleges, as one might expect, and continue to work in their own pace.

 – Generally we can say that the material provided a pleasant atmosphere in the classes. More and more we observed that students help each other, they create complex drawings together, discuss ideas and solutions and they consider the learning material as fun.

5 Future Work

We have already written other modules of the same style for different topics of informatics. Even more textbooks are planned or have already been started.

The first textbook *Lehrbuch Informatik* [5] contains additionally to the introductory programming course in LOGO presented here, two more modules: *History and Concept Formation* and *Methods for Designing Finite Automata*.

6 Conclusion

In this paper we formulated our strategy for creating textbooks and lecture notes and illustrated it by showing a few details of the teaching module *Programming in LOGO*. After that we presented our experience with its use. The main points can be summarized as follows:

1. The length of the text is not necessarily correlated to the time one needs to master the subject presented there. Therefore it is not a good idea to start writing textbooks with given size limits by the publisher. Take as much space as the ideas need to present them understandably.

2. Use the language of the pupils in all explanations and take care on developing it. Also check the success of this effort. Your text has to be suitable for individual learning (similarly as "ETH-Leitprogramme"). After each step forward check and deepen the acquired knowledge by posing questions or exercises.

    The reason of going into detail is not to reduce the interaction between the teacher and the class by using the texts for individual study or to fix the program of the lessons too much. The opposite is true. The detailed lecture notes make the teacher free to use alternative ways of explanations and different didactical approaches. Nothing can go wrong, because if a pupil does not understand everything developed in the lesson, she or he can get full information by reading the lecture notes afterward. These further iteration can be performed by individual speed which is hard to assure when working with the whole class.

3. Test your materials in classes before publishing them. Your experience with possible troubles when teaching complex subjects has to be communicated to the teachers in your textbook. The textbook has to be a valuable source for pupils as well as for teachers.

4. You do not start to think about the choice of the didactic method for particular parts of your lessons before you found a very clear way of approaching your teaching goals from the subject point of view.

References

1. Frey, K., Frey-Eiling, A.: Allgemeine Didaktik (2004)
2. Kalaš, I., Blaho, A.: Exploring visible mathematics with IMAGINE: Building new mathematics calculus with a powerful computational system. In: Learning in School, Home and Community, pp. 53–64 (2002)
3. Kalaš, I., Blaho, A.: Young students and future teachers as passengers on the Logo engine. In: Secondary School Mathematics in the World of Communication Technology, pp. 41–52 (1977)
4. Papert, S.: Mindstorms: Children, Computers and Powerful Ideas, 2nd edn. Basic Books, New York (1993)
5. Hromkovič, J.: Lehrbuch Informatik: Vorkurs Programmieren, Geschichte und Begriffsbildung, Automatenentwurf. Teubner, Wiesbaden (2008)

Informatics as a Contribution to the Modern Constructivist Education

Ivan Kalas and Michal Winczer

Department of Informatics Education
Faculty of Mathematics, Physics and Informatics, Comenius University
842 48 Bratislava, Slovakia
{kalas, winczer}@fmph.uniba.sk
www.edi.fmph.uniba.sk

Abstract. There are many factors – currently not well understood – which influence how efficiently the educational system builds and cultivates *digital literacy* of pupils. Among them is the quality of the educational policy documents, which set the overall strategy from the governmental point; the level of digital literacy of the schools' management and teachers; the level of concern of the pupils and their parents in acquiring competency; the quality and richness of the teaching-learning resources; how dedicated the school is to innovation in general; how is competency implemented in schools – through *Informatics* or *ICT* as a subject, or through ICT integrated in all subjects and the quality of collaboration between teachers of different subjects etc.

In our department we make a great effort to positively stimulate two of these factors: provide modern university pre-service teacher development and produce attractive and inspiring *Informatics* textbooks, educational software and learning resources for children, students and teachers. In this paper we present our current series of *Informatics* textbooks for lower secondary schools. We will analyze in detail the most recent of them: *Informatics Around Us*. We illustrate the contents and style of the book and we reflect on how our textbooks may help stimulate a kind of bottom-up transformation of our schools into creative and motivating learning playgrounds.

1 Introduction

An increasing number of countries have become aware of inconsistencies between (a) the kind of graduates modern society seeks and (b) the kind of graduates produced by the formal educational systems. Governments initiate more or less radical reforms of the general goals of education. Usually they define a short list of the key competencies and specify the process of how schools should build and cultivate them. Among these competencies we can almost always find *information and communication skills* or *digital literacy*. This key competency is then implemented in different countries in one way or another, through *ICT* or *Informatics* or *ICT in subjects*.

There are many factors – currently not completely understood – which interfere with how quickly and deeply this process leads to noticeable results in education. In our department, we thoroughly strive to positively influence two of these factors: provide modern university pre-service teacher development and produce attractive and inspiring *Informatics* textbooks, educational software and learning resources for pupils, students and their teachers. In the following chapters we present our current series of the *Creative Informatics* textbooks for lower secondary schools. We will analyze in detail the most recent of them – *Informatics around Us*. We illustrate the contents and style of the book and we present our strong confidence that modern textbooks of *Informatics* may act as agents for the transformation of the traditional educational system into an attractive constructivist learning environment where new methods of work are applied and new relations between the actors are established.

2 Informatics Education at the Lower Secondary Level [1]

We started building *Informatics* as a separate subject at the upper secondary schools 20 to 30 years ago. Since then this subject has undergone – because of well-known reasons – several major modifications. Since the mid 90s, our department has participated in developing its current concept. We try to implement it as a modern, valuable, self-reliant subject[2], with its overall goals for a student to:

- Become familiar with the concept of information and operations we apply to information,
- Learn to understand, apply and build algorithms and programmes; classify and solve different kinds of problems,
- Become familiar with systems for processing information,
- Become skilled in using applications and understand that they are programmes aimed at solving problems of particular types,
- Be aware of social, ethical and legal aspects of *Informatics* and the information society.

Such goals seem to be adequate. However, it is disappointing and hard to comprehend how many factors affect the real result and product of such a concept. We can influence only some of them from our position as a university for future teachers. We have found that one way to contribute to implementing modern *Informatics* at the upper secondary level is the systematic **development of quality textbooks**.

Recently our conservative educational system has also started to address the need to implement *Informatics* at the lower secondary level[3]. The process has currently slowed down in an unclear mid position: there is an *Informatics* curriculum and many schools would like to use it in their regular teaching, however they often don't have qualified teachers to do so and no space for it in the regular lessons. Thus the subject is often presented as an after-school club or elective subject, with its curriculum frequently deformed into courses of the MS Office or the like. We witness only rarely its proper implementation as a subject, which understands and employs digital

---

[1] We have in mind 10 to 15 years old pupils.
[2] A similar attitude can be found in ISSEP 2006 paper by Hromkovic, see [5].
[3] In parallel to the process of integrating ICT into other subjects, which we initiated through the Infovek project (with all possible successes and failures) more than 8 years ago.

technologies as a means for **transforming the learning process**, with all the potential to develop higher order skills, collaboration, and competencies for self-expression.

This is why we eagerly welcomed the opportunity to be involved in creating new *Informatics* textbooks – this time for the lower secondary level – with respect to our experience in developing modern educational software and experience from several successful international projects where we were acquainted with an actual constructivist approach to the learning process. Therefore we decided to produce a series of textbooks (and/or workbooks) which would accommodate the following facts:

- The series should form an open and flexible set, which could be used in schools in different ways, in partially unprescribed order and with respect for the stage of ICT skills and the level of awareness by the school,
- Children coming to the lower secondary level already have different expectations and different computer and digital literacy,
- New textbooks should lead to complex development of *Informatics* and also contribute to integrating ICT into other subjects, for example through projects etc.,
- New textbooks should employ modern approaches of the constructivist pedagogy (such as learning by discovering, constructing and creating),
- The series should develop skills to communicate and collaborate,
- The series should also develop other competencies, which are considered key to modern education, like critical perception and thinking, higher order thinking skills, decision-making, handling dynamic and unexpected situations etc.,
- The series should be attractive and stimulating for pupils – and their teachers,
- Each part of the series should be a book of well-constructed sequences of activities, supporting the development of all components of modern digital literacy.

Between 2005 and 2007 we (as a wider group of authors) already managed to start this series – titled *Creative Informatics* – by publishing five textbooks[4]. Four of them are devoted to "working with something", namely *First Book on Programming*, *First Book about Working with Pictures*, *First Book about the Internet*, and *First Book about Working with Text*[5]. The fifth and so far the most recent one, *Informatics Around Us*, see [8], is different from the previous books as far as it constitutes a kind of *general guide to modern Informatics*. In the following chapters we will concentrate on this latest book and reflect on our assumptions and goals for it. We will present its contents and style and how we decided to utilize this opportunity to provide schools with an efficient tool to implement Informatics as a modern constructivist subject.

3 Analysis of Similar Foreign Textbooks

Before we started developing the book[6] we deeply and carefully studied similar textbooks from other European countries. In detail we analyzed scores of them (severely limited by most of their foreign languages), devoted to the same age group. Below we list the problems we encountered and recognized (we consider these points as a list of

---

[4] We plan to add some 6 to 7 more.
[5] See [1], [9], [6] and [2].
[6] Which is aimed at mid classes of the lower secondary school, i.e. 12 to 14 year olds.

possible problems and traps, which the authors should be aware of when creating new learning resources for lower secondary pupils and try to avoid them):

- The worst possible – yet rather frequent – alternative is that the textbook is in fact a manual of a certain software tool, most often MS Word, MS Excel or so on,
- Textbooks are often too much "text-oriented", which violates the natural requirement of attractiveness and appeal for the age group,
- Textbooks are often overloaded by the contents. This gives way to improper usage which Papert coined as *Drill and kill*. Most of the stages of the learning process are thus neglected, each page is burdened by too many concepts,
- Textbooks are concentrated too much on the *concepts of the day*, tools and factors (like the actual performance of the processor or actual capacity of the memory, technical details etc.) which will most probably disappear or change soon,
- Those textbooks rarely utilize the potential, which Informatics offers and supports – and may stimulate, for example, projects, cross-curricular activities, high motivation based on attractiveness, space to create, self-express, develop new relations among all actors, learn and work in teams, and support the kind of teacher who in fact is a partner in the process,
- Textbooks often prefer boy-friendly topics to girl-friendly, and thus drive girls away from modern *Informatics* and exciting learning experiences.

We mentioned several weak aspects of most of the current textbooks. However, instead of criticizing them we want to draw the reader's attention to the fact of how hard it is for *Informatics* to find its proper form, how many traps there are for a developer of new teaching/learning resources... and, on the contrary, how many unprecedented opportunities it offers and how difficult it is to reveal its potential for modern education. We have to state that very rare are the examples of the textbooks, which manage to engage *Informatics* as a bridge to new opportunities that is, to attractive, safe and efficient learning.

4 On Our Textbook: *Informatics Around Us*

Our goal is to build respect for *Informatics* as a science and as a subject. We want to give it its proper place in education – it should not substitute for what many subjects do not do. *Informatics* is not about drawing pictures (although through drawing it can develop proper competencies). *Informatics* is not about e-mailing (although through using communication tools it can develop proper competencies) etc.

In our textbook we want to offer a broad view of *Informatics* and its concepts, problems, manifestations, consequences, concerns, applications and challenges – which are **appropriate to the age and knowledge of its readers**. We want to build it in line with the modern constructivist and constructionist approach of Piaget, Papert and others. That is why we present **three stages of working with computers** to the pupils and urge them to get satisfied neither with the first nor with the second of them. We urge them toward the third stage, for we only really know an instrument (foreign language, a tool or a piano) when we can use it to create new things:

I use it ➔ **I understand it** ➔ **I create with it**

In the following parts we present our textbook from four different views: (1) its contents style, (2) different forms of activities illustrated in the book, (3) indirect means to support our educational goals, and (4) how the book tries to support the modern learning process.

4.1 Contents of the Textbook

Its 48 pages have a regular structure of 10 chapters or topics, T1 to T10, with 2 double-pages each (only T3, Digital World, is an exception with 4 double-pages).

These are the topics we carefully decided to include:

- **(T1) Information Around Us** – the goal is to help pupils realize that all activities they do with computers can be perceived as operations with information – such as drawing a picture, sending an e-mail or creating new a command for a Logo turtle. To do so we apply tools, which are being developed and explored by professionals in *Informatics*. We present an informal definition of Informatics (see Fig. 1), and the reasons why we want to preserve information, who produces it (of, course, it is **us**) and who needs it (and it is **us** again). We also put forward our concept of the three stages of working with computers (see above).

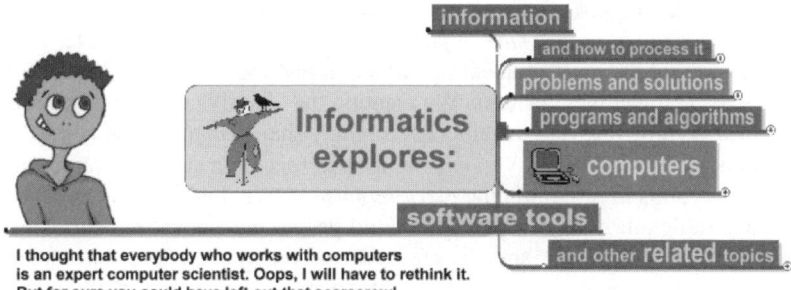

Fig. 1. This is how we specify Informatics for our readers – note both the form and the extent of the definition

- **(T2) Computers Yesterday and Today** – we devote one double-page to the history that led to the invention of modern computers. The other double-page examines different places where we can find computers today and which forms they have. We pay attention to the fact that computers also make the world available to people with special needs. In the historical outline we stress how many different and difficult tasks man had to compute before the arrival of computers (like calendar or sea navigation). However, we use a time line to show how the time lapse between key inventions is shrinking – from centuries to years to months. It is fascinating how recent are such common things as hard disk or notebooks. We encourage pupils to try to guess how computers will look in 10 years and what they will be used for.

- **(T3) Digital World** – more and more devices around us are digital. It means they work and communicate using binary language of 1s and 0s. If we want to use a computer to work with information, we have to convert it into that language first. We mention the light sensor of a digital camera and other sensors, the binary code and binary numeric system, other codes and secret codes. Step by step we explore (a) pictures, (b) sound, (c) numbers, (d) text and (e) different types of information on the screen of a computer. We always ask three questions: How does such information get into the computer? What do we do with it? How does it get out? Here we draw attention to one special type of information (elaborated in detail later in (T5) Programming) – directions to solve a problem, to build a model, to move from one place to another. We ask pupils to list as many *different types of directions* as possible and discuss them. We conclude this topic with an important thought: digital information serves as our memory and cultural heritage to future generations.
- **(T4) Files – Information Inside the Computer** – A file is not a new concept for children of this age, after all they save their pictures into *files with pictures*, Logo projects into *files with projects*, texts into *files with text*... We can say that everything that dwells in the computer is a file and we distinguish two kinds of dwellers: applications or *programmes* such as Calculator, picture editor or Imagine Logo, and *data* such as a composition, a song, a table with collected values etc. Intentionally we (nearly) oversee the files name extensions – nowadays they are often hidden from our sight and different types of files are presented in a different manner. We mention one *super programme*, which administers the whole computer and files. We also present the most frequent operations applied to files. We warn that the size of a file still (sometimes) matters. We mention the "family computer" and rules that are worth keeping if several members of a family share a computer at home.
- **(T5) Programming** – we pay much attention to this topic as far as we consider the attitude of pupils to programming *extra important*. We don't present any particular language in detail; instead we want to build proper understanding, curiosity and a positive relationship. We specify programs as records of procedures (steps) to solve, construct, compute or create something. We show several non-computer records of steps. We also show a wide spectrum of visual and attractive examples in languages like Dragon Pathways (see Fig. 2 and [3]), Scratch, Imagine Logo, Lego MindStorms, Baltik and more. We list three important concepts in programming: (a) *order*, (b) *repetitions* and (c) *conditions*. We explain why we don't use "adult" languages to learn programming[7]. The language we choose should help us think, create and solve interesting problems, should help us discover Informatics. We mention creative robotics and we claim that programming is interesting, hard and beautiful – the same as painting, playing piano or doing hard sport. We advertise modern approaches to learning – by developing your own games or building living compositions, behaviours, events and processes.
- **(T6) Computer as a Construction Kit** – we *carefully* and *briefly* mention the inside of a computer because (a) it often tempts our teachers to use this topic for drill and testing the pupils, which we find inappropriate[8] and (b) this is the field of fast development and integration: more and more functions are integrated directly into

---

[7] People do not learn to swim in the Niagara Falls.
[8] exactly in accordance with Papert's warning: Drill and Kill!

Fig. 2. In the Dragon Pathways, see [3], programming environment children run and build their own interactive games. They populate the screen with different characters and actors and add **picture rules** to specify their reactions and behaviours.

the heart of the computer and it is more difficult or impossible to localise (and name) circuits responsible for them. We talk about which devices help information to get into the computer and out of it. We again mention robots controlled by a computer[9], their sensors and engines, lights etc. We speculate about new tendencies[10] and discuss the task of buying a home computer.

- **(T7) Communication. Computer Network** – we claim that delivering information was crucial in many aspects of ancient and medieval times. We discuss ancient and modern ways of communication, verbal and other, for example, the way the deaf communicate etc. We distinguish communication among people, between us and computers and among computers. We want the communication to be quick, reliable and safe in many senses. We stress that it is not people who should adapt to communication suitable to computers but exactly the opposite. This rule is changing the way we interact with computers. We also present different forms of digital communication and draw attention to questions of security and politeness.

- **(T8) Computers and the Modern School** – we consider this part as a *secret weapon* of the book. That is, we present several modern forms of technology- enhanced teaching and learning – far beyond the scope common in our schools and often unknown to our teachers. We want our pupils[11] to see, what is possible to experience today in school. We want them to long after such an experience. We mention efficient educational software, which helps us to learn by discovering, (see e.g., Fig. 6 or [10]), is visual, interactive, open, and encouraging. We suggest conducting projects (individual, in teams, cross-curricular...) and pupils' research, observations and measurements – employing robotic sets with sensors etc. And we go further – we dream about the school of the near future, where pupils depart for virtual visits and expeditions[12], they virtually take part in dangerous expeditions

---

[9] In Slovakia this area, i.e. *creative robotics for education* – is still waiting for its widespread integration into educational settings. No more than dozens of schools and hundreds of teachers are knowledgeable and enthusiastic about the area; however they are getting little approval and support of the Ministry of Education.

[10] Such as disappearing computers.

[11] And through them also their teachers and parents.

[12] e.g. to the precious Jewish belowground cemetery Chatam Sofer in Bratislava.

etc. Obviously, such activities depend on the level of all actors' level of digital literacy. We also ask pupils to realize that their schooling will never finish[13].
- **(T9) Computer and (Un)Safety** – there are many risks and traps when working with computers, which are good to be aware of. We have to learn to critically evaluate information we find[14], we have to protect our health, we have to learn to protect our work and data in the computer. We also draw attention to the fact that information has become valuable goods. Pupils should also understand that programs have their authors and are sold with certain conditions (licensing) etc.
- **(T10) Information Society** – the way we live is changing. This is also true about *how* and *what* we learn, how we entertain ourselves, how we travel, how we are cured of illness. Computers help us in all parts of life and society. New occupations emerge. In the book, we use fictive interviews with the university students of Informatics: we ask them what they want to do after graduation. Thus we present a wide palette of occupations where quality Informatics education is valid. We send a message to girls – computers are interesting tools for all girls and boys. We examine the role of computers in arts and we conclude the book by an homage to professor Papert and his thoughts (which have been with us for over forty years) that computers can help us learn better and more interestingly – if we understand them and know how to create with them.

When building this content, we carefully observed how many new concepts are introduced in every page and we strove to limit or delete those topics which are likely to become obsolete soon or may easily become unattractive.

4.2 Different Forms of Activities

To efficiently and attractively meet our goals, we have employed several stimulating forms of presentation and activities such as:

- More than 70 exercises, often open-ended and divergent, stimulating discussions, search and research, building presentation or presenting some findings in certain ways. Here are some examples:
  - *What is more: the number of people on the Earth or bits in one gigabyte?*
  - *Try to invent how to count in the binary numeral system*[15].
  - *If we could send and receive only sounds, what kind of information would be difficult to communicate?*
  - *Try to invent an occupation, which doesn't exist at present, but may become real and important in the future. Be creative and witty, give it a name and describe it.*
- Proposals for bigger projects, which may easily grow beyond *Informatics* and initiate interesting cross-curricular activities, programming, development or discovering something related to the topic of the lesson itself, see e.g. Fig. 3. Projects may lead to research and may require a presentation of the findings,

---

[13] As far as they are becoming *life long learners*.
[14] e.g. we draw pupils' attention to www.jbum.com/idt where one can find a fabricated history of computers – thousands of years long.
[15] We give them only light hint: *Notice that* $0 + 0 = 0$, $0 + 1 = 1$ *and* $1 + 1 = 10$.

Fig. 3. An interesting project is to play with colours. *Load a sample picture into a pane, create turtle t1 in it. In the adjacent pane create an identical turtle t2. t1 will jump to a random point of the sample picture, t2 will imitate the same jump, however will...* (see the book). This project has several aspects: (a) programming as an easy yet attractive activity, (b) exploring colours and their transformations, (c) cultivating pupils' interests and horizons and (d) inspiring to do additional similar experiments and transformations.

- Illustrative examples from real scientific projects, which are conducted at our university or elsewhere in Slovakia or another similar cultural environment – with topics, which might be familiar to pupils from the web, from reading or TV,
- Interesting information from events, which are accessible to pupils – either as viewers or actively[16] as contestants, for example in building and programming robots in RoboCup or similar contests,
- False information from the web[17] intentionally used to foster pupils' critical thinking and rational attitude towards information sources,
- Proposals for discussions about interesting and ambiguous topics, such as possible future developments of hardware, the role of ICT in the information society etc.,
- A condensed summary at the end of each topic which recapitulates all new concepts. For us this summary serves also as an audit of the adequacy of new material.

4.3 Indirect Means to Support Our Educational Goals

We employ several additional means to increase the indirect effect of the textbook – to support Informatics education, such as:

- Mind maps as an active, attractive and nonlinear form of presenting certain facts, concepts and relations. As an example one can see Fig. 1 with the definition of Informatics. We frequently use mind maps (or concept maps) to present certain topics and expose pupils and their teachers to this powerful technology for expressing ideas, which in our schools is hardly used so far,
- We often use cartoons and comic characters to present some ideas in the form of jokes or gags, such as in Fig. 4. We borrow some of these from elsewhere[18],

---

[16] Immediately or in the near future.
[17] Naturally, with a hint, which should warn them.
[18] With kind approval of the Swiss Information Society, see www.ictswitzerland.ch.

Files' life is hard.
I really feel for them.
Most of them die
very young. People
simply delete them.
Or copy. Or steal! No wonder they sometimes vanish without trace.

Fig. 4. An anecdote is a good way to present a new concept or idea through exaggerating, misrepresentation, twisting or inversion

- On every page we use numeration of three different kinds, see Fig. 5. Next to the regular page number we add an arithmetic expression in the binary numeral system, which enumerates to the same number. We do not comment or explain this method at all, expecting that there will be pupils eager to explore and perceive such expressions by themselves – we want to give them such a challenge. Next to the expression there is a picture with the binary code of the page number, again without any comment. The sequence of these pictures from page to page may guide the pupils to discover the correct regularity in this visual binary counter,
- We use plenty of diagrams and charts to present some findings, tables of numbers or relations. We want to develop the pupils' skills to understand and use such representations[19] – and let them create similar representations by themselves,
- Often we illustrate things by employing quality educational software – either commercial or experimental (from different research projects, like the one in Fig. 6). We do this with the same goal as mentioned in our ISSEP 2006 lecture, see [7], in the education of future teachers, we want to develop good sense in pupils when working with such software, we want them to be demanding and critical of what they often have to use. That is, we want to resist the *vulgar and naive reduction of educational software to the simple delivering of courses* (of different quality).
- Presented examples often have a secondary motivation. For example, if we are illustrating different kinds of information found on the screen of a computer, we use a screen snapshot from a video editor developed specially for educational reasons and for children of that particular age – we expect our pupils and their teachers to be motivated to do similar projects,
- We have decided to develop a textbook for pupils – and for their teachers. In the past ten years we[20] have managed in this way to supply lower and upper secondary schools with a rich library of attractive resources, which (indirectly, unnoticed and unobtrusively) serve as the means of developing teachers' digital literacy.

34   **10 x (10000 + 1)**

Fig. 5. Three different kinds of numeration – used on each page

---

[19] Based on PISA 2003 and 2006 findings, Slovak pupils scored very poorly in such understanding.
[20] With a team of authors and co-authors from our Department and some other institutions.

4.4 Contribution to Modern Teaching/Learning Strategies

We carefully tried to make it as difficult as possible to misuse our material for traditional teaching. Instead, we wanted to encourage curiosity, explorations, collaborative work, learning by doing and by discovering, projects and discussions. We strove to develop a textbook, which would open the door to modern goals and strategies, such as:

- Developing higher order thinking skills of the pupils,
- Motivating children through attractive activities, which may not at present have strong tradition and support but can be implemented relatively easily – such as building Lego models, their programming and use in small research projects for measuring etc.,
- Giving hints instead of complete material – e.g. presenting only a list of verbs, which characterize what we do with information. Pupils are expected to talk about the operations in their own words, based on their own perception and experience,
- Inviting pupils to virtual walks to museums and galleries, to inaccessible places – far in space or difficult because of other reasons,
- Presenting our views upon Informatics and programming not as the ultimate and beyond any doubt, but to the contrary – as endorsing analytical and critical thinking. Often we reflect the role of Informatics in society. It is more than proper if pupils have diverse opinions of such serious and complex topics. We are open and enthusiastic to learning new attitudes and we want our textbook to spread such an approach among students and teachers as well.

5 Observations and Final Considerations

We are obtaining interesting observations from several doctoral research projects conducted in our department on developing ICT curriculum for lower secondary schools. This research certifies our assumption that Informatics can be implemented as a vehicle for change, as a modern subject, which provides pupils and teachers with valuable opportunities to apply and elaborate new teaching/learning strategies with high motivation, self-responsibility, supporting collaboration, creativity and personality development, see [11] or [4]. In particular, we have observed:

- An exceptionally creative atmosphere in the Informatics lessons, with a high extent of interactions among pupils and teacher(s)[21],
- Pupils effectively learning from other classmates; learning by discovering; collaboratively solving problems in teams,
- Pupils willing to engage in complex projects, which call for searching, problem solving, investigating and experimenting with open-ended, divergent problems.

We assume that quality *Informatics* textbooks may support such learning processes and may help to transform traditional schools into creative and highly stimulating learning environments.

---

[21] This observation confirms that modern Informatics can be implemented in such a way that it gives space to and encourages new relations among the pupils and teachers.

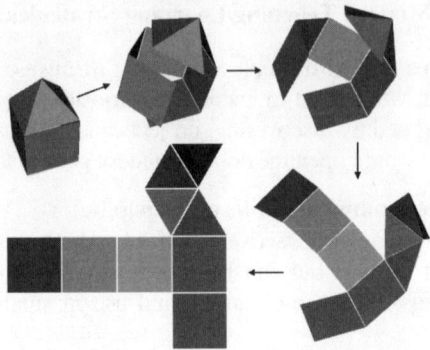

Fig. 6. Experimental educational software environment developed in Elica, see [10]

Acknowledgments. All comic characters, which appear in the textbook and this paper, were created by Martina Kabatova, doctoral student of our department.

References

1. Blaho, A., Kalas, I.: Creative Informatics – First Book on Programming (in Slovak). In: SPN 2005, p. 48, Bratislava (2005) ISBN 80-10-00019-1; Also available in English by Logotron, Cambridge (2004), Also available in Czech by Computer Press, Brno (2006)
2. Blaho, A., Salanci, L.: Creative Informatics – First Book about Working with Text (in Slovak). In: SPN 2007, p. 48, Bratislava (2007) ISBN 978-80-10-00888-9
3. Dragon Pathways. Animated modelling software for 7-11 years old. Logotron educational software, http://www.logo.com
4. Galik, Z.: Investigative Internet Activities And The Development Of Modern Competencies of Pupils, PhD thesis, Comenius University, Faculty of Mathematics, Physics and Informatics, p. 150, Bratislava (2008)
5. Hromkovic, J.: Contributing to General Education by Teaching Informatics. In: Mittermeir, R.T. (ed.) ISSEP 2006. LNCS, vol. 4226, pp. 25–37. Springer, Heidelberg (2006)
6. Hrusecka, A., Varga, M.: Creative Informatics – First Book about Internet (in Slovak). In: SPN 2006, p. 48, Bratislava (2006) ISBN 80-10-00648-3
7. Kalas, I.: Discovering Informatics Fundamentals Through Interactive Interfaces for Learning. In: Mittermeir, R.T. (ed.) ISSEP 2006. LNCS, vol. 4226, pp. 25–37. Springer, Heidelberg (2006)
8. Kalas, I., Winczer, M.: Creative Informatics – Informatics Around Us (in Slovak). In: SPN 2007, p. 48, Bratislava (2007) ISBN 978-80-10-0087-2
9. Salanci, L.: Creative Informatics – First Book about Working with Pictures (in Slovak). In: SPN 2006, p. 48, Bratislava (2006) ISBN
10. Sendova, E., Chehlarova, T., Boytchev, P.: Words are Silver, Mouse-clicks are Gold? Informatics in Education, Vilnius 6(2), 411–428 (2007)
11. Tomcsanyiova, M.: Integrating Logo Programming into Lower Secondary Informatics, PhD thesis, Comenius University, Faculty of Mathematics, Physics and Informatics, p. 149, Bratislava (2008)

New Methodology of Information Education with "Computer Science Unplugged"

Tomohiro Nishida[1], Yukio Idosaka[2], Yayoi Hofuku[3], Susumu Kanemune[4], and Yasushi Kuno[5]

[1] Osaka Gakuin University
nishida@ogu.ac.jp
[2] Iinan Junior High School
idosaka@gmail.com
[3] Shouyou High School
y-hohuku@pen-kanagawa.ed.jp
[4] Hitotsubashi University
kanemune@acm.org
[5] University of Tsukuba
kuno@gssm.otsuka.tsukuba.ac.jp

Abstract. We introduced "Computer Science Unplugged" to our classes in junior and senior high schools. "Unplugged" is an education method of computer science without students using a computer at all. For our classes, we developed original teaching materials and methods for Unplugged. As a result, the students could learn the topics of computer science with interest by using Unplugged. They enjoyed the games in Unplugged and thought about the topics deeply at the same time. We confirmed that students enhanced their motivations, thinking abilities, and imaginations.

1 Introduction

Information education became a common area in Japan by the revision of curriculum guidelines in primary and secondary education in 2002 and 2003. However, many students only learn how to use computers and application software such as word processor, spreadsheet, or presentation in schools. Some teachers do not teach the computer science because they regard computer science as so difficult for students in junior and senior high school.

However, students could be familiar with computer science because they are familiar with mobile phones or video games which include computers in their daily life. On the other hand, it is difficult for students to understand individual topics in computer science such as searching or sorting because they cannot find importance of these things in their daily life.

To solve the problems mentioned above, we introduce "Computer Science Unplugged" [1][2][3] (called "Unplugged" hereafter) which is the education method of computer science without students using a computer at all to classes in schools.

Unplugged provides sophisticated teaching materials and they are suitable for children of a range of ages. Students can enjoy the activities with them and can learn typical computer science topics actively; therefore, they become interested in computer science. The project "Unplugged" was started by Tim Bell (University of Canterbury, New Zealand) et al. He decided to develop the teaching methods and materials about ten years ago because he wanted to show the fascinating aspect of computer science for his five-year-old child.

They published the first textbook [4] in 1998 and now provide the textbook on the Internet [1]. Korean [5] and Japanese [2] versions were also published.

We developed original teaching materials for Unplugged and conducted lessons at schools. As a result, we confirmed that students could learn the computer science topics with interest by using Unplugged. In this paper, we report our lessons and their outcomes.

2 Textbook: "Computer Science Unplugged"

2.1 Contents of the Textbook

The Unplugged textbook contains 12 chapters (Table 1). Each chapter involves an important topic in computer science. In ordinary circumstances, they are too difficult for children. However, even elementary school students can understand them because the textbook provides well-thought explanations and fun activities.

Table 1. Contents of the Textbook

Chapter	Title	Sub title	Ages
1	Count the Dots	Binary Numbers	7 and up
2	Colour by Numbers	Image Representation	7 and up
3	You Can Say That Again!	Text Compression	9 and up
4	Card Flip Magic	Error Detection & Correction	9 and up
5	Twenty Guesses	Information Theory	10 and up
6	Battleships	Searching Algorithms	9 and up
7	Lightest and Heaviest	Sorting Algorithms	8 and up
8	Beat the Clock	Sorting Networks	7 and up
9	The Muddy City	Minimal Spanning Trees	9 and up
10	The Orange Game	Routing and Deadlock in Networks	9 and up
11	Treasure Hunt	Finite-State Automata	9 and up
12	Marching Orders	Programming Languages	7 and up

2.2 Example of the Contents

In chapter 4, they use "Card Flip Magic" to show how to detect and correct an error (Fig.1). We label a girl as Student A and a boy as Student B in the figure. For this demonstration, they use flat magnetic cards that have a different colour on each side.

The procedure of "Card Flip Magic" is as follows.

1. Student B lays out the cards in a 5 × 5 square with a random mixture of sides showing.

Fig. 1. Card Flip Magic

2. Student A says "just to make it a bit harder" and adds another row and column casually.
3. Student B flips over one card while Student A covers her eyes.
4. Student A points out the card which is flipped.

The trick of this magic is a one-bit parity. The cards that Student A added are the key to the trick. Student A must choose the extra cards to ensure that there is an even number of coloured cards in each row and column. The row and column containing the changed card will have an odd number of coloured cards and this will identify the changed card.

Students join this activity without any explanation about the parity bits. Therefore, they try to find the trick of the magic eagerly and want to be magicians.

A teacher explains the trick and the parity bits after most of the students find the trick. After that, they learn "ISBN" and "bar-code" as real-life examples of the check digits. They also calculate ISBNs of books. In closing, the teacher explains the needs of error detection and correction by showing other examples in daily life, e.g., banking.

As described above, by using this method, students can learn topics in computer science without computers. It is difficult for students to have an interest in the parity bits and understand the essence of them only with textbooks and oral explanations. Students might forget the word: "parity bits" even if they learn it by using Unplugged. However, they will remember the essence: "errors can be detected with data for checking" because they had hands-on activities.

In similar way, students can learn various topics in computer science with hands-on activities by using this textbook.

2.3 Significance of Unplugged

(1) "Games" in every learning
   Students can learn through "play." Therefore, they become interested in the topics. Some topics are difficult for students, but they can enjoy them.
(2) Trial-and-error with real things

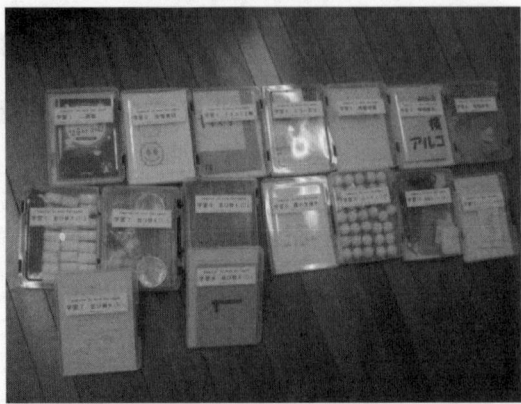

Fig. 2. Original teaching materials packed in small cases

There are many hands-on activities with cards, scale and weights, balls, and so on. They stimulate thoughts of students. Students can habituate themselves to think logically through trial-and-error.

(3) Learning in a group

There are many activities in a group. Students are expected to think deeply because these activities affect one another. They would also be good practices to communicate with others.

(4) Without circumstance

In most cases, students can start their activities with worksheets on the textbook. Teachers can make original teaching materials (Fig.2) at a moderate price if they need. They do not have to use the computer classroom, and they can learn in the regular classroom or out of the classroom.

3 Our Lessons at Schools

In this section, we introduce lessons which we conducted at one junior high school and two senior high schools.

3.1 Lessons at Iinan Junior High School

At Iinan junior high school (Matsusaka city, Mie prefecture, Japan), in the subject of "technology and home economics," one of the authors conducted the classes with Unplugged for two periods: from January through March 2007 and from April through September 2007.

The aim of these lessons was to enhance students' motivations, thinking abilities, and imaginations by using Unplugged. The teacher also expected his students to increase their communication abilities through games in Unplugged.

The purpose of these lessons is not to teach technical knowledge of computer science but to give opportunities that the students think about the essences and

Table 2. Curriculum for Iinan junior high school (second period)

Chapter	Subject
2	Image Representation
3	Text Compression
4	Error Detection & Correction
1	Binary Numbers
6	Searching Algorithms
8	Sorting Networks
10	Routing and Deadlock in Networks
9	Minimal Spanning Trees
11	Finite-State Automata

the fundamental principles of computer science. This policy meets the purpose of "technology and home economics": "developing abilities of innovation and creation in real life." By using Unplugged, the students can enjoy learning these things and their abilities will grow.

Overview of His Classes

At the first period: from January through March 2007, the teacher conducted 10 hours of classes for 3rd grade students (16 students × 4 classes, elective). He taught all chapters of the Unplugged textbook. At the second period: from April through September 2007, he conducted 9 hours of classes for 3rd grade students (12 students × 4 classes, mandatory). Based on his experience in the first period, he selected 8 chapters of the textbook (Table 2).

Fig.3(a) is the scenery of the class of "Colour by numbers" which is the teaching material to explain of image representation. In Fig.3(b), the students are using "scale and weights" to learn sorting algorithms. These materials were made by the teacher.

In Fig.3(c), the students are playing the game "Battleships" to learn searching algorithms. Each student is guessing where her/his partner's ship is. This activity demonstrates three different search methods: linear searching, binary searching, and hashing by using different sheets.

In Fig.3(d), the students are playing "The Orange Game" to learn routing and deadlock in networks. There are two oranges with each student's name except for one student. The teacher distributes the oranges randomly to the students in the circle. Each student has two oranges except for one student who has only one. The students pass the oranges around until each student gets the oranges labelled with their name. Students will find that if they are "greedy" (hold onto their own oranges when they get them); then, the group might not be able to attain its goal. In this activity, they experience "deadlock" and realize the needs for strategy.

Evaluation of the Students

We have conducted enquiries over the students in the second period classes to evaluate the lessons with Unplugged. In Table 3, results of questions "Was the

(a) "Colour by numbers" to learn image representation

(b) Scale and weights to learn sorting

(c) "Battleships" to learn searching

(d) "The Orange Game" to learn routing

Fig. 3. Class scenery at Iinan junior high school

lesson fun?" for each class are shown. We could see that most of the students enjoyed each class. Especially, over 60% of the students evaluated that "The Orange Game" (Routing and Deadlock in Networks) and "Treasure Hunt" (Finite-State Automata) is "Fun(4)" regardless of their difficulty. With respect to this result, we could confirm Unplugged was effective for the students to have an interest in computer science and understand the essence of them. Some students answered "Not fun" for some lessons. They answered that "It is too difficult to understand" in their free description. We must improve the methods for those topics and select topics carefully for next period.

In the free description enquiry, we could find many answers to confirm that we had achieved the desired objective of the classes: enhancing students' motivations, thinking abilities, and imaginations (Fig.4). With respect to this result, we think that Unplugged would be an innovative teaching material. We also observed that students got practical knowledge by connecting Unplugged activities and using computers in their daily life. Unplugged would break the wall between computer science and using computers in real life.

3.2 Lessons at Shouyou High School

At Shouyou high school (Yokohama city, Kanagawa prefecture, Japan), in the subject of "Information B" that is for the scientific understanding of the functions

Table 3. Result of multiple-choice enquiry: Was the lesson fun? (%)

Chapter	Title	4	3	2	1
2	Colour by Numbers	55.3	38.8	5.8	0.0
3	You Can Say That Again!	39.1	45.7	15.2	0.0
4	Card Flip Magic	34.0	48.9	17.0	0.0
1	Count the Dots	41.7	43.8	12.5	2.1
6	Battleships	56.5	41.3	2.2	0.0
8	Beat the Clock	46.8	40.4	8.5	4.3
10	The Orange Game	67.4	28.3	4.3	0.0
9	The Muddy City	39.1	47.8	13.0	0.0
11	Treasure Hunt	62.9	31.4	5.7	0.0

4:Fun,3:Relatively fun,2:Relatively not fun,1:Not fun

Answers relate to motivations
— It was fun. I'd like to do it again.
— I'm interested in "Sending Secret Messages." I'd like solve other problems like this.
— Studying with classmates is more fun than just hearing teacher's explanations.
— I understood how to compress and decompress data.
I'll remember it when I use computers from now.

Answers relate to thinking abilities
— It was difficult, but fun. I've thought much.
— I've thought more than usual. It was difficult but I felt fulfilled after done it.
— I found a pleasure to think and could enhance my thinking ability.
— I think that it was hard to learn it alone because I had to think much.
It's fun to cooperate with classmates.

Answers relate to imaginations
— It's great that bar-codes have lots of meaning.
— I'm happy to find its regularity.
— I'm impressed because I didn't know computers send pictures using numbers.

Fig. 4. Some representative answers from the free description

and mechanism of a computer, one of the authors conducted the classes with Unplugged for 2nd grade students (33 students) from January through March 2007. The teacher taught chapter 6: "Searching Algorithms" for 65 minutes, chapter 7: "Sorting Algorithms" and chapter 9: "Sorting Networks" for 35 minutes.

To mix Unplugged activities with normal classes, she had to prepare for the activities to finish them at short times. She also added deeper contents for senior high school students to acquire their interests.

In the lesson to learn searching, she named the introductory activity "Marriage Meeting Game" (Fig.5). This broke the ice in the class and the activities after that ("Battleships", Fig.6) run smoothly.

In the enquiry after learning searching, representative answers of the students are "I can understand the need of searching (97%)" and "I can understand that there are various kinds of algorithms (91%)." We think that they could understand the characteristic of each searching algorithm in spite of limited time.

In the enquiry after learning sorting with scale and weights, representative answers of the students are "I can understand how to calculate of the maximum

Fig. 5. "Marriage Meeting Game"

Fig. 6. "Battleships" at Shouyou High School

number of swapping data in selection sort (97%)" and "I can understand that there are various kinds of algorithms (94%)." As well as searching, we think they could understand the characteristic of each sorting algorithm.

The result of the question: "Which do you like classes with a computer or Unplugged?" was "Unplugged (60%)," "With computer (7%)," and "Both (33%)." As a result, we could confirm that Unplugged produced the students' motivations. In the free description enquiry, we could find many positive answers: "It's good for brain activation," "It's impressive," "It's fun," "Studying with classmates is good," and "You (teacher) looks fun too."

In these lessons, we could confirm the learning with hands-on activities and without using a computer is effective for information education. There were some students who are not interested in or not good at using computers. However, even such students felt fun, understood the mechanisms, and had good impressions in the Unplugged classes.

3.3 Lessons at Osaka Gakuin Daigaku Senior High School

At Osaka Gakuin Daigaku senior high school (Suita city, Osaka prefecture, Japan), in the subject of programming, one of the authors who usually teaches at a university conducted the classes for 3rd grade students in senior high school (10 students) from April through December 2007. He prepared an original programming environment for novices [6] to learn the basics of computer programming easily. He also desired that his students learn the essential characteristics of computers. Therefore, he introduced Unplugged as materials for introductions of programming exercises. He used "Kid Fax" in chapter 2, "Card Flip Magic" in chapter 4, "Battleships" in chapter 6, and "Treasure Hunt" in chapter 11.

"Card Flip Magic"
In November 2007, the teacher conducted the class to teach "Error Detection & Correction" for 100 minutes. Table 4 shows the lesson plan of the class. In the beginning of the class, he used "Card Flip Magic."

"Telephone Game" is not included in the textbook. However, we think it is important for the students to realize the needs of error correction in real communication. Therefore, the teacher made original work sheets for the game.

The procedure of "Telephone Game" is listed below:

1. The teacher hands the first sheets on which an 11×9 matrix of numbers (0 or 1) is written to the first student of each team. This matrix represents a bitmapped image (Fig.8).
2. The first student tells the matrix to the next student. The next student writes the matrix on his sheet. The teacher gives the instruction that the chance to tell the matrix is only once.
3. The student who had the matrix tells it to the next student. When he has the matrix with parity bits, he can fix it if needed.
4. Last student converts numbers that he heard to a bitmapped image.

Table 4. Lesson plan to learn "Error Detection & Correction"

1. Teacher and students play "Card Flip Magic."
2. Students play "Telephone Game."
3. Students execute a sample program and confirm that an error can detect by parity checking.
4. Teacher explains ISBN, and students calculate ISBN checksums.
5. Students make programs to calculate ISBN checksums.

Fig. 7. Drawing a bitmapped image in "Telephone Game"

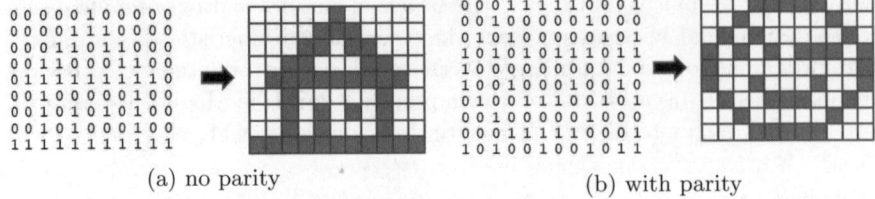

Fig. 8. Data for "Telephone Game"

Ten students were divided into 3 groups (Group A: 3 students, Group B: 3 students, Group C: 4 students). In the first trial, they used the data without parity bits (Fig.8(a)). In the second trial, they used the data with parity (Fig.8(b)) and passed the data in reverse order.

Table 5 shows the results of the "Telephone Game." Two teams succeed in the second trial with parity bits and another team had only one fault. There was a possibility that learning in the first trial influenced the results of the second trial. However, we could see the effect of the parity bit in the "Telephone Game."

In the result of the enquiries: "Did you understand 'Parity check'?" (Table 6), we also could confirm that the students realized the needs of data checking with parity bits.

Effect by Using Unplugged

After the class period ended, we have conducted enquiries that the students freely selected the topics in which they were interested from the list of 11 topics in the programming classes (nine of the students answered). As a result, the most popular theme is "Telephone Game": 7 students (78%) selected that. Moreover, 6 students selected "Battleships" and "Drawing and Redrawing Maps." "Drawing and Redrawing Maps" is the activity expanded upon "Treasure Hunt." In the activity, the students made their own state transition diagrams and translated them to the programs; then, they exchanged their programs and redrew the

Table 5. Result of "Telephone Game"

Team	1st trial	2nd trial
A	failed (19 faults)	failed (1 fault)
B	failed (6 faults)	succeed
C	failed (2 faults)	succeed

Table 6. Result of multiple-choice enquiry: Did you understand 'Parity check'?

Answer	# of students
Understand	6
Almost understand	3
Hardly understand	1
Did not understand	0

other student's map. In contrast, number of students who selected the basic programming topics was three. With respect to this result, we could observe that Unplugged caught students' interest and it gave good effects for programming learning.

On the other hand, there was no student who selected "Searching Program" which related to "Battleships". We guessed that the reason was that "Searching Program" was too complex to understand for the students while "Battleships" was easy. We have to develop the teaching materials, and methods fill the gap between programming education and Unplugged.

4 Conclusion

We reported the outline of "Computer Science Unplugged," the education method of computer science without students using a computer, and results of our lessons with Unplugged in junior and senior high schools.

We could confirm Unplugged was effective for the students because it has the practical teaching materials with various games and hands-on activities. Unplugged includes advanced topics, e.g., "Data Compression," "Searching and Sorting," "Amount of Information," and "Finite-State Automata" which are usually taught at universities. However, the students could learn these topics with interest. Another effect of Unplugged is that we can give a chance to think for students through these activities. In our classes, there were some students who do not like to think. However, they had motivations to learn and thought deeply in Unplugged class.

Unplugged provides 12 or 20 sophisticated teaching materials now and the range of the adjustment of the materials is wide. In our classes, we made original materials included communication channel for "Error Detection & Correction." In this way, we will develop new teaching materials to generalize Unplugged.

There are some related research and activities. Kinesthetic Learning Activities [7] and Non-Programming Resources for an Introduction to CS [8] show the methods for studying computer science by using teaching tools. The shows of Unplugged for high school teachers were held at Carnegie Mellon University [9]. The workshop of Unplugged was also held at SIGCSE 2008 symposium [10]. We would like to cooperate with these activities.

References

1. Bell, T., Witten, I.H., Fellows, M.: Computer Science Unplugged – An enrichment and extension programme for primary-aged children (2005), http://csunplugged.com/
2. Kanemune, S., et al. (translation): Computer Science Unplugged (Japanese Version) (2007)
3. Kanemune, S., et al.: An introduction of Computer Science Unplugged – Translation and Experimental Lessons (in Japanese). In: Proceedings of SSS 2007, pp. 5–10 (2007), http://kanemune.eplang.jp/data/sss07unplugged.pdf

4. Bell, T., Witten, I.H., Fellows, M.: Computer Science Unplugged... off-line activities and games for all ages (1998)
5. WonGyu, L. (translation): Computer Science Unplugged (Korean Version) (2006)
6. Nishida, T., et al.: PEN: A Programming Environment for Novices – Overview and Practical Lessons. In: ED-MEDIA 2008 – World Conference on Educational Multimedia, Hypermedia and Telecommunications (to appear, 2008)
7. Kinesthetic Learning Activities, http://ws.cs.ubc.ca/~kla/
8. Non-Programming Resources for an Introduction to CS, http://csis.pace.edu/~bergin/iticse2000/
9. CS 4 HS Summer Workshop, http://www.cs.cmu.edu/cs4hs/
10. Lambert, L., Bell, T., Cortina, T., Henderson, P.: Computer Science Unplugged. In: SIGCSE 2008 Proceedings of the 39th ACM Technical Symposium on Computer Science Education, p. 553 (2008)

Disciplinary-Pedagogical Teacher Preparation for Pre-service Computer Science Teachers: Rational and Implementation

Noa Ragonis[1,2] and Orit Hazzan[1]

[1] Department of Education in Technology and Science,
Technion – Israel Institute of Technology, Haifa, 32000, Israel
{noarag,oritha}@technion.ac.il
[2] School of Education, Beit Berl College, Doar Beit Berl, 44905, Israel
noarag@beitberl.ac.il

Abstract. This paper presents a case study of an academic course for pre-service computer science teachers that focus on teaching the discipline. The paper specifies and explains the rationale behind the development of the course and its explicit objectives. Achievement of the objectives is explained by describing the subject and content of the lessons, the types of activities integrated into the lessons and the tasks required of the students. All those engaged in teaching computer science: developers of curricula, lecturers in teacher training programs, and lecturers involved in the professional development of computer science teachers, can intend the course model for use.

Keywords: Computer science education, prospective computer science teachers, pre-service computer science teachers training, computer science teacher preparation curriculum.

1 Introduction

The dynamic evolution of the computer science (CS) field poses both educational and pedagogical challenges, including teacher-related issues such as recruitment, pre-service teacher preparation, support for teachers' ongoing professional development, and pedagogical and instructional design of teaching and learning material [20]. For example, in order to support and promote the teaching of CS disciplines, the Computer Science Teachers Association (CSTA) was founded with the rationale that the dissemination of good practices and standards will engage both teachers and students in the CS culture [22].

The ACM K-12 Education Task Force Report draws attention to the need for appropriate CS teacher training programs and notes "teachers must acquire both a mastery of the subject matter and the pedagogical skills that will allow them to present the material to students at appropriate levels." (p.18) [21]. The report recommends that state departments of education have to formulate standards for teacher certification. Such standards will lead to the establishment of teacher preparation programs in which teachers will gain the skills and knowledge necessary to meet the required certification standards.

Hazzan, Gal-Ezer and Blum suggest a model for high school CS education. Teacher preparation programs are one of the four key components of the model, along with a national high school CS curriculum, mandatory CS teachers licensing and research in CS education [8].

Nevertheless, in many places, a CS teaching certificate is not required in order to teach CS. In the US, for example, a survey conducted in 2007 reports that approximately 53% of respondents replied that their state does not require a CS teaching certification [3]. Deek notes that secondary CS courses are usually taught by faculty certified to teach mathematics [4]. Even programs that deal specifically with the training of CS teachers do not necessarily include explicit reference to the teaching of CS. Rather, the training many times refers to teaching in general and, at the best, to principles of teaching science. This might result from the fact that, now, a well-defined, international standard for CS schools curricula and for CS teacher preparation does not exist [1], [17].

In places where CS teacher preparation programs do exist, they include at least one "methods" course, in which prospective CS teachers gain the skills needed to teach CS in high school [1]. However, specific guidelines for the implementation of such courses are rarely provided and most are not up to date [2], [11], [14], [15], [23].

To meet the big challenges of preparing the future CS teachers we present in this paper a case study of the "Methods of Teaching Computer Science" course taught by the Department of Education in Technology and Science at the Technion – Israel Institute of Technology. This case study illustrates the implementation of a course that intends to meet the above-described challenges. The course focuses on broadening the prospective CS teachers' knowledge in many aspects and applies various teaching methods during the course itself.

2 The "Methods of Teaching Computer Science" Course

This section presents the course entitled "Methods of Teaching Computer Science", as it is taught at the Technion's Department of Education in Technology and Science. Following a general overview of the knowledge structure required of pre-service teachers, we describe the course structure, population, and rationale, including detailed objectives. We then present the course syllabus, detailing the topics and contents of each lesson, types of activities integrated into the lessons and a description of the tasks required of the students.

2.1 Background

Teacher preparation programs are usually based on general pedagogical knowledge, subject matter knowledge, pedagogical content knowledge (PCK) and practicum in real classes. PCK refers to what a teacher is required to know in order to teach a certain subject matter: how to make it understandable, difficulties encountered students' preconceptions and misconceptions, and strategies for coping with misconceptions [18], [19]. With respect to CS, Gal-Ezer and Harel claim, "beyond the mastery of core CS material, good CS educators should also be familiar with a significant body of material that will expand their perspectives on the field, and consequently, enhance the quality of their teaching." [5]. Among the issues that they mention are the question What is CS?, a bird's-eye view of the discipline and familiarity with tools and methods for teaching. Hazzan, Gal-Ezer and Blum also claims that teacher preparation programs should include some research elements, such as reading assignments of papers that deal with CS education research and mini-research projects to be carried out by the prospective CS teachers themselves [8].

The course "Methods of Teaching Computer Science" aims at broadening the prospective CS teachers' PCK and sets the basis for the in-school practical training that takes place after it. In a series of papers Lapidot and Hazzan address different topics related to CS teacher preparation, focusing on the "Methods of Teaching Computer Science in High School" course [9], [10], [12], [13]. They refer to different topics that should be included in such a course, like pedagogical approaches for teaching different subjects, tools for assessing pupils' performance, and teaching of social-related issues such as ethics. They also emphasize the need to use active learning when teaching the "Methods of Teaching Computer Science" course. The course described in this paper in detail elaborates on the course described by Lapidot and Hazzan in their papers as well as on its development.

2.2 Course Structure and Population

The course consists of 112 hours of classes and training, divided into two semesters. Each week there are two 2-hour long lessons. Each of the two semesters is devoted to different high school curriculum units. The first semester focuses on the foundations of CS (Units 1-2 of the Israeli high school curriculum) whereas the second semester focuses on more advanced topics, such as abstract data types and computational models (Units 4-5 of the Israeli high school curriculum) [6], [7].

Course participants are students enrolled at the Department of Education in Technology and Science and they usually take the course during their third year of study (out of four years).

The course's academic pre-requisites are relevant CS contents and a major part of the general education and teaching studies. The maximum number of participants in the course is 20.

2.3 Course Objectives

The main course objective is to train pre-service high school CS teachers. The specific objectives derived from this main objective, are to:

1) Enhance prospective CS teachers' professional identity as CS teachers;
2) Heighten prospective CS teachers' awareness to the uniqueness of CS education;
3) Familiarize prospective CS teachers with the national CS curriculum;
4) Expose prospective CS teachers to difficulties encountered by learners when learning different topics from the CS curriculum;
5) Enable prospective CS teachers to master pedagogical skills for teaching CS considering different kinds of learners;

6) Enable prospective CS teachers to master pedagogical tools for teaching CS, including the creation of a supportive and cooperative inquiry-based learning environment;
7) Expose the prospective CS teachers to a variety of CS teaching methods;
8) Expose prospective CS teachers to the research conducted in CS education and to its application in the teaching process.

2.4 Teaching Methods Used in the Course

The teaching methods implemented in the course are varied and their implementation in itself constitutes an essential tier of learning in the course. The course does not only "talk about" but rather it "shows how" to actively apply the teaching principles in the teaching of the discipline. Thus, the course is essentially a workshop and it includes lectures, workshops for developing different teaching materials, hands-on experience with various software programs, practice teaching, and many discussions. Course tasks and assignments are varied and develop simultaneously with the learning process. Task types include, for instance, reading articles and preparing reports, preparing teaching activities, preparing lesson plans, preparing a teaching plan for an entire teaching unit, peer teaching, and writing an entire matriculation exam.

Furthermore, the teaching-learning processes in the course are cooperative in nature. Students present different products before their peers and learn from one another and from feedback they receive from their peers and course instructor. Feedback is given both orally and in writing. In all cases, work products of all of the students are at the disposal of all course participants for use in their course work as well as for future use. The course is accompanied by a website that includes many resources that are available to the students throughout the school year. These resources include links to repositories of learning materials: The website of the Israeli National Supervision of CS education, the website of the National Teachers Center website and links to sites that offer enrichment on topics such as the history of CS, dictionaries of programming languages, information on scientists, and so on. In addition, all contents presented during the course lessons are available on the website.

2.5 Course Syllabus

In order to achieve the course objectives varied of topics are discussed. Some of them are: the curriculum, teaching methods, active learning, developing a lesson outline and social issues of CS. In what follows, due to lack of space, we will present the first semester in details and we will give only a brief description of the second semester.

2.5.1 First Semester – Fundamentals of CS
In this section, we present the course syllabus of the first semester in detail. For each lesson, we present the main topic and for some of the lessons we give a synopsis of the activity undertaken.

Lesson 1: Introduction to the Israeli high school CS Curriculum
Content: The major online sources available to teachers were presented: the websites of the Israeli National Supervision of CS education and of the National CS Teacher Center.

Task: Students were asked to choose an interesting subject that they were exposed to in the CS teachers' website and explain this choice.

Lesson 2: Computer Sciences - What are we Talking About?

Introduction discussion: The essence of CS as a science.

Task: Students worked in groups of 3-4. Each group was asked to plan the content and activity of a first CS lesson in the high school. The groups presented their ideas before the course plenum and a discussion was held.

Lesson 3: Research in Science Education

Introduction lecture: What is science education research and how can it serve teachers? This was illustrated using a research article on the teaching of basic concepts in CS – input and assignment of variables.

Students were referred to databases of studies in CS education.

Task 1: Students worked in pairs and were asked to read a selected research paper that addresses difficulties encountered by novice CS students and write a reflective report. All students uploaded feedback to the course website for use.

Task 2: Students were required to read an article [5] that discusses the diverse knowledge that CS teachers should acquire.

Lesson 4: Reflection and Its Application as a Teaching and Learning Tool

Introduction lecture: What reflection is, how can reflection be used in the teaching process (teacher & students), presenting set of questions that arises reflection. This was demonstrated by an example.

Activity: The teacher as a Researcher – see Appendix.

Lesson 5: Programming Paradigms

Discussion: What is a paradigm? What are thinking paradigms in sciences? What are programming paradigms? Common aspects in families of programming languages according to paradigm. Demonstration of the recursion concept from the paradigm perspective.

Task: Students were asked to illustrate the paradigm differences by writing algorithms for sorting an Array or a List in various paradigms.

Lesson 6: The Fundamentals of Teaching Object-Oriented Programming

Introduction lecture: Emphasize basic object-oriented programming concepts.

Task: Programming exercise - implementation in Java.

Lesson 7: Demonstration of Different Java Development Environments

Activity: Expirience the use of different environments including: visualization environments such as BlueJ (http://www.bluej.org), and animation environments such as Jeliot (http://cs.joensuu.fi/jeliot/index.php).

Discussion: The advantages and disadvantages of the different environments and recommendations for teaching.

Lesson 8: Teaching the Topic of Variables

Group task: What should be taught on the subject of variables? What difficulties can be expected in understanding the concept? Suggest guidelines for a first lesson on the subject; compose three different kinds of questions on the subject of variables and for each question, specify what it examines and what difficulties might be encountered by students during its solution.

Discussion: Tasks were presented before the course plenum. Ways of illustrating variable presentation were discussed, including misconceptions that might be formed due to the use of inappropriate illustrations.

Lesson 9: Types of Questions

Discussion: What types of questions can be posed when teaching CS? Why is it important to vary the types of questions used?

Some thirteen different question models were presented, including question that involve tracking code, checking the correctness of algorithms, completing lines in algorithms, developing a solution to an algorithmic problem, comparing different solutions, describing what an algorithm does, requesting students to compose questions themselves, and so on.

Lesson 10: Teaching Conditional Expressions and Statements

Group task: What should be taught on the subject of conditional expressions and statements? What difficulties can be expected in understanding the subject? Plan a series of 45-min lessons that will reflect the teaching of each subject (simple conditions, nested conditions, complex condition, etc.).

Discussion: The work preformed by the groups was presented and discussed.

Task: Students were requested to compose a summary worksheet that checks the understanding of conditions. The worksheet should take students up to 30 minutes to complete.

Lesson 11: Integrating the Internet into Teaching

Discussion: A short, focused discussion followed by 2 tasks performed in pairs.

Task 1: Choose any topic from the CS curriculum and compose a worksheet that makes use of the internet. The sheet will be used for a 20-min activity. During the development of the worksheet, record guidelines that guided your work. When completed, upload the worksheet to the appropriate course forum.

Task 2: After finishing composing of your worksheet, choose a worksheet composed by two of your classmates and complete it. While working on the worksheet, record your point of view with respect to its contribution to imparting the topic it deals with. *Summarizing discussion.*

Lesson 12: Teaching Loops Statements

Discussion: What kind of loop should be used to begin teaching the subject of loops (while vs. for)? What should be taught on the subject of loops? What difficulties are expected in the understanding of the concept?

Group task: Plan a class activity (not just an exercise) for the first lesson on loops. Prepare student and teacher handouts describing the activity. The teacher's handout was supposed to include detailed didactic instructions so that teachers can read it and apply the activity in their classrooms.

Lesson 13: Participating in the National Teachers Conference for CS Teachers

Out of class activity: Students were invited to participate in the National Teachers Conference for CS Teachers. Students who did not attend the conference were required to visit the National Teachers Conference website and list three lectures/activities that were of special interest to them, specifying the reasons for their choices.

Lesson 14: Integrating Lab Work Into the Teaching Process

Discussion: The CS lab versus labs in other scientific subjects; types of tasks for lab work; organizing the teaching in the lab; guidelines for guiding students in their lab work.

Group Task: Choose any topic from the CS curriculum and compose a lab activity on it. Upload the worksheet to the appropriate course forum.

Lesson 15: Development and Analysis of Algorithms According to "Roles of Variables"

Activity: Students were introduced to the concept through a process of self learning according to the following stages: (1) learn about classification of variable roles, (2) do the "test yourself" activities on the variable roles classification using an online questionnaire (http://cs.joensuu.fi/~saja/var_roles), (3) reflect on the learning (do the students agree with the variable roles classifications? What is their feedback on this kind of class activity? Do they think the topic can be integrated into high school teaching processes and how?)

Lesson 16: Issues of Teaching Memory Organization

Lecture and discussion: The Java memory implementation for: strings, objects, arrays and parameters; is it necessary to teach it to high school students? Potential source for learners' difficulties; recommended teaching methods with respect to those concepts.

Lesson 17: Teaching Methods

Content: Students' difficulties and perceptions; teaching aids; types of exercises.

Lesson 18: The Object-First Approach for Teaching Object Oriented Programming

Lecture and discussion: An overview of approaches and researches; implications of adopting or choosing not to adopt this approach; comparing the various approaches.

Lesson 19: Teaching Arrays

Content: Students' difficulties and perceptions; teaching aids; types of exercises.

Lesson 20: How to Write an Exam

Discussion: The targets of the matriculation exam and ways to meet them.

Workshop: Students worked in pairs and were asked to address the structure of the exam and the type, scope and scoring of the questions. After discussion of the different structures, one of them was chosen and students composed the questions.

Lesson 21: How to Evaluate an Exam

Discussion: The importance of evaluation of exams; evaluation by using an evaluation rubric; the importance of constructing it prior to holding the exam as a way of ascertaining the reliability of the exam questions.

Workshop: Students developed an evaluation rubric for the exam they developed.

Lessons 22-23: Guiding Projects

Content: These lessons were dedicated to discussion and guidance with respect to the teacher's role in guiding large-scale projects written by his or her students. Pedagogic and technical aspects were emphasized as well as class management in such situations.

Lessons 24-28: The Final Semester Paper and Peer Teaching with Respect to It

The final semester paper: The paper objective was to enable each student to independently delve deeper into the construction of a teaching plan for an entire study unit. In their seminar papers, students were expected to express knowledge from different areas studied in the course "Methods of Teaching Computer Science" as well as from other courses. Each student chose a topic from the curriculum, analyzed it and planed a study unit for it. Students were required to address the various resources on the selected topic, including textbooks and at least one research paper in English.

The paper has to include the following sections: (i) Concepts and contents to be taught; (ii) Difficulties expected to be encountered by students when learning the topic; (iii) General division of the topic into several lessons, addressing the recommended teaching sequence; (iv) Building a full lesson plan for two consecutive proposed lessons, specifying the principles guiding the teaching.

The two detailed lesson plans were required to include the following components: (i) Full lesson plan, addressing the lesson objectives and the lesson opening, development and ending; (ii) Description of the activities / questions / tasks / exercises, etc. included in the lesson; (iii) Description of the teaching methods used: frontal teaching, working in small groups, cooperative learning, group or individual independent learning, investigation and discovery, games, etc.; (iv) Description of the teaching aids used: overhead projector, posters, models, computer, learning environment; (v) Suggestion for evaluating students' knowledge after the two lessons, "solution" of the evaluation task, and an evaluating rubric for evaluating the task.

Peer teaching: The final semester lessons were dedicated to individual, 30-min. presentations of their work, given by each of the students. Presentations included two parts: (1) a summary of the research paper dealing with the study unit; (2) introduction of a short excerpt from the planned lesson to the course planner, which was then taught by the student to his or her peers and a description of the considerations involved in the development of this segment of the lesson.

2.5.2 Second Semester – Advanced Topics in CS: Abstract Data Types and Computational Models

The second semester deals with the teaching of advanced contents that, in many places around the world, are not included in formal high school curricula [17]. Lessons held during this semester were related to the following subjects: The teaching of abstract data types (list, stack, queue, and binary tree); the teaching of computational models (deterministic finite automata, push-down automata, Turing machine, languages); the teaching of advanced disciplinary concepts such as recursion, complexity and abstraction; integration of social aspects as ethics and gender in the teaching process; and teaching tools like design patterns and games.

3 Summary

In this paper, we presented a detailed description of a "Methods of Teaching CS" course, which implements the challenges of CS teacher preparation. When examined as a whole, course contents cover and refer to all of the objectives defined in section 2.3. Specifically, the course content is broad and diverse. The course covers the following aspects: the essence of the discipline; disciplinary contents and learners difficulties related to them; research in CS education and ways to use it in lessons planning; several teaching methods; several teaching tools like integrating games, lab, and the internet into the lessons; how to plan tests and how to evaluate them; and more.

Vast and varied knowledge is imparted through active learning and constructivist construction of the pre-service teachers' knowledge. Diversity in teaching methods increases students' interest in the course but, first and foremost, it constitutes a model for implementation in the students' future classes.

Our intention is to further develop this work on CS teacher preparation programs and to foster awareness to its importance. For example, during the 2006-2007 academic year, we integrated in the course a tutoring model that focuses on improving students' skills with respect to the teaching of problem solving, by letting them cope with one-on-one teaching situations [16]. The tutoring activity enabled the students to immediately apply ideas learned in the course. Our aim, in general, is construct a repository of activities for CS teacher preparation programs. Our aim, in general, is construct a repository of activities for CS teacher preparation programs.

References

1. Armoni, M.: Looking at Secondary Teacher Preparation through the Lenses of Computer Science – a Literature Survey (in preparation)
2. Cornwell, L.W.: Crisis in computer science education at the precollege level. In: 13th SIGCSE Technical Symposium on Computer Science Education, SIGCSE Bulletin, vol. 14(1), pp. 28–30. ACM, New York (1982)
3. CSTA: Computer Science State Certification Requirements - CSTA Certification Committee Report (December 2007), http://www.csta.acm.org/ComputerScienceTeacherCertification/sub/TeachCertRept07New.pdf

4. Deek, F., Kimmel, H.: Status of computer science education in secondary schools. J. Computer Science Education 9(2), 89–113 (1999)
5. Gal-Ezer, J., Harel, D.: What (Else) Should CS Educators Know? J. Communications of the ACM 41(9), 77–84 (1998)
6. Gal-Ezer, J., Harel, D.: Curriculum and course syllabi for a high-school CS program. J. Computer Science Education 9(2), 114–147 (1999)
7. Gal-Ezer, J., Beeri, C., Harel, D., Yehudai, A.: A high-school program in computer science. IEEE Computer 28(10), 73–80 (1995)
8. Hazzan, O., Gal-Ezer, J., Blum, L.: A model for high school Computer Science Education: The four key elements that make it! In: 39th Technical Symposium on Computer Science Education, SIGCSE Bulletin, vol. 40(1), pp. 281–285. ACM, New York (2008)
9. Hazzan, O., Lapidot, T.: Social issues of Computer Science in the Methods of Teaching Computer Science in the High School course. Inroads, SIGCSE Bulletin 38(2), 72–75 (2006)
10. Hazzan, O., Lapidot, T.: The practicum in computer science education: Bridging gaps between theoretical knowledge and actual performance. Inroads, SIGCSE Bulletin 6(4), 47–51 (2004)
11. Heeler, P.J.: A master's degree in school computer studies. In: 14th SIGCSE Technical Symposium on Computer Science Education, SIGCSE Bulletin, vol. 15(1), pp. 99–103. ACM, New York (1983)
12. Lapidot, T., Hazzan, O.: Methods of Teaching Computer Science course for prospective teachers. Inroads, SIGCSE Bulletin 35(4), 29–34 (2003)
13. Lapidot, T., Hazzan, O.: Methods of teaching a computer science course for prospective teachers. Inroads, SIGCSE Bulletin 37(4), 79–83 (2003)
14. Moursund, D.: Computer science education for preservice elementary school teachers. SIGCUE Outlook, SIGCSE Bulletin 2(4), 3–10 (1978)
15. Poirot, J., Luerhmann, A., Norris, C., Taylor, H., Taylor, R.: Proposed curriculum for programs leading to teacher certification in computer science. Communications of the ACM, SIGCSE Bulletin 28(3), 275–279 (1985)
16. Ragonis, N., Haazan, O.: Integrating Tutoring Model into Computer Science Prospective Teachers Preparation Program. In: ITiCSE 2008 conference (accepted)
17. Ragonis, N.: Secondary Level Computing Curricula. Encyclopedia of Computer Science and Computer Engineering. John Wiley & Sons, Chichester (assigned for publication)
18. Shulman, L.S.: Those who understand: knowledge growth in teaching. J. Educational Teacher 15(2), 4–14 (1986)
19. Shulman, L.S.: Reconnecting foundations to the substance of teacher education. Teachers College Record 91(3), 300–310 (1990)
20. Stephenson, C., Gal-Ezer, J., Haberman, B., Verno, A.: The new educational imperative: Improving high school computer science education. In: Final report of the CSTA Curriculum Improvement Task Force February 2005, Computer Science Teachers Association, Association for Computing Machinery (2005) (April 2007), http://csta.acm.org/Publications/White_Paper07_06.pdf
21. Tucker, A., Deek, F., Jones, J., McCowan, D., Stephenson, C., Verno, A.: A Model Curriculum for K-12 Computer Science. Report of the ACM K-12 Education Task Force Computer Science Curriculum Committee – Draft (2002) (July 2007), http://www.acm.org/k12/k12Draft1101.pdf
22. White, J.: Computer science teachers association report for ACM's sigs (2004) (December 2007), http://csta.acm.org, http://www.acm.org/sigs/sgb/minutes/agenda100304_3_2.ppt

23. Zur, E., Vilner, T.: Teaching certificate in computer science – didactics workshop. In: 9th ITiCSE Annual Conference on Innovation and Technology in Computer Science Education. SIGCSE Bulletin, vol. 36(3), p. 240. ACM, New York (2004)

Appendix

An Activity: The Teacher as a Researcher

Part A
The following problem is given:
  Write an algorithm that receives array A and array size N and returns *true* if all array members are identical and *false* if they are not.
Write a solution to the problem:

- Keep all drafts from the development process.
- When you are finished, lay your solutions aside and ask for the next task.

Part B
The same problem you solved before is given again:
  Write an algorithm that receives array A and array size N and returns *true* if all array members are identical and *false* if they are not.
Analysis of the question:
  List the CS concepts that you think are manifested in this question.
Following are several different solutions to the same problem. For each solution

- Determine whether it is correct or not.
- If it is incorrect:
    o Describe the mistake.
    o Try to think of the source of the mistake.
    o Try to think how you would help the student understand his or her mistake.
- ** Optional **: Try to present another incorrect solution.

Reflection in Pairs

- Discuss your conclusions from the previous section. Compare the answers – elaborate on your analysis – change it... add to it... correct it...
- Exchange your personal solution to the problem with your partner. Check your partner's solution.
    o Is it correct or incorrect?
    o If it is correct – have you anything to say about the solution in order to develop the capabilities of "your student" in the process of problem solving? Elaborate.
    o If it is incorrect – is it similar to one of the incorrect solutions in your analysis?

Solution1	Solution2

<u>are-equals(A, N)</u>
ok • true
for i from 1 to N do
    if (A[i] ≠ A[i+1]) then
        ok • false
return ok
	<u>are-equals(A, N)</u>
	ok • true
	for i from 1 to N-1 do
	    if (A[i] ≠ A[i+1]) then
	        ok • false
	    else
	        ok • true
	return ok

Solution3	**Solution4**

<u>are-equals(A, N)</u>
ok • true
for i from 1 to N-1 by 2 do
    if (A[i] ≠ A[i+1]) then
        ok • false
return ok
	<u>are-equals(A, N)</u>
	ok • true
	for i from 1 to N-1 by 2 do
	    if (A[i] ≠ A[i+1]) then
	        ok • false
	for i from 2 to N-1 by 2 do
	    if (A[i] ≠ A[i+1]) then
	        ok • false
	return ok

Solution5	**Solution6**

<u>are-equals(A, N)</u>
ok • true
for i from 1 to N-1 do
    if (A[i] ≠ A[i+1]) then
        ok • false
return ok
	<u>are-equals(A, N)</u>
	count • 0
	for i from 2 to n do
	    if (A[i] = A[i+1]) then
	        count • count + 1
	if (count = N) then
	    return true
	else
	    return false

Algorithm – Fundamental Concept in Preparing Informatics Teachers

Ewa Kolczyk

Institute of Computer Science, University of Wroclaw
ul. Przesmyckiego 20, 51-151 Wroclaw, Poland
eko@ii.uni.wroc.pl

Abstract. The concept of the algorithm is fundamental within the computer science (informatics) domain. It is important to introduce it gradually in a spiral manner through all stages of education. Informatics teachers should be able to explain, to give examples and to help understanding the concept of algorithm at an elementary level. Therefore they need some ideas, tools, and didactic concepts to do it. The article presents some examples of tools and techniques, which the future informatics teachers should be familiar with. In teacher training we should deliver meaningful examples and carefully show the stages of building the intuition of the algorithm.

1 Introduction

In the Polish national education system the separate lessons on using computers and ICT are called informatics. Informatics lessons are obligatory in primary schools and in middle schools (*gimnazjum*). In high schools (*liceum*) there is an obligatory subject called information technology (IT) and an elective subject called informatics (computer science). The main goal of informatics classes in primary schools is to prepare students to use computers and their software, mainly to be able to use them in other subjects.

In middle schools (*gimnazjum*), during the informatics classes, students are prepared to use computers, computer networks, and multimedia on a more advanced level. It should give students a more solid background for using ICT in other subjects. Moreover, students are introduced also to problem solving with algorithms. One of possible tools of implementing algorithms is the Logo language.

In high schools (*liceum*) there are two subjects. One of them, called information technology (IT), is the continuation of earlier students' preparation in using computers, networks and multimedia tools for managing information. The stress is put on working with information in a good presentational style, including automation. There is nothing about algorithms and programming. Informatics (computer science) is an elective subject addressed for young people, who are interested in computer science as an element of their future education. The informatics lessons are expecting to show computer science as a discipline connected with designing and implementing new systems of information processing. It should include ways of solving problems in the following stages: analysis of a problem situation, making specification, designing the solution, realization and testing the solution. Students are introduced to classic algorithms, programming languages, theory of data bases, and programming of interactive websites.

The organization of informatics education in the form of obligatory and elective subjects at all levels of education demands the need for preparing teachers for these subjects. Within the group of ICT and informatics teachers I distinguish two separate groups:

- ICT teachers who run informatics lessons in primary and middle school or IT lessons in high school – the main goal for them is to prepare all pupils to use ICT,
- Informatics teachers who run informatics as an elective subject in high school.

The standards of preparing those two groups have been elaborated [9]. The standards could be the common platform for institutions offering in-service training for teachers and teachers themselves who want to improve their qualifications. The standards should meet, on the other hand, the new standards of teachers education published by the Ministry of National Education [10]. The main assumption of the new standards is that the teacher who wants to work at a lower level of education (in primary and middle school) should be prepared for teaching two subjects. This is a great idea for two reasons: the teacher is able to integrate knowledge from different domains in his teaching, and the process of employment the staff for the school is easier. But it is a great challenge for universities to elaborate new study programs, which supply the idea.

Actually the significant part of ICT teachers are teachers for whom teaching informatics is the second specialization, because they are teachers of other subjects which got qualifications to teach informatics during different courses or post-diploma study. So the situation will not change in the future, teachers will merge teaching informatics and teaching other subject e.g. maths, chemistry, physics.

Preparing informatics teachers is more complicated. According to the standards [9] the informatics teachers should demonstrate knowledge at the level of graduates of a computer science department. On the other hand, it is obvious that graduates of computer science don't choose the teacher profession, because of many other job opportunities.

If we look at the algorithm as a fundamental concept, in teacher training there are two situations:

- Teachers, who start to teach informatics as a second specialization, often don't feel confident with the concept of algorithm, so they are very cautious and hesitant about teaching problem-solving and algorithms.
- Graduates of computer science, who become informatics teachers, don't feel the difficulty of the abstract concept for the pupils and often use too complicated examples, or go too fast through the material.

In both situations the teachers should be able to explain, to give examples and to help to understand the concept of the algorithm at an elementary level, so they need some ideas, tools and didactic techniques to do it. During the course of Didactics of Informatics, I show some useful ideas and techniques.

2 Algorithm – Fundamental Concept at Primary Level

The concept of algorithm is fundamental to the computer science (informatics) domain. It is important to introduce it gradually in a spiral manner, before the student has entered secondary education, and has chosen an elective subject. Problem solving with algorithms is included in middle school informatics curriculum. But, in primary school, there are situations when the idea of algorithm, and algorithmic thinking, could be introduced.

The pupils meet the term 'algorithm' first in primary school in math classes, when they are dealing with addition and multiplication algorithms. The pupils are expected to perform the given procedure. They shouldn't write or explain the algorithm, but they have to use it in an effective manner. This is the *first* important observation: *memorizing and performing the procedure is easier than planning, writing or explaining it.*

The first situation, when the pupils are asked to plan the procedure and to write it, is also in primary school, in Polish classes. The pupils are writing the instruction, how to do something, or how to get somewhere, using the enumerated list. This activity from Polish classes could have a natural continuation in informatics lessons. It is an occasion to show how important the sequence is, and the precision of the instruction. In informatics classes, writing the instructions may be concerned with doing tasks on computers, for example the pupils write the instruction, how to arrange a table using word processor, and than other pupils try to perform this instruction. In this activity the pupils use the natural language and they could experience the difficulty in precise formulation of every step of the instruction. Such experience could be used to explain the pupils that the computer requires also precise and exact instructions to perform all actions.

Referring to computers, the pupils know the strategy used in computer games, which I called 'steering on-line'. In this strategy you shouldn't plan the procedure; you simply give the commands and observe the results. The strategy of planning, writing instruction and then performing it is rarely present in popular computer games. This is the *second* observation: *'steering on-line' is easier than planning, writing and then making the computer to perform the instruction.*

ICT teachers should arrange situations, when the pupils can plan, write and then make the computer to perform the instructions. Writing the instruction for the computer requires an introduction to a new language, because the computer doesn't interpret the natural language. For educational purposes it is possible to use in this context a tool – an environment with the hero, the language with limited number of commands and the tasks to be solved using this language. Examples of such environments are easy to point out: Logo with the turtle, Karel the Robot [7], Baltie [1] (with the wizard as a hero, originated from Czech Republic). In the TI'99 software package connected with our textbook for primary schools [3] there is also a program called 'Steering' with a turtle as a hero, who can walk trough the maze, move the treasure from one place to another, and draw lines.

3 Problem Solving with Algorithms at Middle Level

This stage of education is very important for the secondary level, because the informatics lessons, for the last time, are addressed to *all* pupils. It is the occasion to make the pupils conscious what informatics (computer science) is really about, so they can responsibly choose the elective subject in high school. The informatics curriculum for middle schools includes introduction to problem solving with algorithms, but many teachers avoid teaching this part of the curriculum.

Once again, the informatics curriculum should correspond with the curriculum of other subjects. In maths and natural sciences the pupils are expected to solve tasks in which they have to analyze the story and to find what quantities (values) are given and what are we looking for. The mathematical solution includes defining what is given, what result we expect to find and what dependences and equations could be used to find the result. Sometimes there are few equations and they must be merged or transformed to obtain the result. All these steps formulate the algorithm of finding the solution of the task. It is important to show the pupils that the solution of the task taken from maths, chemistry or physics lessons could be written as a list of equations which defines the steps of the algorithm. At this stage in informatics lessons, spreadsheet could be used to write the solution as a data flow diagram [5]. Such an analysis of the task is also the base for an informatics solution of the problem.

Teaching about algorithms should be full of examples of algorithmic procedures known to the pupils from their life and school experience. Once again, the addition (multiplication) algorithm is a good example of a deterministic algorithm. We could show that for the same data the result is always the same, of course, if we have done all steps correctly. The kitchen recipe is a useful example, when we are talking about specification. Some sport contest's regulations and law procedures are good examples for different algorithmic constructions (conditional or iteration statement). The Logo language and the turtle graphics is an inexhaustible source of tasks in which we can show the power of iteration strategy [4].

At this stage, it is important to show how useful simple and natural strategies are in solving problems with a computer. Discovering algorithmic strategies like iteration, binary search or 'divide an conquer' doesn't mean that the pupils should be able to write programs using these strategies. This is the *third* observation: *discovering, understanding and using the strategy is easier than writing it in a formal language*. For example, the game when one person has to guess the number from a given range, and the second person could answer only if the requested number is smaller, bigger or equal. The natural strategy to guess the number in the smallest number of trials is a binary search. The pupils can discover the strategy, but they shouldn't write the algorithm in a formal notation.

The strategy could be discover, also, thanks to the visualization of the algorithm. The classic problem, the Tower of Hanoi puzzle is a nice example. It could be hard for the pupils to find how to move discs in a proper sequence, but the solution could be observed in the visualization [6]. A much more interesting question is, how much time is needed to complete the puzzle for 64 discs, as it was described in the legend [11]. Looking from this point of view, the example is a nice occasion to show how time-consuming solving the problem could be despite the great computing power of present computers. Observing the visualization of the solution could help to find the recursive dependence, how many moves are needed. The pupils could use the spreadsheet to find the result for 64 discs and to calculate, how much time it takes for the performance of such a big number of moves.

4 Didactic Concepts at Secondary Level

In primary and middle school, it is possible to form only the intuition about the concept of algorithm. The examples of formal notation are very simple, because younger pupils are not prepared to advanced manipulation with symbols. It could happen that the pupils haven't had any intuition, and haven't met any example of the formal notation of the algorithm before entering high school. In this situation the informatics teacher should construct the concept very carefully and gradually. Examples from real life, written in natural language should be considered at the beginning. Than, gradually, we start to write algorithmic procedures using more formal notation: the enumerated list of steps, the math notation, the flowcharts and at last the programming language. I mention the programming language at last because it is a formal and artificial language with strict syntax and grammar rules. The latter don't make writing algorithms easier.

Of course, the algorithms written in notations other than a programming language, could not be performed by a computer. But the pupils could perform them using blackboard and chalk. The ability to analyze an algorithm without a computer is very important. Later, it enables for better understanding the semantics of the programming language.

I have mentioned that discovering strategies is easier than writing it in a formal notation. The transition from the idea of the algorithm to the solution in the formal notation meets some barriers [12] but the activities connected with concrete manipulations could help. For example the idea of searching for the minimum a set of numbers is quite natural for the pupils, but the attempt to describe it using a flowchart causes some difficulties. I observed a lesson, where the pupil had to find the shortest pen, using the bag with pens. He didn't see the whole set of pens: he had his hands inside the bag and the only possibility of searching for the shortest pen was to compare two pens by putting them together. After this activity, the pupils started to draw the flowchart of the algorithm for searching for a minimum and than they applied this flowchart to search the shortest person in the classroom. Thanks to these activities the lesson was much more attractive for the pupils, and required the engagement from them. What is more important is that the computers weren't used at this time in the classroom.

The strategy used by the pupils in searching minimum is called a linear search. Implementation of this strategy requires organizing iteration. Identifying what actions should be repeated is the key point in coping with writing the algorithm in a formal notation. In the observed lesson, some pupils managed to identify that iteration in this case is organized almost in the same way as in the other example from the previous lesson when the algorithm of computing the sum of a sequence of numbers was considered. So they successfully used the pattern of the flowchart from the previous example. Using patterns in implementing algorithms is another important idea, which we can consciously use in our teaching.

I start from flowcharts because it is a formal notation which has a graphic representation. This graphic representation is useful to explain algorithmic constructions like iteration, conditional and assignment statements. Another reason is the tool which makes it possible to animate the flowchart. The flowchart is a kind of model of the algorithm. The animation of the flowchart enables us to run the simulation of the model. The tool is named ELI [2]. It is a program in which we can construct the flowchart of the algorithm and where we can run the simulation of this algorithm for different data. We can observe the performance step by step and we can debug the sequence of performed commands and the changes of the variables' values. We are also able to investigate the number of operations performed. So it is a powerful tool for creating, visualizing, and analyzing the algorithms. Using this tool is also a reason to use computers in the lessons concerned with the algorithms.

Another very useful tool for informatics teachers is the implementation of the RAM machine, the simplified model of a computer [8]. This application enables us to write programs in simple programming language and, what is more important, to show the process of compilation. The compiled program is presented in a low-level programming language, and a visualization of running the program is possible.

In the earlier stages of education, the pupils got used to the idea that the computers should be used in every informatics lesson, so it is a good recommendation to think about lessons in which we partly or completely don't use computers at all. The lessons about the algorithms serve as an example that it is possible. In high school, we should introduce the difficult and abstract concepts using the same techniques as we used with younger children: I mean a manipulation with concretes, a visualization, or a graphic representation. We also should make the lessons more attractive by organizing activities which engage the pupils. In the lessons about algorithms is possible to work in groups using brain-storming techniques to find the idea of the solution of given problem. Working with a formal notation is also a good occasion to organize a peer-assisted learning or puzzle groups in which the pupils try to explain to each other the performance of the algorithm.

5 Conclusion

Constructing the concept of the algorithm should be a continuous process through all stages of education. The concept should be present in the curriculum of other subjects, especially in a math's curriculum. The informatics lessons should benefit from lessons of other subjects also in the area of forming the fundamental concepts. In teacher training, it means that we should deliver meaningful examples and carefully show the stages of building the intuition of the algorithmic procedure and algorithmic thinking. We should encourage informatics and ICT teachers to introduce different didactic techniques into their informatics lessons, and not to concentrate only on 'hands-on' computer experiences for their pupils.

References

1. Baltie software's website (accessed 4.01.2008), http://www.sgpsys.com/en/
2. ELI software producer's website (in Polish) (accessed 4.01.2008), http://www.elboxedu.pl/produkty/id,39
3. Gurbiel, E., Hardt-Olejniczak, G., Kołczyk, E., Krupicka, H., Sysło, M.M.: Informatics, textbook for primary school, grades 4-6, WSiP, Warszawa (1999) (in Polish)
4. Hromkovič, J.: Contributing to General Education by Teaching Informatics. In: Mittermeir, R.T. (ed.) ISSEP 2006. LNCS, vol. 4226, pp. 25–37. Springer, Heidelberg (2006)

5. Hubwieser, P.: Functions, Objects and States: Teaching Informatics in Secondary Schools. In: Mittermeir, R.T. (ed.) ISSEP 2006. LNCS, vol. 4226, pp. 106–116. Springer, Heidelberg (2006)
6. Java visualization of Tower of Hanoi puzzle (accessed 4.01.2008), http://www.mazeworks.com/hanoi
7. Pattis, R.: Karel the Robot: A Gentle Introduction to the Art of Programming. John Wiley & Sons, New York (1995)
8. RAM machine software's website (in Polish) (accessed 4.01.2008), http://www.ramachine.webpark.pl/
9. Standards of preparing ICT and informatics teachers (in Polish) (accessed 4.01.2008), http://www.men.gov.pl/edu_infor/dokumenty/standardy1.php#2
10. Standards of teachers' education (in Polish) (accessed 4.01.2008), http://bip.men.gov.pl/akty_pr_1997_2006/rozp_302.php
11. The history of Tower of Hanoi puzzle (accessed 4.01.2008), http://www.cs.wm.edu/~pkstoc/toh.html
12. Weigend, M.: From Intuition to Programme. In: Mittermeir, R.T. (ed.) ISSEP 2006. LNCS, vol. 4226, pp. 117–126. Springer, Heidelberg (2006)

Computer Science Teacher Training at the University of Groningen

Nataša Grgurina

University Center for Academic Learning and Teaching, University of Groningen
Landleven 1, 9747 AD Groningen
The Netherlands
N.Grgurina@rug.nl

Abstract. The University Center for Academic Learning and Teaching (UOCG) provides the University of Groningen with an educational program to train fully qualified secondary school teachers in many secondary school subjects including computer science. This two-year Master's in Education Program consists of teacher training that includes a large internship component and teacher training courses, in addition to those courses provided by the faculties. During the internship, the secondary school where the internship takes place is in charge of a substantial part of the teacher training, while the University's role is mainly a supervisory one.

Keywords: computer science teacher training, University of Groningen, didactics of computer science.

1 The Dutch Educational System

In the Netherlands, high school begins with the seventh grade when students are twelve years old. Although it is common in the lower grades (7 through 9) for a teacher with a *grade two* teaching qualification to teach multiple subjects, in the higher grades the teacher as a rule teaches only one subject, or a cluster of related subjects, e.g., various mathematics subjects. To teach grades ten and higher in the pre-university educational system (the Dutch acronym is VWO), which prepares students for academic studies at a university, and in the senior secondary educational system (HAVO), which prepares students for higher professional education, the teacher needs to be *fully* qualified[1]. This full qualification is obtained by enrolling in a Master's in Education program at a university [5].

In the higher grades of the senior secondary educational system (grades 10 and 11) and in those of the pre-university educational system (grades 10 through 12), the curricula are streamlined into two social and two scientific profiles, which determine for the most part which subjects a student will study. In the ninth grade, each student

---

[1] In this paper, only the secondary senior educational system and the pre-university educational system are discussed since these are the only types of secondary education where a full qualification is required.

selects a profile to follow in grades ten and higher, as well as one or two elective subjects. Computer science is one of these subjects; it is not bound to a particular profile and can be chosen as an elective course by all students [6].

1.1 Computer Science

All students are expected to become computer literate in the lower grades of secondary school [8], so achieving computer literacy is not an objective of the computer science course. This course is not meant as a preparatory course for studying computer science at the higher education level either. Instead, it is meant to give students an overview and understanding of IT concepts, along with a sense of their potential and limitations, all while encouraging cooperative learning on project-based activities [7],[13]. Therefore, besides programming, which is not supposed to take up more than about one quarter of the teaching time [11], students are required to learn about hardware, software, networks, information analysis and databases, system development, project management, and human-computer interaction, in addition to the social and ethical questions involved in the use of IT [11]. The curricula of the two types of secondary schools (senior secondary education and pre-university education) differ only in minor details. It is suggested, however, that in senior secondary education more emphasis should be placed on practical work, while pre-university education should focus more on studying the theoretical aspects of CS. Computer science is one of the very few courses in secondary school that is not a subject in the national exams at the end of secondary education; instead, all assessment takes place at the school level. Currently[2], about sixty percent of all schools offer this elective course, with about ten percent of the students choosing to take it [12].

1.2 Computer Science Teachers

When computer science was first introduced in the senior secondary educational and pre-university educational systems in 1998, there were no qualified teachers. Therefore, a consortium of twelve universities and institutions for higher professional education, CODI[3], was set up to join forces in training teachers. Fully qualified teachers teaching other subjects were encouraged to enroll in this CODI scheme encompassing a two-year in-school training program of about 45 ECTS in order to achieve full qualification for computer science. These teachers were by no means required to have any prior knowledge of computer science; the only requirement was for the teachers to be computer-literate. The program consisted of the subjects listed in Table 1 [10]:

Some of these courses were regular Open University[4] courses, while others were based on those courses taught in computer science degree programs at the college level. And some, notably the Didactics of Computer Science course, had to be built from scratch.

---

[2] The most recent data are from 2006.
[3] CODI is the Dutch acronym for Informatics Teacher Education Consortium.
[4] See: www.ou.nl

Table 1. CODI program

Course	ECTS
Orientation to Computer Science	3.5
Computer Architecture and Operating Systems	0.7
Visual Programming with Java	5.7
Information Systems: Modeling and Specifying	5
Databases	0.7
Telematics	3.5
Software Engineering	5
Man-Machine Interaction	1.4
Programming Paradigms and Methods of Information System Development	1.4
Didactics of Computer Science	5.7
CS Projects	2.8
Practical Teaching Assignment	10

In 2002, when it became clear that the CODI training program would be terminated in 2005 [4], a workgroup was set up to assist in a joint preparation of a regular computer science teacher training program for Dutch universities. In 2004 this workgroup issued its recommendations, including advice, among other things, concerning the didactics of CS that needed to be taught to prospective CS teachers [2]. This will be discussed in more detail in Section 3.2.5 on Didactics.

As of fall 2006, there were five universities in the Netherlands, including the University of Groningen, where a teacher could become fully qualified by following a Master's in Education in computer science.

2 The Teacher Training Program

At the University of Groningen, all teacher training is provided by the University Center for Academic Learning and Teaching (UOCG) [14]. The teachers are trained in the following subjects: Dutch, English, German, French, Spanish, Frisian, classical languages, history, philosophy, geography, social studies, general economics, business economics, mathematics, physics, chemistry, biology and computer science. The two-year Master's in Education (120 ECTS) is generally structured as follows: during the first year the faculty provides subject matter courses for 50 ECTS, and the UOCG provides the Basic Teacher Course for 10 ECTS. During the second year, the faculty provides subject matter courses for 10 ECTS and the UOCG the school-based program for 50 ECTS, half of which is for internship in a high school. Many transfer students do not enroll in this Master's program immediately upon finishing their Bachelor's degree: some have already acquired another Master's degree, some are qualified teachers in a different subject, while others are already working as teachers without any formal teacher training. In such cases it is possible to tailor a study program to fit the individual situation.[5] Those students wishing to become computer science teachers should have a university Bachelor's degree in computer science. Where this is not the case, each student is assessed to determine which courses the student should take so that he or she can enroll in the Master's in Education program. This entails acquiring an adequate body of knowledge pertaining to "software (programming and algorithmics), data (information systems and knowledge systems), hardware (machines and infrastructure), basic principles, (research and) development, context, and computer science as a scientific discipline."[2]

In Groningen, we believe in on-the-job training. A substantial part of teacher training takes place in the classroom. Learning how to teach can best take place in an authentic situation, hence within a school context. The university, in this case the UOCG, sees to it that students are able to merge theory and practice, while familiarizing themselves with the underlying principles of good education.

3 The Role of the University

The UOCG and the faculties provide a number of the modules for teacher training. The parts of the teacher training making up the 60 ECTS provided by the UOCG will be described in Chapter 3.2.

3.1 Bachelor's Degree

Even during their Bachelor's degree, students can get a taste of teacher training. By taking the Orientation for Educational Skills course, students can discover whether the Master's in Education and the accompanying teacher training is to their taste. Within the Faculty of Mathematics and Natural Sciences (this is where computer science is taught) this course is called Communicative Skills and Orientation to Education. During this 5 ECTS course, students become familiar with the basics of teaching methodology and do a short internship in a high school where they observe a dozen or so classes taught by other teachers, teach half a dozen or so classes themselves, and get a first-hand look at the work of a teacher and how schools are organized.

3.2 Master's in Education

During the first year of the Master's in Education, students follow a 10-ECTS Basic Teacher Training Course. The objective of this course is to familiarize students with all aspects of the profession of teacher and to prepare them for teaching independently. This course consists of two parts: Theoretical Support (5 ECTS) and Preparatory School Practice (5 ECTS), which is an extensive internship at a high school. Students teach fifteen to twenty classes and are required to teach at least six successive classes independently. This course concludes with an evaluation that includes an assessment that verifies whether they meet the entry requirements for a school-based program in the second year of the Master's in Education program.

---

[5] In the fall of 2007, a one-year Educational Master's was introduced for students who already have a Master's degree – except for Spanish, philosophy and computer science.

The school-based program (50 ECTS) in the second year represents the core of the teacher-training program. It consists of a number of professionalization exercises: Working at School (25 ECTS), Reflection on Professional Development (2 ECTS), School Subjects (6 ECTS), Learning Processes (3 ECTS), Problem-directed Designing (9 ECTS), Subject Coherence (3 ECTS) and Elective Courses (2 ECTS). Furthermore, there are two themes running through all these professionalization exercises: pedagogical practice and IT in education. There are no exams since the entire assessment is based on rubrics[6]. All the lectures in the second year are scheduled on Mondays, leaving the rest of the week free for internship activities.

3.2.1 Working in a School

This refers to an internship at a high school. In most cases, students are paid during the entire academic year for about one quarter of the regular hours, meaning six to eight classes a week. Throughout the academic year they are fully responsible for teaching their own classes. At least half of the lessons are taught to grades ten and higher. (When it comes to CS, this obviously holds true for all the classes, since CS is not taught earlier than the tenth grade.) In the Collaborative Teacher Education model, much of the teacher training takes place at school. There is a teacher educator in charge of organizing regular meetings with all the student teachers being trained. Every student teacher has a coach – a teacher who teaches the same or a similar subject. The UOCG supplies a tutor whose role it is to visit the school and the student teachers about three times a year and, in cooperation with the teacher educator and the coach, to assess their progress and their level of achievement. The tutor is also in charge of the assessment of the professionalization exercise, Reflection on Professional Development; this will be described in the next section. In this way the UOCG keeps tabs on the quality of the teacher training offered by the secondary school.

3.2.2 Reflection on Professional Development

The student teachers are expected to reflect on their own growth and development as a teacher by writing several reports throughout the academic year. In these reports the student teachers describe and analyze the period just completed and answer several questions.

"What kind of a teacher am I?" In answering this question the student teachers reflect on their level of competence as described in the government's educational standards regulations in terms of interpersonal, pedagogic and didactic competences in the subject they teach, as well as organizational competence; also included are competences relating to their ability to cooperate with colleagues, their environment, and their assessment of their own development as a teacher [1]. Furthermore, the student teachers are expected to elaborate on their own theories about teaching, and on their personal concept of the profession and the subject matter.

---

[6] According to one definition, "a rubric is an authentic assessment tool used to measure students' work. It is a scoring guide that seeks to evaluate a student's performance based on the sum of a full range of criteria rather than a single numerical score." (See: http://edtech.kennesaw.edu/intech/rubrics.htm)

"What kind of a teacher do I want to become?" The student teachers describe their objectives for the coming period, and paint a complete picture of the kind of teacher they want to become.

Personal development plan: this part of the report contains specific objectives and how they will be attained.

During the school visits the tutor discusses these reports with the student teachers, the teacher educator, and the coach. The tutor is in charge of assessing this professionalization exercise.

3.2.3 Learning Processes
The prospective teachers need to familiarize themselves with learning and teaching theories and they should be able to interpret and implement them in their own teaching practice while taking into account the way students learn and develop.

3.2.4 Problem-Directed Designing
This is a professionalization exercise where the Master's students combine research with creating an education analysis and a final product. In every secondary school there are problems just waiting to be tackled. The student spots a problem, preferably one that is not confined to a single class or subject, analyzes it, and comes up with a solution meant to improve education.

For example, one student noticed a lot of resistance when high school students were required to log their activities in a logbook while working on a practical assignment. It turned out that this resistance to logbooks was commonplace throughout the entire curriculum, so the student decided to look into it and come up with recommendations to alleviate this problem.

3.2.5 School Subject (Didactics)
This professionalization exercise is about teaching and learning the school subject. Specifically, it concerns the content and objectives of the subject, the place of the subject within secondary education as a whole. It also deals with the question of how a student learns the subject, how this subject is assessed, and how to create a good learning environment. If the situation were ideal, a prospective teacher would be supplied with a range of ready-made methods and techniques to enable him or her to teach every detail of the subject in the best way possible. When it comes to CS, however, this is not so easy. The main objective of this professionalization exercise, therefore, is to equip the prospective teacher with those methods that will enable him or her to make choices and decisions as to how best to teach CS.

In 2004 the workgroup making recommendations about what regular CS teacher training would involve stated that "Computer science is a completely new subject both in terms of its content and its didactics; it entails *concepts* concerning information and communication, automation and informatization, the relationship between *IT* and *society*, and more specifically the use of IT in industry. The learning outcomes of this course are described [...] on a rather highly abstract level, which implies that further *breakdown needs to take place in practice (at the school level)*." [2] Furthermore, the way CS is set up in high schools (with no national exam, and assessment largely based on practical assignments often involving a group effort) gives the teacher the chance to differentiate among the students. All this freedom, of course, brings with it a responsibility to be explicit about all the choices and decisions made, and then for the teachers to be able to explain what motivated them to make the choices they did. The workgroup goes on to state: "CS is a discipline that is in a constant state of development. We therefore assume that fully qualified CS teachers will need to play a major role in the development of this school subject as well." In conclusion, the workgroup stressed that "the school subject CS has its own didactics that are in part still in development; as a result, a fully qualified CS teacher must be able to contribute to the development of the subject". [2]

Development of the professionalization exercise entailed in School Subject (Didactics) for CS follows the recommendations of this workgroup. Prospective teachers learn about general didactics issues, such as various student activities and how to tailor their teaching to the needs of individual students. At the same time, they are encouraged to reflect on the content and the methods used in their work, etc. When it comes to the didactics of CS in general, they are expected to become skillful at developing their own teaching materials and assessment methods, along with selecting, adjusting and using existing teaching materials, and writing their own teaching plans. They should be able to recognize which CS concepts and skills are (relatively) constant, and which ones are new and need to be added to the curriculum. They are encouraged to set up interdisciplinary projects in cooperation with teachers of other subjects. They are expected to develop their own vision of CS as a secondary school subject and to recognize their role and responsibility in contributing to its development. Furthermore, they are encouraged to cooperate with colleagues from other schools (since there is usually only one CS teacher per school) and with online CS teacher communities such as www.informaticavo.nl.

More specifically, prospective teachers learn how and when to use IT in their lessons, how to deal with the software and hardware limitations of the school network and they receive advice on practical matters such as the relationship with the school management and system administrators. They learn how to design their lessons, and how to support the learning process of their students in terms of learning specific CS issues [14]. Since this school subject is so new, in many cases there is still no agreement on the best approach to teaching it, so prospective teachers need to learn how to make their own well thought-out decisions. The issue of how to teach programming is a good example of this. Should the students, for instance, be encouraged to use the top-down approach to tackle a problem, or bottom-up, or yet another method entirely? The 2007 Dutch Secondary Education CS Curriculum[7] left all options open in the way it included "programming" in the curriculum term about software: "Software: The student should be familiar with simple data types, program structures and programming techniques." [11] The textbooks currently on the market add to the confusion by offering teaching materials for Java, Visual Basic, Delphi and Gamemaker, among others. At the same time, in the semi-formal circuit (such as the online community on www.informaticavo.nl) additional teaching materials can be found for Logo, NQC for Lego Mindstorms and Pascal. Individual schools have been reported using yet other languages, such as Python, Robolab or Scratch, to name just a few. Under these circumstances, instead of prescribing how to teach programming, a prospective teacher

---

[7] This is the CS curriculum for senior secondary education and pre-university education.

is presented with an overview of teaching approaches and is encouraged to look for the method that best fits the given situation and then to justify the choices made.

CS teachers face a similar range of possibilities when it comes to teaching most other topics comprising CS, so the principle goal of the professionalization exercise is how to prepare prospective teachers to make appropriate decisions.

To accomplish the objectives entailed in the professionalization task, students study the literature, and work on a number of smaller and larger assignments. The major assignments deal with what is expected from the everyday practice of teaching, such as examining and evaluating textbooks or designing and teaching a series of lessons. Since the numbers of students are small, there is ample room to adjust the contents of the professionalization exercise to suit the individual needs of the students.

3.2.6 Subject Coherence

Interdisciplinary assignments and projects, as well as cooperative and project-based learning, have been receiving increased attention in high schools, and prospective teachers need to be prepared for them. For this professionalization exercise, students of biology, computer science, physics, chemistry and mathematics work together. The assignment is to design teaching activities and materials for a *profile afternoon* where secondary school students in the scientific profiles in the higher grades (ten and higher) work on an interdisciplinary project. These teaching materials are made available to the high school students through an Electronic Learning Environment,[8] and there are also written instructions for the teachers.

Each student group is coached individually; there are only two lectures for this professionalization exercise. The first lecture is dedicated to an explanation of the task and the formation of the groups. In the final lecture, all the groups come together and discuss their projects.

One example is illustrative of the projects designed by the students. This particular group was made up of two biology students, two mathematics students and a computer science student. Their goal was to illustrate the scientific method, a topic that is by no means limited to one single scientific discipline. The biologists observe a phenomenon, such as the spread of a disease or gossip. The computer scientist then programs a model[9] that provides a dynamic visual representation with variable parameters. The mathematicians construct the formulae that correspond to this dynamic discrete model. These are then, in turn, assessed by the biologists, thus going full circle.

3.2.7 Elective Courses

The students can choose from a range of possibilities. These include courses offered by their own faculties, such as Capita Selecta, and also school-related themes such as student counseling, quality management at school, design and development of school programs and plans, IT management in schools, multicultural education, etc.

---

[8] The UOCG uses BrainBox, as do some secondary schools. Many other schools have chosen to work with the learning environments Moodle, TeleTop, "it's learning", etc.
[9] In Greenfoot, a Java IDE.

4 The Role of the School

In the Collaborative Teacher Education model there is a teacher educator present at school. He or she organizes regular meetings with the student teachers, preferably weekly, and provides support for all the practical aspects of class management: teaching, taking part in school events, etc. The coach is closely involved with the teaching of a particular subject. Students are expected to observe other teachers' lessons, and to have their own lessons regularly observed and analyzed, with a number of them recorded (on tape). Even though the UOCG has no direct influence on the content of this training, the results are evaluated by the tutor during the assessment of the professionalization exercises Working at School and Reflection on Professional Development, as discussed in sections 3.2.1 and 3.2.2.

The majority of schools where the UOCG students do their internships have a teacher educator and, when there isn't one, this role is assumed by a mentor. This is a UOCG lecturer who organizes weekly meetings with the students and does all the work that would otherwise be done by the teacher educator.

5 The Numbers

A more appropriate title for this chapter would be *The Number*. So far there has been exactly one student who has graduated as a fully qualified computer science teacher at the University of Groningen. There are no more than a dozen students enrolled at the present time in all of the five Dutch universities offering this training combined[10]; regrettably none of these are enrolled in Groningen. This raises several questions.

Why are there so few students? Don't the Computer Science Bachelor's students find the Master's in Education, and thus a career in education, attractive? At the moment there is a wide-ranging shortage of teachers in the Netherlands and the situation is expected to get worse in the years to come. [9] The factors behind this situation are thought to be the low social standing of the teaching profession in general, the booming economy, and, in the case of computer science specifically, the fact that there are very few schools that can offer a CS teacher a full-time position. Currently, an estimated three out of ten computer science teachers lack the relevant qualifications [4], [12]. Why then are so few of them studying to become properly qualified? There has been no research into this question, but several factors appear plausible. A teacher wishing to become fully qualified is likely to keep on teaching more than the required six to eight weekly lessons while studying for his Master's degree, a situation that would require enormous time and effort. This situation becomes even more onerous if the teacher in question does not already have a Bachelor's degree in CS and has to obtain that first. Finally, the reward for all this labor is a questionable one; the teacher is more than likely to remain in exactly the same job situation after obtaining the full qualification. In other words, the incentive to go back to school is lacking.

So, what consequences will this have for the future of computer science in Dutch high schools? The situation described is perceived as a serious threat. Suggestions have been made to alleviate the problem by introducing various shorter routes to

---

[10] That is, in December 2007.

achieving a full CS qualification, possibly by reintroducing the CODI scheme, but no clear solution has yet been found [12].

It would be interesting to know whether experiences have been similar in other countries, and if so, how they are dealing with them. The answer to this question would be of great interest, but regrettably this lies beyond the scope of this paper.

References

1. Besluit bekwaamheidseisen onderwijspersoneel. Staatsblad van het Koninkrijk der Nederlanden 460 (2005)
2. Barendsen, E., Dijk, B.v., Hacquebard, A., Hartsuijker, A., Korten, J., Meijer, H., et al.: Startdocument Eerstegraads Lerarenopleiding Informatica (2004)
3. CODI:Het (profiel-) keuzevak Informatica in de Tweede Fase van havo en vwo vanaf 2007 (2006), http://www.informaticavo.nl/voorlichting/informaticadocenten.doc
4. CODI (2007), http://www.informaticavo.nl/scripts/voorlichting.php#codi
5. Eurydice: The Education System in the Netherlands 2006/2007. Eurydice, Directorate-General for Education and Culture (2007)
6. Grgurina, N., Tolboom, J.L.J.: The Dutch Secondary School Informatics Curriculum - Another Polder Model, Broad in Scope, But Not Too Deep? In: Benzie, D., Iding, M. (eds.) WG 3.1 & 3.5 Joint Working Conference: Informatics, Mathematics and ICT: a 'golden triangle', College of Computer and Information Science Northeastern University, Boston, MA, USA (2007)
7. Hacquebard, A., Zwaneveld, B., van Dijk, B., van Leeuwen, H., Timmers, J.: Keuzevak Informatica in de Tweede Fase HAVO en VWO, Opstap naar de kennismaatschappij. CODI (2005)
8. Hulsen, M., Wartenbergh-Cras, F., Smets, E., Uerz, D., van der Neut, I., Sontag, L., et al.: ICT in Cijfers (ICT in Figures) Nijmegen: IVA – ITS (2005)
9. MinOC&W: LeerKracht! Den Haag: MinOC&W (2007)
10. MinOC&W: Omscholing informatica Cfi. In: UITLEG Gele Katern, vol. 14(7), p. 22 (1998)
11. Schmidt, V.: Handreiking schoolexamen informatica havo/vwo. SLO, Enschede (2006)
12. Schmidt, V.: Vakdossier 2007 Informatica SLO, Enschede (2008)
13. Stuurgroep Profiel Tweede Fase: Advies Examenprogramma's havo/vwo Informatica. MinOC&W, Den Haag (1995)
14. UOCG: Lerarenopleiding (2007), http://www.rug.nl/uocg/onderwijs/lerarenopleiding/index

Distance Learning Course for Training Teachers' ICT Competence[*]

Valentina Dagienė, Lina Zajančkauskienė, and Inga Žilinskienė

Informatics Methodology Dept., Institute of Mathematics and Informatics
Akademijos str. 4, LT-08663 Vilnius, Lithuania
{dagiene, lina.zajanckauskiene, ingasolyte}@ktl.mii.lt

Abstract. Nowadays teachers are required to meet social, pedagogical and objective requirements related to the information and communication technology (ICT). This is the main reason to pay more attention to teachers' training by means of ICT and render opportunities for them to get access to topical information, to learn while working. Distance education is one of the learner-friendly ways to give them the necessary knowledge and to develop ICT skills. The paper deals with a distance learning course designed for teachers who are working at secondary schools in Lithuania. The course is developed to improve teachers' computer literacy and educational skills of ICT application. The main requirements to regulating teachers' ICT literacy competence, the results of researches on ICT in education, the basic requirements and principles for creating distance education courses are also discussed. Finally, the structure of the distance education course is presented.

Keywords: Teacher training, ICT competence, ICT integration, distance learning course.

1 Introduction

Requirements to teachers' competences on information and communication technology (ICT) have been formulated and approved by the Ministry of Education and Science of the Republic of Lithuania [10]. A necessity to realize the goals and objectives has appeared. The main problem is integration of ICT in education – how to prepare user-friendly courses and how to train teachers. [2] The paper deals with the problems of ICT integration in the education course development and implementation, a designed project and its results are represented. Besides the Strategy for the introduction of ICT into Lithuanian education for 2005–2007 [11], there is a General Computer Literacy Standard [4] as well as requirements on creating programs for teacher training. The requirements are oriented to developing and improving teachers' ICT competence. The aim of this paper is to acquaint readers with the new requirements and with distant education courses developed on the basis of these requirements.

---

[*] This contribution has been implemented within the framework of eStart project (Digital Literacy Network for Primary and Lower Secondary (K-9) Education) under contract 2006 - 4530/001-001 ELE ELEB11.

The General Computer Literacy Standard has been developed in Lithuania in order to reduce the general education gap in the field of information technologies which has occurred due to a rapid development and spread of ICT and because of the need for lifelong learning. The purpose of the Standard is to set uniform requirements and recommendations for the qualification of computer literacy of the population, and to legitimize the principles of certifying computer literacy [4].

A computer literacy qualification may be essential and minimal: 1) the basic qualification of computer literacy shall include ICT knowledge and skills sufficient to use a computer in professional activities at the user level. 2) the minimal qualification of computer literacy shall include ICT knowledge and skills. Basic needs may be met by using the services available in the electronic space – preparation, search, and delivery of information and communication. The special requirements to teachers' ICT literacy were prepared as well. These requirements provide competences to be achieved by teachers while learning [10]:

1. Teachers should creatively individualize the teaching and learning process.
2. Teachers should purposefully use ICT.
3. Teachers should purposefully apply methods in teaching and learning.
4. Teachers should organize ICT resource management for teaching and learning.
5. Teachers should plan ICT resource use for teaching and learning.
6. Teachers should evaluate and reflect on topics regarding the use of ICT.

To train these competences an educational course of ICT has been prepared.

Since the requirements to teachers' ICT competence have changed, in the lapse of several years some new software and programs for learning in Lithuanian appeared. That is why it was necessary to change distant education courses that were prepared for teachers in 2004 [2]. It was necessary to reorganize the course contents, to add new features and new recommendations in line with the new competences and new requirements to distant education courses.

2 Specific Features of ICT in Education

It is always necessary to know how to use ICT in education with a view to improve school life. It is clear that, if we wish to integrate ICT into education, it is necessary to pay more attention to teacher training in this area. Every teacher should be able to work with ICT in his or her class, to sense its advantage, to notice changes in teaching his or her subject. ICT is indispensable in everyday life. The main attention is paid to using ICT in education: we hope that when using ICT, the quality of the learning process will be better, the motivation of pupils will be higher, and the connection between practice and theory will be stronger. Some problems have not been solved as yet: not all pupils have got skills to work on their own, whereas to those that have got good skills, less attention is paid than they still need. Some schools are able to partially solve the problems with lessons when teachers are ill. Distance education and virtual learning environments are one of the methods to solve those problems. [14]

Teachers should be able to use ICT while teaching and learning. It is necessary for them to know pedagogical, social, ethical, and cognitive ICT issues and its influence on education. It is rather difficult because the main attention should be paid to the whole process. The students 'learn to learn' – this is the main paradigm of the present education.

There are several studies and recommendations on the main topics that should be analyzed with a view to apply ICT in education in the most successful way [1, 14]:

- The ways and methods of ICT application in education,
- Psychological aspects of ICT in education,
- Improvement of the learning process of students with special needs by ICT,
- Development of an information society and its coherence with education,
- Social and ethical problems of ICT in education,
- Organization of the learning process by using ICT,
- Preparation, dissemination, and presentation of curricula using ICT.

These topics had a great influence while building a project of teachers' ICT literacy education. The goals of this part were as follows:

- Motivate the use of ICT in education and show its importance,
- Analyze the ways, possibilities and methods of using ICT for learning and teaching and learn to apply them.

One leading principle of the courses is the subject orientation, to enable teachers to work jointly on ICT (of all school types) applications to their specific school subject [5]. Therefore there are lots of recommendations for teachers of all the subjects on the course material.

One of the key objectives is to give each teacher the opportunity to take his point of departure in his educational and social context. Another one of the founding principles of the pedagogical thinking of the European Pedagogical ICT license is that knowledge and competences do not arise through the transfer of information from one person to another, but that learning is a result of collaborative learning through contributing, creating and acting.

When developing the content for a Pedagogical ICT License, the following main objectives must always be paid due attention to:

- Development, process and teamwork are key issues,
- No use of ICT-tools without a pedagogical rationale.

The Pedagogical ICT license has to:

- Substantially contribute to meet the needs for ICT-pedagogical competences of the teachers,
- Contribute to improve the pedagogical practice of participants in relation to the integration of ICT,
- Contribute to an increased use of e-learning that meets the needs and qualifications of an individual teacher [12].

The didactical concept aims at supporting active, self-organized learning of the participants with several real face-to-face meetings during the entire course. [5]. A teacher's professional development normally includes continued education, individual development, curriculum writing, in-service education, peer collaboration, coaching, mentoring, and study groups. [13]. If teachers' own education is limited, they lack the confidence, knowledge and skills to teach much more than they were taught themselves, or to teach in a different way. Quality matters as much as quantity. To do their job well, teachers need to possess a mastery of their subject matter they are to teach and to be skilled in the process of teaching [9].

If we compare the course contents and recommendations of international experts and educational policy makers, we can notice that most of these topics are included in our course contents [6, 7]. Every topic is applied to the Lithuanian situation and there are some practical recommendations how to use ICT in education in the best way.

3 Requirements to the Distance Learning Course

The course is based on communication and collaboration: it has some components which need to collaborate in groups, discuss, search for information, evaluate the progress, to fulfil tasks in groups and so on. The main attention is paid to training of computer literacy in education: to get skills in managing information, analyzing it, acquiring knowledge. Two types of requirements (pedagogical and organizational) to the distant course on teacher training have been developed.

According to the pedagogical requirements the distance course should be:

1. Discursive: teachers and students should have some agreements according to the course goals and achievements;
2. Applicable: the course contents should be structurized so that everyone was able to manage its material;
3. Interactive: the learners try to achieve the goals, teachers should seek feedback;
4. Reflexive: teachers should analyze the teaching and learning process and the learners receive feedback on his (her) learning process.

According to the organizational requirements, the distance education course should be:

1. Negotiation lives up to resources: teachers and students should agree on individualized access to resources;
2. Coordination: the learners should have a possibility to collaborate with other learners, connect with groups, control with whom to share the resources;
3. Observation: the teacher should have a possibility to observe the teaching and learning process and to connect with discussion groups, observe the completed tasks when necessary and so on;
4. Individualization: the learners should have a possibility to use his (her) own resources, plan his (her) learning process, to act individually;
5. Self-organizing: the learners should have an opportunity to use a virtual learning environment, and to form groups separately from the teachers;
6. Adjustment: the teachers should have a possibility to give individual material to each student, according to his (her) progress. [3]

4 The Structure of the Distance Learning Course for Teachers

The distance learning course consists of modules with following properties (Fig. 1):
- each module has some syllabus which is presented in two ways:
  - text for reading,

- video file.
- The material for reading is given in PDF format;
- All video files are given in SCORM format;
- There are self-control tasks and tasks for reflection in each module (tests, questions);
- There are textual documents that briefly acquaint teachers with the contents of the module;
- There are activities for the communication among the course participants.

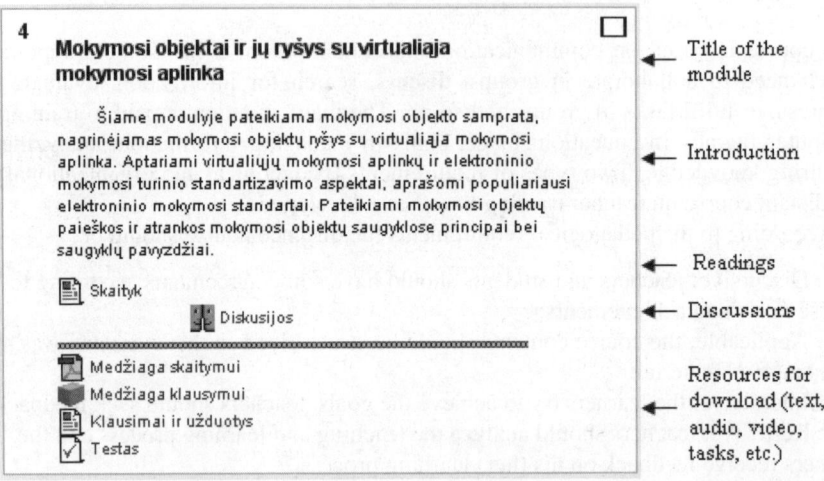

Fig. 1. The view of a module

The teachers who want to learn are divided into groups; every group has its own lecturer (course tutor). He or she coordinates the learning process during all the learning time: responds to any letters received, coordinates discussion in forums, gives necessary information, explains any questions, and evaluates the homework. The learning process contains three parts:

1. The introductory seminar – the first meeting of teachers and tutors will be face to face. Its aim is to acquaint teachers with the principles of working on the course material and the results they are expected to achieve. The tasks are discussed.
2. Learning by distance.
3. The final seminar – presentation of the results and discussions.

The structure of the developed distance course and the way of using it is shown in Fig. 2.

The distance education course contains 8 modules:

1. ICT for general education: experience and perspectives for development.
2. ICT for general education: creating presentations.
3. Learning objects and their relationship with a virtual learning environment.

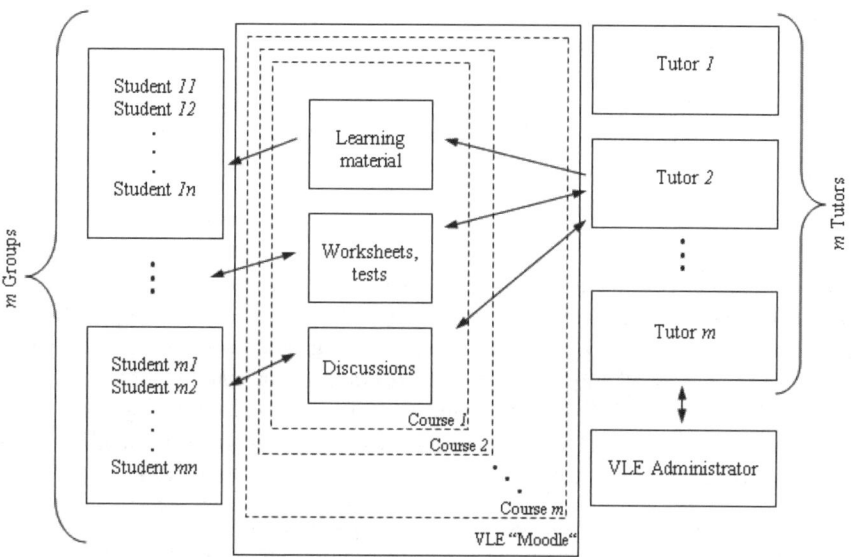

Fig. 2. Interaction between the activities while learning by distance

4. Using the learning objects at the lessons.
5. Using the learning objects – websites – at lessons.
6. Presenting personal experience of using ICT.
7. Innovative methods for learning and teaching.
8. Using the virtual learning environment (Moodle).

We will try to give a short description of each module referring to its contents and how it helps a teacher to achieve the necessary competence.

Each module is intended to develop the teachers' ICT competence which includes technological and educational parts.

1st Module. *ICT for general education: experience and perspectives for development.* The module generalizes the experience and perspectives for the development of ICT in basic, secondary, and special needs education. Teachers are acquainted with ICT strategic points of reference in education, general ICT planning, principles of integration in other subjects. The importance of purposeful ICT application and planning in education is emphasized. The examples of these activities are given as well. The possibilities for teachers, parents and pupils to communicate using ICT are discussed. The danger related with ICT and the prevention are discussed. The problems of disabled people are discussed and the ways of solving them using ICT are presented. The addresses of courses and the courses for special education are given.

2nd Module. *ICT for general education: creating presentations.* The module corresponds to a competence provided by teachers' ICT literacy to creatively individualize the teaching and learning process. This competence is evaluated at three levels, therefore the material of this course is divided into three parts. The first part contains the methodology of how teachers could enrich the learning process using presentations.

The main methodic recommendations are discussed according to the presentations created. The second part corresponds to the second level of competence and gives examples how teachers could use ICT for presentations and mini projects. The last part contains particular elements which could help teachers apply ICT (3rd level, Table 1). The examples of particular presentations are given for mathematics, physics and other subjects.

3rd Module. *Learning objects and their relationship with a virtual learning environment.* A definition of the learning object is given as well as the relationship with the virtual learning environment (VLE). The aspects of VLE and standards of the electronic learning content as well as the most popular standards are discussed. The principles of search for learning objects in storages and addresses of the storages are given. The examples of publishing the electronic learning contents (using SCORM) into a VLE are presented. By means of this module we tried to train teachers' competence to purposefully use ICT and plan ICT activities. Teachers get familiar with a new type of the learning object (SCORM) that can be used only in VLE.

4th Module. *Using the learning objects at the lessons.* The main competence that is trained in this module is to plan and organize ICT in education, to organize ICT resources in education. The ICT competence here is related to the learning objects and their creative application in practice. The methods how to look for the learning objects, download and install them are presented. Several examples of learning objects are given. General principles of working with an interactive whiteboard are described. Teachers are acquainted with the general programs suitable to work with interactive whiteboards.

5th Module. *Using the learning objects – websites – at the lessons.* The main competence that is trained in this module is to individualize the learning process of particular subjects. This competence is evaluated at three levels and particular indices are given: a) to enrich the learning material with possibilities to apply ICT in education (1st level, Table 1), b) to integrate the themes, related to students' ICT literacy, into the subject (2nd level, Table 1), c) to prepare the syllabus related to ICT application in education (3rd level, Table 1).

The use of internet resources, websites is attractive and available without difficulty. Teachers should talk about websites that contain the learning material or just information for learning and about the websites which have software, programs, and technological resources for learning.

6th Module. *Presenting personal experience of using ICT.* This module contains an explanation of digital culture, analysis of electronic blogs and digital folders and their use for presentation of personal experience. A definition of an electronic blog and its purpose are given. The possibilities of using electronic blogs while planning the learning process and evaluation of pupils' achievements and progress in the use of digital folders are indicated. The examples of electronic blogs and digital folders are presented.

The module complies with competences given in the requirements on the programs of teachers' ICT literacy: to plan ICT in the learning process, evaluate and reflect on using ICT in education. The competences are evaluated at two levels and particular indices are given: a) a teacher plans ICT application, uses the experience and material of research, evaluates their purposefulness, prepares presentations on the personal experience of ICT in education, and applies several tools, i.e., electronic folders (e-portfolio), internet blogs, to present his(her) experience; the material that he or she has applied in planning later activities (2nd level, Table 1), b) helps colleagues to plan ICT proceedings, related to improving students' learning, communicates with colleagues discussing on the learning achievements; evaluates the school state on ICT in education, gives recommendations for planning school activities. (3rd level, Table 1).

7th Module. *Innovative methods for learning and teaching.* A definition of innovative methods of teaching is given in this module as well as a short review, and the material of famous scientists reported at the forums of Innovative teachers forums. The main topics are about innovations in education, the characteristics an the innovative teacher, the peculiarities of group work, and the methods of forming groups. This module complies with the competences given in the requirements on the programs of teachers' ICT literacy: a) to individualize the learning process in a creative way, b) to apply the learning and teaching methods in a creative and reasonable way.

The first competence is evaluated at three levels, and the necessary indexes are given: a) a teacher enriches the learning and teaching process with possibilities to use ICT (1st level) b) he integrates the necessary themes related to the requirements of the students' ICT literacy standard (2nd level), c) a teacher prepares the syllabus related to possibilities of applying ICT (3rd level).

The second competence is evaluated at three levels as well and the following indexes are provided: a) a teacher uses ICT to improve or extend traditional methods of education, to organize projects (1st level), b) by means of ICT a teacher realizes distance education, selects methods that satisfy a constructive paradigm (integration methods, projects, learning in collaboration) (2nd level), c) helps colleagues to choose the methods properly (3rd level).

8th Module. *Using the virtual learning environment (Moodle).* The module conforms to competences given in the requirements on the programs of teachers' ICT literacy: to organize ICT resources in education. All the competences are related to a virtual learning environment, its application in education and creative use of its abilities. Some information is given on work with the virtual learning environment Moodle, and some examples are presented how to organize lessons using Moodle.

Each module is developed so as to train at least one competence. There are some modules designed to train two competences.

The organizers of the distance education course conceive the sessions on the basis of what is actually known and practicing today, having built a dynamic framework for teaching and learning activities. In this way it is possible to describe and demonstrate vividly the essential elements, processes, and mechanisms of ICT-based teacher education. The innovative methods are useful to apply in running the distance course as well [8].

Each competence should be evaluated on three levels. The relations between modules, ICT competence, and levels are shown in Table 1.

Table 1. Relations among distance course modules, ICT competence and levels

Module	Competence	1st level	2nd level	3rd level
		Teacher...		
(1) ICT for general education: experience and perspectives for development. (3) Learning objects and their relationship with a virtual learning environment.	Purposeful usage of ICT in education	applies	uses	helps colleagues
(2) ICT for general education: creating presentations. (5) Using the learning objects – websites – at lessons.	Individualization of education in a creative way	enriches	integrates	applies methodically
(7) Innovative methods for learning and teaching.	Purposeful application of learning and teaching methods	uses	applies picks up	helps colleagues
(4) Using the learning objects at the lessons.	Plans ICT usage		plans; uses the experience, evaluates	helps in planning
(8) Using the virtual learning environment (Moodle).	Organizes ICT resources		is able to organize	prepares virtual groups
(6) Presenting personal experience of using ICT.	Evaluates and reflects on ICT usage in education		prepares presentations	gives recommendations

5 Conclusions

At present, the methodology of teaching and learning is different and teachers should be able to teach children to learn, applying ICT in education in the most powerful and purposeful way. This is the main reason why scientists should pay attention to teachers and let them always learn. This is possible by using virtual learning environments, ICT, and creating powerful courses that show teachers' abilities of ICT, available Internet resources, creative ways of applying ICT in education in the classroom and at home.

The distance education course for teachers has been prepared following the requirements to teachers' competences on ICT and the principles of projecting and creating distant courses. While learning teachers improve their ICT competence and can use it in everyday life at school. The course is available for all the teachers. This means that every teacher has a chance to learn at any time with a view to improve the ICT competence and make lessons more powerful and innovative.

The course content is located on a server which belongs to the Centre of Information Technology of Education using the VLE Moodle technology (http://vma.emokykla.lt/moodle). The modules are prepared using sounds, animation, as well as text and multimedia resources. All the resources are downloadable.

The course was started in March 2008 and a framework of research on the training and syllabus is scheduled. Once the research has been completed, the analysis of the learning material as well as improvements will be made.

Acknowledgements

The course material was developed in pursuance of the EU Structural Fund support for Lithuania on behalf of the Educational Development Centre in Vilnius, Lithuania, 2007. This contribution has been implemented within the framework of eStart project (Digital Literacy Network for Primary and Lower Secondary (K-9) Education) under contract 2006 - 4530/001-001 ELE ELEB11.

References

1. Cornu, B.: Didactics, information and communication technologies, and the teacher of the future. In: Taylor, H., Hogenbrick, P. (eds.) The Bookmark of the School of the Future, pp. 51–79. Kluwer Academic Publishers, Boston (2000)
2. Dagienė, V., Valavičius, E.: Teacher Training via Distance Learning Focused on Educational Issues of Information Technology. Informatics in Education 3(2), 179–190 (2004)
3. Dagienė, V., Jasutienė, E., Jevsikova, T., Zajančkauskienė, L., Žilinskienė, I.: IKT taikymas pradiniam ir specialiam ugdymui: nuotolinio kurso pedagogams projektavimo aspektai. Lietuvos matematikos rinkinys, 47, spec. nr., Vilnius, pp. 161–167 (2007) (in Lithuanian)
4. General Computer Literacy Standard (2004), http://www.emokykla.lt/admin/file.php?id=185
5. Gorny, P., Daldrup, U.: Guenther-Arndt H. How to Teach Teachers to Teach with New Media: Initial and Further Teacher Education in a Web-Based Collaborative Distant Learning Environment. In: Bachmann, G., Haefeli, O., Kindt, M. (eds.) Die virtuelle Hochschule in der Konsolidierungsphase, pp. 137–142. Münster u. a, Waxmann (2002)
6. van Weert, T., Anderson, J. (eds.): Information and communication technologies in education: A curriculum for schools and programme of teacher development. Division of Higher Education, UNESCO (2002)
7. Resta, P., Semenov, A. (eds.): Information and communication technologies in teacher education: A planning guide. Division of Higher Education, UNESCO (2002)
8. Jucevičienė, P., Brazdeikis, V.: Educators' ICT Competence: Searching for the Evaluation Strategy. In: Dagienė, V., Mittermeir, R. (eds.) Information technologies at School. Proc. of the 2nd International Conference "Informatics in secondary school: evolution and perspectives", Vilnius, Lithuania, November 7–11, 2006, pp. 40–52 (2006)
9. Perraton, H.D.: Distance Education for Teacher Training. Routledge, London, New York (1993)
10. Reikalavimai mokytojų kompiuterinio raštingumo programoms (2007), http://www.emokykla.lt/lt.php/dokumentai/kompiuterinio_rastingumo_standartai/52

11. Strategy for the Introduction of Information and Communication Technologies into the Lithuanian Education for 2005–2007. Ministry of Education and Science of the Republic of Lithuania (2004), http://www.emokykla.lt/en.php/documents/lithuanian_policy_documents/1126
12. The European Pedagogical ICT Licence (EPICT) (30/04/2008), http://www.epict.org/
13. Weiss, B.: Professional Development Courses For Teachers (30/04/2008), http://www.moxie-drive.com/articles/article.php/03-08-2007Professional-Development-Courses-For-Teachers.htm
14. Williams, D., Coles, L., Wilson, K., Richardson, A., Tuson, J.: Teachers and ICT: Current use and future needs. British Journal of Educational Technologies 31(4), 307–320 (2000)
15. Zajančkauskienė, L.: Distance education at secondary school. Creation and management of e–courses using ATutor. In: Dagienė, V., Mittermeir, R. (eds.) Information technologies at School. Proc. of the 2nd International Conference Informatics in secondary school: evolution and perspectives, Vilnius, Lithuania, November 7-11, 2006, pp. 626–631 (2006)

Teaching Information Technology and Elements of Informatics in Lower Secondary Schools: Curricula, Didactic Provision and Implementation

Valentina Dagienė

Head of Informatics Methodology Dept., Institute of Mathematics and Informatics, Akademijos
str. 4, LT-08663 Vilnius, Lithuania
dagiene@ktl.mii.lt

Abstract. In Lithuania, teaching and learning informatics in general education has more than twenty years of history. Starting from a theoretical informatics subject now we have a combination of using information and communication technologies (ICT) while learning many subjects with some basic elements of informatics (computer science). The general curricula of information technologies (IT) for lower secondary schools in Lithuania were essentially revised and renewed. The paper deals with the goals and approach of introducing ICT into general education. It discusses the competencies and values to be developed while teaching and learning IT and with IT. The links with other school subjects and the relationship between the compulsory IT course and the integrated parts as well as optional modules are described. Educational standards on IT for lower secondary schools are presented.

Keywords: ICT in education, IT curricula, teaching informatics, didactics, educational standards for IT.

1 Introduction

The implementation Strategy of ICT into Lithuanian education for the years 2005-2007 [11] states that modern technologies are penetrating more and more into education, influence teaching and learning different disciplines, methodologies and the whole process of education – a new stage of school computerisation is forming which is qualitatively stronger. The Strategy has set out the analysis of introduction of ICT into the Lithuanian education system, the mission of the strategy, the goals, the tasks and the indicators for assessment of the progress. The objective of the Strategy is integration of ICT into all levels of teaching and learning processes in order to improve general education and vocational training in the Lithuanian education system.

Students as well as teachers must perceive an advantage of using modern technologies in the process of education: a breakthrough of ICT in the teaching process of some subjects has been planned. While implementing these provisions one of the main works is intensive development of ICT capabilities in the lower grades of secondary education, namely grades 5-10 (in the Lithuanian education system it is entitled as basic school). This is envisaged in the Strategy as one of the factors of the breakthrough of ICT in the educational process.

Rapid penetration of computers and computer technologies in schools as well as in other educational institutions, libraries and households forces a revision of the curricula and educational standards prepared earlier [5, 6]. According to international and national research data a lot of school-age children spend a major part of their time at the computer. It becomes necessary to take the appropriate measures that would enable to include ICT into all possible stages of education in order to form a qualitatively new phase of teaching and learning. The comparative study on ICT development in schools suggested by UNESCO [1] identifies that Lithuanian schools are in the transmission between applying and infusing approaches. The first one is linked with schools in which a new understanding of the contribution of ICT to learning has developed. The infusing approach is linked with schools that use a range of computer-based technologies, teachers explore new ways in which ICT changes their personal productivity, the curriculum begins to merge subject areas to reflect real-world applications. We would like to move towards the stage of understanding how and when to use ICT tools to achieve a particular purpose. This stage is linked with the infusing and transforming approaches in ICT development. It is expected that after the revision of the IT curricula it will turn to be more helpful in forming the learning pattern of life in school and will encourage moving towards holistic general education.

The teaching of informatics has a profound tradition in Lithuanian schools; a rich experience in the field has been accumulated. The model of compulsory course of teaching informatics in upper secondary schools (grades 11 and 12) has been developed [4]. After some time the compulsory teaching of the subject "began to shelve down" – into grades 9 and 10 [2, 3]. One of the main tasks posed in the Strategy on implementation of ICT into Lithuanian education is to teach younger school-age children to use ICT. This task becomes natural and important in order to improve and modernise the whole education. The objective goes even further: ICT must penetrate more and more deeply into the educational process and become an inseparable part of the educational content.

Internet and usage of mobile communications became everyday tools. It is important to create conditions for the students to satisfy their modern learning and self-education needs. It is necessary to seek that children could develop their information skills and find material suitable for versatile learning, that teachers would advise what to use and how, would relate the academic knowledge with the interests of students and the social needs [9].

As it is pointed out in the UNESCO recommendations, the content of the ICT course in schools has an extremely important role [1]. If the main competencies of the last century were regarded as a combination of "three R" – Reading, wRiting, aRithmetics – our time invites us to search for something fundamental and necessary. An IT course emphasizes three main parts: information search, text processing, and work with numerical data. These three are relevant everywhere and for everybody. Consequently, these are the things that should draw the main part of an IT school course compulsory for all pupils [3].

With regard to the changed role of the ICT as well as with respect to the needs of pupils and school communities the curricula – general programmes – of all subjects in lower secondary schools (grades 5-10) were substantially revised and renewed. Therefore, the new IT curriculum for lower secondary schools was developed and approved by the Ministry of Education and Science of the Republic of Lithuania [7].

2 IT Curricula: Competencies and Values to be Developed

The main purpose of an IT course for basic education is to direct the technological knowledge and abilities of students towards better understanding of the computer possibilities and application, development capability and the desire for co-operation not only within the school community and the family but also with students all over the world. ICT suggest especially extensive opportunities for the development of the everyday intellectual activities of students promoting continuous personality development and co-operation in order to develop independence, for continuous search of knowledge and processing of information, for planning of everyday activities, forming logic and systematic thinking.

The fundamental objective of teaching IT is to create conditions for the students to acquire skills, knowledge and experience in usage of modern technologies and to relate this to improvement of the learning process of students and their integration into life in the knowledge society. When implementing this objective, the goal must be that students acquire the basic ideas and concepts of IT, acquire skills that would help them in their everyday activities and develop values. Computer literacy and information culture must be developed by each student, particularly stressing abilities, skills, knowledge and experience related to the informational activities [7].

Students are being prepared for their future life as citizens of the information and knowledge society who are capable of using the modern technologies and adapting in the changing society and who are ready to improve their life-long professional skills.

In grades 5-10 of lower secondary school (basic education) the IT course is obligatory. When implementing the IT curriculum the following goals must be achieved. Students should:

- Apply ICT in all fields of their activities and purposefully learn;
- Expand diverse communication by using ICT;
- Be capable of using the opportunities provided by ICT while looking for information, processing and presenting the information;
- Be capable of planning their activities, of creatively and purposively improvising, and of trusting their strengths;
- Develop their curiosity related to innovations, be disposed to learn newer and more efficient methods of activities and be interested in new technologies;
- While purposefully using ICT, be able to receive, sort, handle, transfer and accept digital, textual and visual information.

Information education and encouragement to efficiently and properly use ICT forms not only the computer literacy and skills of the modern work of students but also, if the content and methods of education and self-education are properly prepared, develops their values. A teacher should help and encourage students to flexibly and creatively use the advantages of modern technologies for improvement of their everyday activities. The following fundamental values must be nurtured:

- Curiosity about innovations, disposition to learn newer and more efficient methods of activities, interest in modern technologies;
- Respect for the legal rules regulating information technologies;
- Respect for the norms of ethics and moral;
- Self-esteem and respect for others;
- Need to continuously improve the character and style of the personal informational activities;
- Trust in personal strengths, creativity, and responsibility for one's actions;
- Abilities to work in a team;
- Abilities to communicate in the digital world.

If students became systematically familiarised with ICT starting with the lower grades and the ICT were consistently integrated with different subjects and issues, education of students on modern competences would qualitatively improve. Students would more rapidly acquire competences necessary for better learning. ICT are very effective when developing communicative, cognitive, working and practical abilities and competences, thus the main abilities and competences were pointed out when developing the IT curricula for lower secondary schools [7].

Communicative abilities and competences:

- to be able to maintain civilized communication using different ICT tools and technical equipment;
- to correctly use the main terms of computer and information technologies, to be able to explain them, and to understand their meaning.

Cognitive abilities and competences:

- To be aware of the significance and importance of ICT to the continuous change of the modern society and cultural development;
- To see ICT relations in the analyzed processes;
- To apply the acquired knowledge in ICT when learning different school subjects;
- To associate the acquired knowledge in ICT with the existing life experience and to apply it in solving real-world problems;
- To be capable of recognizing and applying the acquired knowledge when using new computer tools.

Working and practical abilities and competences:

- To be aware of the purpose and the principles of computer technologies;
- To be capable of using the basic software for processing information;
- To use the computer aids in order to improve learning;
- To develop systematic, structural and critical thinking and to take decisions;
- To be capable of searching information according to the set goals;
- To analyze, critically evaluate, and summarize information and to convey it to others.

3 Didactic Provisions

One of the essential features of the IT course in lower secondary school is orientation towards the reasonable and purposeful application. It is important to show schools how ICT change teaching and learning and assist in different subjects. This creates one of the basic attitudes of organisation of information education – association of ICT with the entire school life and all subjects. It is important to actively and meaningfully apply modern ICT in lessons of different subjects. ICT methods may also be applied for modelling of natural and social phenomena and performing technical and humanitarian research. Integration of ICT and their inclusion into the courses of different subjects is in essence the development of the style of information activities. Thus the goal of association of ICT with practical activities is implemented: when teaching IT, priority is attached to practical information activities and work with different technologies.

It is important to apply various forms of communication in the class (discussions, considerations, short presentations), to prepare papers, summaries, annotations, to use different sources of information (books, video and audio records, CDs, databases etc), to use the computer when calculating, writing or illustrating essays, or visually presenting data.

It is very important to use ICT for development of creativity, curiosity, skills of purposeful activities not only during the lessons on information technologies. In this respect the project preparation method is especially worthwhile. Opportunities for application of ICT allow students to carry out projects on any topic interesting for them. Thus the learning motivation is strengthened and practical and differentiated teaching of IT is implemented. It is important to try to complete projects and not to stop after making initial mistakes – to correct them, to improve the work until the goal is achieved. This is important both for development of abilities to achieve the goal and for cultivation of the sense not to be afraid of mistakes and to have self-confidence. Common projects of the students' team should be encouraged and skills of collective work, its planning, and distribution of works should be developed. The project preparation method enables natural integration of different topics. In addition, it implements the most relevant didactic aspect, meaningful learning. Bigger or smaller projects of all disciplines should be very carefully co-ordinated in order not to overload pupils with the project works.

It is very important to teach to create open projects, to prepare them structurally, to plan, to start from simple problems and then step by step to learn solving more complicated ones, and to encourage common projects of several subjects in order to relate different knowledge about the psychical and the physical world surrounding us into one whole.

New technologies are always related to the abundance of new words. The computer field has especially many terms. One of the main aspects of education in general school is nurturance of the Lithuanian language. It is necessary to follow the development of computer and information technologies' terminology, to use correct terms, to avoid slang.

While using modern technologies, certain legal regulation of human relations related to information is forming. It is necessary to implant into students respect for the legal norms regulating information technologies, for example, copyrights, to provide information about the rights of a person to receive data about him or her and so on. Whereas the internet is more and more significant in social life, it is essential to give permanent attention to the social and ethical aspect of information usage.

4 Description of the Curriculum Implementation Model

One of the fundamental tasks of the Strategy for the Introduction of ICT into the Lithuanian Education is to seek implementation of information technology skills in lower grades of basic education. Several levels of teaching of this course are differentiated: (1) Initial cognitive usage of information technologies; (2) Partial integration of information technologies; (3) A separate course on information technologies.

The cognitive course prevails in grades 1–4 of primary education. The general curriculum of primary schools seeks naturally, without special accentuation, to show the child a variety of forms of information, to create an opportunity to experience and manipulate them. On the stage of primary education, integrated education on IT should dominate. Schools may at their own discretion propose to children optional after-school activities related to IT or similar forms of education.

During the lessons of the mother tongue, mathematics, music and art, students acquire an elementary perception of language, alphabet, sounds and letters denominating them, quantity and numbers denominating it, sentences and mathematical symbols, other tools for expression of images and sounds, their internal order and rules of use. Rational usage of books and other sources of information along with the familiarisation with the computer starts.

The curriculum on IT for lower secondary schools is aimed at co-ordination of a separate course on IT with application of these technologies for different purposes and partial integration is performed. Usage of IT is especially recommended during the lessons of Lithuanian and foreign languages, art, mathematics and natural history.

The education programme of lower secondary schools, starting with the fifth grade, includes a separate course on IT, a part of which will be integrated with other subjects in the future.

It is proposed to appoint a total of 68 hours in grades 5-6 for the course on IT and 34 hours integrating IT with other subjects. Integration with art (topic "Drawing with the computer") and mother tongue as well as foreign languages (topic "Internet and electronic messages") is suggested. The analysed topics are directly related with the aforementioned things. Nevertheless, other things are also recommended, particularly the project activities combining several subjects.

34 compulsory hours and 68 integrated hours for IT are suggested in the course designated for grades 7-8. Integration with other subjects is recommended, for example: mother tongue (topic "Creation, editing and publishing a text document"), art (topic "Preparation and demonstration of presentations", subtopic "Elements of design in the Web pages") and mathematics (topic "Elements of table preparation"). Teaching of other subjects using ICT during the lessons or after-school activities is also encouraged.

The course on IT in grades 9-10 is aimed at summarising and systematising students' knowledge, to purposefully use their skills, drawing attention to the right application of the technologies and their legitimacy. For those who wish to grasp the principles of computer work and its management, an optional module on algorithms shall be proposed (at the moment it is included in a compulsory IT course). For the course on IT in grades 9-10, 34 obligatory hours, 17 optional hours and 17 integrated hours are recommended. The IT course designated for grades 9-10 is more specific, intensive and requires systematic summarisation of knowledge.

Once again it should be stressed that the proposed integration of lessons is relative. If a school has other teachers who effectively apply ICT during their lessons or other educational activities, part of the integrated lessons should be allocated to these subjects. For example, part of the lessons on the topic "Internet and electronic messages" may be integrated with geography, biology or history subjects, the subtopic "Simple formulas" may be integrated with physics or chemistry.

Integrated lessons may be conducted commonly by teachers of both IT and main subjects, at least in the beginning. It is essential to carefully consider the course of a lesson or a cycle of lessons, to co-ordinate actions, to envisage the specific tasks. Thus, only the knowledge of the lesson may be efficiently conveyed, the respective skills of pupils properly developed and knowledge delivered. A teacher of IT, when communicating with teachers of other subjects, will be able to envisage what skills are necessary for students in the lessons of other subjects. Recording all tasks performed by students into CDs or other storage is recommended so that a student can supplement his or her computer folder (portfolio).

IT lessons, both separate and integrated, shall be conducted in the computer labs. During the practical trainings the work should be performed using different software: keyboard simulators, systems developed for preparation of texts and graphical material, students become familiar with the internet, e-mail, searching on the Web, fundamental concepts of the computer, etc. Application of educational aids developed for teaching different subjects is especially recommended.

Distribution of the curriculum implementation model according to the years and the planned number of hours per week is presented in Table 1.

Table 1. Gradual change of IT subject in lower secondary schools

School year	5th grade	6th grade	7th grade	8th grade	9th grade	10th grade
2005–2006	1 OB				1 OB	1 OB
2006–2007	1 OB	1 OB			1 OB + 0.5 IN	1 OB
2007–2008	1 OB + 0.5 IN	1 OB + 0.5 IN	1 OB		1 OB + 0.5 IN	1 OB
2008–2009	1 OB + 0.5 IN	1 OB + 0.5 IN	1 OB + 0.5 IN	1 IN	1 OB + 0.5 IN	1 OB
2009–2010	1 OB + 0.5 IN	1 OB + 0.5 IN	1 OB + 0.5 IN	1 IN	1 OB + 0.5 IN	1 OB
2010–2011	1 OB + 0.5 IN	1 OB + 0.5 IN	1 OB + 0.5 IN	1 IN	1 OB + 0.5 IN	1 OP

OB – obligatory IT course; OP – optional IT course; IN – integrated IT course.

Starting with the school year 2005-2006 one hour per week of an IT course appeared in the fifth grade, in school year 2006-2007 the obligatory course on IT was conducted both in grades 5 and 6 as well as in grades 9-10. Starting with the school year 2007-2008 the obligatory course on IT is conducted in all grades of lower secondary schools (5-10). Integrated courses appear gradually in grades 5, 6 and 9. In grade 10 a test for students on computer literacy is arranged [10].

The new model will completely enter into force starting with the school year 2010-2011. Then the tenth grades will not have the obligatory IT course – only optional one consisting of several elective modules. The modules should introduce various basic aspects of informatics to students, by "bridging the gap" between fundamentals and the dynamic world of computing [8]. Programming is an important and purposeful activity, therefore it is planned that at least one optional module for programming should be presented to grades 9-10 (Table 2).

Table 2. Optional IT course: programming module

Grades 9–10	Basic topics
Elements of algorithms and programming	Conception of algorithm, ways of writing
	Programming languages, compilers
	Preparation of algorithms, coding and running the program
	Dialog between program and user
	Entering and output of data, printing formats
	Main actions of algorithms: assignment, loop
	Simple data types
	Stages of program development
	Control data and correctness of program
	Programming style and culture
	Simplest algorithms and their programming

The IT course for upper secondary grades 10-12 is being essentially revised. Several optional modules, mostly oriented to the requirements for study courses in higher educational institutions, are being developed.

Since the number of computers in schools is increasing, schools have faced problems on practical application of education on ICT; this can be particularly said about their integrated usage in different fields of activities of teacher and student.

5 Educational Standards for Information Technology

Educational standards for IT describe the results of learning – basic knowledge and skills – which have to be acquired by the majority of students who have completed the respective grade. The standards are developed for students, teachers, and managers of educational institutions. The standards are oriented towards the values of information technologies, abilities, knowledge and skills which are essential for a citizen of modern society and which are intended to be conveyed by the obligatory course on IT and by supplementary training, in the event a school (a school council) thinks that it is worth creating conditions for a major part of students to seek better results.

For the meantime the educational standards just to grades 5-8 are prepared (Table 3). After wide discussions between experts, schoolteachers and schools agreed on seven topics for learning and using IT: one of them concerns just grades 5-6, two concern just grades 7-8.

Table 3. Educational standards: student abilities

IT topics	Basic abilities for grades 5–8
Working with the computer	To be capable of using a computer.
	To understand and apply hierarchical structure of information storage in the computer.
	To know and regard the copyrights of software and products developed using computers.
Drawing with the computer (only for grades 5-6)	To be able to use the main drawing tools and to independently create a picture.
	To perform the main actions with a picture (copy, cut, rotate, flip).
Creation, editing and publishing a text document	To be able to prepare a text document.
	To be able to prepare a text document for printing.
Internet and electronic messages	To know at least one search engine and to use it when searching for information, according to a word or group of words.
	To know the main ethical principles of information usage and communication in the computer networks.
	To read, write, and send electronic messages with attachments.
	To be aware of the risks of viruses and to know tools protecting the computer information from viruses.
	To be able to connect to chat sites and to communicate in them.
Design and modelling	To be able to consider and prepare a project: drawing or animation.
	To understand the main actions (repeating, description of new commands, usage of variables) and to be able to apply them.
	To be able to create algorithms for drawing geometrical shapes.
Elementals of table preparation (only for grades 7-8)	To make simple tables using a spreadsheet. To process simple statistical data using a spreadsheet. To be able to make charts from a data table.
Preparation and demonstration of presentations (only for grades 7-8)	To know and be able to use the advantages of programs for making presentations.
	To know the main requirements for the structure of presentation.
	To be able to demonstrate and comment on the presentation.

The educational standards were based on the fundamental level for grades 6 and 8, which is the main level of information literacy describing good results on the subject sufficient for further successful learning (Table 4). This level should be achievable by the majority of students. After achieving it, students must perceive the basic concepts and terms of information technology, be able to use ICT when performing practical tasks according to the provided instructions, and be able to formulate conclusions and summarise the knowledge they have.

The educational standards are formulated in a way that the achievements can be easily measured. Blind and straightforward teaching, when teachers merely follow the requirements described in the standard, should be avoided. Therefore, continuous work with teachers is needed. They should understand the didactic provisions and teaching methods. The educational standards are just a landmark for the development of students' skills.

Table 4. Educational standards: student achievements that should be reached in grades 6 and 8

IT topics	Achievements in grade 6	Achievements in grade 8
Working with the computer	Uses keyboard, mouse and printer. Can use simple software and educational programs. Finds and runs familiar programs. Chooses necessary storage device, disk, directory or file. Creates a directory, rename or remove it. Can control program windows: open, close, minimize, maximize, and use the scroll bar. Knows the main tools for health safety of those who work with computers.	Knows ways of opening the main programs and files. Can apply hierarchical structure of information in the computer for storage of products. While working in one program can copy objects (fragments of text, pictures) and edit the copies. Can transfer fragments of documents prepared from one file to another using different programs. Performs actions with objects: creates, removes and applies formats. Describes the copyrights.
Drawing with the computer (only for grade 6)	Can find and run a simple program for preparation of graphics (drawings). Opens existing drawing file. Saves the created drawing into the storage device. Uses different drawing tools: pencil, paintbrush, eraser, tool for drawing geometrical shapes. Can change the properties of drawing tools. Uses tools for drawing curves. Can copy or cut the necessary part of the picture to insert it into other place. Can change the size of the inserted copy. Performs symmetric transformations (rotates, flips).	
Creation, editing and publishing a text document	Uses the keyboard levels, chooses a keyboard of the required language. Opens and closes the text editor. Opens a text file, creates a new document and saves it. Types a simple text using the keyboard following the rules for text writing. Chooses a proper font, its style (bold, italic) and size. Recognizes the main elements of the text – symbol, paragraph and heading – and can change their formats. Can keep evenly aligned (formatted) paragraphs. Copies and cuts a fragment of text, inserts it into other place. Can insert images into text. Prepares a small document for printing.	Can describe how to prepare a more complicated document. Can set the margins of a page. Can select the necessary fragment of a document and copy (insert), remove, move and format it: change the font and its style, size, color. Can change the spacing of text and use subscript, superscript, underlining effects. Can set the language of text and use the spelling tools. Can find the necessary word and phrase in a text and change it into another using the text formatting tools. Knows the main rules for computer document layout and applies them in practical work. Knows the text formatting and layout concepts.

Table 4. (*continued*)

Internet and electronic messages	Finds and runs the browser. Uses the main menu items of the browser. Uses the Internet to search for information. Can download the necessary document or image from the Internet. Describes the main ethical principles of information usage in the networks and risks of the Internet. Reads, writes and sends electronic messages. Encloses an attachment to the message (file). Is aware of the risks of computer viruses and names several tools which help to avoid viruses. Communicates in the chat sites following the principles of ethics.	Understands the hierarchical principle of making the Internet address. Performs a search for information, if necessary using not only the main but supplementary keywords. Applies other options in the search engine. Finds, saves, and uses different information (textual, graphical, video, audio).
Design and modelling	Can draw by using several technologies: stamping, photographing. Can use drawings created using other graphical programs. Explores behavior of object using the simplest programs. Can create objects (for example, program buttons). Can distinguish serial and parallel actions. Understands principles of animation, can use moving objects in his or her projects.	Understands the purpose of programs, procedures and can present examples. Can perform the main actions, such as repeating, case selection. Understands the concept of variable and can use it. Can use procedures and their parameters. Reads and understands the simplest recursive algorithms. Creates simple geometrical algorithms, uses procedures with parameters. Can plan and complete a geometrical drawing.
Elementals of table preparation (only for grade 8)	colspan	Knows the main concepts of the spreadsheet: cells, their co-ordinates, address of the cell. Can create simple tables using the spreadsheet and do the necessary formatting. Can enter, change and delete data in the tables. Can select and delete columns and rows. Applies the simplest formulas of addition, deduction, multiplication and calculation of mean and can correct and copy them. Processes simple statistical data using the spreadsheet. Can make bar, pie and column charts from a data table.
Preparation and demonstration of presentations (only for grade 8)		Can use the program to make presentations and independently creates a presentation. Can set the desired type of slide and change it if necessary. Can choose the background color and fill in for a slide. Can choose a design template, apply and correct it when preparing a presentation. Can insert a copied text, picture, and table into the slide. Knows the main requirements of the logical structure of the presentation and follows them when working independently. Can demonstrate and comment on the presentation.

6 Discussion and Conclusions

Teaching and learning with ICT is one of the main concepts in Lithuanian general education. Starting from the small separated course of informatics in schools we gradually improved provision of computers for schools, installed computer networks, taught teachers, created educational aids, made revision of the IT curriculum, elaborating and changing it several times.

To obtain holistic education and learning, based on ICT (UNESCO names it as transformation approach), we gradually have to plan our steps and foresee the sustainability of various measures and actions. No matter how strong our desire is, we cannot impetuously pass from the academic teaching of separate subjects to integration. It is even more complicated to form the learning pattern of life and culture in school. In a limited number of schools these aims could be implemented in quite a short time, but we are seeking for the changes in the whole country, in all or almost all schools.

Therefore the gradual model of IT teaching and use in grades 5-10 was prepared. The separate IT course is being combined with the integration of ICT into other subjects. Furtheron the optional modules are being formed.

The model covers the competences and values of students to be developed as well as it introduces the didactic provisions. It took much time to agree on the main fields of IT teaching and the basic abilities. The described educational standards were prepared after long discussions with teachers and policy makers. It is not supposed that they are already perfect, certainly not. However, they provide general directions for ICT teaching and learning in schools.

References

1. Anderson, J., Weert, T.: Information and Communication Technology in Education. A Curriculum for Schools and Programme of Teacher Development. Division of Higher Education, UNESCO (2002)
2. Dagiene, V.: Curriculum for Introducing Information Technology in Lithuanian Primary Education: Role of Logo. In: EuroLogo 2005: the 10th European Logo Conference. Digital Tools for Lifelong Learning, Warsaw, August 28–31, 2005, pp. 211–218 (2005)
3. Dagiene, V.: Teaching Information Technology in General Education: Challenges and Perspectives. In: Mittermeir, R.T. (ed.) ISSEP 2005. LNCS, vol. 3422, pp. 53–64. Springer, Heidelberg (2005)
4. Dagiene, V.: The Model of Teaching Informatics in Lithuanian Comprehensive Schools. Journal of Research on Computing in Education 35(2), 176–185 (2002-2003)
5. General Curriculum and Education Standards: Pre-school, Primary, and Basic Education. Ministry of Education and Science of the Republic of Lithuania, Vilnius (2003)
6. General Curriculum for General Education School in Lithuania and General Education Standards for Grades XI-XII, Vilnius (2002)
7. General Programme for Basic Education on Information Technologies. Ministry of Education and Science of the Republic of Lithuania (2005)
8. Haberman, B.: Teaching Computing in Secondary Schools in a Dynamic World: Challenges and Directions. In: Mittermeir, R.T. (ed.) ISSEP 2006. LNCS, vol. 4226, pp. 94–103. Springer, Heidelberg (2006)
9. Herring, J.E.: Teaching Information Skills in Schools. Library Ass. Pub., London (1996)
10. Students' General Computer Literacy Standard. IT at School, Vilnius (2002)
11. Strategy for the Introduction of Information and Communication Technologies into the Lithuanian Education for 2005–2007 (2004),
    http://www.emokykla.lt/en.php/documents/lithuanian_policy_documents/1126/

Spreadsheet Knowledge and Skills of French Secondary School Students

Françoise Tort, François-Marie Blondel, and Éric Bruillard

UMR STEF – ENS de Cachan - INRP, UniverSud
94235 Cachan cedex, France
francoise.tort@ecogest.ens-cachan.fr,
francois-marie.blondel@inrp.fr,
eric.bruillard@creteil.iufm.fr

Abstract. The aim of our research project called *DidaTab – Didactics of Spreadsheets* – is to get a more comprehensive picture of ICT uses in French schools and to obtain a better knowledge of students' spreadsheet competencies. The exploratory study of curricula and practices shows very sparse use during secondary education. To achieve a more precise estimation of what students can do with spreadsheets, we identified detailed competencies and designed computer performance tasks to serve as a basis for tests. The analysis of the results of a few groups indicates that in most cases students' knowledge and skills are rather low. A deeper investigation of students' work shows close links between lack of confidence with spreadsheets and lack of knowledge in mathematics and informatics.

Keywords: ICT competencies, informatics curriculum, spreadsheet software, computer tests.

1 Introduction: From ICT to Spreadsheet Focus

In many European countries, ICT is included in the prescribed curricula (see for examples, Eurydice [5] p. 24), but very few data about effective practices in classrooms and ICT competencies of students are available. National or international surveys have been carried out in order to evaluate ICT competencies: PISA Feasibility Study [8] ECAR [7], Eurostat [4]. Various indicators have been identified, including the ability to use professional software: word processing, spreadsheet, communication, web searching.

Concerning spreadsheets, several surveys indicate significant variations in their use by university students. In a survey carried out in 2004 for EDUCAUSE by Kvavik & Caruso [7], students declared that they spent 2 hours per week on average "Creating spreadsheets or charts (Excel, etc.)", but, they ranked themselves at a lower level of skill with applications like Excel than Word. In Australia, in a survey of students enrolled in first-year units at his university, Lim [9] found that a significant proportion of them – 9% to 18% – report "having no knowledge of spreadsheet skills".

Spreadsheet programs have often been mentioned as a key component of ICT literacy [12]. Spreadsheet competencies are often demanded in job requirements and appear in many vocational schools programs. Pemberton and Robson [11] pointed out the importance for companies of their employees' spreadsheet skills. Moreover, some famous and big companies seriously wonder about costly errors made in spreadsheet files that are manipulated and designed by their employees [10], [3]. These questions have been under debate since the earlier 90's in a community of firms and researchers, called the European Spreadsheet Risks Interest Group (see http://www.eusprig.org/).

So spreadsheets seem to be a focus of interest in several countries and we decided, three years ago, to launch a research project called *DidaTab - Didactics of Spreadsheets* [1][2]. Considering that it is not meaningful to take into account ICT as a whole, we focused on spreadsheets.

Studying the use of spreadsheet software is particularly interesting. It covers a large range of uses and functions: spreadsheet design, calculation, data graphing, data record-keeping. Moreover, the programming side of spreadsheets is often hidden but undeniable. Tabulating data and implementing dynamic calculus need to master data types, variables, operators, functions, references... that are all basic programming concepts. As a consequence, looking at spreadsheet competencies may give interesting indications of general competencies in informatics.

Our aim in this part of the DidaTab project was to identify these general spreadsheet competencies and estimate how far they are developed by high school students.

In this paper, we first present the spreadsheet competencies we identified and the performance tasks we built as materials for computer tests. In order to investigate students' skills and knowledge more deeply, we then focus on case studies, extracted from the DidaTab Project. We explore the results of 4 tests designed for specific student groups. We show the main results. We finally discuss what a deeper analysis of students' interaction with spreadsheet software reveals about their knowledge of spreadsheet and the links with mathematics and informatics.

2 Spreadsheet Uses and Students' Competencies

In the current state of French education, ICT appears explicitly in the prescribed curriculum for junior high school (grades 6 to 9)[1], in the so-called "technology" classes. It is a subject among others, in a course that takes only one hour period per week.

For most of high school students (grade 10 to 12), the basics of informatics, like programming, systems, etc. are not taught at all. Some specific parts of informatics are only introduced in the technological stream, like databases in management or programming in engineering. Most of the time, informatics is encountered by way of computer applications that are considered as tools to be used in the context of a particular subject matter. As a consequence, spreadsheet software appears only in some classes: mathematics, physics, chemistry, biology, geology, economics, engineering, management...

---

[1] Remember that education is compulsory until the age of 16, corresponding to grade 9.

2.1 Spreadsheet in the French Curricula

In order to get a better view of the place given to spreadsheets in the curriculum, we choose a set of classes in which we assumed that spreadsheets could be involved in teaching or learning. For each of these 10 classes, we analyzed the official instructions (the planned curriculum) and the most important educational resources (textbooks and websites). These analyses were completed by interviews of 29 teachers and 70 students about their uses of spreadsheets at school and at home, (see [13] for details).

In junior high schools, spreadsheet skills are taught at grade 7 as an introduction to ICT, in the "technology" classes, for a total amount of about 15 hours. Teaching is done through practical activities with computers and most teachers use activity sheets that focus on basic functionalities and elementary skills.

In senior high school, spreadsheets are considered as a tool among other software applications which can be used to organize, sort and present data, to make simple calculations and display graphs or charts, depending on subject matters, but in most of the official texts, the use of spreadsheet is only recommended and the recommendations put the emphasis on the competencies rather than knowledge.

As a result, very sparse uses of spreadsheet during secondary education can be observed, except in some specific streams like management.

Interviews with students have shown very sparse spreadsheet uses outside of school. This demonstrates the importance of what school can offer in this domain. But interviews of teachers reveal their difficulty in using spreadsheets during school time.

This raises important questions about students' practices and competencies: How do they manage with activities involving spreadsheets? What do they learn from these activities? And, at the end of high school, what are their final competencies?

2.2 Spreadsheet Competencies

Most surveys on ICT competencies are based on self-assessment techniques whose major drawback is that users largely over-estimated their own skills. To investigate spreadsheet competencies of high school students, we preferred working on a method based on the analysis of students' productions in situations where they are asked to perform specific tasks involving spreadsheets.

This type of analysis implies that: (i) spreadsheet competencies are explicitly stated, (ii) tests related to these competencies are produced, with the objective of investigating how deep students' knowledge about spreadsheet concepts is and whether they are able to perform tasks involving these concepts.

Use of spreadsheets in high schools mainly consists of making simple calculations, graphing relations between variables, displaying business forms and charts, selecting and sorting data, and, for some students, doing statistics or performing financial calculations. To reach this level of mastery, students have to acquire general software competencies but also more basic and domain-independent spreadsheet knowledge and skills.

Available documents that could be used to identify general spreadsheet competencies are very scarce. The most comprehensive one is the module 4 of the European Computer Driving License Foundation (ECDL) Syllabus which is declined in two versions, basic and advanced. But the phrasing of the syllabus is too close to the performance tasks associated with spreadsheet and could not easily be transformed to produce indications for designing general skills and competencies.

Starting from a previous work of Vandeput and Colinet [14], we identified a set of basic spreadsheet skills taken from what is taught in general training for beginners, and what we have seen about spreadsheet uses in high schools.

Every skill is described as a specific ability to use basic features to perform general but simple tasks. Based on these elements, the whole set of 87 basic skills is organized in 5 main categories and 23 sub-categories as follows:

1. **Cells and Sheets Editing and Formatting.** This category covers: select and edit cells, format data types, copy and paste values, and autofill. With 22 skills listed, this category is a basis for most of the others because it contains all basic manipulation of the objects displayed in a spreadsheet.
   Example: "Copy the value of a cell or a range of cells"
2. **Formulas.** This category covers: write a formula with operands, operators and commonly used functions, relative and absolute referencing, use of auto-fill effects on referencing, identify errors. This category that contains 24 skills is the core of spreadsheet development.
   Example: "Write a formula with mathematical functions"
   "Use the effect of autofill on cells referencing"
   "Translate a calculation described in natural language into a formula"
3. **Graphs and Charts.** This category covers: create a graph of data from one or two series, use the main available types of graphs, edit graph display features. It contains 13 skills.
   Example: "Graph data with a suitable chart type"
4. **Data Tables.** This category covers: sort a table by one or more levels, filter a table, search a table, extract from a selection. It contains 15 skills.
   Example: "Choose a criterion to sort using one key"
5. **Modeling.** This category covers: identify cell status, organize values and calculation, structure for printing. It contains 13 skills. It is the most difficult to develop because it deals with high level abilities which are often dependant of the domain of application of the spreadsheet, like accounting, business or communication.
   Example: "Differentiate values obtained by formulas from others"

In the definition process, functionalities which were too specific, like financial functions or solver were deliberately put aside because they have been designed to meet specific professional requirements (accounting) or scientific needs (statistics).

Describing what students may know about spreadsheet in terms of skills implies also a minimum knowledge of concepts. For instance, "write a formula with mathematical functions" requires knowing the syntax of formulas, the references to cell value and also the existence of basic mathematical functions.

3 French High School Students' Competencies

To assess competencies, the idea was to develop a series of various tests made of typical performance tasks. Each test is built for a particular group of students enrolled in a particular stream, general, technological or vocational. To be able to allow comparisons, the design of tests follows a general framework. We will first focus on computer-based performance tasks and then on tests.

3.1 Performance Tasks

In a typical *performance task*, students are given a spreadsheet that contains data taken from a very simple real life example. They have to either change or transform the appearance of the given spreadsheet (enlarge a column, bold some cells, sort columns), or make calculations from data, or create new objects like charts or tables.

Each task is related to a *limited number of skills*, typically from one to three, all in the same category.

A collection of about 100 performance tasks has been built to serve as a basis for building tests. The general objective was to have several performance tasks of various difficulties available for assessing one skill.

	A	B	C	D	E
1	Change data display below, so that population numbers appear with only one digit after the decimal point.				
2					
3			year	population	
4			2001	59.042	
5			2002	59.342	
6			2003	59.635	

Fig. 1. Task fmb-40 - To change the display format of a decimal number. Assessed skill is "Display formats for each category of data: numeric, date/hour, text".

	A	B	C	D	E	F	G	H	I	J	K	L	M	N	O
1	Cell O5 automatically displays the sum of the values entered in the cells of columns A to N.														
2															
3	Write the suitable formula in O5														
4															
5	22	15	63	84	25	31	76	40	92	49	13	54	65	10	

Fig. 2. Task ft-28 - To write the sum calculation of a vector. Assessed skills are "Write a formula with mathematical functions", "Use cell reference relatively to the current cell".

	A	B	C	D	E
1	The table below gives in column C the tax-free amounts of expenditures. Write in D6 the formula that calculates the corresponding tax and copy it down to D7 and D8.				
2					
3			Tax rate	0.196	
4					
5			Amount	Tax	
6		Paper	42		
7		Photocopy	137		
8		Renting	129		

Fig. 3. Task fmb-14 – To calculate a tax using absolute reference. Assessed skills are: "Use cell reference relatively to the current cell", "Use absolute cell reference", "Use the effect of autofill on cells referencing".

	A	B	C	D	E
1	The table below gives the number of points obtained by candidates during a competition.				
2	Display the table such that the best candidates appear at the top.				
3					
4		Name	Points		
5		Alexia	317		
6		Arno	285		
7		Chloe	109		
8		Ely	484		
9		Emilie	508		
10		Gregory	459		

Fig. 4. Task ft -17 - Simple sort. The skill is: "Choose a criterion to sort using one key".

The analysis of students' productions in tasks related to a particular skill should provide enough elements to assess this skill. The small number of skills involved in a particular task should facilitate the analysis of students' responses, reducing the range of possible interpretations. Some examples are given below (Fig. 1 to 4).

Students may think of various solutions and apply several techniques to perform a task. The variety of solutions provides interesting indicators of the level of knowledge of the student and of her or his understanding (or misunderstanding) of spreadsheet concepts and functionalities. For instance, in the task on Fig. 2, foreseeable solutions for a formula giving the expected result may include: constant values or cells references, SUM function or "+" sign, or any combination of these options.

3.2 Tests and Skills

During the 2006 and 2007 school years, 12 different computer tests have been designed. Each test was administrated to a separate group of students belonging to the same class, giving a total of 241 tested students. We report here on the results of 87 students, belonging to 4 groups listed below:

- 22 students at the end of *junior high school*, in a *general stream of study*, aged 15, code **JG**
- 30 students at the beginning of *senior high school*, in a *general stream of study*, aged 16, code **SG**
- 22 students in the middle of *senior high school*, in a *"Humanities" stream of study*, aged 17, code **SH**
- 13 students at the end of *vocational school*, in a *"Business" stream of study*, aged 18, code **SV**

Students may have very few uses of spreadsheets, and some of them may be specific to their curricula. Thus, it is more appropriate to build one specific test per group, than to use the same test for all groups. In that way, each test was designed in order to be consistent with the estimated level of skills of students and to allow discriminating among respondents' skills.

Each test lasted one hour and included 8 to 10 performance tasks that cover all the categories of skills with various levels of difficulties (See exact distribution in Table 1). See [13] for a detailed description of the methodological framework and tools used for test design.

Table 1. Tests Composition – Number of Tasks per Skill Categories

Category \ Test	JG	SG	SH	SV
1. Editing Cells and Sheets	2	1	2	3
2. Writing Formulas	4	4	5	4
3. Creating Graphs	1	1	1	1
4. Managing Tables	1	1	1	2
5. Modeling	0	1	0	0
Total	8	8	9	10

Students had to work directly within a given spreadsheet file and to record their work at the end of the test. Collected data include: students' recorded files, direct observations of working students, and, for some cases, automatic video screen captures.

3.3 Low Competencies, Teacher and Stream Effects

First, we will report on the achievement of skills and, in the following section, on some particular concepts. Table 2 reports, for each test, how many students achieved the most important skills. Results are grouped by sub-categories of skills.

Students succeed rather well in tasks linked to the "formatting cells" category (Table 2, row 1). More precisely, 100% of them succeed in formatting tasks like italic and bold, but less than 100% are able to change a column width. These tasks concern superficial manipulations of spreadsheet objects that do not need specific knowledge.

The success rate decrease slightly when the tasks require more understanding of spreadsheet objects and functionalities, as is the case for tasks concerning graphs and tables (Table 2, 3 lower rows).

Most of the students are able to create a bar graph, the default graph type in spreadsheet software, but very few of them are able to choose another type of graph, like pie chart or scatter plot, when it is more suitable.

The success rate is lower for tasks on data sorting (less than half of students). Note that the sorting task was not obvious (see Fig. 4): a decreasing sort on a criterion based on the values of the second column of the given table.

Table 2. Tests Success – Number of students achieving skills[2]

Sub-Category of skills	JG	SG	SH	SV
Number of students	22	30	22	13
1.1 Formatting cells	22	–	22	10
1.2 Displaying numbers (format)	4	18	17	1
2.1 Writing simple formulas	9	30	22	2
2.2 Using cells reference	9	28	22	2
2.3 Using basic functions	3	3	6	3
2.4 Using absolute reference	–	9	10	0
3.1 Creating a bar graph	14	25	22	4
3.2 Choosing a suitable graph	0	3	8	–
4.1 Sorting out data	10	19	13	6

---

[2] The "–" sign means that we collected no information on this skill.

These tasks are more discriminating among the different groups' results. Junior high schools students (JG) and vocational students (SV) have lower success rates, than senior high school students in both "general" (SG) and "humanities"(SH) groups. These students have certainly already done such tasks at school.

But the more discriminating tasks are those which test formula writing skills. Tasks related to the skills of the sub-categories "Writing simple formulas" and "Using relative cell references" (for instance writing "=A2*C1"), are well performed by a minority of the junior high school (JG) and vocational students (SV), respectively 9 out of 22 and 2 out of 13 (Table 2, rows 3 & 4), when all senior high school students succeed in it. This gap between groups is similar to the one observed on tasks concerning display format of numbers (Table 2, row 2), where students were asked to display a decimal number with a fraction format.

The explanation may partly rely on lack of competencies in mathematics, as already shown in [6] for the vocational stream students. However, other competencies may be implied. Students in the "Humanities" group (SH) are able to write syntactically correct formulas, even if they have mathematic difficulties. For instance, when they are asked to write the calculus of an increase of a given rate (a formula like "=C10*1,043"), 19 out of 22 students write formulas which are syntactically correct, even if 7 of these are mathematically wrong

Some differences can also be explained by the teacher's attitude and practices. For instance, students in the "Humanities" group perform rather well, perhaps unexpectedly, in formula writing, because their maths teacher often use spreadsheets in class.

Finally, all students have low performance on skills that require a deeper knowledge of the core of formula writing: functions and absolute cells references (Table 2, rows 5 & 6).

More precisely, very few of them use the SUM function, even if the situation suggests it. Table 3 reports on the students' use of functions and operators. The figures indicate how many students used the SUM function (row 1) or the + operator (row 2) for the task ft-28 (See Fig. 2). In this task, because of the number of values to sum, it is more appropriate to use the SUM function, but most of the students use the + operator, probably because they don't know that such a function is available. The same applies to problems involving other functions. For instance, when students are asked to calculate the average of 4 marks, very few of them use the AVERAGE function (row 3). Most of them write a formula where the sum is divided by a constant, like "=(A1+B1+...)/4" or "=SUM(...)/4". (row 4).

Table 3. Use of functions or operators for one task

Functions	JG	SG	SH	SV
Number of students	*22*	*30*	*22*	*13*
SUM function	2	0	6	2
+ operator	9	26	15	1
AVERAGE Function	5	0	7	-
+ and / operators	8	26	13	-

The results show that these students don't know what a library of functions is. Perhaps they have already used the SUM function. But they probably don't link it with a set of pre-defined functions available for formula writing.

3.4 Diversity of Solutions, Underlying Knowledge

A deeper analysis of students' productions gives interesting indications on their misunderstanding, or lack of understanding of spreadsheet concepts and functionalities.

Confusion between display value and internal value: It is interesting to look at the various solutions found by the junior high schools students (JG) on the task where they had to change the display format of decimal numbers (see Fig. 1). 15 out of 22 propose a solution but only 4 produced the expected one: keep the actual value 59.042 in the cell and choose the "one digit after the point" option as display format. The 11 other students change the value of the cell. Some of them erase the digits after the point, others change the position of the point. Some of them finally change the display format. One adds tabulations before the value in order to get it truncated by the right border of the cell.

Students in the "Humanities" group (SH), who have good results on this task (17 successes out of 22), hesitate in another task when they have to display a percentage. 17 give a correct formula to calculate the percentage (like "=B4/B9"). But they use three different display solutions: "standard" display format option, add "*100" in the formula, add a % sign at the end of the value in the cell.

These points show that these students cannot make a clear distinction between the internal value and the displayed value of a cell, in relation to the format.

This confusion may be strengthened by the software's behavior. In general, entering a value in a cell has two effects: to set the internal value and to set the display format. For instance, entering "12%" in a cell sets the internal value to 0.12 and the display format to percentage. This feature which has been designed to facilitate the user's work, cannot help the beginners to understand the underlying concepts and functionalities.

Misunderstanding of what functions are: In section 3.3, we pointed out the fact that students don't know the library of functions. Some of their productions also show that they do not understand what a function is. Indeed, several students, from 1 to 5 in each tested group, have surprising non-standard uses of functions in formulas. They mix function and arithmetic operators in such a way that the function is totally useless (see Table 4).

Table 4. Formulas written by some students – useless functions and arithmetic operators

Formulas	Comments
=SUM(A1+B1+C1) =PRODUCT(B6*C6)	The used functions match with the calculus to be done, but they are useless in the written formula
=SUM(D6-E6) =SUM(C12*10)	Although the calculus is not a sum, the student uses the SUM function
=PRODUCT(B6)*0.38	Here the function is used in place of the first operand of the * operator.

It seems that these students do not clearly understand the meaning of a function and do not know how to use it. They work as if any formula must begin with a function call. Because they don't really know the syntax of the function, they fill it out with expressions using operators, instead of cell references. For cases were the SUM function is used, the error may have been encouraged by the "sigma" button, available from the tool bars. A click on the button causes "=SUM()"to appear in the selected cell, with the cursor into the brackets ; the user has just to fill it out. As a consequence, the students use the function as a skeleton to be filled out with the mathematical operations.

This wrong use may be strengthened by the fact that no error occurs when they enter their formulas. Indeed, all these formulas are syntactically correct and give a correct result.

Inadequate selection of cells before an action: In some tasks, we have observed that students obtain wrong results because they apply an operation to a wrong selection of cells.

For instance, in a task were they are asked to graph a series of percentages given in a column, the last figure being the total of 100%, 11 students in the SG group create a graph including this last value (100%).

In another task, looking like ft-28 (Fig.2), students are asked to enter the calculus of the sum after the last cell of the series. They are also asked to enter the calculus of the average in the next cell. Some students calculate the average of the series of data including the sum.

In both cases, the error is due to the "extension of selection" which is automatically performed by the software. The students select one cell and click on the action button (the graph button or the sigma button). Then the software extends the selection to the whole range of cells and applies the operation to this selection. As they are not aware of this, students do not check the result nor the behavior of the software interface.

Misunderstanding of what data tables are: Another interesting mistake is observed in tasks where students are asked to sort a data table. For instance in the task ft-17 (Fig. 4), some students (4 or 5 per groups) sort only the second column of the table or the two columns independently instead of sorting the whole data table.

It seems that these students do not understand that the given spreadsheet is not just a list of independent values but a data table, i.e. a collection of tuples (in rows) that have the same attributes (in columns). They may have already sorted values in a spreadsheet, but they probably not learned to manage data tables.

4 Conclusion

In France, very little informatics is taught in secondary schools but, in the official texts, a significant place is given to software use in subject matters. The general discourse is that students will receive some minimal training at one stage and then will encounter ICT usage in every subject during their scholarship. The underlying idea is that a regular use of software is sufficient to acquire the related knowledge and skills.

Focusing specifically on spreadsheets, the DidaTab project explored school practices and showed scarce uses of spreadsheet software by students both at school and at home.

Findings from computer tests on spreadsheet show various levels of achievement from one tested group to another. Some case studies show that students who have a good level in mathematics have fewer difficulties with writing formulas, or using cell references. Also, case studies show that these students' level of confidence with the software may be linked to the teachers' attitudes or practices during classes.

But findings from computer tests show for all groups of students very few skills and knowledge. If the best students have rather good results on very basic skills, all of them have difficulties on tasks that need deeper knowledge on spreadsheet concepts and features: the role of a library of functions, the cells referencing system, managing data tables, etc.

A deeper analysis of students' productions reveals that their difficulties with spreadsheets are tightly linked to their lack of informatics competencies. Students don't master basics concepts of variables, data types, functions, data tables, which are central in spreadsheets.

Moreover, students don't master basics principles of software interface, like selection-action procedure, definition of default parameters, automatic behavior of software, shortcuts for a series of actions, all principles that they should master to be able to anticipate results of their action on the interface.

According to us, these findings show that occasional use of software is not sufficient for students to acquire the basic knowledge and skills. It raises the issue of what curriculum on spreadsheet software, based on informatics fundamentals, should be followed in French secondary school. This requires an exploration of the intertwined relationships between mathematics, informatics and spreadsheets, and to establish a progression over concepts and competencies.

References

1. Blondel, F.-M., Bruillard, E.: Analysis of the uses of spreadsheets at home and in schools by French students. In: ECER 2006 (European Conference on Educational Research), Transforming Knowledge, Geneva (September 2006)
2. Bruillard, E., Blondel, F.-M., Tort, F.: DidaTab project main results: implications for education and teacher development. In: McFerrin, K., Weber, R., Carlsen, R., Willis, D.A. (eds.) Proceedings of Society for Information Technology and Teacher Education International Conference, SITE 2008, pp. 2014–2021. AACE, Chesapeake, USA (2008) ISBN: 1-880094-64-9
3. Croll, G.: The Importance and Criticality of Spreadsheets in the City of London. In: EuSpRIG conference (2005)
4. Demunter, C.: How skilled are Europeans in using computers and the Internet, Eurostat, European Communities, 17/2006 (2006)
5. Eurydice, Key Data on Information and Communication Technology in Schools in 2004 (2004), http://www.eurydice.org/ressources/eurydice/pdf/048EN/004_chapB_048EN.pdf
6. Haspekian, M., Bruillard, E.: What role does mathematics play in students' spreadsheet competencies? A case study of French students skills in a vocational school. In: Proceedings of Informatics, Mathematics and ICT, IMICT 2007, College of Computer and Information Science Northeastern University, Boston, USA (2007) ISBN 13: 978-0-615-14623-2

7. Kvavik, R.B., Caruso, J.B.: ECAR Study of Students and Information Technology, 2005: Convenience Connection, Control and Learning, vol. 6 (2005)
8. Lenon, M., Kirsh, I., Von Davier, M., Wagner, M., Yamamoto, K.: Feasibility Study for the PISA ICT Literacy Assessment. In: ACER 2003 (2003)
9. Lim, K.: A Survey of First-Year University Students' Ability to use Spreadsheets. In: Spreadsheets in Education, 1, 2, pp. 71–85 (2004)
10. Panko, R.: Spreadsheet Errors: What We Know. What We Think We Can Do. In: Proceedings of the Spreadsheet Risk Symposium; European Spreadsheet Risks Interest Group (EuSpRIG), Greenwich, England, July 17-18 (2000), http://panko.shidler.hawaii.edu/SSR/Mypapers/EUSPRIG_2000.htm
11. Pemberton, J.D., Robson, A.J.: Spreadsheets in Business. Industrial Management & Data Systems 100, 379–388 (2000)
12. Snyder, L., Aho, A.V., Linn, M.C., Packer, A., Tucker, A., Ullman, J., Van Dam, A.: Be FIT! Being fluent with information technology. National Academy Press, Washington, DC (1999)
13. Tort, F., Blondel, F.-M.: Uses of spreadsheets and assessment of competencies of high school students. In: Benzie, D., Iding, M. (eds.) Proceedings of Informatics, Mathematics and ICT, IMICT 2007, College of Computer and Information Science Northeastern University, Boston, USA (2007) ISBN 13: 978-0-615-14623-2
14. Vandeput, E., Colinet, M.: Utiliser le tableur en toute autonomie. In: Pochon, L.-O., Bruillard, E., Maréchal, A. (eds.) Apprendre (avec) les progiciels: Entre apprentissages scolaires et pratiques professionnelles, pp. 73–98. Neuchâtel: IRDP & Lyon: INRP (2006)

Harmonization of Informatics Education – Science Fiction or Prospective Reality?

Peter Micheuz

Klagenfurt University, Institute of Informatics Systems, Informatics Didactics,
A-9020 Klagenfurt, Austria
Peter.micheuz@uni-klu.ac.at

Abstract. Starting from the influential Common European Framework of Reference for Languages, this paper presents a synopsis of current frameworks and curricula in terms of (informatical) education at the secondary school level. Some initiatives from well known organizations and institutions show the global and national efforts to structure the fragmented field of computing at the school level. The definitive answer as to whether a perceptible process of harmonization seems to be realistic in the near future cannot yet be given, but there are some positive indicators.

1 Introduction

Recently, a growing concern for unifying European education can be observed. This process is endorsed by the Bologna agreement [4] which mainly applies to organizational and administrative aspects in higher education. These measures of harmonization should lead to better comparability and possibilities for mutual participation, exchange and cooperation.

Concerning the content of education in secondary schools, a unifying tendency has already found exemplary representations in the form of international comparative research activities on educational achievements. Among them, PISA is undoubtedly the most prominent. Obviously, but not incidentally, this study still does not cover the area of ICT and Informatics.

Apparently, the main reason can be identified as the lack of a European Framework for ICT and Informatics education as a basis for an elaboration of curriculum guidelines, syllabi, examinations, etc.

What are the reasons why such a widely accepted IT-framework was not established until now? Perhaps a quote from Isaac Asimov, well known for his works of science fiction, can give an answer: "The only constant is change, continuing change, inevitable change, which is the dominant factor in society today. No sensible decision can be made any longer without taking into account not only the world as it is, but the world as it will be." Probably, this applies to the dynamics of informatics, and to all related fields, more than to all other traditional educational areas. Seemingly, the digital gap between pupils and students worldwide is exceeded only by the gaps among the policy makers in their (non)efforts to establish reasonable strategies to consolidate and harmonize informatics education in elementary and secondary schools.

It is true that the recent decades of an accelerated development to a digital and computerized society went hand in hand with changing technologies and didactical approaches to informatics education on all levels, and moreover, less than ten years ago, just thinking of a common standardizing framework for informatics education at the secondary level would have been like hitting a moving target. But after more than thirty years of practical computing experience in schools and theoretical reflections about its characteristic periods of development [20], the pillars of informatics in an educational context do consolidate and become gradually visible. An initiative for the development of a common, widely accepted framework as a guideline for comparable curricula and educational standards on a worldwide, at least on a European level, is overdue.

2 Looking across the Borders of Our Discipline

There is much evidence that in the case of computing in schools, encompassing the interwoven triad of IT, Informatics, and E-Learning, uncertainty and diversification among European countries and even within countries is unusually high. As a small comfort, traditional disciplines such as language learning, maths and even physical education undergo a discussion about pedagogical challenges as well, and moreover, lack empirical data resulting from insufficient educational research.

2.1 The Common European Framework for Languages

As already mentioned in the introductory remarks, probably the most successfully elaborated framework in an educational context is the Common European Framework for Languages of School Education (CEFR) [5]. It was launched and developed over a period of nine years – "No great thing is created suddenly (Epictetus)" – under the patronage of the Language Policy Division of the Council of Europe (CeO, Europarat). Evidently, this framework exerts an unparalleled impact on the European educational system in terms of language learning.

Language learning can be categorized into the activities of understanding (listening, reading), speaking (spoken interaction, spoken production) and writing, each described by clearly defined proficiency levels:

A   Basic User (A1-Breakthrough, A2-Waystage)
B   Independent User (B1-Threshold, B2-Vantage)
C   Proficient User (C1-Effective Operational Proficiency, C2–Mastery)

Further details of this framework consider qualitative aspects of spoken language such as range, accuracy, fluency, interaction and coherence.

Finally published in 2001, the CEFR is the fruit of ample linguistic research, and constitutes a completely new approach aimed at redefining language teaching objectives, contents and methods. More importantly, it can serve as a common, transnational base for the design of programmes, curricula, syllabi, certificates, and educational standards. Moreover, it can be used as a solid basis for assessment criteria, even at lower levels, which can be stated in terms of positive achievements rather than negative deficiencies. Last but not least it supports the planning of self-directed learning, including raising the learner's awareness of his or her present state of knowledge and skills, the self-setting of feasible and worthwhile objectives, the selection of materials and self-assessment.

The CEFR is generally considered as being comprehensive, transparent and coherent. Coherent in this context means that the framework specifies the full range of language knowledge, skills and use.

2.2 The NCTM Standard for Mathematics

Another well known, widely accepted and influential example of a framework stems from the National Council of Teachers of Mathematics, in short NCTM, located in Reston, Virginia, USA. In its mission statement, the NCTM, claims to be "the public voice of mathematics education, providing vision, leadership and professional development to support teachers in ensuring equitable mathematics learning of the highest quality for all students." The NCTM is the biggest and most influential nongovernmental organization in terms of mathematics education in North American schools. Its best known publication and framework, "Principles and Standards for School Mathematics", published in 2000 and the result of many years of conceptual work of many scientists and practitioners, outlines the essential components of a high-quality program of school mathematics [23].

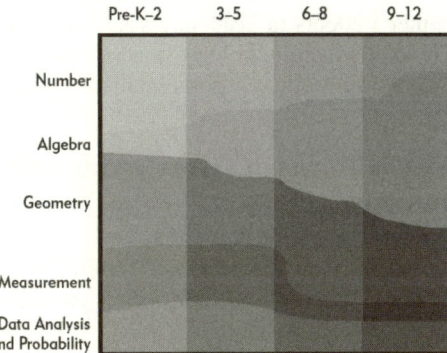

Fig. 1. Content standards and grade bands of the NCTM-Standard

2.3 Harmonization of Physical Education in Europe

"Against a background of perceived threats to physical education, an investigative world-wide survey of the state and status of physical education in schools funded by the International Olympic Committee was carried out in the years 1998 and 1999. The survey findings, based on data collated from a globally administered semi-structured questionnaire and an extensive literature survey, reveal that physical school education is in a perilous position in all continental regions of the world." This statement, part of the abstract from [12], is remarkable in two different respects.

First, it is interesting to observe that physical education with its long and seemingly untouched tradition and position in the canon of obligatory disciplines such as language learning and mathematics, is in a threatened situation. It cannot be excluded that sometimes informatics education has been implemented at the expense of physical education in some schools, whether autonomously or centrally regulated by the Ministries of Education. In any case, the introduction of a new discipline normally implies a predatory competition, unless the general number of lessons in schools is increased.

The proponents and policy makers of physical education in schools cannot be really amused if they have to sacrifice valuable hours of physical education for hours of informatics instruction in thr form of too much sedentary occupation in front of computers. It seems easier to find other subjects which are replaced by ICT and informatics lessons.

Second, as pointed out in [12], the need for harmonization is obvious, not least due to the international data collated, which provide a "distorted continental regional and individual national picture of physical education in schools". In this context it is remarkable that a world-wide survey has been sponsored by the International Olympic Committee. "I have to urge caution in interpretation of data because [...] there is too much of a gap between the promise and the reality. Survey data generated from governmental-level agencies tend more often than not to reflect policy principles rather than the realities of actual implementation and practice." [13]

The author can confirm this statement referring to a recent online-survey which had been conducted in 2007 [20]. Apart from the fact that Austria's Ministry of Education evidently lacks detailed data regarding Informatics education, even hard facts such as the ratio computer:students in academic secondary schools are reported in a very flattering way. The real situation, at least in academic secondary schools is evidently worse than indicated in European reports such as "Education at a Glance".

3 Major Initiatives in Terms of Overviewing and Structuring Informatics Education

This section reviews exemplary and influential efforts of well-known organizations and institutions to structure and consolidate informatics education are reviewed.

3.1 UNESCO/IFIP and ACM/CSTA

The UNESCO/IFIP curriculum, published in 2002 [16], can be seen as an ambitious approach to structure ICT education at the secondary level.

"Information and Communication Technology (ICT) has become, within a very short time, one of the basic building blocks of modern society. Understanding ICT and mastering the basic skills and concepts of ICT are now regarded by many countries as part of the core of education alongside reading and writing. This area of study sometimes goes under the all-embracing name of informatics. [...] It provides a practical and realistic approach to curriculum and teacher development that can be implemented quickly and cost effectively, according to available resources. [...] The curriculum is designed to be capable of implementation throughout the world to all secondary age students."

The introduction in the foreword of this international framework stresses the all-embracing term ICT, including informatics as "the science dealing with the design, realization, evaluation, use, and maintenance of information processing systems, including hardware, software, organizational and human aspects, and the industrial, commercial, governmental and political implications of these."

It is disputable if this generalization is fruitful for a common international understanding of the terminology. The challenge is how to resolve the semantic problem that arises with the term computer science as the anglo-saxon counterpart of informatics, and IT as the more generic term than ICT. The working group of UNESCO has solved this seemingly academic question very pragmatically.

Looking closer at the four areas of ICT–competence [ICT Literacy], [Application of ICT in Subject Areas], [Infusing ICT across the Curriculum], [ICT Specialization], it is obvious that ICT Literacy is, except for the last two modules, equivalent to the ECDL Core, which contains Basic Concepts of ICT, Using the Computer and Managing Files, Word Processing, Working with a Spreadsheet, Working with a Database, Composing Documents and Presentations, Information and Communication, Social and Ethical Issues, Jobs and/with ICT.

Furthermore it seems to be an unfortunate allocation that the advanced modules Spreadsheet Design and Database Design are placed within the Application of ICT in Subject Areas. These important subject matters of informatics education should be categorized into the area ICT Specialization, together with programming and software design. In the author's opinion this framework needs some revision.

In the UNESCO/IFIP publication "Information and Communication Technologies in Schools" with the subtitle "How ICT can Create New, Open Learning Environments" [26], published in 2005, we find the recommendation: "At every level of schooling, ICT are not a closed or self-contained subject to be taught and learned independently from other subjects. Rather, ICT are a subject that, by its very nature, should be treated as interdisciplinary, integrative, and cross-curricular […]. Of course, some elements of ICT can be taught in a dedicated time."

This proposal is a slap in the face for all who endeavor to establish informatics as a mandatory subject among the canon of the traditional disciplines. Many relevant publications point out that the integrative approach of ICT is not successful and stress the need for informatics lessons of its own.

Regarding higher education, an insightful overview is given in the overview report of the Association for Computing Machinery (ACM) [1], where clarification in the computing disciplines, computer engineering, computer science, information systems, information technology and software engineering, are specified.

While higher education permanently deals with itself in refactoring its degree programs and in aiming at consolidation and clarification of its confusing terminology, the current situation in elementary and secondary education (not only in the USA) is not better, but even worse.

Unlike the IFIP Curriculum, the (American) Computer Science Teachers Association (CSTA) [6] distinguishes clearly between Computer Science, Information Technology, and Fluency. The comprehensive model curriculum proposes four categories [Foundations of Computer Science], [Computer Science in the Modern World], [Computer Science as Analysis and Design], [Topics in Computer Science, including AP Computer Science, Courses Leading to Industry Certification].

AP means "Advanced Placement" Computer Science and encompasses advanced, object-oriented programming methodology with an emphasis on problem solving and algorithm development, binary trees, recursive data structures and dynamically allocated structures. AP Courses are offered by the College Board to high school students as an opportunity to earn college credit for a college-level computer science course.

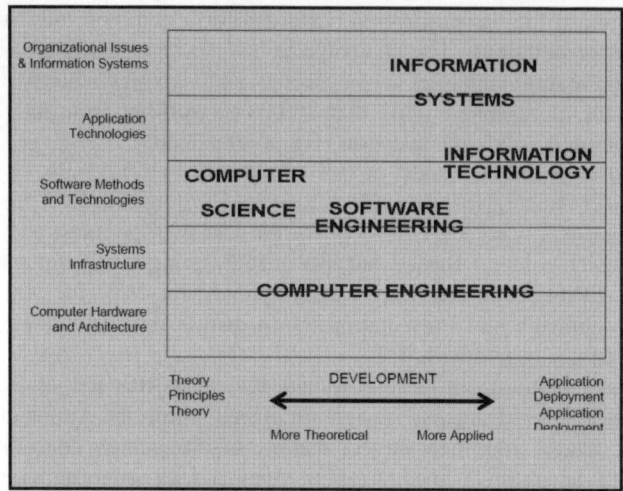

Fig. 2. ACM's classification and allocation of computing disciplines

A recent National Academy Study (National Research Council, 1999) defines an idea called IT fluency as something more comprehensive than IT literacy. Moreover, IT fluency also includes the active use of algorithmic thinking (including programming) to solve problems, whereas IT literacy is more limited in scope. It is based on the three orthogonal categories: concepts, capabilities, and skills. [6, p. 6].

3.2 OECD and PISA

PISA, the world's largest comparative study in the educational area, launched by the Organisation for Economic Co-Operation and Development (OECD) [2], assesses how far students near the end of compulsory education have acquired some of the knowledge and skills in the area of language, math and science that are essential for full participation in society. ICT competencies have not been tested so far, but there is a feasibility study [19] which indicates that it is likely that, at the latest in 2012, ICT-competencies will be tested. Magenheim classifies the first proposals for the test items as completely insufficient. Puhlmann and Humbert [15][25] and Friedrich [11] go a step further and, on their part, develop models and construct assignments.

The integration of testing ICT-Skills and informatics competence in a future PISA-study has to be considered as the most effective step in harmonizing informatics education at the lower secondary (compulsory) level. The reason is evident. No politician would be amused to see his/her country at the low end of the world's most famous educational ranking list.

Developing such a test in a field where apparently "the only similarity is its diversity and the only constant is change", is perhaps the most responsible task ever in the context of standardizing ICT and informatics.

3.3 CEPIS and ECDL

At this point we leave the input-oriented meta level of frameworks and curricula and enter the world of output-measuring certificates on a commercial level. One of its most prominent representatives is the organisation CEPIS (The Council of European Professional Informatics Societies), located in Amsterdam and responsible for two leading European IT Skills certifications, the ECDL® (European Computer Driving License) EUCIP (Certification of Informatics Professionals) [9].

Whereas the EUCIP does not play any role in secondary education, the ECDL, although originally designed for adults, is offered also for pupils and students at the secondary level. At present, there are no comprehensive studies about the penetration of the ECDL in secondary education.

The ECDL Foundation is the organisation behind the world's leading end-user computer skills certification programme. Internationally recognised in about 150 countries, it has attracted by now over 7 million candidates to its range of 10 certification programmes, among them the ECDL Core as the most accepted [9]. The seven modules of the ECDL Core and the first seven modules of the IFIP Curriculum in terms of ICT Literacy are the same.

When talking about assessments and standards regarding basic IT skills, the ECDL cannot be ignored. The decision to introduce the (external) certificate ECDL in secondary education is a challenge for all school decision makers, particularly as it is connected with costs and the worry of reducing teaching just to mere product training.

Educational decisions should always be based on a set of reliable arguments. But what are the substantial arguments to justify offering external, costly certificates at schools? Some important theses can be found in [17], where the CEO of the association, which organizes ECDL-tests at schools in Austria, among other arguments, appraises the ECDL as a normalizing instrument for pupils at the transition from lower to upper secondary education.

Whereas the ECDL plays a considerable role in standardizing informatics education in Austria, the current spread of the ECDL in German schools is still inferior. Presently, five of all sixteen Ministries of Education of the German federal states, among them Bavaria, recommend the ECDL for secondary education. It will be interesting to observe in the near future if the business model of the ECDL will yield an increasing demand among students and teachers.

4 National Initiatives in Germany and Austria

Two interesting empirical studies were recently conducted at the Technical University of Dresden by the department of Didactics of Informatics.

The first study [21] draws an impressive picture of the enormous diversity in terms of informatics education within the 16 federal states of Germany. Even intensive efforts in form of recommendations and resolutions of such influential institutions as the German Society for Informatics (GI e.V.) have still little effect, although the importance of a coherent informatics education and its implementation in schools is pointed out.

The second study [3] is a synopsis and comparison of informatics education in 13 countries, including three non-European countries: Japan, New Zealand and the Philippines. The study shows clearly the different national strategies to implement ICT in secondary education. It is remarkable, that in the course of a major school reform in 1999, Poland considerably reinforced informatics education at the secondary level. Is it coincidence or a logical consequence that Poland has seen a significant rise in reading performance since PISA 2000?

Both studies must be seen as an indispensable basis for an evidence-based policy. Moreover they should suggest further empirical research on the basis of well-elaborated methodologies.

A recently conducted nationwide study [27], surveying and investigating all Austrian academic secondary schools, yielded an extremely fragmented picture of informatics education even in this type of schools. One can hardly find two schools with an identical offering of formal informatics classes in lower secondary education. The result is an undue digital gap among the pupils at the end of the lower secondary level, where exactly one third did not even attend one hour of formal ICT and informatics instructions. At this point, initiatives for improvement in the form of implementing educational standards at the end of lower secondary general education are not supported by the Ministry of Education. Interestingly, an Austrian competence model for applied informatics in upper secondary vocational education, based on the ECDL, but going further and deeper, has been developed recently [7].

This strategy of building a house top-down resembles remarkably the German equivalent of implementing uniform final exams for the subject of informatics at the end of secondary education "Einheitliche Prüfungsanforderung in der Abiturprüfung (EPA)" [8].

In conclusion, a proposal for a very complex framework in terms of educational standards for informatics at the lower secondary level should be mentioned. Since 2003 in Königstein, the German conference INFOS 2003 in Munich [14][15][25],

Table 1. Comparison/Analogy NCTM-Standard - German Informatics Standard

Mathematics (NCTM)	Informatics (German Group)
Content Standards	
Number and Operations	Information and Data
Algebra	Algorithms
Geometry	Languages and FiniteAutomata
Measurement	Informatics Systems
Data Analysis and Probability	Informatics, Humans and Society
Process Standards	
Problem Solving	Modelling and Implementing
Reasoning and Proof	Reasoning and Evaluating
Communication	Structuring and Networking
Connections	Communicating and Cooperating
Representation	Representing and Interpreting

about 80 contributors from Germany, Switzerland and Austria worked in many informal meetings on this model. "Principles and Standards for Informatics in Schools" (Grundsätze und Standards für die Informatik in der Schule), has been published as a draft paper and comprehensive supplement of the German journal "Login" [18] and draws its title not incidentally from "Principles and Standards from School Mathematics", the showcase project from the NCTM. Finally there was an agreement on five content standards and as many process standards. Table 1 shows the result of this German approach in comparison to the NCTM standard.

This major contribution for consolidating and structuring school informatics at the lower secondary level is more than an ambitious framework which is available for a broad discussion among teachers, school practitioners, scientists and policy makers. A translation into English and a global distribution among teachers of informatics for international discussion would be appreciated.

5 Conclusion

Without doubt, harmonization has a positive connotation, and is a worthwhile goal in many respects. This applies to the fragmented and seemingly chaotic organization of informatics education worldwide and often even within countries and schools, more than to traditional subjects. Closing the digital gap should not only address the students' different ICT-related competencies, but as pointed out in this paper, it should address the different gaps in terminology and in the perception of informatics, that often lead to an undesirable organizational patchwork at the level of continents, countries, regions and even schools.

A comparative study such as PISA, with consideration of ICT-related assessments, could be helpful to accelerate the process of harmonization and standardization. Although a Common European Framework for Informatics would not guarantee automatically quick organizational and educational improvements, it is absolutely necessary in an international context, even if its major impact would only serve as a guideline for sophisticated PISA assignments.

References

1. ACM Computing Curricula – The Overview Report (2005)
2. http://www.oesz.at/index_mula.php?language=en (2008-03-15)
3. Blumich, S.: Schulsysteme und informatische Bildung im internationalen Vergleich, Diplomarbeit, Technische Universität Dresden (2007)
4. http://ec.europa.eu/education/policies/educ/bologna/bologna.pdf (2008-03-15)
5. http://www.coe.int/t/dg4/linguistic/CADRE_EN.asp (2008-03-15)
6. A Model Curriculum for K–12, Computer Science: Final Report of the ACM K–12 Task Force Curriculum Committee (October 2003)
7. Dorniger, C.: IT-Bildungsstandards, Das Kompetenzmodell Angewandte Informatik für die Sekundarstufe II (2008-03-15),
   http://pcnews.at/default.aspx?Id=14467
8. EPA-Standards (2008-03-15), http://www.kmk.org/doc/beschl/EPA-Informatik.pdf
9. ECDL – Homepage (2008-03-15), http://www.ecdl.org

10. http://ec.europa.eu/education/policies/2010/doc/basic-skills_en.pdf(2008-03-15)
11. Informatik und PISA – vom Wehe und Wohl der Schulinformatik. In: Hubwieser, P. (Hrsg.) Informatische Fachkonzepte im Unterricht. INFOS 2003, GI-Edition LNI, pp. 133–144 (2003)
12. Marshall, Hardman: The State and Status of Physical Education in Schools in International Context. European Physical Education Review 6, 203–229 (2000)
13. http://www.aehesis.de/PhysicalEducation/index.htm (2008-03-15)
14. Humbert, L., Puhlmann, H.: Essential Ingredients of Lieracy in Informatics. In: Magenheim, J., Schubert, S. (eds.) Concepts of Empirical Research and Standardisation of Measurement in the Area of Didactics of Informatics. GI-Dagstuhl-Seminar, September 19-24, 2004. Seminar-Edition, Lecture Notes in Informatics, vol. 1, German Informatics society (GI) (2004)
15. Humbert, L., Puhlmann, H.: Informatische Bildung und PISA Standards – zur Umsetzung für die informatische Bildung. In: CD Austria, Sonderheft Nr. 5/2004, pp. 21–24 (2004)
16. IFIP (2008-03-15), http://wwwedu.ge.ch/cptic/prospective/projets/unesco/en/curriculum2000.pdf
17. Karner, E.: Zertifikate in Schulen - sind denn unsere Noten nichts mehr wert? In: CD Austria, Sonderheft Nr. 5/2004, pp. 21–24 (2008-03-15), http://www.gym1.at/schulinformatik/standards/buecher/standards.pdf
18. LOGIN, Heft Nr. 146/147, 27. Jahrgang (2007)
19. Magenheim, J.: Towards a Competence Model for Educational Standards of Informatics. In: WCCE 2005 - Proceedings of the 8th IFIP World Conference on Computers in Education, University of Stellenbosch, Cape Town, Juli 4-7, 2005 (2008-03-15)
20. Micheuz, P.: Informatics Education at Austria's Lower Secondary Schools Between Autonomy and Standards. In: Mittermeir, R.T. (ed.) ISSEP 2006. LNCS, vol. 4226, pp. 189–198. Springer, Heidelberg (2006)
21. Weeger, M.: Synopse zum Informatikunterricht in Deutschland Analyse der informatischen Bildung der allgemein bildenden Schulen – durchgeführt auf der Basis existierender Lehrpläne und Richtlinien, TU Dresden (2007)
22. Mulder, F., van Weert, T.: IFIP/UNESCO's informatics curriculum framework 2000 for higher education. ACM SIGCSE Bulletin 33(4), 75–83 (2001)
23. http://www.nctm.org (2008-03-15)
24. http://www.pisa.org (2008-03-15)
25. Puhlmann, H.: Informatische Literalität nach dem PISA-Muster. In: Hubwieser, P. (ed.) Informatische Fachkonzepte im Unterricht. INFOS 2003. GI-Edition LNI – Lecture Notes in Informatics, Bnd P-60, pp. 79–89 (2005)
26. UNESCO/IFIP Information and Communication Technologies in Schools, A Handbook for Teachers, p. 183 (2005)
27. Micheuz, P.: Some Findings on Informatics Education in Austrian Academic Secondary Schools. Informatics in Education, Journal, Lithuanian Academy of Sciences, Vilnius (to appear, 2008)

Development of E-Learning Design Criteria with Secure Realization Concepts

Christian J. Eibl and Sigrid E. Schubert

Didactics of Informatics and E-Learning
University of Siegen
Hölderlinstr. 3, 57076 Siegen, Germany
{eibl,schubert}@die.informatik.uni-siegen.de

Abstract. This article introduces design criteria for e-learning systems based on implications from the disciplines of educational science, software engineering, and information security. Theoretical realization concepts to implement stated requirements are discussed. A conceptual implementation of a proxy server realized within this research project is also presented. This proxy server demonstrates the feasibility of stated concepts and enables outsourcing of security-related tasks to an automated process.

Keywords: e-learning, information security, educational science, design criteria, proxy server.

1 Introduction

This paper reports findings from research, currently in progress, concerning the design of appropriate security architectures for e-learning. The motivation for this research assignment with partners in South Africa (von Solms, University of Johannesburg) comes from higher education of informatics, especially the course of media informatics in education. In this course we teach in the context of e-learning:

- educational requirements,
- various models of learning, e.g., distant learning, computer supported collaborative learning (CSCL), blended learning,
- development of secure informatics systems.

Most of these terms are not appropriately defined. Here e-learning is used to refer to learning enhanced with informatics systems. It deals with both, the methodologies in learning and with associated technologies using:

- distributed computing (computers that are communicating over a network),
- interactive multimedia (compound of audio, animation, video and interactivity),
- the World Wide Web (an information system which accesses interlinked, hypertext documents via the Internet).

The research methodology [4] is similar to software engineering with the phases analysis, design, and implementation. Therefore, we analyzed the related work of educational science and of informatics. Here in particular criteria of software quality and information security are analyzed, which are necessary to realize selected implications from educational science (Section 2). Based on interdisciplinary requirements of education and informatics we propose a theoretical realization of design criteria of appropriate security architectures for e-learning (Section 3). On account of the complexity of the whole architecture we evaluate our theoretical approach in a stepwise manner. A prototype for the practical realization of a proxy server for automated security processes in the learning management system "Moodle" is the first case study (section 4). In further work an advanced version of the prototype will become a component of the security architecture for e-learning.

2 Design Criteria for E-Learning Systems

This section deals with requirements from three affiliated disciplines. The analysis is started with an investigation of the application field e-learning, i.e., educational science aspects (A). Afterwards, aspects of software quality (B) as well as of information security (C) will be presented.

A. Implications from educational science

In the following, six criteria are presented to show the necessity of certain program parts and requirements to improve learning success for all participants.

A1. Equal opportunities

Goals of e-learning usually mentioned are:

- to guide through information or to communicate information to the student;
- to help students perform specific tasks or learn a procedural skill in which they are expected to increase proficiency.

Therefore, e-learning is an essential part of education in the knowledge society. As human rights include equal opportunities in education we have to guarantee equal opportunities in e-learning, too. This leads to the criteria of usability (B3), portability (B6), and availability (C1) of e-learning systems.

A2. Social support by co-operation and communication

Situated learning considers the social situation and the communication context of learners to be of major importance [11]. This approach demands especially communication capabilities to be implemented and sufficient to share knowledge and to get in contact with other learners in order to succeed. It is both, psychological needs to have social contacts as well as advantages in learning. Sharing thoughts and explaining learning matter to other learners is motivating and important. To fulfil such needs, e-learning systems must not cut off communication, but encourage it and assist in co-operative learning. As this is crucial for sustained learning, students need a competence framework with the competences to co-operate and to communicate by means of informatics systems (ICT). It is very important to be able to discuss with others to verify and refine their own theories and to receive confirmations or correction hints concerning their learning steps [9]. Communication technologies are used in e-learning, such as email, chat sessions, and discussion boards, to engage students in the exchange of ideas or information. Today the term e-learning 2.0 refers to the increasing use of co-operative software, such as blogs and wikis which are gaining popularity as writing and publishing facilities for multiple users. This leads to the criteria efficiency (B4: with the sub-criteria time behaviour and resource behaviour) and confidentiality (C3) of e-learning systems.

A3. Activities of students as important steps of the learning process
The notion of learning as cognitive process has changed significantly. In constructivism, learning is no longer considered as externally transfusing knowledge, but as a constructive process in each learner. This implies learning is considered as an active process. Regarding learning theories it gets obvious that they cannot be implemented with comparable effort, since a theory of learner's complexity in gathering knowledge implies an appropriate complexity of methods to interact with learners in e-learning systems. Consequently, e-learning systems for complex learning theories like constructivism must give all possibilities to become active and enable learners to take part in directing their own learning process. This leads to the criteria functionality (B1: with the sub-criteria suitability, accuracy, interoperability, compliance, and security) and access control (C4) in e-learning systems.

A4. Priority to meet learning objectives
E-learning primarily aims at supporting the described learning objectives but not the use of informatics systems per se [8]. Hence, it is absolutely essential to guarantee the objectives of an equivalent traditional learning process. This leads to the criterion of usability (B3) of e-learning systems.

A5. Flexible learning
Current models of learning propagate a shift of responsibility from teacher to learner, i.e., learner-centred scenarios are to be developed. "The design aims towards a user-centred, trainee-centred, interactive, collective, collaborative structure for the web-based learning environment that allows the individual to collect, organize and re-contextualize knowledge." [10, p. 1]. This is one cause for the requirement of changeability of the informatics systems in such a learning environment. Another cause is the gap between previous knowledge and new expectations of a course. The teacher or tutor knows the previous knowledge and skills of the students and the intended learning outcomes which can be expressed in terms of competences. Hence, each e-learning system has to be adapted to the special target group of learners. This leads to the criteria maintainability (B5) and integrity (C2) of e-learning systems.

A6. Integration of e-learning in the learning environment
Learning is a process which needs a carefully designed learning environment. The mainstream of e-learning develops toward blended learning. This means, traditional education and e-learning are merging. But ICT supported learning should

not automatically be named blended learning. Stacey and Gerbic analyzed numerous definition attempts in literature and created a valuable definition: "In our application of the term blended learning, ICT may be used to either enhance the dominant mode of face-to-face on-campus interaction and or may provide a blend of synchronous and asynchronous media (that can also include face-to-face classes) to complement a dominant mode of distance education." [15, p. 3]. This leads to the criteria reliability (B2: with the sub-criteria maturity, recoverability, fault tolerance), availability (C1), and access control (C4) of e-learning systems.

B. Implications from software engineering

Software quality is classified in a structured set of criteria and sub-criteria as follows: functionality (B1), reliability (B2), usability (B3), efficiency (B4), maintainability (B5), and portability (B6). We only discuss B1 and B5 in detail because their role in the context of e-learning could be misunderstood.

B1, functionality, is a set of attributes that bear on the existence of a set of functions and their specified properties. Sub-criteria are suitability, accuracy, interoperability, compliance, and security. Security aspects increased importance correlated with the wide spread usage of informatics systems and increasing interconnections [13]. Unfortunately, most of the literature found for information security are books that address either the field of security in a holistic way by using examples like military or financial environments [3], or specialized publications that only address single aspects of security, e.g., cryptography [14]. All of these publications concentrate only on technical security issues. Even articles directly concerning the area of privacy and security in e-learning are mostly focused on technical issues like traffic analysis, cryptography, or distributed logging mechanisms.

B5, maintainability, is a set of attributes that bear on the effort needed to make modifications. Sub-criteria are stability, analyzability, changeability, and testability. B5 is the key to reusability and standardization of learning objects in e-learning systems. The two main concepts are "Learning Object Metadata" (http://ltsc.ieee.org) and "Sharable Content Object Reference Model" (http://www.adlnet.org).

C. Implications from information security

In the early 1980s, Voydock and Kent [17] wrote about security in "High-Level Network Protocols". Their disjunctive subdivision of the security problems "unauthorized release of information", "unauthorized modification of information", and "unauthorized denial of resource use" lead to today's widely used security services "confidentiality", "integrity", and "availability".

"Security of e-learning is not to be restricted to the technical system. It is necessary to cover the entire environment, including the organizational process of teaching, administration and examining." [18, p. 22]. Hence, for sensible security considerations all affiliated users have to be integrated. It is "always a combination of objectives, people, procedures, and tools." [12, p. 32] Using this cognisance, Åhlfeldt et al. [1] introduced an extended security model aiming at organizational problems. The resulting TFI model (three main parts for security: TFI = Technical-Formal-Informal Security) considers the technical security as only one third of the whole security investigation. In addition to this, formal security like external regimentation, e.g., law, or superior policies as well as internal regimentation with local adaptations and more fine-grained policies fitting the exact situation need to be investigated, stated, and verified to keep an environment secure. The informal security as third part of the model aims at the users of the system. Security policies are only valuable, if all participants are conscious of their meanings and do not try to circumvent them. Hence, this informal security considers clarifying about security concerns to prevent users from undermining necessary mechanisms. We use the following definition of security of e-learning:

An e-learning system is described as secure if it guarantees availability (C1), integrity (C2), and confidentiality (C3) for all users in combination with access control (C4).

C1. Availability: An e-learning server is called available if it is reachable over a network almost every time it is needed with sufficient resources. Service intervals must be kept short and announced adequately in advance. Failures, if any, should only lead to short interruptions.

C2. Integrity: Modifications of transmitted or stored data must be detectable. If reasoned by technical defects, fault tolerance and error correction can be applied. If reasoned by fraudulent usage, originator and context should be disclosed.

C3. Confidentiality: For individual information security (privacy), e.g., learning progress, data must be kept secret. It is in the decision of the learners themselves to discard or submit their solutions and problems while learning to other parties like teachers.

C4. Access control: Users cannot transfer or increase the received privileges even if they collaborate without the perpetrator being identified.

Coming to the interdisciplinary research for security in e-learning, there are only few publications that address this special domain. Within this, Weippl [18], for example, gives an overview of this field in a superficial way. He regards risk analysis processes as well as informal subjective requirements as seen from the viewpoint of different roles in the system, i.e., authors, managers, teachers, and students. In addition to this, general introductions to access control mechanisms as well as to cryptography mentioned and sketched coarsely without closer discussion about the complexity of application and their respective implementation in e-learning environments.

Graf [7] discusses web-based assessment and the necessity of deliberations. He developed for this a software environment to be used in controlled learning environments that exchanges RMI-messages (RMI = Remote Method Invocation) between Java applets on the client-side and a Java application on the assessment server. With this approach he can assure critical elements of assessment like time-fairness and continuation after abort if still in time. Due to the focus on assessment, usually necessary investigations about privacy protection and communication and co-operation capabilities in e-learning are explicitly neglected by Graf [7, p. 2].

Deliberations concerning privacy protection demands in educational environments can be found in [2]. Alicia Anderson investigated privacy protection in present universities using informatics systems to administer several tasks and to hold personal information. As major problem she states the fact that "the academic culture often puts a lower priority on information security in relation to openness" [2, p. 16]. This "culture of openness" often considers security and privacy as hindering technologies, although numerous incidents showed up the organizational value and need for protection of privacy.

3 Theoretical Realizations of the Design Criteria

This article primarily aims at information security investigations in e-learning. Hence, other related implications and approaches from software engineering and human-computer-interaction will be neglected in this place although relevant, too, for implementing qualitative good and well usable systems.

A1: Equal opportunities

Treating all learners equally from a security point of view primarily demands that availability and especially the quality and performance of available systems must be ensured. Within this, a main problem besides technical failures will be denial-of-service (DoS) attacks by creating a lot of traffic or provoking system failures. For this, filtering malformed packets, load balancing on incoming requests, and quality of service settings (QoS) for network connections should be taken into account. In addition, productive environments must be built redundantly with fall-back systems, such that erroneous parts can be easily replaced by others, i.e., ensure "business continuity" [18]. For the case of security incidents appropriate response deliberations must be at hand like a team of experts to analyze the attack for disclosing the problem and circumvent it in other systems [19]. In addition, computer forensic work enables criminal prosecution of attackers.

A2: Social support by co-operation and communication

For enabling learners to communicate and co-operate adequately with an e-learning system we must ensure efficient data exchange. Hence, to communicate just in time, delays must be minimized which again is related to QoS and DoS as mentioned above. In addition, reliability concerns must be managed, such that established communications will not be disconnected regularly and collaborative results can be stored reliably with only negligible risk of data loss.

Closely coupled to the results of collaborative work is data integrity. The system must guarantee that no one can fraudulently modify results interchanged between participating learners at least without getting disclosed. Integrity also is important concerning the correctness of learning material as well as personal data. Especially relevant information for issuing a certificate must be unaltered. Digital signatures can help disclosing manipulations by third parties as well as hashing mechanisms or error correcting codes can be sufficient for accidental changes or alterations because of technical reasons like malfunctions.

For keeping results private until submission the data confidentiality is essential. Confidentiality of transmitted data can be solved with methods provided by cryptographic researches. Sometimes anonymity is considered as part of confidentiality, too. Especially the secrecy of connection data that could be disclosed by traffic analysis can be relevant for commercial participants with background of economical impact.

A3: Activities of students as important steps of the learning process

Enabling a high degree of interaction and activity increases the complexity of a system significantly and thus security issues must be considered accordingly. Most relevant are access privileges for possible tasks and activities in the e-learning system. With respect to hierarchical structures in traditional teaching role based access control seems best applicable. Roles in general can be centrally managed by the system administrator. He can adjust their privilege settings and assign users to special roles. Hence, with sufficiently detailed and appropriate privilege settings, learners can be active without disturbing others and without being distracted by unauthorized interventions.

A4: Priority to meet learning objectives

To keep the learners focused on their learning process, the e-learning system should remain hidden behind easily reachable functionality. Especially information security mechanisms must be comprehensive to be accepted and used sensibly. For this, besides well explaining dialogues, education concerning the informatics systems and possible threats is reasonable.

With respect to authentication processes it makes sense to use already existing and well approved systems. The service of authentication is vital to all other security services, since only with appropriate authentication, privileges and identities can be assigned to the user correctly. It is sensible to use well known and easily applicable authentication systems with sufficient security mostly based on cryptography. No password or otherwise sensitive data for an authentication process must be discernible by eavesdropping the network. Sophisticated authentication methods like biometrics or challenge-response methods, e.g., using digital signatures, are reasonable but not applicable in all environments. However, necessities to authenticate can interrupt the learners in their current thought, so using central authentication services, e.g., using Shibboleth, Kerberos, or directory services, allow single sign-on solutions where learners have only to authenticate once and can access all functionality according to their privileges.

A5: Flexible learning

Highly flexible learning environments enable close adjustments to a specific target group. Concerning access control as introduced above a two-sided approach with global and local roles is sensible. Global roles can be used for general course-independent privilege settings, whereas inside of courses teachers should be able to create and manage local roles to allow a more fine-grained privilege setting, since for every affiliated person or group a special setting can be used. Desirable for this is a system that audits the whole role and privilege structure to disclose contradictions and inconsistencies.

A6: Integration of e-learning into the learning environment

For a seamless integration of e-learning into existing learning environments such a system must be as fast and reliable as possible, and available with such high quality that it clearly shows to be advantageous for learning. Information security with all facets mentioned must therefore be considered and applied in order to guarantee almost equal quality and reliability as other (traditional) learning sources would do.

4 Practical Work on a Proxy Server for Automated Security Processes

At the author's institute a proxy server for digitally signing e-learning content is being developed [5]. Such a proxy server primarily aims at being sort of a personal secretary in such a way that it can perform certain security related tasks for the learners to keep them concentrated on their learning process. Proxy servers run logically on the application layer, i.e., ISO/OSI layer 7, and therefore, they can examine and alter packets passing them just like the users themselves could do.

First of all, the implementation aims at a small and fast program that is available for most platforms, i.e., platform independent implementation, and that can be integrated in almost every network without noticeable constrains. In this context a main realization goal is the conformity to the Hypertext Transfer Protocol in version 1.1 (HTTP/1.1) as specified in [6]. This ensures easy embedding even in complex network architectures as long as the other components are compliant to this standard as well. In conjunction with the functionality of the network, the proxy server has to cope with several simultaneous connections. Otherwise, the first connection would block the proxy server and no other connection could take place before the first one has been reset. Due to the demand of high degree of freedom and little constraints this must be prevented. For the sake of performance of established connections, and therefore, the quality of use, we propose a restricted storage of packets by forwarding data as fast as possible to the e-learning system. Hence, payload data needs to be forwarded immediately while the signature can be computed on a stored copy of the whole message and afterwards be appended to the stream. A high configurability of the proxy server is necessary for using it in the wide variety of networks used in practice and to allow individual users' adjustments.

This proxy approach offers many possibilities for establishing security tasks or cryptographic processes concerning exchanged data. In the first step, we were implementing digital signing routines to ensure integrity of learning content and communication messages. For this case we propose a university wide public key infrastructure (PKI) that supports the users in generating and administering their pair of keys. Regarding the functionality of the proxy, it must, of course, have access to the private key of the user. The private key can be stored on a smart card with own signing functionality, a USB stick, or, if created on the currently used computer, locally on the hard disk drive. Since private keys should be protected by a pass phrase or other authentication methods, the proxy will have to demand the identification of the user. After this step, the proxy signs all messages sent to a learning management system and verifies signatures embedded in requested contents. For evaluating embedded signatures it needs access to corresponding public keys that can be provided by a key server managing all known public keys of the university wide PKI.

Since the proxy server has to communicate in some scenarios like warning the user if an incoming message was altered fraudulently, this should preferably take place in the language of the learner for being as comfortable as possible. For the way of communication there exists the possibility of building a graphical user interface or the approach of modifying the HTTP stream, i.e., the proxy server can add some message text or colour bar for example on top of the requested web page to signalize the security status of this site. To manage transparency for all users and to not distract other learners, it is sensible to store the signature in a way that learners or teachers not using the described proxy server cannot see the cryptographic signature code at first sight. For achieving this, it has to be stored in tags that are not displayed. Since most learning management systems contain a content management system filtering user entries, there is no general solution how to hide those signatures.

The concept of using a proxy server as secretary is very flexible. Therefore, in a further step, the authentication process could be automated as well. As far as the pass phrase for the private key of the user is strong and kept secret, the digital signature can be used as authentication method in challenge-response scenarios where the server sends a randomly generated string and gets an encrypted version of this string as answer. This enables a cryptographically secure authentication method that cannot be repeated by an eavesdropper.

5 Conclusions

We introduced six main criteria for designing e-learning offerings with respect to findings from educational science. Since every criterion applied in implementing such a system increases the system's complexity, this undoubtedly leads to further demands for information security investigation to meet newly emerging security issues. This article discussed theoretical realization aspects addressing those security concerns. As proof of concept, a prototypical implementation of a proxy server was introduced. This proxy server is implemented at the authors' institute for the task of digitally signing messages sent to a learning management system. Although the current prototype shows the feasibility of applying and implementing stated design criteria, further research is necessary to concretize relevant criteria for necessary parts of a learning environment integrating e-learning.

References

1. Åhlfeldt, R.-M., Spagnoletti, P., Sindre, G.: Improving the Information Security Model by using TFI. In: [16], pp. 73–85
2. Anderson, A.: Effective Management of Information Security and Privacy. Educause Quarterly Journal (1), 15–20 (2006)
3. Anderson, R.: Security Engineering – A Guide to Building Dependable Distributed Systems. Wiley Computer Publishing, New York (2001)
4. Eibl, C.J.: Information Security in E-Learning. In: Abbott, C., Lustigova, Z. (eds.) Information Technologies for Education and Training. Proc. of IFIP iTET, University of Prague, pp. 204–213 (2007)
5. Eibl, C.J., von Solms, S.H., Schubert, S.: Development and Application of a Proxy Server for Transparently, Digitally Signing E-Learning Content. In: [16], pp. 181–192 (2007)
6. Fielding, R., Gettys, J., Mogul, J., Frystyk, H., Masinter, L., Leach, P., Berners-Lee, T.: Hypertext Transfer Protocol. HTTP/1.1. Request for Comments (RFC) 2616 (1999)
7. Graf, F.: Lernspezifische Sicherheitsmechanismen in Lernumgebungen mit modularem Lernmaterial. Dissertation thesis (German), TU Darmstadt (2002)
8. Hamid, A.A.: e-Learning: Is it the "e" or the learning that matters? Internet and Higher Education 4(3), 311–316 (2002)
9. Hills, P.J.: Teaching and Learning as a Communication Process. Croom Helm, London (1979)
10. Koulountzos, V., Seroglou, F.: Designing a web-based learning environment. The case of ATLAS. In: Benzie, D., Iding, M. (eds.) Informatics, Mathematics and ICT: A golden triangle. Proceedings, Boston, USA, June 27-29 (2007) ISBN-13: 978-0-615-14623-2
11. Lave, J., Wenger, E.: Situated learning: Legitimate peripheral participation. Cambridge University Press, New York (1991)
12. McCarthy, M.P., Campbell, S.: Security Transformation: Digital Defense Strategies to Protect Your Company's Reputation & Market Share. McGraw-Hill, New York (2001)
13. National Research Council (U.S.): Computers at Risk: Safe Computing in the Information Age. National Academy Press, Washington, DC (1991)
14. Schneier, B.: Applied Cryptography, 2nd edn. Wiley, New York (1996)
15. Stacey, E., Gerbic, P.: Teaching for blended learning. How is ICT impacting on distance and on campus education? In: Kumar, D., Turner, J. (eds.) Education for the 21st Century-Impact of ICT and Digital Resources: Proceedings of the IFIP 19th World Computer Congress, TC-3, Education, pp. 225–234. Springer, Boston (2006)
16. Venter, H., Eloff, M., Labuschagne, L., Eloff, J., von Solms, R.: New Approaches for Security, Privacy and Trust in Complex Environments. IFIP sec2007. Springer, New York (2007)
17. Voydock, V.L., Kent, S.T.: Security Mechanisms in High-Level Network Protocols. ACM Computing Surveys 15(2), 135–171 (1983)
18. Weippl, E.R.: Security in E-Learning. Springer, New York (2005)
19. Yasinsac, A., Manzano, Y.: Policies to Enhance Computer and Network Forensics. In: Proceedings of the 2001 IEEE Workshop on Information Assurance and Security, United States Military Academy, West Point, NY, June 5-6 (2001)

On the Technological Aspects of Generative Learning Object Development

Robertas Damaševičius and Vytautas Štuikys

Kaunas University of Technology,
Software Engineering Department,
Studentų 50-415, Kaunas, Lithuania
robertas.damasevicius@ktu.lt, vystu@if.ktu.lt

Abstract. Learning Objects (LOs) are digital resources that can be used (and reused) to support the learning process. Generative Learning Objects (GLOs) are generic and reusable LOs from which the specific LO content can be generated on demand. We discuss the technological aspects required for implementing the GLOs: (1) variability modeling using feature diagrams, (2) multi-dimensional separation of the LO design concerns, (3) multiple languages for implementing a LO specification, (4) an external metalanguage for implementing parameterization, generalization and modification of a LO, and (5) heterogeneous metaprogramming techniques for generating LO instances from the generic LO specifications on demand. An example of a GLO for teaching array sorting algorithms in a programming curriculum is presented.

1 Introduction

Currently, an instructional technology, called "*learning objects*" (LOs) [1], is leading as technology of choice for e-Learning support due to its potential generativity, adaptability, and scalability [2]. The concept of LO is the most important concept in the learning domain due to many reasons:

- A learner needs to know why and what to learn.
- A teacher needs to know and understand why, what to teach and how to deliver the content to the learner.
- A course designer needs to know and understand what to design and how to represent the content for storing and sharing.
- Curricula developers need to know and understand why, what and how to plan and additionally - where and when - the courses are integrated into teaching plans.

LOs are generally understood to be digital entities deliverable over the Internet where they can be accessed and used simultaneously by many learners. Furthermore, LOs are intended to be reused multiple times in different contexts, used independently or grouped into larger collections of content, including traditional course structures.

Though reusability was in the focus of the researchers for long time, so far it was understood narrowly, mostly in terms of component-based reuse. However, in recent years there is a noticeable trend to enhance LO reusability by introducing novel approaches, such as glass-box LOs [3], aspect-oriented LOs [4], adaptive LOs [5] or LOs based on object programming concepts [6].

The main idea of LO is to break educational content down into small chunks that can be reused in various learning environments [7]. When reused, such small chunks of educational content are combined in various ways leading to a great variability of the learning content. Such variability cannot be modeled using UML [8], which has no adequate means for expressing different variants of configurations of a system. The development of LOs still remains a vague issue, because there is no clearly defined and widely adopted LO specification and development methodology as, e.g, in software engineering, where classes and objects are modeled using UML, a standardized graphical specification and modeling language.

Currently, technology advances enable teachers and course designers to create the content in a variety of versions. Modifications, changes and adaptations of the content are common reuse activities. The need for adaptation increases with technological advances and expansion of the e-Learning domain. If adaptations are done *ad hoc*, this may lead to the uncontrolled growth of similar versions causing additional difficulties in storing, sharing and reusing LOs. If adaptations can be done automatically, we have a more powerful kind of reuse, called *generative reuse*. Recently T. Boyle *et al.* [9, 10] have proposed the concept of Generative Learning Objects (GLOs), which is based on separating the LO design from the instantiation of the LO content and using templates as a generative technology. The approach provides more capabilities LO design, focuses on LO quality issues, and introduces a solid basis for a marked improvement in LO design productivity.

To extend the reusability of LOs, we need a more attentive look to the LO domain itself from the reuse perspective; or more precisely, we need to analyze commonality and variability of LOs systematically. Though learning theories [11, 12] actually recognize and consider many features that might be conceived as commonality and variability, they emphasize the pedagogical or psychological viewpoint only, without explicit representation of variability and without any intent of using generative technologies explicitly. As LOs represent the content that may vary across different courses and the delivery of content relates also to pedagogical aspects (e.g., motivation, scenarios, teaching theories, etc.), social aspects (e.g., teachers' preferences, students' abilities, collaborative e-Learning, self-learning, etc.), and technological aspects (e.g., representation in e-Learning, or in m-Learning, etc.), the boundaries of variability may be extremely large.

Our approach is based on the concept of GLOs already introduced in the domain [9, 10], instructional design [7, 11], Scope-Commonality-Variability (SCV) analysis [13] of related LOs, explicit representation of interface and functionality in the LO model [14], and the heterogeneous metaprogramming techniques [15, 16].

This paper is a continuation of a work on the development of GLOs [17]. Here we further extend on GLO technological implementation aspects using feature diagrams for feature modeling of LOs, and heterogeneous metaprogramming techniques for generating LO instances on demand from the generic LO specification (in Section 2). An illustrative example on the development of sorting algorithm GLO is presented in Section 3. Section 4 summarizes and evaluates the capabilities of the approach and presents indications on some limitations and tasks for future work.

2 Technological Aspects of GLO Development

2.1 Variability Modeling Using Feature Diagrams

Given the likelihood of the broad deployment of LO-based technology and the dangers of employing it in an instructionally unprincipled manner, there is a clear need for a solid methodological and technological background. In such context, we propose using *feature diagrams* for modeling learning content. Originally, feature diagrams were introduced in the FODA (*Feature Oriented Domain Analysis*) methodology in 1990 [18]. Since then, they have undergone several extensions [19, 20] intended to improve their expressiveness and extend their semantics. Feature diagrams first were applied in the context of industrial manufacturing product lines, e.g., for modeling car assembly lines. Later, the idea was extended to software product lines. A software product line is a set of software systems that share a common, managed set of features satisfying the specific needs that are developed from a common set of core assets in a prescribed way [21]. The concept, if applied systematically, allows for dramatic increase of software design quality and productivity, provides a capability for mass customization and leads to the "industrial" software design [22].

Based on the success of feature modeling and product lines in the industrial manufacturing and software engineering domains, we propose using *feature diagrams* in the e-Learning domain for specification, representation and structuring of learning content. We hope that feature modeling of learning content would ease maintenance of learning content, reduce its redundancy and duplication, allow for easy customization when applying for different teaching aims, student groups, and e-learning environments, and provide a global framework for coordinating the re-engineering and reuse of LOs.

Furthermore, feature diagrams are also important for constructing domain ontologies by providing views on ontologies [23, 24] in order to acquire a common understanding of the learning domain. Ontology is a conceptual specification that describes knowledge about a domain [25]. The construction of such ontologies allows providing shared and common understanding of a specific domain and facilitates knowledge sharing and reuse.

There are several definitions of what a feature is. Informally, features are key distinctive characteristics of a system. FODA defines a feature as a prominent and distinctive user visible characteristic of a system [18]. ODM (*Organization Domain Modelling*) defines feature as a distinguishable characteristic of a "concept" (e.g., artifact, area of knowledge, etc.) that is relevant to some stakeholders (e.g., analysts, designers, and developers) [26]. When comparing to other conceptual abstractions (such as function, object, and aspect), features are externally visible characteristics, whereas functions, objects, and aspects have been mainly used to specify the internal details of a system. Therefore, feature modeling focuses on identifying externally visible characteristics of products in terms of commonality and variability, rather than describing all details of a system.

The result of feature modeling is a *feature model*. Features are identified and classified in terms of capabilities, domain technologies, implementation techniques, and operating environments. Capabilities are user visible characteristics that can be identified as distinct services, operations, and non-functional characteristics. Domain technologies represent the way of implementing services or operations. Implementation techniques are generic functions or techniques that are used to implement services, operations, and domain functions. Operating environments represent environments in which applications are used.

Features are primarily used in order to discriminate between LO instances. Common features among different products are modeled as *mandatory* features, while different features among them may be *optional* or *alternative*. Optional features represent selectable features for products of a given domain and alternative features indicate that no more than one feature can be selected for a product.

A feature diagram is a graphical AND/OR hierarchy of features that captures structural or conceptual relationships among features. A feature diagram consists of a set of *nodes*, a set of directed *edges* and a set of edge *decorations*. The nodes and edges form a *tree*. The edge decorations are drawn as arcs connecting subsets or all of the edges originating from the same node. The root of a feature diagram represents a concept. Features (see Table 1) can be mandatory (and-features), optional, alternative (or-features, case-features). *And-features* are denoted with a filled circle. *Or-features* are denoted with an empty circle. *Extension points* are features that have at least one optional subfeature, an edge ending in an empty circle, or at least one set of direct or-(sub)features. Extension points with optional features are simply denoted as edges ending in an empty circle. Extension points with or-features use a filled decorated edge arc, the edges ending in a filled circle to denote the mandatory features.

Three types of relationships are represented in a feature diagram. The *composed-of* relationship is used if there is a whole-part relationship between a feature and its sub-features. In cases where features are a generalization of sub-features, they are

Table 1. Feature attributes for feature model representation

Feature type	Definition and formal description	Graphical notation
Mandatory	Feature B (C, D) is included if its parent A is included **if** A **then** B; **if** A **then** B **and** C	
Optional	Feature B (C, D) may be included if its parent A is included **if** A **then** B or *no feature* **if** A **then** B **or** C **or** *no feature*	
Alternative (case-selection)	Exactly one feature (B or C or D) has to be selected if its parent A is selected **if** A **then** *case of* (B, C, D)	
Alternative (or-selection)	At least one feature (B, C or D; or B and C; or B and D; or C and D; or B and C and D) has to be selected if its parent A is selected **if** A **then** *any of* (B, C, D)	

organized using the generalization/specialization relationship. The *implemented-by* relationship is used when a feature (i.e., a feature of an implementation technique) is necessary to implement the other feature. Moreover, features have *dependencies*: the selection of one feature may rule out (mutual exclusion) or assume (requires, includes) the inclusion of another feature.

Aggregation of features represents all variability within the scope of the domain and it is used to construct the domain feature model, or feature model. The derivation of a product consists of traversing the feature tree in an orderly manner and selecting the optional features. The result is a product description containing all the features in the product (a feature configuration). In product line terminology, a product is fully specified when all of its variation points are bound; that is the product specification is complete when all features have been selected.

Feature diagrams provide a concise and explicit representation of variability. They guide the choices to be made for determining the features of specific products and facilitate the reuse of software components implementing these features. We apply feature diagrams as a tool for representing learning content and connecting between learning aims, teaching materials and LOs.

2.2 Multi-language Design

The educational, pedagogical, managerial, and knowledge theory aspects of the GLO model have already been discussed in [17]. Here we extend on the technological implementation aspects of the GLO model.

From the technological point of view, the proposed LO model is based on the paradigm of *multi-dimensional separation of concerns* [27], which claims that multiple dimensions of concerns in a design should be implemented independently. The separation of concerns is a usual way to deal with complex problems in a system design. We claim that different concerns of a design are best implemented when using separate languages for different purposes as follows:

1) Domain language(s) implement various aspects of domain functionality.
2) External language(s) (e.g., preprocessing, scripting, meta-language) implement generalization of the repetitive design features, introduce variations, and integrate components into a design.

Using multiple languages that are more suitable and efficient for the specification of subsystems of a large system is called the multi-language design [28] paradigm. The multi-language design introduces a clear separation of concerns in a design by using different languages in the multi-language specification(s) [29] from which a LO is composed of.

With the arrival of the internet-based technologies, the multi-language design gained the popularity. The examples of multi-language specifications are JavaScript, Java applets and servlets embedded in HTML documents, CGI (Common Gateway Interface) programming, dynamic web page generation using PHP, JSP (Java Server Pages) or ASP (Active Server Pages), mobile code systems, etc. For example, in CGI programming, the concerns are clearly separated between "interface" (HTML forms) and "information processing" (PERL commands for text file processing). In Java servlets, different languages represent different levels of abstraction. Java is used for processing user requests and generating HTML code. HTML is used for GUI interfacing and reading user requests. Therefore, we have a clear separation of concerns "interface" and "request processing".

Such separation of concerns is also important in the LO-based learning, where the representation aspects of learning content should be separated from the content itself and from any embedded functionality. Such separation allows achieving higher reusability and portability of LOs between various e-Learning platforms and environments.

2.3 Metaprogramming

The genericity and generativity aspects of GLOs are supported by a metalanguage, which supports parameterization, creation of generic components in a domain, domain code generation and other metaprogramming techniques.

In general, metaprogramming is defined as a manipulation with programs as data [15]. A common usage of metaprogramming is to provide mechanisms for writing generic code, i.e. explicitly implementing generalization in the domain. Domain language implements commonalties in a domain, while a metalanguage allows developers to specify variations to be implemented in the domain system, and to synthesize customized implementations by composing domain code fragments. Generalization is achieved by the parameterization of differences in different domain program representations, which allows representing domain components with many commonalties in a compact way.

Genericity is usually achieved by the parameterization of differences in different program representations, which allows representing components with many commonalties in a compact way. This simple feature of metaprogramming allows improving reusability substantially by providing parameterized components, which can be instantiated into target programs for different choices of parameters.

The basis of metaprogramming is a separation of the domain artifacts from the knowledge how to customize and glue them together. The higher-level program (metaprogram or metaspecification) uses pieces of lower level constructs as data and allows representing variability of domain artifacts at a higher level of abstraction concisely. This allows achieving generalization and automatic creation of the customized programs.

Metaprogramming can be implemented in several ways. At the abstraction level, we need to analyze the capabilities of the language and separate the concerns, which relate to implementing the basic functionality from those, which allow expressing generic solutions and customized specifications. This separation may be accomplished, for example, implicitly using only the internal capabilities of a given domain language, or explicitly either introducing some extensions to the domain language (*homogeneous metaprogramming*) or using an *external metalanguage*.

In this paper, we use the *heterogeneous metaprogramming* techniques, which combine two different languages in the same specification: a *metalanguage* is used at the higher layer of abstraction for representing manipulations on domain language source code, and a *domain language* is used for representing domain program instances. As LO instances are typically represented in XML (or HTML, XHTML, etc.) format they are actually domain programs.

2.4 Development of a Generative (Generic) Specification

The development of the generative specification (metaprogram or GLO) using the metaprogramming approach consists of the following stages:

1) Introduction of a model for representing a GLO;
2) Application of a LO model for representing LO instances;
3) Identification of commonality-variability in the explicit form for the given family of related LO instances;
4) Selection of a metalanguage;
5) Introduction of a metalanguage constructs into the LO specification leading to the development of the GLO specification;
6) Testing and validation of the GLO specification; and
7) Incorporation of the GLO into an e-Learning environment.

We have selected our own metalanguage Open PROMOL [12] because: 1) it contains a wide spectrum of commands for the manipulation with text; 2) it is based on the use of the functional approach and its functions are close to the syntax of most known programming languages; 3) we have a long experience in using it in teaching and learning; and 4) it has a clear (human readable and computer readable) metainterface. The latter is the most essential requirement for the LO domain because the LO user is usually not a programmer.

We distinguish between the metadata which is the metainterface of the GLO specification, and the LO instances generated from the GLO. Variability parameters are represented as metaparameters at a higher level of abstraction in the GLO metainterface, while the commonality-variability relationships are coded at a lower-level within the body of the GLO metaspecification. The role of the metainterface is to allow an educator to select the parameters of the GLO which reflect different features and variability of the GLO. Selection of the different values of these parameters can be used for LO personalization and tuning for different teaching tasks and student proficiency levels.

The body of the GLO is hidden from the end-user (because the technological details of meta-programming are important only for a GLO developer/programmer). The GLO is usually accessible only for an educator and is stored on the LO server repository. By selecting the metaparameters of GLO and using the metalanguage processor, the GLO is instantiated, i.e., the specific LO instances are generated. The role of LO instances is to present a specific personalized learning content to the students. These LO instances can be aggregated with other LO instances to make up a course topic (lecture). Therefore, students can access LO instances using an internet browser and can use it for learning course topics as well as for performing individual course tasks during course lab hours.

3 Case Study: Development of a GLO for Teaching Array Sorting Algorithms

In our case study, we consider the array sorting algorithms implemented in various programming languages as LOs. Such LOs could be used in different programming teaching courses to demonstrate the principles and effectiveness of the array sorting algorithms within the internet-based e-Learning environment independently from a particular programming language. As there are many similarities in the description and implementation of such LOs, they could be described as a single GLO, from which the specific LO instances could be generated at any time.

Sorting GLO has many variable features, which can be represented using a feature diagram (see Fig. 1): learning objective (principles or effectiveness), and algorithm, and demonstration. Demonstration features include sorting order (ascending or descending), and implementation language (Pascal, C++, Java, or any combination of these languages can be used for demonstration of sorting algorithm implementation), and platform (Desktop or Mobile). These features form a feature space of the GLO.

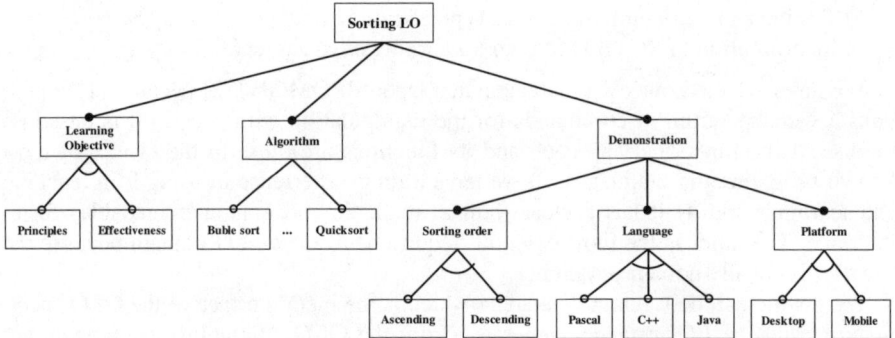

Fig. 1. Feature diagram of array sorting algorithm LO

Based on the feature diagram of sorting GLO, a GLO specification is developed. The values of the parameters to implement the generalization are described in the meta-interface of the GLO specification (see Fig. 2). The user (lecturer, teacher) can select different learning objectives (e.g., demonstrate the principles of sorting for a particular algorithm, or its effectiveness in terms of operations), select a particular sorting algorithm, select a sorting order (either descending or ascending), and a programming language for an example of implementation (Pascal, C++, Java). Different combinations of selected values can lead to 216 (216=2·9·2·3·2) different LO instances generated from this single GLO metaspecification.

```
$
"Identify the learning objective:
      1- principles, 2- effectiveness"        {1,2}       goal:=2;
"Select a sorting algorithm:
      1- Bubble Sort, 2- Selection sort,
      3- Insertion sort, 4- Shell sort,
      5- Merge sort, 6- Heapsort,
      7- Quicksort, 8- Bucket sort,
      9- Radix sort"                          {1..9}      algorithm:=1;
"Select a sorting order:
      1- descending, 2- ascending"            {1,2}       order:=2;
"Select an implementation language:
      1- Pascal, 2- C++, 3- Java"             {1,2,3}     language:=1;
"Select target platform:
      1- Desktop(HTML), 2- Mobile(xHTML)"     {1,2}       platform:=2;
$
```

Fig. 2. Example of GLO metaspecification in Open PROMOL (interface only)

Using the specified interface options, the metalanguage processor generates a LO implemented in HTML+Javascript, which can be distributed over the Internet. The HTML part of the LO is used for presentation of the natural language description of a sorting algorithm and for presentation of its implementation in a specific programming language, while Javascript is used for demonstration of the principles or effectiveness of a specific sorting algorithm.

The examples of the generated specific sorting algorithm LOs as seen via the PC's standard internet browser or mobile phone are given in Fig. 3. The LO introduces the student with the description and implementation of the Bubble sort algorithm, and demonstrates it in action. The array for sorting is generated after pressing the button "Generate". And then the sorting process is demonstrated after pressing the button "Bubble sort".

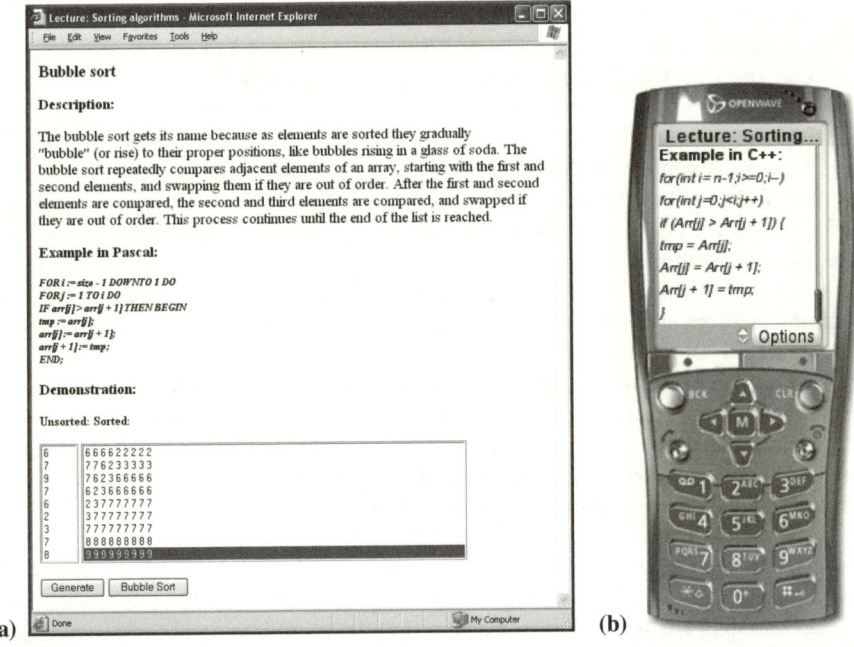

Fig. 3. Examples of LOs: (a) Bubble sort; Pascal; Desktop; and (b) Bubble sort; C++; Mobile (a fragment)

4 Conclusions and Future Work

Reusability is a fundamental feature of LOs. Though reusability aspects, such as the component view to LOs or the role of granularity for reusable components and models, were at the focus of researchers for long time, the efforts to enhance these aspects towards generative reuse are expanding only now. Examples of this shift are the introduction novel models that support adaptation of LOs (e.g., glass-box reuse model, aspect-oriented LOs, adaptive LOs, LOs based on object programming concepts) and the concept of Generative Learning Object (GLO).

In this paper, we have discussed the technological aspects required for implementing GLOs. These include: 1) LO variability modeling using Feature Diagrams (FDs), 2) multi-dimensional separation of LO design concerns, 3) multiple languages for implementing a LO specification, 4) an external metalanguage for implementing parameterization, generalization and modification of a LO, and 5) heterogeneous metaprogramming techniques for generating LO instances on demand from the GLO metaspecifications.

FD can be seen as a means for: 1) graphical representation of knowledge of the entire family of related LOs by providing domain ontologies using feature concepts, their types, values and relationships; 2) specification of variability-communality relationships of LOs at a higher level of abstraction in order to develop and implement GLOs systematically; 3) analysis and better understanding of the learning domain itself because FDs enable to express granularity, compositionality and context explicitly to support reusability of learning content.

The advantages of using GLOs are as follows: 1) higher LO quality due to GLOs that could be developed and tested by experts; 2) increase in productivity due to automatic on-demand generation of the LO instances from the GLO metaspecification; 3) managing of related LO instances within a CMS (Content Management System) is simpler, because they are generated from a single meta-specification and then distributed to the learners in a variety of instances automatically; 4) flexibility for LO modification enabled by the selected generative technology; 5) even the same material within the educational systems can be easily tailored to both students' and teachers' individual needs and represented as a GLO; 6) the GLOs may be a part of the metadesign environments of the e-Learning systems (in the sense of the G. Fisher's *et al.* [30] *metadesign* concept).

The disadvantages of the approach are: 1) higher development costs due to the need of additional efforts for analysis; 2) the need of the additional tool support for the generative technology; 3) more complicated testing of GLOs; 4) the need for extensive experimentation in order to achieve a higher maturity; 5) the generative approach requires more precise explicit LO models.

As the related learning content may have a large variability dimension, a GLO can be viewed as a concise specification of the whole family of related LO instances. But it is not quite clear what the size and granularity of GLOs should be and what scope of GLO variability is optimal. The mechanism of explicit integration of learning units within a GLO is to be further extended, as well as the external composition of smaller LOs into larger GLOs. To enhance reusability, GLOs and their supporting environment are to be integrated into e-Learning systems. These problems require further research.

References

1. Learning Technology Standards Committee. IEEE Standard for Learning Object Metadata. IEEE Standard 1484.12.1. IEEE, New York (2002)
2. Wiley, D.A.: Learning Object Design and Sequencing Theory. PhD Thesis, Department of Instructional Psychology and Technology, Brigham Young University (June 2000)

3. Fournier-Viger, P., Mayers, A., Najjar, M., Nkambou, R.: A Cognitive and Logic Based Model for Building Glass-Box Learning Objects. Interdisciplinary Journal of Knowledge and Learning Objects 2, 77–94 (2006)
4. Pankratius, V.: Aspect-Oriented Learning Objects. In: Proc. of the 4th IASTED Int. Conf. on Web-Based Education (WBE 2005), Grindelwald, Switzerland, February 21-23 (2005)
5. Berlanga, A., Garcia, F.J.: A Proposal to Define Adaptive Learning Designs. In: Proc. of Workshop on Applications of Semantic Web Technologies for Educational Adaptive Hypermedia (SW-EL 2004) in AH 2004, Eindhoven, The Netherlands, August 23, 2004, pp. 354–358 (2004)
6. Mohan, P., Brooks, C.: Engineering a Future for Web-based Learning Objects. In: Cueva Lovelle, J.M., Rodríguez, B.M.G., Gayo, J.E.L., Ruiz, M.d.P.P., Aguilar, L.J. (eds.) ICWE 2003. LNCS, vol. 2722, pp. 120–123. Springer, Heidelberg (2003)
7. Wiley, D.A.: Connecting learning objects to instructional design theory: A definition, a metaphor, and a taxonomy. In: Wiley, D.A. (ed.) The Instructional Use of Learning Objects (2000)
8. Fowler, M.: UML Distilled: A Brief Guide to the Standard Object Modeling Language, 3rd edn. Addison-Wesley, Reading
9. Leeder, D., Boyle, T., Morales, R., Wharrad, H., Garrud, P.: To boldly GLO - Towards the Next Generation of Learning Objects. In: World Conference on e-Learning in Corporate, Government, Healthcare and Higher Education, Washington, USA, November 2004, pp. 28–33 (2004)
10. Morales, R., Leeder, D., Boyle, T.: A Case in the Design of Generative Learning Objects (GLO): Applied Statistical Methods GLOs. In: Proc. of World Conference on Educational Multimedia, Hypermedia and Telecommunications (ED-MEDIA 2005), Montreal, Canada, June 27-July 2, 2005, pp. 302–310 (2005)
11. Merrill, M.D.: Instructional Transaction Theory (ITT): Instructional Design Based on Knowledge Objects. In: Reigeluth, C.M. (ed.) Instructional-Design Theories and Models: A New Paradigm of Instructional Theory. Lawrence Erlbaum Associates, Mahwah (2000)
12. Štuikys, V., Damaševičius, R.: Scripting Language Open PROMOL and its Processor. Informatica 11(1), 71–86 (2000)
13. Coplien, J., Hoffman, D., Weiss, D.: Commonality and Variability in Software Engineering. IEEE Software, 37–45 (November/December 1998)
14. Sametinger, J.: Software Engineering with Reusable Components. Springer, Heidelberg (1997)
15. Sheard, T.: Accomplishments and Research Challenges in MetaProgramming. In: Taha, W. (ed.) SAIG 2001. LNCS, vol. 2196, pp. 2–44. Springer, Heidelberg (2001)
16. Štuikys, V., Damaševičius, R., Montvilas, M.: A Metaprogramming-Based model for Generation of the eLearning-Oriented WEB Pages. In: Boyle, T., Oriogun, P., Pakstas, A. (eds.) Proc. of 2nd Int. Conf. on Information Technology: Research and Education (ITRE 2004), London, England, June 28-July 1, 2004, pp. 64–68 (2004)
17. Štuikys, V., Damaševičius, R.: Towards Knowledge-Based Generative Learning Objects. Information Technology and Control 36(2), 202–212 (2007)
18. Kang, K., Cohen, S., Hess, J., Novak, W., Peterson, S.: Feature-Oriented Domain Analysis (FODA) Feasibility Study. Technical Report CMU/SEI-90-TR-21, Software Engineering Institute, Carnegie Mellon University (November 1990)
19. Eisenecker, U.W., Czarnecki, K.: Generative Programming: Methods, Tools, and Applications. Addison-Wesley, Reading (2000)
20. Kang, K.C., Lee, J., Donohoe, P.: Feature-Oriented Product Line Engineering. IEEE Software 19(4), 58–65 (2002)

21. Clements, P., Northrop, L.: Software Product Lines: Practices and Patterns. Addison-Wesley, Boston (2002)
22. MacGregor, J.: Requirements Engineering in Industrial Product Lines. In: Proc. of Int. Workshop on Requirements Engineering for Product Lines REPL 2002, Essen, Germany, pp. 5–11 (2002)
23. Czarnecki, K., Kim, C.H.P., Kalleberg, K.T.: Feature models are views on ontologies. In: Proc. of 10th Int. Software Product Line Conference (SPLC 2006), Baltimore, Maryland, USA, August 21-24, 2006, pp. 41–51 (2006)
24. Štuikys, V., Damaševičius, R., Brauklytė, I., Limanauskienė, V.: Exploration of Learning Object Ontologies Using Feature Diagrams. In: World Conference on Educational Multimedia, Hypermedia & Telecommunications (ED-MEDIA), Vienna, Austria, June 30-July 4 (2008)
25. Guizzardi, G.: On Ontology, ontologies, Conceptualizations, Modeling Languages, and (Meta)Models. In: Vasilecas, O., Edler, J., Čaplinskas, A. (eds.) Frontiers in Artificial Intelligence and Applications, Databases and Information Systems IV. IOS Press, Amsterdam (2007)
26. Simos, M., Creps, R., Klingler, C., Lavine, L.: Software Technology for Adaptable Reliable Systems (STARS). Organization Domain Modeling (ODM) Guidebook, v. 1.0 (1998)
27. Ossher, H., Tarr, P.: Multi-Dimensional Separation of Concerns and The Hyperspace Approach. In: Aksit, M. (ed.) Software Architectures and Component Technology: The State of the Art in Software Development. Kluwer Academic Publishers, Dordrecht (2000)
28. Kleinjohann, B.: Invited Talk: Multilanguage Design. In: Proc. of Int. IFIP WG 10.3/WG 10.5 Workshop on Distributed and Parallel Embedded Systems (DIPES 1998), Paderborn, Germany, pp. 23–38 (1998)
29. Damaševičius, R., Štuikys, V.: Separation of Concerns in Multi-language Specifications. Informatica 13(3), 255–274 (2002)
30. Fischer, G., Giaccardi, E.: MetaDesign: A Framework for the Future of End-User Development. In: Lieberman, H., Paternò, F., Wulf, V. (eds.) End User Development - Empowering People to Flexibly Employ Advanced Information and Communication Technology. Kluwer Academic Publishers, Dordrecht (2004)

Informational Technologies for Further Education of Latvian Province Teachers of Informatics

Jurijs Lavendels, Vjaceslavs Sitikovs, and Kaspars Krauklis

Riga Technical University,
Faculty of Computer Science and Information Technology,
Institute of Applied Computer Systems,
Meza 1/4, LV-1048, Riga, Latvia
jurisl@cs.rtu.lv

Abstract. This is a review of the procedure, technologies and process of further educational courses within the framework of the ESF project "Informational Technologies for Further Education of Latvian Province Teachers of Informatics". The objective of these courses is to clarify the method of teaching of algorithmization and basic programming in secondary schools. The technological realization of the courses was based on online e-teaching using costless VoIP Skype network based software. Summarizing results of e-teaching courses imperfection considerations regarding unsolved problems of virtual communication as a new way of cooperation were made.

1 Introduction

Within the framework of the ESF project "Informational Technologies for further education of Latvian province teachers of informatics" in May and June 2007 courses of raising the level of proficiency for secondary school teachers of Informatics were organized. For the courses' provision, online e-teaching methods were actively used. The teaching process realized had its educational, economic and trial reasons.

A direct aim of the education mentioned was to clarify the method of teaching algorithmization and bases of programming in secondary schools. It is based on high school lecturers' observations of first year students' understanding of the usage of programming technologies, which fundamentally differs from Riga Technical University´s (RTU) accepted programming and algorithmization paradigms.

Obviously, students' understanding is based on knowledge and skills which have been learnt during Informatics lessons at secondary school.

Since 1991 Latvia suffers demographic a crisis. Consequently the amount of secondary school graduates has decreased during the last years. High schools fight for attracting new students. Students of Riga and Riga districts' secondary schools are well informed about study opportunities at RTU through Open Door Days, exhibitions etc. However, students from distant regions and country areas mostly are poorly informed about both, study opportunities at RTU, and the science course "Computer-based systems". For attracting entrants to study at Riga Technical University the decision to form and strengthen contacts with Informatics teachers of regional secondary schools' was reached. This method provides an opportunity to communicate with students not directly, but with school staff mediation. To enable mutual interest an e-teaching course "Programming and algorithmization bases" was accomplished.

Online e-teaching for the teaching process is not enough studied and it is rarely used. Implementation of such a technical solution in real teaching process is a nontrivial activity both technically and psychologically. Usage of WEB conference software and service in regular lessons is also an economically disadvantageous activity. In search of alternatives a research [1] of free software and service which are based on VoIP Skype for providing virtual communication was made. Separate solutions were implemented in providing an e-teaching course.

2 Process of Courses Preparation

To realize further education courses first of all it was necessary to prepare teaching materials, to study and invite audience – province school teachers of Informatics, as well as to provide technical part of activity.

2.1 Course Participants

Participants of the courses are teachers of Informatics from different regions of Latvia. Exploration of schools, distribution of invitations to courses, registration of participants would be quite a labor-consuming process which does no guarantee success. To provide invitation and management of the courses' participants, five coordinators (teachers of informatics) were involved in this project. The organizational part of the courses provision was performed by following the scheme, outlined in Fig. 1.

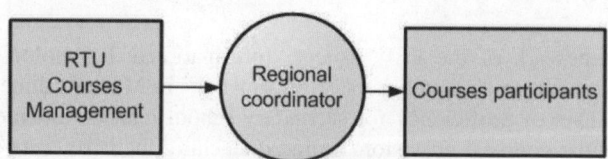

Fig. 1. Enrolment of participants of courses

With the mediation of a coordinator the following information was distributed to the audience:

- guidelines about usage of electronic aids,
- guidelines about necessary steps to allow participation in online lessons,
- the time of the first online lecture and other information.

The auditory of teachers is territorially dissipated within the limits of city, province, and state. The specificity of work is also concerned with the address of place of employment. It is not always possible to realize further education courses regionally covering 40 km territorial radius.

According to Latvian legislation teachers are obliged to raise their level of proficiency regularly. The realization of teachers' training courses is possible in the following ways:

- Studying at night classes or extra-mural courses;
- Studying during holidays and vacations at intensive training courses;
- E-teaching.

Further education courses' auditory is more than 35 secondary school teachers of Informatics from different Latvian regions, geographically covering possible auditory in a radius 200 km from Riga Technical University. The average amount of listeners at the online e-teaching lesson is 20 persons. Teachers' interest to participate in those courses is based on the following reasons:

- Regular raising level of proficiency is duty of each teacher;
- The teaching process is lead by experienced high school lecturers and programming practitioners;
- Courses do not have a participation fee;
- Electronic teaching courses distinctly decrease both time and finance expenses in comparison with fulltime courses.

2.2 Development of Multimedia Aids for the Course

The content of electronic teaching aids for the course is based on adoption of aids used at high school for the level of secondary school. To provide teaching process multimedia, e-learning aids which were based on a previously accepted concept were developed. The aids developed include MS PowerPoint slides about all given themes and specially edited records of life presentations. For recording the program Screen-Flash [2] was used. The usage of this software provides:

- Recording of screen picture and mouse cursor manipulations;
- Voice record;
- Editing of records;
- Inserting table of contents and other managerial elements;
- Exportation of records from SWF format to AVI and EXE formats.

As a result, a batch of teaching aids was developed and placed in the Internet.

2.3 Technical Solution of Online Lessons

To realize an online teaching process, it was necessary to define what requirements must be satisfied before choosing appropriate software. For providing online lessons the following requirements were set:

- Participants must have an opportunity to see all actions taking place in the course lecturer's computer screen during the lecture;
- Participants must have opportunity to hear lecturer during the lecture;
- Participants must have an opportunity to ask the lecturer or other course participants questions using voice broadcasting devices;
- Online text messages must exchange between all course participants.

To fit the requirements within the limits of the project, criteria of functional conformity, applicability and minimal expenses were set. Together with course participants several experiments to find reasonable solution of realizing online lessons were made. For the technical solution the following software and services were used:

- VoIP Skype client software for providing text messages and voice broadcasting;
- HighSpeedConferencing [3] service for providing conference call management;
- "PrettyMay Call Center for Skype" [4] for rerouting calls in case of low quality of signal;
- "ScreenStream" [5] for transmission of screen picture and mouse manipulations.

The Solution scheme applied is shown in Fig. 2.

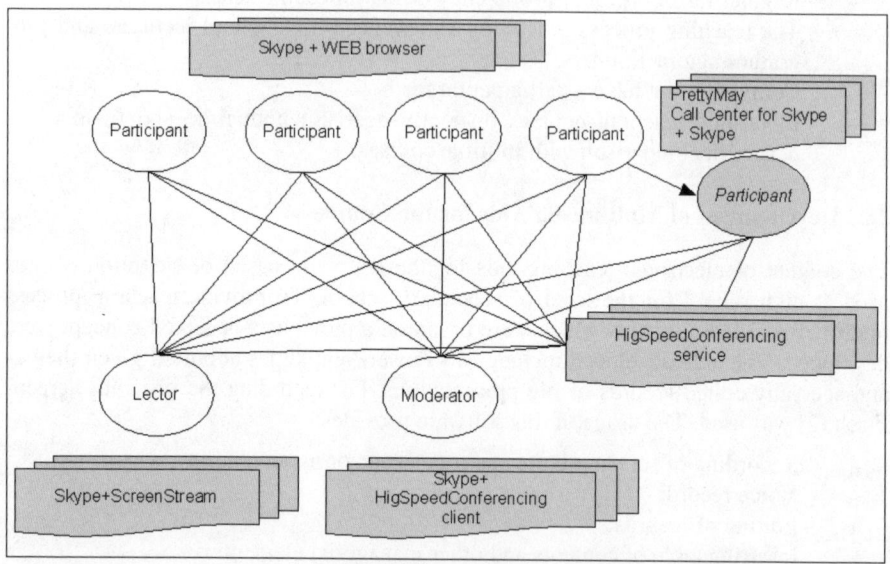

Fig. 2. Online lectures' solution scheme

During the online lectures from broadcasting party two participants are involved - lecturer and moderator, where the last responsible for technical part of event. For broadcasting a special workstation with broadband optical Internet connection are used.

3 Teaching Process Activities

The teaching process included definite synchronous and asynchronous teaching components:

- Independent acquisition of electronic aids;
- Online lectures;
- Independent development of electronic aids;
- Presentation of developed teaching aids during the online lessons.

3.1 Online Teaching Process

Online lessons were started at a time previously agreed upon with the teachers. With the mediation of Skype's text message transfer service all course participants and course administration greeted each other and started exchanging messages on a free theme. When there were enough audience present and the lecture's technical side was provided, the moderator of the lecture gave information about picture broadcasting URL and voice conference call number in a Skype text message window. The lecture started. Provision of the lectures process is shown in Fig.3.

Fig. 3. E-learning online lecture

Online lectures were used for presentations, for demonstrations of work with integration development environment, as well as audience test work presentations. Lectures mainly were based on previously prepared MS PowerPoint presentations and demonstrations in Borland Pascal for the Windows development environment. At the same time messages between course participants and moderator group were exchanged. Thereby participant were discussing the theme or asking the lecturer questions. They also asked the moderator to give them the microphone so they will have an opportunity to ask questions over the cyberspace. The lecturer received information about questions and uncertainty, gave answers and explanations. At the end of the lecture extra discussion was initiated and each participant was asked to take the microphone and speak.

To pass a test in the course teachers had to fulfill the exercise which consists of two parts:

- To prepare electronic teaching aids about any informatics' theme;
- To present prepared aids during the online lecture.

To fulfill the exercise course participants used the following software:
- MS Office batch for teaching aids and presentations;
- Movie Maker [6] for video clips;
- Screen Flash for teaching clips.

Prepared files were allocated in a place available for each person. Each course participant can use them in his/her teaching process. When a file was prepared, it had to be presented during the online lecture. The participant, which wanted to present the work, sent it to the moderator, then received rights to use a microphone and started the presentation. After presentation was finished, other participants used text messages for broadcasting reactions or took the microphone to ask questions and give comments.

The teaching scheme is shown in Fig. 4.

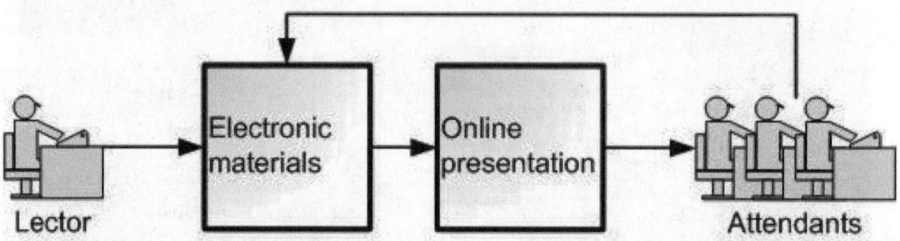

Fig. 4. E-learning lectures cycle

3.2 Participants Questionnaire

At the last section of online lectures a questionnaire for teachers were made. The aim of this questionnaire was to get the participants' evaluation of the technical side of the teaching process and Internet connection parameters. Results of this questionnaire are shown in Table 1.

Table 1. Results of participants' questionnaire

Parameter	Value
Participants	24
Upload speed (avg.)	1046 Kb/s
Download speed (avg.)	2048 Kb/s
Real IP address	52%
Voice call quality	3.38 of 5
Video traffic quality	4.58 of 5

The results of the questionnaire might be interpreted in a following way:
- Up/Download speeds of participants' Internet connection are different. Consequently connection quality is also different;
- Approximately half the audience for connection use a real IP address;

- Evaluation of voice signals was middling. The reason of such quality was usage of HighSpeedConferencing freeware version.

4 Evaluation of Technical Solution

The solution used has both advantages and disadvantages which are based on the solutions expenses, VoIP Skype architectural and specific character, and e-learning course working results.

Solution advantages:

- Usage of free software and service versions decreased total expenses;
- Because of VoIP Skype as architectural and technological solution, high voice broadcasting and text messages exchanging service accessibility was provided.

Solution disadvantages:

- Usage of HighSpeedConferencing free service in several cases provided dissatisfactory quality of voice broadcasting;
- To participate in courses, the audience had to install Skype client software on their computers and to know how to connect to HighSpeedConferencing.

5 Problems of Virtual Communication

Usage of electronic communication resources for supporting a teaching process has several psychological and managerial problems.

The majority of e-learning course participants are unacquainted with each other. It is difficult or even impossible to establish and strengthen close cooperation between members of the group. Online lessons are the only opportunity for participants to team up. In such a situation it is difficult for participants to exchange ideas, express and maintain their opinions, because they do not feel feed-back. Other participants' opinions and attitude in most cases are not known.

Participants are not well motivated to communicate actively during the lesson, because each is sitting at home near the computer screen. In groups where the amount of participants is more than 10 people, the majority of participants can take part as passive listeners.

Elder people find it very difficult to start using new electronic communications and teaching resources.

Management of virtual lessons is a psychologically complicated process and it is difficult to control it. The lecturer of such a course must speak to an audience which he/she does not see and does not hear, hoping that any of the course participants would express their opinions by text messages or would ask for a microphone to speak.

6 Conclusion

Education based on online e-learning has both advantages and disadvantages. For secondary school teachers from different Latvian provinces it was a very good opportunity to get the necessary certificate of their level of proficiency with minimal financial and temporal expenses. They also get acquainted to teaching methods in high schools, had opportunity to get to know their colleagues and exchange information with them. They also participated in an experiment of using new teaching technologies and had experience in online public presentations over Internet.

Organizers of this course had the opportunity to influence the teaching process of informatics in Latvian schools. They also expanded contact circle and continued investigation and implementation of online e-learning.

Usage of new technologies had the following problems:

– Course participants were not acquainted to online communications; virtual communication cannot replace real communication;
– Technical solutions based on the Internet environment are not reliable;
– Feed-back between lecturer and audience was not felt;
– Verification of knowledge and skills was difficult;
– Difficulty to have effective work with elder people.

Usage of a technological solution based on VoIP Skype and free software is not the most appropriate choice. The reasons of it are architectural solutions of a P2P net for providing double-sided voice traffic and quick changes at free software market. A more appropriate solution for online lessons might be special educational client-server software. The management method of online e-learning is one of the approaches weak sides. For more detailed development an extra investigation is necessary.

References

1. Krauklis, K., Sitikovs, V.: Software solutions for provision of collaboration between users within VoIP Skype environment (in Russian). In: Education and Virtuality 2007, Yalta, Ukraine, September 17-21, 2007, pp. 245–252 (2007)
2. ScreenFlash, Unflash.com (2007), http://unflash.com/
3. High Speed Conferencing by Vapps, Vapps LLC (2006),
   http://www.highspeedconferencing.com/
4. PrettyMay Call Center for Skype - Overview, PrettyMay Team (2007),
   http://www.prettymay.net/callcenter/index.htm
5. Download Desktop Screen Sharing Software, NCH Software (2007),
   http://www.nchsoftware.com/screen/index.html
6. Windows Movie Maker - Wikipedia, the free encyclopedia, Wikimedia Foundation, Inc. (2007), http://en.wikipedia.org/wiki/Windows_Movie_Maker

Author Index

Adamaszek, Michał 192
Aoki, Hiroyuki 63, 75
Averbuch, Haim 180

Benaya, Tamar 161
Blondel, François-Marie 305
Blonskis, Jonas 204
Bruillard, Éric 305

Chrząstowski-Wachtel, Piotr 192

Dagienė, Valentina 19, 204, 282, 293
Damaševičius, Robertas 337
Diks, Krzysztof 31

Eibl, Christian J. 327

Freiermuth, Karin 216
Futschek, Gerald 19

Ginat, David 87
Grgurina, Nataša 272
Gruber, Peter 134

Haberman, Bruria 180
Hazzan, Orit 253
Hofuku, Yayoi 241
Hromkovič, Juraj 216
Huang, Shih-Lung 53
Hubwieser, Peter 142

Idosaka, Yukio 241

Kalas, Ivan 229
Kamada, Toshiyuki 63, 75
Kanemune, Susumu 75, 241
Kolczyk, Ewa 265
Kovatcheva, Eugenia 99
Krauklis, Kaspars 349
Kuno, Yasushi 75, 241

Kurebayashi, Shuji 63, 75
Kwiatkowska, Anna Beata 1

Lavendels, Jurijs 349

Madey, Jan 31
Martin, Fred 41
Micheuz, Peter 317
Muller, Orna 180

Niewiarowska, Anna 192
Nikolova, Nikolina 99
Nishida, Tomohiro 241

Ragonis, Noa 253
Rhine, Don 41
Romeike, Ralf 122

Schubert, Sigrid E. 327
Schulte, Carsten 110
Sendova, Evgenia 99
Sitikovs, Vjaceslavs 349
Stefanova, Eliza 99
Steffen, Björn 216
Štuikys, Vytautas 337
Sysło, Maciej M. 1

Tort, Françoise 305
Tseng, I-Chih 53

Weigend, Michael 151
Winczer, Michal 229
Wu, Cheng-Chih 53

Yamamoto, Yoshikazu 63
Yovcheva, Biserka Boncheva 171

Zajančkauskienė, Lina 282
Žilinskienė, Inga 282
Zur, Ela 161

Printing: Mercedes-Druck, Berlin
Binding: Stein+Lehmann, Berlin

Lecture Notes in Computer Science

Sublibrary 1: Theoretical Computer Science and General Issues

For information about Vols. 1– 4750
please contact your bookseller or Springer

Vol. 5130: J.v.z. Gathen, J.L. Imaña, Ç.K. Koç (Eds.), Arithmetic of Finite Fields. X, 209 pages. 2008.

Vol. 5103: M. Bubak, G.D. van Albada, J. Dongarra, P.M.A. Sloot (Eds.), Computational Science – ICCS 2008, Part III. XXVIII, 758 pages. 2008.

Vol. 5102: M. Bubak, G.D. van Albada, J. Dongarra, P.M.A. Sloot (Eds.), Computational Science – ICCS 2008, Part II. XXVIII, 752 pages. 2008.

Vol. 5101: M. Bubak, G.D. van Albada, J. Dongarra, P.M.A. Sloot (Eds.), Computational Science – ICCS 2008, Part I. XLVI, 1058 pages. 2008.

Vol. 5092: X. Hu, J. Wang (Eds.), Computing and Combinatorics. XIV, 680 pages. 2008.

Vol. 5090: R.T. Mittermeir, M.M. Sysło (Eds.), Informatics Education - Supporting Computational Thinking. XV, 357 pages. 2008.

Vol. 5065: P. Degano, R. De Nicola, J. Meseguer (Eds.), Concurrency, Graphs and Models. XV, 810 pages. 2008.

Vol. 5062: K.M. van Hee, R. Valk (Eds.), Applications and Theory of Petri Nets. XIII, 429 pages. 2008.

Vol. 5059: F.P. Preparata, X. Wu, J. Yin (Eds.), Frontiers in Algorithmics. XI, 350 pages. 2008.

Vol. 5058: A.A. Shvartsman, P. Felber (Eds.), Structural Information and Communication Complexity. X, 307 pages. 2008.

Vol. 5050: J.M. Zurada, G.G. Yen, J. Wang (Eds.), Computational Intelligence: Research Frontiers. XVI, 389 pages. 2008.

Vol. 5038: C.C. McGeoch (Ed.), Experimental Algorithms. X, 363 pages. 2008.

Vol. 5036: S. Wu, L.T. Yang, T.L. Xu (Eds.), Advances in Grid and Pervasive Computing. XV, 518 pages. 2008.

Vol. 5035: A. Lodi, A. Panconesi, G. Rinaldi (Eds.), Integer Programming and Combinatorial Optimization. XI, 477 pages. 2008.

Vol. 5029: P. Ferragina, G.M. Landau (Eds.), Combinatorial Pattern Matching. XIII, 317 pages. 2008.

Vol. 5028: A. Beckmann, C. Dimitracopoulos, B. Löwe (Eds.), Logic and Theory of Algorithms. XIX, 596 pages. 2008.

Vol. 5022: A.G. Bourgeois, S.Q. Zheng (Eds.), Algorithms and Architectures for Parallel Processing. XIII, 336 pages. 2008.

Vol. 5018: M. Grohe, R. Niedermeier (Eds.), Parameterized and Exact Computation. X, 227 pages. 2008.

Vol. 5015: L. Perron, M.A. Trick (Eds.), Integration of AI and OR Techniques in Constraint Programming for Combinatorial Optimization Problems. XII, 394 pages. 2008.

Vol. 5011: A.J. van der Poorten, A. Stein (Eds.), Algorithmic Number Theory. IX, 455 pages. 2008.

Vol. 5010: E.A. Hirsch, A.A. Razborov, A. Semenov, A. Slissenko (Eds.), Computer Science – Theory and Applications. XIII, 411 pages. 2008.

Vol. 5008: A. Gasteratos, M. Vincze, J.K. Tsotsos (Eds.), Computer Vision Systems. XV, 560 pages. 2008.

Vol. 5004: R. Eigenmann, B.R. de Supinski (Eds.), OpenMP in a New Era of Parallelism. X, 191 pages. 2008.

Vol. 4996: H. Kleine Büning, X. Zhao (Eds.), Theory and Applications of Satisfiability Testing – SAT 2008. X, 305 pages. 2008.

Vol. 4988: R. Berghammer, B. Möller, G. Struth (Eds.), Relations and Kleene Algebra in Computer Science. X, 397 pages. 2008.

Vol. 4985: M. Ishikawa, K. Doya, H. Miyamoto, T. Yamakawa (Eds.), Neural Information Processing, Part II. XXX, 1091 pages. 2008.

Vol. 4984: M. Ishikawa, K. Doya, H. Miyamoto, T. Yamakawa (Eds.), Neural Information Processing, Part I. XXX, 1147 pages. 2008.

Vol. 4981: M. Egerstedt, B. Mishra (Eds.), Hybrid Systems: Computation and Control. XV, 680 pages. 2008.

Vol. 4978: M. Agrawal, D. Du, Z. Duan, A. Li (Eds.), Theory and Applications of Models of Computation. XII, 598 pages. 2008.

Vol. 4975: F. Chen, B. Jüttler (Eds.), Advances in Geometric Modeling and Processing. XV, 606 pages. 2008.

Vol. 4974: M. Giacobini, A. Brabazon, S. Cagnoni, G.A. Di Caro, R. Drechsler, A. Ekárt, A.I. Esparcia-Alcázar, M. Farooq, A. Fink, J. McCormack, M. O'Neill, J. Romero, F. Rothlauf, G. Squillero, A.Ş. Uyar, S. Yang (Eds.), Applications of Evolutionary Computing. XXV, 701 pages. 2008.

Vol. 4973: E. Marchiori, J.H. Moore (Eds.), Evolutionary Computation, Machine Learning and Data Mining in Bioinformatics. X, 213 pages. 2008.

Vol. 4972: J. van Hemert, C. Cotta (Eds.), Evolutionary Computation in Combinatorial Optimization. XII, 289 pages. 2008.

Vol. 4971: M. O'Neill, L. Vanneschi, S. Gustafson, A.I. Esparcia Alcázar, I. De Falco, A. Della Cioppa, E. Tarantino (Eds.), Genetic Programming. XI, 375 pages. 2008.

Vol. 4967: R. Wyrzykowski, J. Dongarra, K. Karczewski, J. Wasniewski (Eds.), Parallel Processing and Applied Mathematics. XXIII, 1414 pages. 2008.

Vol. 4963: C.R. Ramakrishnan, J. Rehof (Eds.), Tools and Algorithms for the Construction and Analysis of Systems. XVI, 518 pages. 2008.

Vol. 4962: R. Amadio (Ed.), Foundations of Software Science and Computational Structures. XV, 505 pages. 2008.

Vol. 4961: J.L. Fiadeiro, P. Inverardi (Eds.), Fundamental Approaches to Software Engineering. XIII, 430 pages. 2008.

Vol. 4960: S. Drossopoulou (Ed.), Programming Languages and Systems. XIII, 399 pages. 2008.

Vol. 4959: L. Hendren (Ed.), Compiler Construction. XII, 307 pages. 2008.

Vol. 4957: E.S. Laber, C. Bornstein, L.T. Nogueira, L. Faria (Eds.), LATIN 2008: Theoretical Informatics. XVII, 794 pages. 2008.

Vol. 4943: R. Woods, K. Compton, C. Bouganis, P.C. Diniz (Eds.), Reconfigurable Computing: Architectures, Tools and Applications. XIV, 344 pages. 2008.

Vol. 4942: E. Frachtenberg, U. Schwiegelshohn (Eds.), Job Scheduling Strategies for Parallel Processing. VII, 189 pages. 2008.

Vol. 4941: M. Miculan, I. Scagnetto, F. Honsell (Eds.), Types for Proofs and Programs. VII, 203 pages. 2008.

Vol. 4935: B. Chapman, W. Zheng, G.R. Gao, M. Sato, E. Ayguadé, D. Wang (Eds.), A Practical Programming Model for the Multi-Core Era. VI, 208 pages. 2008.

Vol. 4934: U. Brinkschulte, T. Ungerer, C. Hochberger, R.G. Spallek (Eds.), Architecture of Computing Systems – ARCS 2008. XI, 287 pages. 2008.

Vol. 4927: C. Kaklamanis, M. Skutella (Eds.), Approximation and Online Algorithms. X, 289 pages. 2008.

Vol. 4926: N. Monmarché, E.-G. Talbi, P. Collet, M. Schoenauer, E. Lutton (Eds.), Artificial Evolution. XIII, 327 pages. 2008.

Vol. 4921: S.-i. Nakano, M.. S. Rahman (Eds.), WALCOM: Algorithms and Computation. XII, 241 pages. 2008.

Vol. 4919: A. Gelbukh (Ed.), Computational Linguistics and Intelligent Text Processing. XVIII, 666 pages. 2008.

Vol. 4917: P. Stenström, M. Dubois, M. Katevenis, R. Gupta, T. Ungerer (Eds.), High Performance Embedded Architectures and Compilers. XIII, 400 pages. 2008.

Vol. 4915: A. King (Ed.), Logic-Based Program Synthesis and Transformation. X, 219 pages. 2008.

Vol. 4912: G. Barthe, C. Fournet (Eds.), Trustworthy Global Computing. XI, 401 pages. 2008.

Vol. 4910: V. Geffert, J. Karhumäki, A. Bertoni, B. Preneel, P. Návrat, M. Bieliková (Eds.), SOFSEM 2008: Theory and Practice of Computer Science. XV, 792 pages. 2008.

Vol. 4905: F. Logozzo, D.A. Peled, L.D. Zuck (Eds.), Verification, Model Checking, and Abstract Interpretation. X, 325 pages. 2008.

Vol. 4904: S. Rao, M. Chatterjee, P. Jayanti, C.S.R. Murthy, S.K. Saha (Eds.), Distributed Computing and Networking. XVIII, 588 pages. 2007.

Vol. 4878: E. Tovar, P. Tsigas, H. Fouchal (Eds.), Principles of Distributed Systems. XIII, 457 pages. 2007.

Vol. 4875: S.-H. Hong, T. Nishizeki, W. Quan (Eds.), Graph Drawing. XIII, 402 pages. 2008.

Vol. 4873: S. Aluru, M. Parashar, R. Badrinath, V.K. Prasanna (Eds.), High Performance Computing – HiPC 2007. XXIV, 663 pages. 2007.

Vol. 4863: A. Bonato, F.R.K. Chung (Eds.), Algorithms and Models for the Web-Graph. X, 217 pages. 2007.

Vol. 4860: G. Eleftherakis, P. Kefalas, G. Păun, G. Rozenberg, A. Salomaa (Eds.), Membrane Computing. IX, 453 pages. 2007.

Vol. 4855: V. Arvind, S. Prasad (Eds.), FSTTCS 2007: Foundations of Software Technology and Theoretical Computer Science. XIV, 558 pages. 2007.

Vol. 4854: L. Bougé, M. Forsell, J.L. Träff, A. Streit, W. Ziegler, M. Alexander, S. Childs (Eds.), Euro-Par 2007 Workshops: Parallel Processing. XVII, 236 pages. 2008.

Vol. 4851: S. Boztaş, H.-F.(F.) Lu (Eds.), Applied Algebra, Algebraic Algorithms and Error-Correcting Codes. XII, 368 pages. 2007.

Vol. 4848: M.H. Garzon, H. Yan (Eds.), DNA Computing. XI, 292 pages. 2008.

Vol. 4847: M. Xu, Y. Zhan, J. Cao, Y. Liu (Eds.), Advanced Parallel Processing Technologies. XIX, 767 pages. 2007.

Vol. 4846: I. Cervesato (Ed.), Advances in Computer Science – ASIAN 2007. XI, 313 pages. 2007.

Vol. 4838: T. Masuzawa, S. Tixeuil (Eds.), Stabilization, Safety, and Security of Distributed Systems. XIII, 409 pages. 2007.

Vol. 4835: T. Tokuyama (Ed.), Algorithms and Computation. XVII, 929 pages. 2007.

Vol. 4818: I. Lirkov, S. Margenov, J. Waśniewski (Eds.), Large-Scale Scientific Computing. XIV, 755 pages. 2008.

Vol. 4800: A. Avron, N. Dershowitz, A. Rabinovich (Eds.), Pillars of Computer Science. XXI, 683 pages. 2008.

Vol. 4783: J. Holub, J. Žďárek (Eds.), Implementation and Application of Automata. XIII, 324 pages. 2007.

Vol. 4782: R. Perrott, B.M. Chapman, J. Subhlok, R.F. de Mello, L.T. Yang (Eds.), High Performance Computing and Communications. XIX, 823 pages. 2007.

Vol. 4771: T. Bartz-Beielstein, M.J. Blesa Aguilera, C. Blum, B. Naujoks, A. Roli, G. Rudolph, M. Sampels (Eds.), Hybrid Metaheuristics. X, 202 pages. 2007.

Vol. 4770: V.G. Ganzha, E.W. Mayr, E.V. Vorozhtsov (Eds.), Computer Algebra in Scientific Computing. XIII, 460 pages. 2007.

Vol. 4769: A. Brandstädt, D. Kratsch, H. Müller (Eds.), Graph-Theoretic Concepts in Computer Science. XIII, 341 pages. 2007.

Vol. 4763: J.-F. Raskin, P.S. Thiagarajan (Eds.), Formal Modeling and Analysis of Timed Systems. X, 369 pages. 2007.

Vol. 4759: J. Labarta, K. Joe, T. Sato (Eds.), High-Performance Computing. XV, 524 pages. 2008.